U.S. MARINES IN VIETNAM

THE WAR THAT WOULD NOT END

CHARLES D. MELSON
MAJOR USMC (RETIRED)

HELLGATE PRESS
CENTRAL POINT, OREGON

THE WAR THAT WOULD NOT END

U.S. MARINES IN VIETNAM, 1971–1973

Published by Hellgate Press, an imprint of PSI Research, Inc.
©1998 by Charles D. Melson

For information or to direct comments, questions, or suggestions regarding this book and other Hellgate Press titles, contact:

        Editorial Department
        Hellgate Press
        P.O. Box 3727
        Central Point, OR 97502

        (541) 479-9464 *telephone*
        (541) 476-1479 *fax*
        info@psi-research.com *email*
        http://www.psi-research.com *Web site*

Cover design: Steven Eliot Burns
Cover photography courtesy: Marine Corps Historical Collection

Library of Congress Cataloging-in-Publication Data

Melson, Charles D.
    The war that would not end : U.S. Marines in Vietnam, 1971–1973 /
Charles D. Melson.
      p. cm.
    Rev. ed. of : U.S. Marines in Vietnam : the war that would not end,
1971–1973 / by Charles D. Melson and Curtis G. Arnold. 1991.
    Includes index.
    ISBN 1-55571-420-X (paper)
    1. United States.   Marine Corps. --History--Vietnamese Conflict,
1961–1975. 2. Vietnamese Conflict, 1961–1975--Campaigns.
I. Melson, Charles D. U.S. Marines in Vietnam. II. Title.
DS558.4.M46 1998
959.704'345--dc21   97-42531
                                          CIP

Printed and bound in the United States of America
 Printed on recycled paper when available.

TABLE OF CONTENTS

FOREWORD

This volume details the activities of Marine Corps units after their departure from Vietnam in 1971 of III Marine Amphibious Force through the 1973 ceasefire, and includes the return of Marine prisoners of war from North Vietnam. Written from diverse views and sources, the common thread in this narrative is the continued resistance of the South Vietnamese Armed Forces, in particular the Vietnamese Marine Corps, to Communist aggression. This book is written from the perspective of the American Marines who assisted them in their efforts. Someday the former South Vietnamese Marines will be able to tell their own story.

By July 1971, less than 500 U.S. Marines, mostly advisors, communicators, and supporting arms specialists remained in Vietnam. It was thought at the time that the success of "Vietnamization" of the war would lessen even this small number, as it was hoped that the South Vietnamese could continue fighting successfully. This hope vanished in spring 1972, dashed by a full-scale North Vietnamese Army invasion. The renewed combat saw the U.S. Marines return once more to Southeast Asia in a continuation of the war that now seemed to have no end. The fighting proceeded into the fall, and only ceased with the signing of peace accords in Paris in January 1973.

The War That Would Not End is the product of a collaboration of two career Marines, who brought a total of 42 years of service experience to the project while assigned to the History and Museums Division of Headquarters Marine Corps. Lieutenant Colonel Curtis G. Arnold began the task. A native Alabamian, Lieutenant Colonel Arnold enlisted in the Marine Corps in 1950 and served with the 1st Marine Division in Korea. Discharged in 1953, he remained in the Marine Reserve in inactive status while he attended Auburn University. Following graduation, Lieutenant Colonel Arnold was commissioned in January 1958. He attended the Communication Officers Orientation Course at Quantico, Virginia, and served as a communications officer for much of his career. He served in Vietnam with the 3d Marine Division from 1966 to 1967, receiving the Bronze Star Medal. He was aide to Assistant Commandant of the Marine Corps General Lewis W. Walt from 1968 to 1969. He then attended Marine Corps Command and Staff College at Quantico and remained there at the Marine Corps Schools as an instructor. He joined the History and Museums Division in 1973 and retired from the division and the Marine Corps in 1975. Lieutenant Colonel Arnold's efforts are reflected in the themes of chapters 2 through 9, based on interviews and then-available records. He played a critical part in the location and recovery of the Marine Advisory Unit records just prior to the fall of Saigon. Lieutenant Colonel Arnold also contributed to this project through his review of the comment edition and with further advice and encouragement until his untimely death in 1990.

The project was completed by Major Charles D. Melson. From California, Major Melson entered the Marine Corps Reserve in 1967 and in 1970 both graduated from Sonoma State University and was commissioned. Following Basic School, he served overseas as an infantry officer with assignments to Vietnam in 1972 with the 9th Marine Amphibious Brigade. He was awaiting orders to Sub Unit One, 1st ANGLICO, when the war ended in 1973. Major Melson spent a large portion of his career in combat and reconnaissance units in both Fleet Marine Forces Atlantic and Pacific. He has decorations for military merit, combat action, and humanitarian service. Beginning in 1982, he was an instructor at the U.S. Naval Academy and earned a master of arts degree from St. John's College, Annapolis, Maryland. Major Melson subsequently was assigned to Headquarters Marine Corps, first to the Command Center and then, in 1986, to the History and Museums Division. Major Melson wrote the remaining eight chapters and shaped the volume into its final form. This included revising Arnold's manuscript to make use of much additional material. Major Melson left active service in 1990, but was recalled to active duty with the division, including duties with the U.S. Central Command during the Persian Gulf War.

E. H. SIMMONS
Brigadier General, U.S. Marine Corps (Retired)
Director of Marine Corps History and Museums

PREFACE

In the more than five years since the publication of the first edition and the 25 years since these actions took place, nothing has changed the basic tale of men in battle in the service of their country. It is with great pleasure that I take the opportunity to introduce this story to a new and larger group of readers.

Ernest Hemingway wrote about war in *A Farewell to Arms* in 1929, contending that, "Abstract words such as glory, honor, courage, or hallow were obscene beside the concrete names of villages, the numbers of roads, the names of rivers, the numbers of regiments and the dates." For many reasons, this observation holds true for this narrative. The variety and scope of U.S. Marine participation in the final phase of the Vietnam War makes this an account of units and individuals as part of the activities of the other Services or of the South Vietnamese forces. This is reflected in the sources used to tell this story; the author had to rely on diverse material for information. In fact, most events discussed are drawn as exceptions from the normal process of records-keeping and availability: ad hoc units and mixed-service, or even multinational formations were the norm. This suggested the use of commenters who could bring together otherwise dispersed records to support the volume. Interviews from recorded and transcribed and other oral formats were also especially valuable. A draft of this book was sent to key participants, 231 individuals. Of these, 114 replied. They are listed in the appendix and referenced repeatedly in the text. Interviews from recorded and transcribed and other oral formats were also especially valuable. Most of this original material has been archived for use by Marines and other scholarly researchers.

Military evolutions are the product of teamwork and this book is no exception. It should be noted that the theme for the story came from Lieutenant Colonel Curtis G. Arnold who got the ball rolling. Thanks to Colonel John E. Greenwood of the

Marine Corps Gazette and Colonel John G. Miller of the *U.S. Naval Institute Proceedings* for their kind words and support. I would like to particularly recognize Dale Andrade of the U.S. Army Center for Military History and Howard C. H. Feng of the National Archives and Records Administration for their critical interest in Vietnamization and the Spring Offensive. Their continued exchange of comments and documents kept me writing.

I am indebted to my colleagues in the historical agencies of the U.S. Army, Navy, Air Force, and Joint Chiefs of Staff, all of whom provided information and opinion, and made documentation available for analysis. Thanks to all those who reviewed the various drafts and provided comments, corrections, and insights only available from those who took part in the events described.

At the Marine Corps Historical Center, the following members of Brigadier General Edwin H. Simmon's staff gave valuable contributions of time and effort: Robert V. Aquilina, Major Leonard A. Blasiol, Slyvia Bunyasi, Colonel Marguerite J. Campbell, Joyce M. Conyers, Danny J. Crawford, Captain David A. Dawson, Major George R. Dunham, Major John T. Dyer, Jr., Major Arthur F. Elzy, Evelyn A. Englander, Ann A. Ferrante, Dr. V. Keith Fleming, Jr., Benis M. Frank, Shelia P. Gramblin, Captain Meredith P. Hartley, William S. Hill, Lena M. Kaljot, Catherine A. Kerns, Jamie Koepsell, Soudarak S. Louangkhot, David A. Melson, Patricia E. Morgan, Sergeant Kevin L. Parker, Lieutenant Colonel Michael L. Powell, Henry I. Shaw, Dr. Jack Shulimson, Robert E. Struder, and Colonel James R. Williams.

CHARLES D. MELSON
Major, U.S. Marine Corps (Retired)
Kent Island, Maryland

LIST OF MAPS AND CHARTS

PART I

VIETNAMIZATION

CHAPTER ONE
FROM THE DELTA TO THE DMZ

Nixon's Doctrine • Contingency Forces • Flexibility and Response • Command Relations • Residual Force • Marine Security Guard, Saigon • The Marine Air Contol Squadron Detachment • Sub Unit One, 1st Air and Naval Gunfire Liason Company

Nixon's Doctrine

For over a decade, decisions by three presidents transformed America's role in South Vietnam from a few advisors to a full-blown massive battlefield effort, reaching a maximum troop-level of 549,000 during 1969. The U.S. Armed Forces found themselves involved in a long and unpopular war. With the Nixon Doctrine of July 1969, however, the U.S. began its essential disengagement from Vietnam. The United States would meet its treaty commitments, but expected South Vietnam to assume the greater portion of its own defense through "Vietnamization."[1]

By July 1971, Marines in the Pacific Command (PacCom) had once again become a combat force-in-readiness, leaving behind in Vietnam only residual forces. General Robert E. Cushman, Jr., Commandant of the Marine Corps (CMC), observed that the Marine Corps during this epoch witnessed "the emergence of new forms of force, some overt, some more difficult to recognize or define, and fewer purely military in character than before." He went on to conclude that properly balanced and properly deployed amphibious forces provided "an effective means — and at times the only means — of exerting influence on situations where our interests are involved."[2]

Yet for Marines stationed in the Western Pacific (WestPac), Vietnam was a war that would not end. A war whose continued prosecution was carried on throughout Vietnam, Southeast Asia, the Pacific, and even from the continental United States of America. Although officially known as the "Ceasefire Campaign," this period is better known for the central event of the time, the Spring or Easter Offensive in South Vietnam.[3]

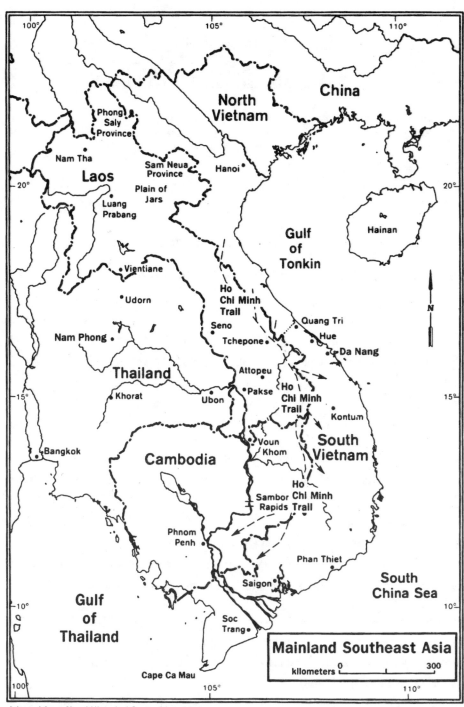

Mainland Southeast Asia

Adapted from Naval Historical Center Material

Contingency Forces

With the Marine Corps strength in Vietnam limited to a few hundred, the III Marine Amphibious Force (III MAF) in the Western Pacific reverted to a responsive posture with the U.S. Navy Seventh Fleet. Marines served in Marine Detachments on board carriers, cruisers, and command ships. With the exception of these Marines assigned to ships' detachments, Marine units made up the fleet landing force.[4] The usefulness of deployed landing forces had been apparent since Marines first went on ships. During the Vietnam war these forces consisted typically of a battalion landing team (BLT) supported by a composite helicopter squadron, forming a basic air-ground team. Seventh Fleet's landing force, called the Special Landing Force or SLF, made 72 amphibious landings in Vietnam through 1969. The Seventh Fleet assigned the SLF mission to the 3d Marine Division on Okinawa in late 1969. The 4th and 9th Marines provided battalions and marine medium helicopter squadrons (HMMs) came from Marine Aircraft Group (MAG) 36 to serve with the fleet amphibious forces.[A] Navy amphibious squadrons were administrative organizations while the amphibious ready group (ARG) was the specific task organization for a particular mission.[B] The amphibious ready groups deployed in two independent configurations. ARG Alpha was organized around a helicopter carrier and ARG Bravo centered on an amphibious transport dock. Another BLT remained on Okinawa as the air-transportable contingency battalion.[5]

After 21 November 1970, the term SLF was changed to Marine amphibious unit (MAU) and Headquarters, 31st Marine Amphibious Unit deployed continuously with Amphibious Ready Group Alpha.[C] As amphibious ready groups were the building blocks of the Navy's amphibious forces, the MAU was the foundation of the landing force. Commanded by a colonel, this was a standing headquarters that provided command, control, and continuity for ground and air units that deployed in rotation. The war did not cease for the 31st MAU with III MAF's departure from Vietnam in April 1971. The 31st MAU was kept within a 120-hour travel time of Military Region 1 (MR 1) and BLT Bravo was no more than 168 hours away from commitment to operations in MR 1. In May and June 1971, the 31st MAU with BLT 1/9 and HMM-164 was on 72-hour standby in support of the departure from Da Nang of the 3d Marine Amphibious Brigade, the last remaining Marine combat unit in Vietnam.

(A) A composite squadron generally consisted of 4 heavy-cargo lift CH-53As, 14 personnel lift CH-46Ds, and 4 utility UH-1Es.

(B) An amphibious squadron generally consisted of an amphibious assault ship (LPH), two amphibious transport docks (LPD), two landing dock ships (LSD), two or three tank landing ships (LST), and an amphibious cargo ship (LKA).

(C) The terms SLF and Special Landing Force continued to be used informally. As of 1989, the MAU was changed to MEU for Marine Expeditionary Unit, a return to a more traditional designation for Marine deployed forces.

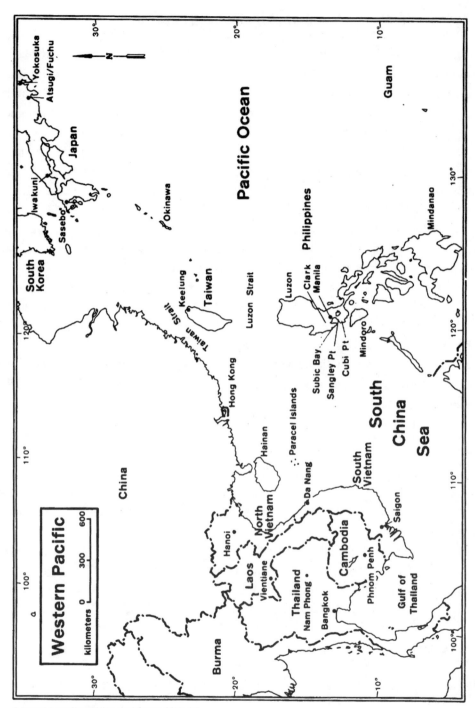

Adapted from Naval Historical Center Material

By July 1971, freed from direct operations in Vietnam, III MAF was the Pacific Command's immediate reserve. Lieutenant General Donn J. Robertson as III MAF commander, had operational control of the 3d Marine Division (3dMarDiv), the 1st Marine Aircraft Wing (1st MAW), and the 3d Force Service Regiment (3d FSR). III MAF was now a regional force with theatre concerns ranging from Vietnam to the Philippines and Korea, concerns corresponding with the Seventh Fleet area of operations. As crises occurred, the Marine units afloat were among the first U.S. tactical units to respond. Regional responsibilities brought new problems and concerns to General Robertson. One issue was the reduction of Pacific Fleet amphibious shipping from six to four squadrons during the year, severely constraining the ability of the Seventh Fleet to commit amphibious forces.[6]

The 31st MAU served as the forward element of a Marine amphibious brigade (MAB), based on General Robertson's conclusion that this was the size of force that available Seventh Fleet transport could move. Existing contingency plans reflected incremental deployment as shipping became available. General Robertson's staff planned for at least one additional battalion landing team to be flown into an objective area to reinforce a deployed brigade. The III MAF planners assumed that additional Marine units could mount out within two weeks if supported by the Eastern Pacific amphibious ready squadron. Within another two weeks the arrival of two additional amphibious squadrons could double the available shipping for amphibious operations.[7] When not on ship for contingencies, exercises, and port visits, Marine units trained ashore at III MAF's "MAU Camp," in the Philippines using the nearby Subic Bay and Zambales training areas.[D] Upon joining a new Marine battalion and squadron, the ARG and MAU conducted amphibious landing exercises to rehearse and validate operation and landing plans. At the same time port calls to Hong Kong, Taiwan, Singapore, and Japan caused deployments to take on aspects of pleasure cruises.

In August 1971, Fleet Marine Force Pacific (FMFPac) established a table of organization for a Western Pacific "ready" brigade. The following month, the 9th MAB formed a cadre staff from personnel of the three Okinawa-based Marine commands to plan and prepare for a scheduled exercise, Golden Dragon II, with Rear Admiral Walter D. Gaddis's Task Force 76. This nucleus staff embarked on the task force's flagship, the USS *Blue Ridge* (LCC 19). That fall BLT Bravo (BLT 1/9) deployed to Camp Fuji, Japan, while the 31st Marine Amphibious Unit with BLT 2/4 and HMM-165 on the USS *Tripoli* (LPH 10) remained at sea or at Subic Bay with Amphibious Ready Group Alpha.

(D) The presence of Philippine security forces and Communist New People's Army units made these training areas literally live-fire areas.

War between India and Pakistan broke out during this period. Vice Admiral William P. Mack of the Seventh Fleet assigned the 31st MAU to Task Force 74 for the evacuation of Americans threatened by the fighting in Pakistan. The MAU interrupted its preparations for Exercise Fortress Light II in the Philippines and the ARG proceeded towards the crisis area. It was replaced in December 1971 by the provisional 331st Marine Amphibious Element of Major Raymond M. Kostesky, known as "Ray's MAE" at III MAF. This consisted of a headquarters, rifle company, and helicopter detachment all aboard the USS *Denver* (LPD 9). The India-Pakistan emergency required combined Marine and Navy staffs to develop planning data for the air deployment of company-sized to brigade-sized units to assist in the evacuations. This planning effort provided the basis for later III MAF evacuation contingencies the following year.[8]

Admiral John S. McCain, Jr., CinCPac, declared the crisis resolved on 7 January 1972 and the 9th MAB nucleus staff resumed planning for Exercise Golden Dragon. Lieutenant General William K. Jones, as FMF Pacific commander, drew three observations from the crisis: first, the separation of individual ready group ships for more than 30 days reduced Marine readiness to carry out the mission of amphibious assault by fragmenting the 31st MAU; second, Marines had to supplement ship's crews because Navy manning levels did not account for 24-hour combat operations, and finally an increased use of "special category"[E] message-traffic reduced the flow of necessary information needed for effective planning. These observations proved valuable in the months to come as amphibious forces returned to Vietnam.[9]

The 1972 New Year, the Year of the Rat in the Tet calendar, began with Lieutenant Colonel William R. Von Harten's BLT 3/4 assuming duties with the 31st MAU, now under Colonel Walter C. Kelly, and Lieutenant Colonel Phillip B. Friedrichs' BLT 1/9 continuing as BLT Bravo. In another change, Lieutenant General Louis Metzger relieved III MAF commander General Robertson.[F] In March 1972 BLT 1/9 loaded ARG Bravo ships at White Beach, Okinawa for the crisis-delayed Exercise Golden Dragon II, by way of port visits to Hong Kong and the Philippines. At this same time the assistant commander of the 3d Marine Division, Brigadier General Edward J. "E. J." Miller, joined the staff on the *Blue Ridge* as brigade commander for the exercise.

(E) This message traffic was usually highly controlled and thus unavailable to most who needed the information.

(F) III MAF remained a lieutenant general billet through 1972.

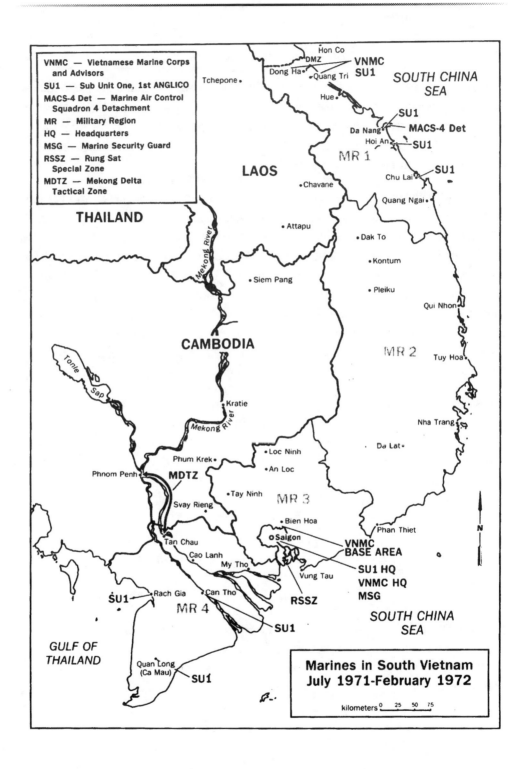

VNMC — Vietnamese Marine Corps
  and Advisors
SU1 — Sub Unit One, 1st ANGLICO
MACS-4 Det — Marine Air Control
  Squadron 4 Detachment
MR — Military Region
HQ — Headquarters
MSG — Marine Security Guard
RSSZ — Rung Sat
  Special Zone
MDTZ — Mekong Delta
  Tactical Zone

Marines in South Vietnam
July 1971-February 1972

kilometers 0   25   50   75

Flexibility and Response

During the last half of 1971, the main activity of III MAF aviation units in Southeast Asia was presence at sea with the Seventh Fleet amphibious groups. Marine Medium Helicopter Squadrons 164 and 165 supported the 31st MAU in rotation as "composite" squadrons; the BLT with ARG Bravo was supported with a detachment from Marine Light Helicopter Squadron (HML) 367.

In Vietnam, a detachment of air controllers from 1st MAW at Da Nang. Another "in-country"[G] aviation activity was the combat evaluation of the North American YOV-10D Bronco gunship. A detachment of two aircraft and 21 Marines flew with the U.S. Navy's Light Attack Squadron 4 (VAL-4) at Binh Thuy.[H] The modified OV-10s mounted a 20mm gun and an infrared sight, the night observation gunship system (NOGS). The Marines flew 200 combat missions denying the cover of darkness to the Communists in MR 3 and MR 4. By 31 August 1971 testing was completed, and the Marines departed. As a result of the evaluation, Lieutenant General William K. Jones, commanding FMFPac, adaptation of the OV-10D was recommended by the Marine Corps.[10]

Strict Department of Defense limits on the entry of combat aircraft and personnel into Vietnam meant that 1st MAW's major contribution during 1971 was as part of the CinCPac strategic reserve. For the air units stationed in Japan and Okinawa this brought an emphasis on reconstructing material stocks eroded over the years of combat and filling training gaps which had developed because of the demands of operations. In December 1971, when the USS *Coral Sea* (CVA 43) arrived for a Western Pacific cruise with Marine All-Weather Attack Squadron 224 (VMA[AW]-224) attached to the carrier air wing, which provided an added capability. The character of Marine air deployments remained stable through the first three months of 1972.

Command Relations

Seventh Fleet, Seventh Air Force, and the remaining advisory, administrative, and logistical units with the Military Advisory Command Vietnam (MACV) continued to support the South Vietnamese in their war against the North Vietnamese. The Seventh Fleet provided strategic deterrence and sea control. In accordance with Washington's policy, senior American commanders in the Pacific increased the logistic and combat support to South Vietnam, but at the same time continued to withdraw American troops from the embattled nation.[11]

(G) Term referring to the geographic confines of South Vietnam.

(H) Deployed from 1 June 1971.

Command relations varied depending upon the mix of forces.[1] Operations at sea were under the control of Seventh and Pacific Fleets. For operations in South Vietnam, MACV, as a subordinate of CinCPac, exercised control of units through regional assistance commands. The 1st Regional Assistance Command (FRAC) was assigned to MR 1. Seventh Air Force controlled air operations in South Vietnam as MACV's deputy for air. In contrast, air operations over North Vietnam were controlled by either Seventh Fleet or Seventh Air Force under CinCPac. For the redeploying Marine units this meant defining operational control ("Opcon") and administrative control ("Adcon") depending upon where they were and who they worked for. Complex command relations required that the greatest attention be paid to coordination at the tactical level (see appendices). General Metzger commented that most, if not all, major deployments and actions during this period originated from the Joint Chiefs of Staff passed through the chain of command to the "action agency," III MAF, and that FMFPac "could only serve as an advisor" to CinCPac and Pacific Fleet to "sell" a specific course of action.[12]

Residual Forces

In South Vietnam, Keystone Oriole Alpha Increment, the seventh increment of President Nixon's phased withdrawal program, was completed on 30 June 1971, marking, for the time being, the end of the U.S. Marine ground units' active combat role in the Vietnam War. However, as the sun rose over the South China Sea on the morning of 1 July 1971, United States Marines were still to be found, nevertheless, throughout the length and breadth of the Republic of Vietnam. These Marines were charged with diverse roles and missions. Some were combat-experienced advisors; others possessed detailed technical knowledge; a few had broad training in computer communications and data theory; but they all had one common denominator — they were U.S. Marines.

Not since March 1963 when they had numbered 532, had there been so few Marines in-country. The largest group, with a total of 195 Marines, was Sub Unit One, 1st Air and Naval Gunfire Liaison Company (ANGLICO) with Lieutenant Colonel Eugene E. Shoults as officer-in-charge. The next larger group was the Marines who guarded the American Embassy in Saigon and the Consulate in Da Nang. These were the 156 men of Company E, Marine Security Guard Battalion (MSG). The Marine Advisory Unit of the Naval Advisory Group was the third in size with 68 Marines serving as advisors to the Vietnamese Marine Corps (VNMC). The smallest unit was the 20-man detachment of Marine Air Control Squadron 4 (MACS-4), 1st MAW, which had

---

(I) This was complicated by an "advisory" command operating in support of the Government of South Vietnam.

remained behind at Da Nang to operate the Marine Tactical Data Control Center known as the Southeast Asia Tactical Data System Interface (SEATDSI). The remaining 107 or so Marines were assigned duties as advisors to the Army of the Republic of Vietnam (ARVN), the Vietnamese Navy (VNN), the Territorial Forces, and as members of the Military Assistance Command, Vietnam staff.[13]

Marine Security Guard, Saigon

In a less than dramatic, but no less meaningful role than the fleet or advisory units, was the special mission being carried out by the Marine Security Guard (MSG) at Saigon and by the detachment at Da Nang. Five officers and 151 enlisted Marines guarded the U.S. Embassy in Saigon and the U.S. Consulate at Da Nang. Their primary mission was to "provide protection for all classified material and equipment and other administratively controlled matters at the Department of State's Foreign Service Establishments." In addition, these Marines were "to provide protection for U.S. personnel and Government property under the direct control of the Chief of Diplomatic Mission." Because of the large-size of the Vietnam security guard, it was designated Company E of the Marine Security Guard Battalion.[14]

All Marines on State Department duty in Vietnam had successfully completed the necessary training and had met the stringent qualifications required while undergoing the five-week academic and physical training course at the Marine Security Guard School at Henderson Hall in Arlington, Virginia. They had been trained in subjects ranging from protocol to counterespionage. Qualification with a new series of small arms was mandatory since Marine Corps-issued weapons were not used in embassies. A joint board of both State Department and battalion personnel had the final word as to whether a Marine was accepted for embassy or consulate duty. One out of four trainees was eliminated. The tough school was necessary for the demanding subsequent assignment of security guard Marines to one of 117 embassies and consulates located in 96 countries.

The Marines of Company E did not restrict themselves exclusively to security tasks. As much as the political and military situation would allow, they formed a viable bond of comradeship with the Vietnamese people, particularly the children, in and around "The Marine House"[(J)] compound near the Ambassador's residence. They had "adopted" the children at Hoa Khan Hospital, as well as the orphans at Hoi Duc Anh.

On 3 July 1971, Dr. Henry Kissinger, special advisor to President Nixon, arrived at Saigon to confer with Ambassador Ellsworth Bunker, South Vietnam's President, Nguyen Van Thieu, and other U.S. embassy and military dignitaries. The MSG

(J) Generic name for the lodging for MSG Marines in Company E.

Marines performed a myriad of tedious and demanding chores related to providing security for Dr. Kissinger's safety. That same month, on 13 July, an electrical fire developed in offices of the United States Agency for International Development (USAID) in Saigon, trapping mission employees on the fifth through ninth floors. Seventy-five Marines, both officers and enlisted, responded to USAID's call for assistance. Disregarding their own safety, the Marines entered the building, located the trapped employees, and immediately started guiding them to safety. Time and again the embassy Marines entered to make certain all persons were clear of the building and that all classified material was secured. After ascertaining these two facts, the Marines turned their full efforts toward fighting the fire. Their quick response prevented the fire from spreading beyond the fourth floor.

The political and military situation in Saigon during the last half of the year had become very tense as the date for national elections neared. Routinely scheduled training was canceled during this period of unpredictable activity, not only by the enemy but also by the diverse factions within the city of Saigon. In the month of August, the city of Saigon was in a full alert as the Vietnamese went to the polls to elect their representatives to the Republic of Vietnam's lower house. On 26 September 1971, Sergeant Charles W. Turberville was killed and four other Marines wounded during a terrorist attack on U.S. Embassy personnel in Phnom Penh, Cambodia. This necessitated the transfer of five Marines from Company E, under Master Sergeant Clenton L. Jones, to Phnom Penh to bolster the embassy guard there.[15]

On 28 October 1971, a new commanding officer, Major Edward J. Land, reported to Company E, relieving Captain William E. Keller. Major Land, a native of Nebraska with an easy-going, midwestern manner, had enlisted in the Marine Corps in 1953 at the age of 17. Before being commissioned in 1959 he served as a drill instructor for two years in San Diego and was a distinguished marksman with both the rifle and pistol. His first tour in South Vietnam had been spent with the 1st Marine Division at Da Nang as officer-in-charge of a scout-sniper platoon. Major Land faced some of the biggest challenges of his Marine Corps career as he took charge. During the fall, the Company's "Scramble Reaction Team," designed to react to any kind of an emergency, responded to 140 bomb threats and 29 bomb detonations, as approximately 122 enemy rockets fell within Company E's area.[16] On Christmas Day 1971, a Communist-terrorist threw an M26 fragmentation grenade into the Marine House compound in Saigon, injuring Sergeant Michael L. Linnan and Salay Mag, a local security guard. Despite this, Major Land's mission was still diplomatic, other Marine units were more directly involved in the continued conduct of the war.

The Marine Air Control Squadron Detachment

The smallest and most concentrated unit of U.S. Marines in South Vietnam was a detachment on top of "Monkey Mountain" on the Tien Sha Peninsula northeast of Da Nang. The 20-man detachment of Chief Warrant Officer Guy M. Howard was from Marine Air Control Squadron (MACS) 4, 1st MAW. Its job was to operate and maintain the Southeast Asia Tactical Data System Interface (SEATDSI) and had stayed behind when the air wing departed Vietnam. These Marines were highly trained operators and technical specialists of the Marine Tactical Data Communications Center (TDCC), a component of the Marine Air Command and Control System which was originally known as the Marine Tactical Data System (MTDS).

Developed by an exclusively Marine Corps research and development effort, MTDS was designed specifically for amphibious warfare and to be compatible with the systems of the other services as well as the North Atlantic Treaty Organization (NATO) system. It was designed to be "an advanced, mobile, landbased, semiautomatic tactical air defense and air control capability." The system made full use of computers integrated with a display system to process volumes of information rapidly. It was a case of space age technology being fully utilized in a "brush fire war."

This system, which was operational in South Vietnam in July 1967, enabled the squadron to establish a data-quality interface with units of the Seventh Fleet. This was the first combat employment of such a system and allowed the integration of MTDS with the Navy's shipboard and airborne tactical data systems (NTDS & ATDS). Shortly after being established on Monkey Mountain, the unique capabilities of the TDCC were recognized and expanded to provide assistance for all American services as well as other allied forces.

In December 1971, CinCPac approved the deployment of an Air Force unit to Udorn, Thailand, that would provide an air-to-ground digital-link capability as well as ground terminal equipment that could be linked to and integrated with the Marine SEATDSI at Da Nang. This vital data link and interface also automatically transmitted radar surveillance provided by Air Force and Navy elements operating over the Gulf of Tonkin and North Vietnam. The information developed was transmitted instantly to the Task Force 77 Anti-Air Warfare Coordinator and the Air Force Air Defense Commander. The SEATDSI was also used to rendezvous, refuel, and monitor air strikes over North Vietnam and to provide the vital coordination between naval gunfire missions and air strikes that were being conducted near each other.

Because of the special capability of the Marine TDCC to understand clearly data messages from both the Air Force and Navy data systems, it was imperative that a detachment of Marines remain in Vietnam to continue to provide an interface between the incompatible Air Force and Navy systems. All three systems were used to monitor the location and disposition of friendly air and to detect, identify, and direct intercept efforts against the hostile air threat which still prevailed in the north. This small Marine detachment with its unique equipment substantially contributed to the capability of both Air Force and Navy units to operate on a regional basis.[17]

Sub Unit One, 1st Air and Naval Gunfire Liaison Company

The single largest and most dispersed U.S. Marine unit in Vietnam was Sub Unit One, 1st Air and Naval Gunfire Liaison Company (ANGLICO). Much like the motto of the U.S. Armed Forces Radio and Television Network in Vietnam, Sub Unit One (SU1) covered "From the Delta to the DMZ." Marine naval gunfire spotters on top of outpost Alpha-2 from Gio Linh just south of the Demilitarized Zone (DMZ) kept a close eye on any movement to the north, while as far south as the Ca Mau Peninsula on the Gulf of Siam, spotters assisted territorial forces with their naval gunfire (NGF) requirements. Unlike the hand-picked U.S. Marine advisors, the ANGLICO Marines and naval personnel had received neither language training nor formal instruction on Vietnamese culture, yet were called upon to serve in ARVN units. They were quite capable, however, of putting high-explosive naval ordnance on target. According to Lieutenant Colonel D'Wayne Gray, who, on 19 July 1971, had relieved Lieutenant Colonel Shoults as officer-in-charge of the unit, "the Marines came through in good style."

Lieutenant Colonel Gray, a prematurely gray, pipe smoking Texan, was well qualified for this assignment. He was knowledgeable of the Vietnamese, their language, and their culture. In 1964 he had attended the Vietnamese Language School at the Foreign Service Institute in Arlington, Virginia, and had served a previous tour in Vietnam in 1965 as advisor to the Chief of Staff of the Vietnamese Marine Corps, then Lieutenant Colonel, Bui The Lan. After his return to the United States he organized the first Marine Corps Vietnamese Language Course at Quantico, Virginia. He taught Vietnamese language for one year before being assigned to Headquarters Marine Corps (HQMC) and took over the Vietnam Desk in the Joint

Planning Group. In addition to this extensive Vietnamese background, he was a qualified aerial observer (AO) with broad experience in supporting arms.[K] [18]

As Gray assumed command of Sub Unit One at a platoon-sized ceremony in Saigon, he was concerned with two matters. First, he was determined to supply the South Vietnamese all the naval gunfire and air support they needed to stand off the northern forces. Second, he also wished to see his Marines and sailors continue to work well with the Vietnamese as well as the Koreans and Australians. He later stated that the possibility of a major involvement with North Vietnamese forces never crossed his mind, "things were winding down; this was going to be a quiet period."[19]

ANGLICO was charged with the coordination of naval gunfire and air support in any form for U.S. Army and allied forces. In Vietnam, ANGLICO was responsible for obtaining and controlling the fire of Seventh Fleet's destroyers and cruisers along the country's entire coastline. In addition, the ANGLICO Marines assigned a brigade tactical air control party to the Korean Marine Corps units. Sub Unit One's headquarters was in Saigon adjacent to the MACV compound, but its spot and liaison teams were positioned at eight sites throughout the coastal areas. Lieutenant Colonel Gray felt that his teams knew how to shoot and communicate; that they were above average in intelligence; and that they possessed the initiative necessary to carry out their responsibilities of advising senior officers on fire support matters. The teams were ready, but there were some obstacles.

When coordinated, naval gunfire, artillery and air support complemented each other. Naval gunfire was generally accurate and effective under a variety of weather conditions and helped fill the gap left by departing U.S. artillery. These naval gunfire missions, however, had to be coordinated to prevent interference with air strikes in the same area. It was standard procedure to coordinate activities of both air liaison teams and tactical aircraft with naval gunfire support ship missions. The Marine tactical data system interface capability, mentioned earlier, provided this vital coordination and control of supporting arms.[L]

The problem for ANGLICO teams was the necessarily detailed coordination of supporting fires to combat units. At the time, artillery and NGF were not permitted to

---

(K) The AO, a naval aviation observer (tactical), was a Marine Corps phenomenon — that used ground officers in light aircraft and helicopters to control supporting arms and to report on enemy activities. At times, a warrant officer or lieutenant found himself controlling the firepower of a major general. These qualified, and occasionally colorful, individuals served with ANGLICO, observation squadrons, artillery regiments, and the division intelligence section.

(L) The basic organization for employment was a tactical air control party (TACP) with airborne or ground forward air controllers (FACs) and a shore fire control party (SFCP) with naval gunfire spot teams and liaison teams. These task units combined to form an air-naval gunfire platoon.

fire at the same time that close air support missions were being flown in the same area. This problem was addressed daily, but no agreement was reached to use the Marine's restrictive fire plan that allowed simultaneous air and gunfire use. Gray recalled the U.S. Air Force "just refused to consider any alternative ... and the U.S. Army, all the way to the top, let them get away with it." Consequently, when the aircraft made their runs, the artillery and naval gunfire simply had to stop firing. Although it was a coordination nightmare, the situation was tolerable during this slack period as there were no really worthwhile targets of opportunity or pressing needs for gunfire support.[20]

The range of the naval guns was also a major deficiency. Almost three years earlier on 15 March 1969, the battleship USS *New Jersey* (BB 62) with her 16-inch guns, had returned to the United States for decommissioning. The preponderance of naval guns that remained were mounted on destroyers and were of 5-inch bore diameter. The older 5"38 guns, with their limited range and manual loading were reserved for areas near the coastline. The newer automated and long-range 5"54 gun was used on targets which were either farther inland or which called for heavy, fast concentrations. The 5"54 also fired a rocket-assisted projectile (RAP),[(M)] which extended the normal range of the American gunfire support ships. This round, however, was not very accurate or effective at maximum range. Despite limitations, the support ships, working hand-in-glove with the spotters, formed an array of combat power which was a deterrent to enemy movements and activities along coastal areas.

Liaison and staff integration between ANGLICO and supported forces presented a real, but lesser, problem. ANGLICO detachments, headed by junior Marine and Navy officers and enlisted men, often were confronted by senior American Army and Air Force officers to provide the most appropriate supporting arm to employ in a given situation and how best to utilize it. Often the rank differential was extreme, such as the time a U.S. Army lieutenant general landed his helicopter on a fire support base in MR 1 to discuss naval gunfire with the senior American present, a U.S. Marine lance corporal.

The challenge of communications for the widely dispersed ANGLICO and fire-support units was met by Master Sergeant Donald E. Heim and his team of communicators. Heim, a former Marine artillery officer and to Gray "a superb staff NCO," was constantly at work holding together a radio network plagued by areas marginal high frequency wave-propagation and extended distances that taxed the capabilities of his equipment. The network, however, was unusual in that it provided

---

(M) This projectile was fired from a gun-tube as though it was an ordinary round. At a certain point after leaving the gun a rocket ignited and gave the ordnance extra propulsion to extend its maximum range. Keep in mind that effective use of naval gunfire is within the first three-quarters of range of the gun fired.

an alternate means of voice-communications among Marines throughout South Vietnam. This network later was to prove significant in tying together an otherwise disparate group of Marines.[N]

Fire Support teams were supporting the United States, Vietnamese, and Australian armies and the Korean and Vietnamese Marines. In MR 1 a liaison team with XXIV Corps in Da Nang supported U.S. Army units. Shore Fire Control Parties were with the 1st, and later the 3d, ARVN divisions at Quang Tri; spotters worked with VNMC units and their U.S. Marine advisors along the DMZ and with the American 23d (Americal) Infantry Division at Chu Lai. In MR 2 a liaison team was maintained at Nha Trang; spotters were flown in on rare occasions when needed. A liaison team was at MR 3 regional headquarters in Long Binh and spot teams were with the U.S. Army's 3d Brigade, 1st Cavalry Division, at Bien Hoa and with the Australian forces at Nui Dat. In the Mekong Delta in MR4, a liaison team was assigned to the regional headquarters at Can Tho. Two Marine AO's flying with VAL-4 at Binh Tuy and a shore fire control party with the 21st ARVN Division at Ca Mau completed Sub Unit One's dispositions. During the next few months, Gray shifted his teams to meet the differing needs of the supported units.

Near Hoi An in MR 1, the largest ANGLICO contingent in South Vietnam was assembled under Major Edward J. "Jim" Dyer. With this northernmost and most heavily threatened of the country's military regions, ANGLICO Marines supported the 2d Republic of Korea Marine Corps (ROKMC) Brigade and were charged with not only control of naval gunfire support but also with arranging for and controlling all allied air support. ANGLICO personnel were attached to the companies of the brigade so that when the Koreans needed air strikes, helicopter support, or medical evacuation, the planes could be requested and directed in English. This policy was necessary because the helicopters belonged to the U.S. Army and the tactical close air support was provided by the U.S. Air Force, U.S. Navy, and South Vietnamese Air Force (RVNAF). English was the only common language.

Major Dyer, a former Naval officer, was an especially qualified Marine. While in the Navy, he had been a naval gunfire liaison on Okinawa with the 3d Marine Division. During his first tour in Vietnam, he was an advisor to the Vietnamese Navy's junk force. At the end of 1965, he requested an inter-service transfer to the Marine Corps, was commissioned in Saigon, and reported to the Marines for a full tour of duty as a 105mm howitzer battery commander in Vietnam. In June 1971, Major Dyer was in Vietnam again for his third tour, his second as a Marine, and was right at home with his naval gunfire platoon in support of the ROK Marines.

(N) Because ANGLICO operators were with a variety of units and in equally varied locations, MACV's Deputy Assistant Chief of Staff, J3 (Operations), Brigadier General William H. Lanagan, Jr., a Marine himself and a personal friend of Lieutenant Colonel Gray, had a Marine-manned communications system that extended the whole length of South Vietnam.

The Korean camp and outposts were examples right out of a field manual — immaculate in every way with every sandbag in place. It was apparent to Major Dyer that the "Blue Dragon" Marines were thoroughly professional: they kept their hair cut close, wore their uniforms with pride, appeared physically ready.

During July 1971, despite Typhoons Harriet and Kim, the cruiser USS *Oklahoma City* (CLG 5) fired repeatedly in support of the ROKMC. Staff visits to the ship by both ROKMC staff officers and ANGLICO personnel ensured coordination and technical understanding among all parties concerned. Briefings were held on the area of operations, friendly positions, common radio frequencies, intelligence targets, and target lists. Enemy activity was generally light, but the ROKMC had scattered contact while on a cordon and search operations in the foothills of the Que Son Mountains. In the field with the ROK Marines, Corporal Anthony Sandoval provided the communications link and control necessary for NGF and air support. Most of his efforts were directed toward controlling helicopters flying logistic support missions.

Military Region 1 was the area that, on a day-to-day basis, provided the most return for the expenditure of money, ammunition, time, and manpower. Although it was difficult to assess damage done and enemy killed, many targets along the Demilitarized Zone were fired upon daily. In addition, Marines in the northernmost province served as an early-warning, instant-response, reaction element. Lieutenant Colonel Gray called them "disaster preventers." Time was to prove him correct.

Elsewhere, when things were quiet, Marines were idle, and this idleness presented a problem. The apparent enemy inactivity and the lack of a need to respond was countered by a vigorous training and crosstraining program and enrollments in Marine Corps Institute correspondence courses in forward observer techniques. Communicators were sent to the 3d Marine Division Naval Gunfire School at Subic Bay, Philippines, and NGF spotters were trained in communications procedures and equipment while in Vietnam. Many Marines, including Gray and First Sergeant Ernest Benjamin, both of whom were over 40, underwent parachute jump training at the ARVN Airborne Division Training Center at Tan San Nhut, while some Marines completed similar training on Okinawa given by the 5th Special Forces Group (Airborne). The physically demanding preparation for such training occupied the otherwise slack time and built an "Airborne" esprit within Sub Unit One.[0] It also created an atmosphere of mutual respect between ANGLICO and the ARVN Airborne Division it supported.

Along the northeast sector of the DMZ, the NGF area of responsibility shifted inland to the west. Naval gunfire spotters shared common locations with the U.S. Marine

---

(0) Members of ANGLICO units were required to be parachute trained in order to carry out their mission in support of joint and combined operations, in this case with the ARVN Airborne Division.

advisors on such hilltop outposts as Alpha-1 and Alpha-2 (Gio Linh) just below the DMZ. A spurt of enemy activity during the latter part of August gave the spotters the opportunity to call up to 10 missions a day. Most of the missions were suppressive fires targeted against enemy mortar and rocket positions. Supporting the Marine spotters on the ground as well as the 1st ARVN Division were ANGLICO aerial observers flying from the airfield at Dong Ha in both U.S. Army and RVNAF aircraft. Lieutenant General Welborn G. Dolvin, commanding XXIV Corps, expressed his satisfaction with the naval gunfire support rendered in his area of responsibility during this period.[21]

Despite the fact that areas became devoid of enemy activity and obvious enemy movements, Lieutenant Colonel Gray was insistent that his men be gainfully employed. Drugs, racial unrest, inter-service rivalry, and bad weather threatened morale and challenged his unit's leadership. In a letter to Headquarters Marine Corps recommending a reduction of the unit's manning level, Lieutenant Colonel Gray said, "No Marine should remain in Vietnam who does not have a full day's work to do every day." The proposal to reduce was made in order "to make these Marines available for more productive employment and to remove them from this environment where idle minds create problems at a higher rate than found in a normal devil's playground."[22] These reductions were made feasible by dissolving all ANGLICO units in MR 2 and MR 3, while still maintaining mobile spot teams prepared to re-enter those areas on short notice.

For example, during late September 1971, a flare-up in Tay Ninh Province, MR 3, and across the border in Cambodia, challenged the responsiveness as well as boosted the morale of Sub Unit One. Enemy activity in that area appeared to threaten the city of Tay Ninh. Intelligence reports caused the MACV Deputy J-3 for Operations, Brigadier General William H. Lanagan, to ask for an additional tactical air control capability along the Cambodian border. The USAF was tasked with providing the forward air controllers (FAC) and ANGLICO to supply the communicators and FAC teams to direct and control USAF aircraft inland.

In less than an hour, Master Sergeant Heim had the men and equipment staged. At first light the next morning, Lieutenant Colonel Gray, Master Sergeant Heim, and the Marine teams boarded helicopters, flew to Bien Hoa, picked up three USAF ground forward air control officers, and then flew to Tay Ninh City. There they took up three positions around the city. During the next several days, the teams received sporadic rocket fire in and near their positions. Although they did not control any air strikes, the teams were in place and were ready and communicating with the orbiting aircraft. An emergency had been met with dispatch.[23]

By October, the winter monsoon had come to the northern provinces. Weather conditions were so severe from 4 to 13 October that there were no naval gunfire support ships available. During the rest of the month the weather remained so miserable that neither friend nor foe did much moving. On 23 October 1971, Typhoon Hooster, with gusts up to 85 miles-per-hour, was uprooting trees and flooding the Da Nang, Chu Lai, and Quang Ngai areas. The communications equipment with the liaison-spot teams was damaged by the weather, while the Marines themselves suffered no injuries.

By November 1971, as the adverse weather conditions subsided, suitable targets for naval gunfire increasingly appeared. Still, the employment of naval gunfire ships decreased as ARVN artillery took up more of these fire missions. By 29 November, the Army's 23d Infantry Division had departed Vietnam. As the 2d ARVN Division relocated to Chu Lai to assume that tactical area of responsibility, Shore Fire Control Party "I-3" at Quang Ngai moved with it. The ANGLICO platoon at Hoi An prepared to stand down as the Korean Marine Brigade made preparation for its departure in early December.[24]

On the night of 22 December 1971, MACV Advisory Team 17 personnel observed a sizable enemy troop movement north of Duc Pho village in Quang Ngai. The enemy seemed to be moving in the direction of the town, and the advisors wanted the ANGLICO operators to "do something about it."[25] The liaison team located with the 2d ARVN Division at Chu Lai was called into action. Team commander Lieutenant (jg) Aaron D. Garrett, USN, responded by calling in high-explosive, variable-timed fragmentation, and smoke projectiles into the middle of the enemy's disposition. The Army advisors jubilantly radioed back that the mission was a success. Because of the cover of darkness, the Communists had displayed uncharacteristic boldness and were caught moving across the open terrain. When the rounds hit, the enemy formation was broken, and they quit the field in a rout. An early morning sweep did not reveal any bodies, but blood trails and abandoned equipment were in evidence.

By the end of 1971, Vietnam's Navy had four deep-draft ships with naval gunfire capability, albeit limited when compared to the larger, more heavily armed U.S. ships. Nevertheless, an attempt was made toward Vietnamization of naval gunfire support.[P] Vietnamese fire control personnel readily grasped the rudiments of NGF, but the indirect fire capability of the VNN ships was severely limited by the existing gunfire control system and close-in support of friendly troops was therefore marginal. ARVN officers were trained and did control some fire in the Mekong Delta, but as a whole, the effort was ineffective.[26]

(P) Attempts to organize a South Vietnamese ANGLICO-type unit within the VNMC were turned down by the VNN, ARVN, and VNAF.

During January 1972, Sub Unit One continued to provide support for ARVN units in MR 4. Naval gunfire provided support for the construction of fire bases in the southern portion of the Ca Mau Peninsula. As the fire bases were completed, ARVN artillery was moved into position. Both naval gunfire and artillery then concentrated on bringing fire to bear on suspected enemy control points, staging areas, and probable base camps. By early March, field artillery was programmed to provide complete coverage of the Delta Region. A gradual and consistent reduction of naval gunfire requirements appeared to be reasonably certain.

In order to extend the range of naval gunfire inland, on 2 February 1972, the American destroyer USS *Morton* (DD 981) sailed into Da Nang Harbor to fire into Elephant Valley, an enemy staging area west of the city. Such a mission had been considered previously, but this was the first time it had actually been carried out. While its operations were difficult to coordinate within the confines of the bay, the destroyer's presence provided moral support in and around the Da Nang area.[27]

By 24 March 1972, there were no U.S. ground spotters on an assigned basis anywhere in Vietnam except along the DMZ. There, Marines remained in the observation tower at Gio Linh Alpha-2 along with their ARVN counterparts. From other ANGLICO personnel, additional spot teams had been organized to respond to an emergency or any unusual situation. Lieutenant Commander Richard M. Kreassig, USN, the ANGLICO liaison officer for XXIV Corps, had even drawn up a contingency plan to cover the possible evacuation of exposed Alpha-2 during an emergency, particularly during the February Tet period. A Tet offensive anticipated by MACV did not materialize, however, and allied forces stood down from their alert. Now, because of Lieutenant Colonel Gray's persistent recommendations, Sub Unit One's authorized personnel strength was reduced from 185 to 89 men, effective 1 May 1972.

It appeared that peace indeed had come to South Vietnam; the market places in the Cam Lo village just south of the DMZ were scenes of active trading. Bru Montagnards were once again planting their crops in the Ba Long River Valley with a reasonable hope of harvesting them without Viet Cong interference. One could drive alone from Quang Tri Province to the bustling capital city of Saigon and southward to Ca Mau in the heart of the Delta without fear of ambush or confrontation. The canals in the U Minh Forest were open to civil use with relative assurance of safety. South Vietnam, with its natural wealth in forests, paddies, and rivers, seemingly had begun to prosper once more.[28]

CHAPTER ONE ENDNOTES.

Unless otherwise noted, all unpublished Marine Corps documents consulted in preparation of this study are held in the custody of the Archives Section, Marine Corps Historical Center (MCHC), Washington, D.C. Unless otherwise noted, the narrative is derived from CinCPac, Command History 1971 through 1973, hereafter CinCPac ComdHist [year]; USMACV, Command History 1971 through 1973, hereafter MACV ComdHist [year]; ComNavForV, Command History 1971 through 1972, hereafter NavForV ComdHist [year]; ComSeventhFlt, Command History 1971 through 1973, hereafter SeventhFlt Comdhist [year]; HqFMFPac, Operations of U.S. Marine Forces Southeast Asia, July 1971-March 1973, hereafter FMFPac MarOpsSEA; and respective Marine Corps unit command chronologies and after-action reports.

Nixon's Doctrine

1 "US Objectives/Military Objectives in SEAsia, CMC Reference Notebooks 1973, Tab I-F-1; The President's Report to Congress on Foreign Policy," 9Feb72. Also, Marshall Green, "The Nixon Doctrine: A Progress Report," *Department of State Bulletin*, 8Feb71.

2 Gen Robert E. Cushman, Jr., "To the Limit of Our Vision and Back," *United States Naval Institute Proceedings*, May 74, p. 121.

3 CMC msg to ALMAR dtd 1Jul71; Plans and Operations memo dtd 24Jan74, Tab A, HQMC(C/S), "Major Accomplishments, 1972-1973."

Contingency Forces

4 FMFPac MarOpsSEA, pp. 1-1 to 1-6.

5 Marine Corps Command Center, hereafter MCCC, Landing Forces-7th Fleet dtd 18Nov70, Tabs 43-1 to 43-3.

6 Marine Corps Museum script, "Time Tunnel" Case 19 (MCHC, Washington, D.C.).

7 SeventhFlt ComdHist72, passim. For the period covered this included Amphibious Squadrons 3, 5, and 7.

8 Col Raymond M. Kostesky, comments on draft ms, dtd 22Jan90 (Vietnam Comment File).

9 FMFPacMarOpsSEA, pp. 1-7 to 1-9.

Flexibility and Response

10 FMFPac, Operations of U.S. Marine Forces in Vietnam, May–June 1971, p. 19.

Command Relations

11 VAdm Stansfield Turner, "Missions of the U.S. Navy," *Naval War College Review*, Mar-Apr74, pp. 2-17; BGen Edwin H. Simmons, "The Marines: Now and in the Future," *Naval Review 1975*, May75, pp. 102-117; "Marine Corps Operations in Vietnam, 1969-1972," *Naval Review 1973*, May73, pp. 196-223; and Cdr Robert C. Schreadley, "The Naval War in Vietnam, 1950-1970," *Naval Review 1971*, May71, pp. 180-209.

12 LtGen Louis Metzger, comments on draft ms, dtd 8Dec89 (Vietnam Comment File).

Residual Forces

13 MACV ComdHist71, vol. ii, p. F-9. Also, Bob Heim, "Tell Them We're Here," *Leatherneck*, Aug72, pp. 24-29.

Marine Security Guard, Saigon

14 MSGBn ComdC 1971, passim. Also, SSgt M.M. Patterson, "Leathernecks With a Special Mission," *The Observer* [MACV], 15Dec72.

15 MGySgt Harry G. Lock, comments on draft ms, dtd 3Jul90 (Vietnam Comment File).

16 Ibid.

The Marine Air Control Squadron Detachment

17 FMFPac MarOpsSEA, p. 21

Sub Unit One, 1st Air and Naval Gunfire Liaison Company.

18 LtGen D'Wayne Gray, comments on draft ms, dtd 9Nov89 (Vietnam Comment File).

19 Col D'Wayne Gray intvw dtd 18Mar75, Tape 6021 (OralHistColl, MCHC, Washington, D.C.). Also, MajGen D'Wayne Gray ltrs to BGen Edwin H. Simmons dtd 25Aug71, 14Sept71, 3Nov71, 13Feb72, 24May72, and 28Apr83 (Vietnam Comment File).

20 Gray comments.

21 SU1 ComdC, Aug71.

22 SU1 msg to CMC dtd 30Aug71 (Vietnam Comment File).

23 SU1 ComdC, Sep71.

24 SU1 ComdC, Oct71, Nov71.

25 Ibid.

26 SMA ltr to FRAC dtd 7Sept72, SMA memo dtd 9Oct72, and SMA memo dtd 26Dec72 on NGF training and support, MarAdvU Turnover Folder, (MarAdvU File).

27 MACV ComdHist71, p. V-42.

28 Gray intvw.

CHAPTER TWO
THE ADVISORS

Naval Advisory Group, Naval Advisory Units • The Rung Sat Special Zone • The Mekong Delta Tactical Zone • Naval Advisory Group, Marine Advisory Unit • 'Trusted Friends' • • Winding Down • Along the DMZ

Naval Advisory Group, Naval Advisory Units

By the mid-1971, the main thrust of the U.S. policy in Vietnam centered around the advisory effort. Most Marine advisors were concentrated within the framework of the Naval Advisory Group (NAG) under the Commander Naval Forces Vietnam, Rear Admiral Robert S. Salzer. This included the Marines who quietly served their tours unheralded in the Mekong River Delta Region of MR 4. This river plain, to the east, south, and west of Saigon, accounted for almost a quarter of the total area of South Vietnam. A grid of rivers and canals dominated this relatively flat region, where boats and helicopters provided the most practical mode of transportation. Otherwise, a traveler faced an exhausting struggle on foot through a quagmire of murky water, oozing mud, and practically impenetrable tropical vines and roots. Under French colonial rule, the delta was criss-crossed with a well-developed road and canal system for ease of regional movement. Because of the importance of this network to the economies of both Vietnam and Cambodia, it was vital to keep these highways open.

From as early as 1954, the thick mangrove jungles provided a place of refuge for the Viet Cong (VC) guerrillas as they waged their war of terror upon the region's hamlets and river commerce. After each attack, the VC could return to the relative safety and seclusion of their base camps. However, operations conducted by both Regional (RF) and Popular (PF) Forces which began in 1964, over the years had reduced the enemy activity from a major threat to minor harassment. Since July 1964, when Major Edward J. Bronars was assigned as the first U.S. Marine advisor in the region, Marines had worked with these government troops in assisting the villagers in base, village, and hamlet security. Within this delta, Marines were assigned to both the Rung Sat Special Zone and the Mekong Delta Tactical Zone.[1]

The Rung Sat Special Zone

The Rung Sat Special Zone (RSSZ) was an area of approximately 480 square miles southeast of Saigon, extending to the South China Sea. Rung Sat, which means "Forest of Death," was an area of great concern to the South Vietnamese because the Long Tau River ran through its center. The Long Tau, or Royal River, could accommodate deep-draft ships up to 720 feet long. The river banks were low and lined with dense mangrove marsh and swamps. It was the main shipping channel leading to Saigon and much of the logistic and economic support of South Vietnam depended on the river remaining open. The RSSZ command was charged with keeping this waterway open and functioning.

By October 1971, enemy activity had been brought under control. Combined U.S. Marine, Navy, and Army advisors, under the supervision of the Senior Advisor, RSSZ, U.S. Navy Commander Douglas A. Stewart, worked with the local forces in operations designed to keep the enemy off balance. At the same time they assisted the civilians in reconstruction, public health, education, and other aspects of nation-building. With some sense of security, the fishermen, woodcutters, and farmers once again were following the roles of their forefathers as an ominous peace settled over Rung Sat, the Forest of Death.

Major James M. Tully was Commander Stewart's assistant senior advisor and was specifically charged with tactical ground and air operations. The zone was divided into two districts, Can Gio on the east and Quang Xuyen on the west. Each district had a U.S. Marine advisory team assigned to it. The Quang Xuyen District team was headed by Captain Ronald S. Neubauer, while Captain David W. Blizzard headed the team in the Can Gio District. Daily, Vietnamese and Americans shared food, hardships, and work as they patrolled the waterways of the Rung Sat. With his assignment to the swamps of the RSSZ, Captain Neubauer, a lean, red-headed Marine from Norwalk, Connecticut, was far removed from the pageantry of his previous duty station. While assigned to the Marine Barracks, Washington, D.C., he had served as parade adjutant and as a social aide at the White House.[2]

To cover their vast districts each captain was assisted by six enlisted advisors and one Navy medical corpsman. The enlisted Marines, on occasion, were called upon to advise Vietnamese officers while the Navy corpsmen were often required to perform functions or to give treatment that would normally be expected of a physician. The enlisted Marines were often communications, intelligence, and engineer specialists. They assisted in all forms of military and civil operations, but the counterinsurgency effort was their forte. Each man on the team worked closely with his counterpart in an effort to develop a comprehensive program to pacify the entire Long Tau shipping channel.

In such an undertaking, each meter of river was as vital as the next. Friendly forces had to be as mobile and as flexible as possible in order to counter the Viet Cong threat. Operations ranging from multi-company helicopter and waterborne assaults down to squad-size interdiction missions were carried out repeatedly and with such effectiveness that enemy activity had been reduced to practically nothing. Advisors accompanied the Vietnamese on operations, assisting the commanders on the ground in talking with the command and communications helicopters, providing aerial observation, close air support, naval gunfire support, troop lifts, and medical evacuation.

Marine Staff Sergeant Freddie L. Murray was assigned to work with the Regional Force militia in late 1971. Murray assisted the Vietnamese with communications between ground units, arranged for boats to move through the waterways, and for U.S. Navy or Army helicopter support. There was not much excitement in the Rung Sat, only hard, dirty work of slogging through knee-deep mud and swamp under a blistering sun. Murray felt that progress had been made and the advisors no longer went on field operations "unless they have a specific target to hit."[3]

There were times when Marine advisors gave more than just morale or communications support. On 9 November 1971, Captain Blizzard accompanied a Vietnamese PF squad in the Can Gio District that walked into an enemy ambush. One "PF" was hit by the initial burst and fell seriously wounded. While directing the other Vietnamese to secure a helicopter landing zone, Captain Blizzard radioed for a medical evacuation helicopter. With the helicopter on the way, he ran 50 meters to the fallen soldier and, while a burst of enemy fire tore the ground around him, hoisted the wounded man to his shoulders and carried him 300 meters to the secured zone. After the "Medevac," Captain Blizzard rallied the Vietnamese and led them in an assault on the enemy position. For his bravery, he was awarded the Silver Star Medal. Later, he was to go north to join the fighting in MR 1 with the Vietnamese Marines.

The Mekong Delta Tactical Zone

To the northwest along the Cambodian border, things had not been quiet. Late in 1970 the North Vietnamese and Viet Cong had made an effort to isolate Phnom Penh, the capital of the Khmer Republic, by closing all lines of communications including the vital Mekong River between Tan Chau, Vietnam, and Phnom Penh, Cambodia. Early in 1971, the oil tanker *Mekong* was sunk while transporting petroleum upstream. After this attack the Cambodian Government asked the United States and South Vietnam to provide protection for the river convoys between Tan Chau and Phnom Penh. This was not to be an easy task, for convoy protection required close cooperation among nine military services of the three nations.

After a request of the Cambodian government, Operation Tran Hung Dao 18 was initiated for the Mekong Delta Tactical Zone (MDTZ). The primary objective of this operation was to organize and coordinate ground and air support for convoys which carried military cargo and petroleum products from Tan Chau to Phnom Penh. The vital river route passed through more than 100 kilometers of dense jungles, high river banks, and several narrow gorges affording the enemy ideal ambush positions at almost any point.[4] On 18 January 1972, Major Donald R. Gardner relieved Commander Arthur St. Clair Wright as senior advisor, Tran Hung Dao 18 (THD-18), area coordinator; and commander, Task Group 116.15. Major Gardner, wearing a Silver Star Medal from a previous tour of duty in Vietnam and after serving nine months in the Chau Doc Province, was embarking upon an assignment that had political and cultural implications unavoidable even at the advisory level.

Traditionally, Vietnamese and Cambodians neither liked nor respected one another. It was Major Gardner's task to minimize this historic antagonism through a continuous liaison and coordination effort. As he recalled, only "the good working relationship, in spite of ethnic differences, between the FANK (Cambodian Army), 4th ARVN Ranger Group, and the THD-18 made this possible."

In addition to the Vietnamese Navy commitment of ships, tankers, tugs, and barges to haul fuel and other supplies to Phnom Penh, there was a constant requirement to support the ARVN ground forces that provided river bank security. Originally, the VNMC had been tasked with these duties, but, ultimately, the ARVN 4th Ranger Group of the 44th Special Tactical Zone were assigned this mission. In cooperation with the Cambodian 4th Infantry Brigade, the ARVN Rangers were successful in preventing the enemy from closing the river supply route.[A]

Major Gardner's VNN counterpart, Commodore Nghiem Van Phu, a graduate of the U.S. Army's Command and Staff College, had run convoys on the Red River in North Vietnam prior to 1954, before Gardner was old enough to wear a uniform. He was a naval professional in every sense and expected no less from his officers and men. Under the Commodore's tutelage, the slow-talking Gardner from Tennessee quickly became accustomed to "brown water navy" techniques.[B] Major Gardner learned the customs of the delta people, visited their families, and made efforts to improve

(A) MajGen Donald R. Gardner later noted that this "was the only source of supply for Phnom Penh. Had it failed, Cambodia would have fallen in 1971." (Gardner comments)

(B) "Brown water navy" is a phrase used to describe riverine and coastal operations as opposed to the "blue water navy" of the ocean-going forces.

sanitary and living conditions. The people-to-people effort took on a new meaningone day when on a sampan, he delivered a child. Every day seemed to present new challenges.

In February and March 1972, allied forces uncovered caches of arms and supplies near outlying bases along the Cambodian border indicating that Communist infiltrators had prepared for more than guerrilla-type harassment actions. Air strikes by American, Vietnamese, and Cambodian forces provided some convoy protection, but the Communists, however, repeatedly made their presence known. In early 1972 there were more than 60 ambushes against shipping to Phnom Penh. During this time, the enemy sank one barge and damaged other vessels with rockets. Communist antiaircraft fire downed three helicopters providing escort air cover.[5]

Naval Advisory Group, Marine Advisory Unit

While individual Marines served Vietnamese forces within Naval and MACV advisory units, one group of Marine advisors had caught the Corps' popular image as "The Marine Advisors." These were the officers and men of the Marine Advisory Unit[(C)] who served with the Vietnamese Marine Corps. The VNMC was formed with the 1954 ceasefire that established North and South Vietnam. An elite unit by any standard and closely associated with the U.S. Marine Corps, the VNMC had been fighting the Communists for more than 20 years. Marines selected to serve as advisors with them were considered fortunate for being among the only Marines in combat and for the exotic nature of their assignment. As advisors, the Americans wore the same distinctive green beret and "tiger stripe" field uniform of the Vietnamese. Under the supervision of a Senior Marine Advisor (SMA), Marines were assigned to VNMC battalions, as well as to brigade and division staffs.

The VNMC had its beginning in October 1954 when Lieutenant Colonel Victor J. Croizat helped organize the VNMC from former colonial-era commandos, who had come south under the provisions of the Geneva Conference agreements.[(D)6] A division-sized service since 1968, the VNMC boasted nine infantry battalions, three artillery battalions, and three brigade headquarters designated Marine Brigades 147, 258, and 369. Each of the brigades was originally formed with the infantry battalions which made up its numerical designation i.e., Marine Brigade 258 originally had the 2d, 5th, and 8th battalions under its control. In practice, a brigade headquarters controlled whatever mix of units it was assigned. The VNMC, along with the ARVN Airborne,

---

(C) Abbreviated at the time as the MAU, but hereafter MarAdvU, to avoid confusion with the Marine Amphibious Unit (MAU) of the Seventh Fleet.

(D) 1st and 2d *Battaillons de Marche*, in accordance with Decree 991-QP/ND of 13Oct54.

formed the Joint General Staff General Reserve of the Republic of Vietnam, and, as such, were employed in any of the four military regions. Additionally, a VNMC battalion or a task force could be attached to any of the corps tactical zones or army divisions to serve as a reaction force. From April 1971, two brigades operated in Quang Tri Province first under the operational control of the 1st ARVN Division headquarters and later with the newly formed 3d ARVN Division. The Marine division headquarters and the remaining brigade were located in Saigon.

By now, many of the U.S. Marines reporting to the advisory unit in Saigon for duty were returning to Vietnam for their second and third times. Some had completed the Army's Military Assistance Training Advisor (MATA) Course at Fort Bragg, North Carolina, or the Marine Advisor Course at Quantico, Virginia. A few advisors were fluent in Vietnamese and most could converse at a basic level. Upon arrival in Saigon, the new advisors could tell that the city was prospering. The open markets were doing a rushing business; street vendors were hawking their wares; nightclubs abounded; and there was a swarm of people constantly in motion on small but noisy motorscooters. As the advisors made their way north to join their battalions, they were surprised at the peaceful appearance of the countryside. During the latter part of 1971, both Americans and Vietnamese moved throughout the area with little trepidation. No one felt the necessity of wearing a helmet or flak jacket and few Marines actually carried a magazine loaded in their weapons. The Vietnamese seemed happy and in good physical shape, many would greet the Americans in English when they passed.

After the initial briefing in Saigon by the Senior Marine Advisor, those Marines assigned to the brigades operating in the north often made their way there by serving as mailmen and couriers to Marines already in the field. While all the advisors' mail came into Saigon, the way it got to the other end of the country was not predetermined. For example, when Captain Ray L. Smith checked in and was assigned to the 4th VNMC Battalion at Mai Loc, he carried four bags of mail with him. It was relatively easy to catch an aircraft from Saigon to Da Nang, but from that point on the itinerary was erratic. After spending a day at Da Nang, Smith was able to catch a plane to Phu Bai. Because of the monsoon rains, Major Walter E. Boomer, senior advisor to the 4th VNMC Battalion, met Captain Smith at Phu Bai in a Jeep. Smith was wary as the two traveled from Phu Bai through Hue, Quang Tri, and Dong Ha, right up to the position where he was to be stationed. It seemed to be a different kind of tour from his first in Vietnam.

Some Vietnamese Marine officers had been trained in the United States and spoke English. They had been in combat for years and often did not feel the need for an American advisor. Because of this, the American Marines often felt more like a fire

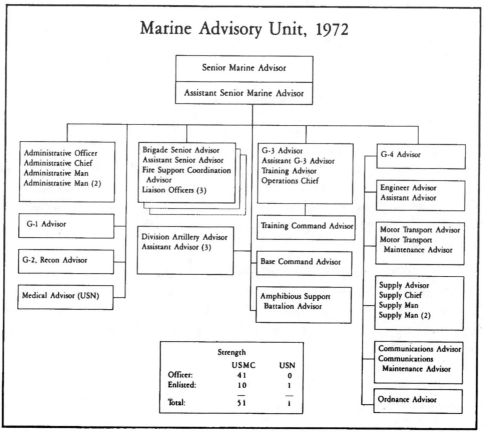

Marine Advisory Unit, 1972

Senior Marine Advisor

Assistant Senior Marine Advisor

Administrative Officer
Administrative Chief
Administrative Man
Administrative Man (2)

Brigade Senior Advisor
Assistant Senior Advisor
Fire Support Coordination
Advisor
Liaison Officers (3)

G-3 Advisor
Assistant G-3 Advisor
Training Advisor
Operations Chief

G-4 Advisor

G-1 Advisor

Division Artillery Advisor
Assistant Advisor (3)

Training Command Advisor

Engineer Advisor
Assistant Advisor

G-2, Recon Advisor

Base Command Advisor

Motor Transport Advisor
Motor Transport
Maintenance Advisor

Medical Advisor (USN)

Amphibious Support
Battalion Advisor

Supply Advisor
Supply Chief
Supply Man
Supply Man (2)

Communications Advisor
Communications
Maintenance Advisor

Ordnance Advisor

	Strength	
	USMC	USN
Officer:	41	0
Enlisted:	10	1
Total:	51	1

Adapted from Marine Advisory Unit Material

support coordinator than an advisor. In fact, during this period Colonel Joshua W. Dorsey III, who had relieved Colonel Francis W. Tief as senior advisor, was making plans to pull the advisors from the battalion level. He wanted to consolidate them at each brigade, thus forming a "liaison team" that could be responsive as the needs arose.[7]

'Trusted Friends'

The Marine advisors with the battalions in the field had a "fairly comfortable" life. They lived in bunkers, slept on cots, and shaved and bathed out of their helmets. There were kerosene lamps for light and gasoline stoves which took the damp chill out of the air, particularly during the monsoon season with its penetrating cold. Rats in the bunkers, however, did nothing for peace of mind. Their number was constantly multiplying, along with hordes of mosquitoes. One Marine advisor killed 34 rats in his area in an evening.

Marine advisors routinely shared the Vietnamese food of their counterparts' mess, which together with attempts to converse in Vietnamese, did more to foster good personal relations than anything else. Eating Vietnamese food, however, initially could be an unsettling experience. "Nuoc Mam," a fermented sauce made of fish and salt, was served with practically every meal as a source of protein. When of poor quality, it had a strong, offensive smell to most foreigners. Luckily, battalion commanders usually had the high quality variety which was quite tasty. Special occasions called for exotic foods such as coagulated duck blood pudding with peanuts on top, a delicacy unknown to most Americans.

Vietnamese Marine methods of food procurement differed from the orderly, industrialized, logistical procedures of the USMC. The battalion commander was given an allocation of funds to buy food for his troops. He would do his purchasing in the local markets and from individual farmers. Although the government provided bulk rice and canned goods, the preponderance of the food prepared in the battalion messes was obtained from the local area. When resupply runs arrived, any meat would be cooked immediately in order to preserve it since there was no refrigeration. This would provide meat for the next few days without any problems unless it became flyblown and maggot infested. Occasionally, in the mountain regions, a deer or a wild boar would be shot and find its way into the battalion's cooking pots. If the battalion was operating along the coast, the menu might include crab and other seafoods. Farm produce was also cheaper there than it was inland. The American advisors often made contributions to their counterparts' mess by sharing packages from home. The results could be unpredictable. Captain Ray Smith recalled receiving a large can of lobster meat and turning it over to his counterpart's chef who was in the process of preparing the evening meal. Eagerly anticipating the rare delicacy, he sat down to dinner to find it on the menu all right ... submerged in turnip soup.

Although the Americans made every effort to know their counterparts better by living with them and sharing their lot, they took pains not to become involved in certain aspects of Vietnamese military procedures. One such area was the administration of discipline. A Vietnamese Marine found guilty of an offense was awarded punishment that might seem harsh to the observing advisor and certainly would not be found in the Uniform Code of Military Justice or even the "Rocks and Shoals" of the old Corps. It was, in short, immediate and extremely corporal. Strict discipline contributed to the high morale of the closely-knit VNMC battalions. Another positive indicator was the Marines' intense personal loyalty to their commanders, especially battalion commanders. Their relationship was long standing and it was not unusual for a Marine to have served in the same battalion for as long as 15 years. It was only natural for the Vietnamese emphasis on the family to extend into professional life.[8]

Winding Down

During June 1971, VNMC Brigade 147 defeated NVA assaults during which the enemy had used tear gas and had reached the Marines fighting holes.[E] One U.S. Marine advisor, Captain Dennis M. Dicke, was mortally wounded on Operation Lam Son 810 while serving with the 7th VNMC Battalion. The outcome of the battle was doubtful until artillery and close air support turned the tide in favor of the Marines. By July 1971, the situation in South Vietnam seemed quiet enough, although Marine battalions in MR 1 had beaten back enemy attacks during the preceding three months. By mid-year, however, activity had subsided and newly arrived advisors were reporting to their battalions in the field with a feeling that this was going to be a quiet period indeed.

During this time, battalions spent about three months in MR 1 and then rotated to Saigon for refurbishing, training, and rest and recuperation with their families. Each of the battalions had a designated base camp near Saigon which served as a permanent home for the unit where administration, supply, and training activities took place. In addition, many of the Marines' families lived nearby. Upon arrival in Saigon, the Vietnamese Marines were granted a 10-day leave with their families. Often when a battalion was due to return north, men who had overstayed their leave reported in packed and ready to go. After fighting a long war, the advisors learned the important thing was to be there when the unit departed for the "fronts" and they usually were.[9]

(E) Vietnamese Marines, whose senior officers had come from the north, referred to their enemy as Communists or Viet Cong (Vietnamese Communists) and did not use the American term NVA (North Vietnamese Army) or the Communist's PAVN (People's Army of Viet Nam).

After leave, training was the order of the day. Some of the training was undertaken within the base camp areas, while formal schools were conducted at the Vietnamese Marine Training Command at Thu Duc, northeast of Saigon. This camp included recruit-training facilities, ranges, and housing with adequate facilities to accommodate 2,000 students simultaneously. Indoor classrooms, a confidence course, infiltration course, mine and boobytrap course, and a 300-meter bayonet course provided individual training.[10]

American Marines were assigned to the training command to assist in the management of the instruction program. With the withdrawal of American units from Vietnam, much U.S. Marine Corps equipment was turned over to the Vietnamese Marines. Marine advisors concerned themselves with teaching the VNMC personnel the use and care of the surplus equipment.[11] On one occasion to facilitate this training, the 3d Marine Division sent a mobile training team from Okinawa to Thu Duc. This team spent six weeks training the Vietnamese in utilization of the equipment left by III MAF, including the 106mm recoilless rifle and the multi-channel radios, the AN/MRC162s and 163s. These two items of equipment played important roles in the events which were to follow.[12]

On 12 August 1971 at 0900, Admiral Salzer, as Commander Naval Forces Vietnam, presented the advisory unit with its second Naval Unit Commendation.[F] At the same time, a major effort was being made in the reorganization of the VNMC. Historically, the involvement of American Marines had been on the battalion level, giving tactical advice to their counterparts in the field. Colonel Dorsey wanted to shift the emphasis on the U.S. Marine advisors from one of rendering tactical advice to one of resource management.

Colonel Dorsey wanted to accomplish two major objectives during 1972. Along with Major Donald B. Conaty, the G-3 advisor to the VNMC Division, Colonel Dorsey worked to foster a greater sense of unity between the Vietnamese Navy and the VNMC in order to build a viable amphibious assault team. Their chief aim was to have the division plan and execute a brigade-size landing. They also planned to organize and use tactical operations centers (TOCs) at the brigade as well as division level. These centers would also include a fire support coordination center (FSCC) capable of coordinating artillery, air strikes, and naval gunfire. Finally, a division command post exercise was to be conducted to test each aspect of the reorganization. To this point, the VNMC had not operated as a division-level force and lacked necessary command and control personnel and equipment. Even though a VNMC division headquarters had been committed in Laos during Operation Lam Son 719, there was very little command experience above the brigade level.[13]

(F) For the period of 1 July 1969 to 1 July 1971, extended through 31 December 1971 in lieu of a third award.

Along the DMZ

South Vietnamese defenses along the demilitarized zone consisted of a string of positions developed in part from the previous American defenses oriented along the main avenues of approach from the north and the west. These stretched from the coast,inland across National Highway 1 (QL-1), turning south across Highway 9, and tied in with a string of fire support bases guarding the highland valley approaches from the west. American Marines recalled this as the "Leatherneck Square" bounded by Gio Linh, Con Thien, Cam Lo, and Dong Ha. Now these locations were know by Vietnamese names or more anonymous alpha-numeric appellations. On 6 October 1971, a U.S. Army liaison team from MACV arrived at Alpha 4 (Con Thien) to inspect the position before the newly formed 3d ARVN Division assumed responsibility for the DMZ. The 1st ARVN Division, which had tactical responsibility for the DMZ, was scheduled to displace south in early November. MACV Advisory Team 155, under Colonel Donald J. Metcalf, USA, the senior advisor, was tasked with providing American support to the commanding general of the 3d ARVN Division. Team 155, which was primarily billeted at Quang Tri, consisted of more than 200 men. Of this number, less than 20 U.S. Army advisors were actually in the field with ARVN units. With its hot food, bar, and showers, Team 155 was an oasis to the U.S. Marines serving with the VNMC in northern MR 1.[14]

Throughout this period there had been occasional enemy contact, generally of platoon-size, but no major enemy encounters. On 23 October 1971, elements of the 4th VNMC Battalion made contact with an estimated enemy platoon east of Alpha 4. In the resulting action three Vietnamese Marines were wounded. In spite of a raging rain storm, an Army helicopter piloted by 1st Lieutenant Scott Livingston, USA, flew in to evacuate the wounded Marines. The weather was so bad that, on taking off, the helicopter was forced down at Mai Loc Combat Base where it had to remain overnight. According to Major Boomer, the wounded Marines were evacuated the next morning in spite of the fact that "... helicopters don't fly in weather like that."[15] On a lighter note, all the American Marines in the north gathered at Charlie 1 to join with Marines all over the world in celebrating the 196th birthday of the Corps, on 10 November 1971. Birthday cakes were flown up from Saigon and the Vietnamese Marines joined in the big celebration. There was plenty of beer for everyone, but the cake made a number of Marines sick.[16]

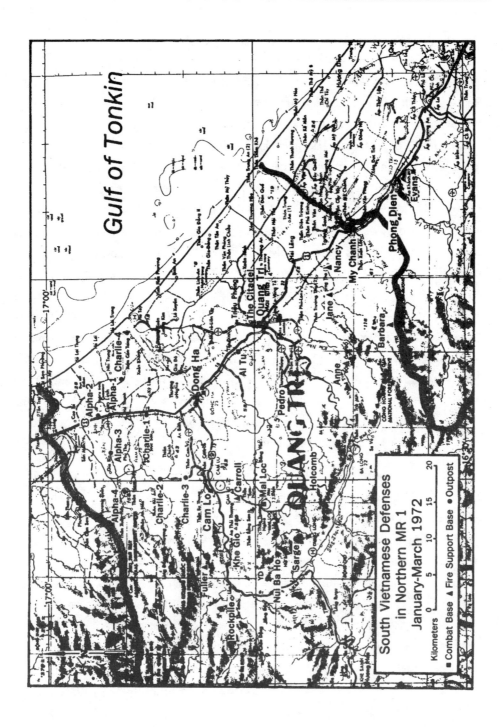

South Vietnamese Defenses in Northern MR 1, January–March 1972

Activity along the DMZ was almost at a stand still. It was an ideal time to consolidate the advisors at the brigade level, but as Colonel Dorsey remembered:

> ... something was going on; particularly up north there was a feeling of foreboding. The fire support bases were at minimum strength, whereas the USMC had these same bases fully manned. The ARVN strength was insufficient, and they were not actively patrolling, although the VNMC did a little — but not enough. I couldn't help but feel that something was going to happen. It seemed like a charade. The weather was bad; it was really cold. The FSBs [fire support bases] were socked in.[17]

The weather was indeed terrible along the DMZ. It was miserably cold and everybody, including the North Vietnamese Army was preoccupied in trying to keep warm and dry. Major Boomer, with the 4th VNMC Battalion, said he never had been so cold in his whole life. He was having some second thoughts on why, when given a choice of assignments upon arriving at Saigon, he had chosen an infantry battalion instead of a staff job at division headquarters. It was tough, but it would get tougher. Factors other than the weather were slated to deteriorate.

A significant attack occurred on the night of 12 December 1971 — 3,000 meters to the east of Charlie 3. The NVA failed in their assault of a Regional Force company, losing 17 men in the process. The next morning the dead NVA were laid out in Cam Lo village. From that time on, the road from Cam Lo to Charlie 2 did not seem quite so secure. On 21 December, just after the 5th VNMC Battalion, with Major Donald L. Price as senior advisor, replaced the 4th VNMC Battalion, the enemy fired more incoming rounds on the newcomers than the 4th Battalion had received all that fall.[18] Late one evening, Major Price and Captain Marshall R. "Skip" Wells looked north into the DMZ and observed the sparkle of signal flares, assuming that even the NVA had "to train before an offensive."[19]

Major Robert F. Sheridan, senior advisor to the VNMC Brigade 369, expressed his concern at this time to brigade commander Colonel Phan Van Chung about the lack of mobility resulting from maintaining fixed locations. Colonel Chung, who had a reputation as an outstanding commander who utilized his staff and appreciated his American advisors, conducted battalion-size operations west of Highway 9. Two consecutive sweeps from the Rockpile south to the Ba Long Valley revealed no sign of the enemy, but they were indeed out there, Major Sheridan even talked to one of them on Christmas Eve.

The Marine advisors had two channels of communications: at brigade, the advisor had an AN/MRC83 radio Jeep which he used for his twice-weekly checks with advisory unit headquarters in Saigon. The other channel was the local "Gunga Din" network which linked the advisors in the local area. Although it was a secure net utilizing the tactical cryptographic device, the KY38, the Marines would usually transmit in the clear mode as they conversed over the "party" line. It was quicker and used less power from the radios' batteries. After the nightly electronic "advisor conference" on 25 December 1971, Major Sheridan wished all a Merry Christmas. To everyone's surprise an Asian voice in perfect English came up on the air and replied, "Merry Christmas to you," and this general conversation followed:

> **S:** Who is this?
>
> **NVA:** Oh, I listen to you all the time. Where are you? Mai Loc? Sarge? or Fuller?
>
> **S:** I can't tell you where I am.
>
> **NVA:** You are American Marine. Why don't you go home?
>
> **S:** I'll go home when you guys go home.
>
> **NVA:** Well, maybe we will all go home some day. Are you married?
>
> **S:** Yes.
>
> **NVA:** How many children do you have?
>
> **S:** Too many.
>
> **NVA:** That's good. I have five girls in Hanoi which I haven't seen in nine months.
>
> **S:** Maybe the next time you go to Hanoi you can make a boy.

Both laughed and then talked about the poor weather. Finally the enemy signed off with, "I must go now. Merry Christmas! I hope the war ends soon." Yes, the enemy was out there, and furthermore; he was listening, so deficient communications security took on a whole new meaning.[20]

By January 1972, the 3d ARVN Division had responsibility for everything north of Highway 9, including Dong Ha and Fire Support Base Fuller. The division commander, Brigadier General Vu Van Giai, visited his troops in the field every day. General Giai's U.S. Army advisors were oriented on training and logistics and were not present at units below the regimental level. Giai also dropped in on the VNMC units, which were under his operational control and oriented to the west of Quang Tri. He seemed to enjoy speaking in English with the Marine advisors.

The 3d ARVN Division, newly formed and occupying unfamiliar terrain, was beset with many problems. The ARVN soldiers, who included a mix of soldiers of varied quality, were untrained as a unit. Lieutenant Colonel William C. Camper, USA, a MACV Team 155 advisor with the 2d ARVN Regiment, observed that "we were getting college students who had evaded the draft for long periods, also interpreters who had worked for U.S. forces." These were "big-city slickers" who did not compare to the average ARVN soldier from a rural background. Camper concluded, "they definitely had an effect on morale and adequacy of training."[21]

On 27 January 1972, a USAF gun ship, patrolling Highway 9 to Khe Sanh, was shot down at 5,000 feet right over the Khe Sanh air strip, by an SA-2 missile. During February, enemy activity started to pickup to the west. Fire Support Base Fuller was hit with rocket fire almost daily. Both the outpost at Nui Ba Ho and FSB Sarge, along with Fuller started reporting ground contacts. South Vietnamese troops in the vicinity of the Rockpile, north of Highway 9, reported hearing tracked vehicles and trucks moving at night. Lieutenant Colonel Camper recalled that he accompanied an air cavalry "Pink Team" in a Hughes OH-6 Cayuse ("Loach") helicopter, landing in several locations behind the Rockpile, finding "fresh tracks from tracked vehicles in a number of locations," but seeing no enemy troops and receiving no enemy fire.[G]

Directives and warnings from Saigon required a high state of readiness during Tet, the national holiday period celebrating the lunar new year. Both MACV and ARVN staffs predicated that the North Vietnamese would challenge Vietnamization in 1972. General William C. Westmoreland, as Chief of Staff of the U.S. Army, had visited South Vietnam in early 1972 for the Chairman of the Joint Chiefs of Staff and the Secretary of Defense. After touring all four military regions and talking with General Creighton W. Abrams and Chairman of the Vietnamese Joint General Staff, General Cao Van Vien, he concluded they were confident "that they can handle the situation" that existed.[22]

Communist troop buildups were identified along the DMZ and Laotian border areas west of Quang Tri and Thua Thien Provinces. The North Vietnamese high command had organized a corps-level headquarters to carry out the attack on South Vietnam's MR 1. Identified as the *Tri Thien Hue Front* with the *702d Command Group Headquarters,* it crossed over previous front and military region boundaries to undertake the Spring Offensive. It was commanded by Major General Le Taug Tan and his political deputy Le Quang Dou. This coincided with a multidivision threat in

---

(G) U.S. Army Pink Teams were composed of five helicopters. Two OH-6 "Loach" light observation helicopters acted as scouts while two Bell AH-1 Cobra gunships provided an attack capability. A UH-1 provided the flight's command and control.

the tri-border region west of Pleiku.[H] Like most intelligence predictions, the questions of when, where, and in what strength were left to the local commander to determine. American commanders and advisors in MR 1 were directed by General Abrams to determine likely avenues of approach and assembly areas to pre-plan Arc Light strikes, as he wanted "no delays due to targeting procedures when the time comes to go with these strikes."[23]

Other reports indicated that big guns were being moved west of the Marines' positions and groups of 20 to 30 enemy were observed moving openly during the daytime.[24] Incidents of road mining were being reported. Captain George Philip III, advisor to the 1st VNMC Artillery Battalion, narrowly escaped death from vehicle mine detonation. While returning to the battalion command post and instead of crossing a bridge just south of Mai Loc, he drove his jeep in the stream to wash it. A vehicle full of ARVN artillery officers drove over the bridge Captain Philip had delayed crossing. The bridge exploded killing them all. This incident was cause for instituting the "two-jeep" policy which made it mandatory for at least two vehicles to move in convoy at all times in case of an enemy ambush or mine incidents.[25]

On 5 March 1972, the South Vietnamese began an operation to clear the area around Fire Support Base Bastogne east of Hue City and met heavy resistance from elements of the *324B NVA Division*. This generated a flurry of response with B-52 "Light" bombings and tactical air sorties, but the appearance here of NVA troops was not seen as part of a concerted buildup of forces in MR 1. Indications were that the main threat was directed at MR 2. This was the prevailing view held by MACV and the American Embassy in Saigon.[26] The Vietnamese I Corps commander, Lieutenant General Hoang Xuan Lam, and his latest American counterpart, Major General Frederick J. Kroesen, Jr., USA, commanding the newly formed 1st Regional Advisory Command, viewed the situation with concern.[I] Dispositions by the 3d ARVN Division and the VNMC units in MR 1 remained along key terrain and avenues of approach along Highway 9 from the west, where the North Vietnamese threat had been from in the past. Although the positions along the DMZ had always been within range of artillery, they were not considered worthy of a conventional attack by combined arms.[27]

During the last week in March, VNMC patrols in Quang Tri Province began finding caches of mortar and B-40 rocket rounds. People were spotted moving supplies and a Vietnamese was captured in the Ba Long Valley carrying mortar rounds. By this time

---

(H) At the American Embassy was Edwin W. Besch, a medically retired Marine captain, who followed the activities of NVA and VNMC units as an intelligence analyst for the Central Intelligence Agency at the American Embassy. He recalled that, "in fact, the first firm indication of the impending offensive in South Vietnam was the infiltration into the western highlands of the *320th NVA Division*" from north of the DMZ in January 1972, followed by the 2d NVA Division from Laos. (Besch comments)

(I) FRAC was established on 19 March 1972.

every friendly location that had an artillery position was taking enemy incoming artillery and rocket rounds regularly. The U.S. Air Force and Navy flew support missions every day, weather permitting, but many times during the day visibility was almost zero. The U.S. Army's 8th Radio Research Field Station (8th RRFS) at Phu Bai reported that an NVA artillery headquarters was located only six kilometers southwest of Fire Support Base Sarge.

From Sarge, Major Boomer had briefed General Giai on everything the Marines had been seeing and their concern over the buildup of enemy forces. Boomer proposed offensive action west of Sarge in the belief that this would provide "more accurate information on the enemy's intentions and possibly disrupt his plans." General Giai "casually dismissed" this proposal.[28] Major Boomer, in retrospect, said that it was obvious that the enemy was stockpiling ammunition and supplies at the base of the hill that FSB Sarge was located on. By now, enemy contacts and artillery fire "grew heavier," and it was clear that a major enemy build-up was taking place.

On 28 March 1972, an NVA soldier noted he was with a unit "in a staging area in the jungle very close to the enemy. In spite of his daily patrols, the latter is unaware ....We take advantage of a heavy downpour to cross the Ba Long River." His objective was the cloud-shrouded firebase "Dong Toan," known to the Americans as Sarge.[29]

CHAPTER TWO ENDNOTES

Unless otherwise noted, material in chapters two through nine is derived from: Vietnamese Marine Corps/Marine Advisory Unit Historical Summary 1954-1973, hereafter VNMC HistSum; Marine Advisory Unit Historical Summary, 1972, hereafter MarAdvU HistSum72; Marine Advisory Unit Monthly Historical Summary, hereafter MarAdvU ComdC [date]; *The Covan* newsletter, hereafter *Covan* [date]; and Marine Advisory Unit files received from the VNMC Logistics Branch, Navy Division, DAO, hereafter MarAdvU File (cited by subject and page, folder, and file). Also, Standing Operating Procedures for Marine Advisory Unit, MAUO P5000.1A, n.d.; Marine Advisory Unit, NAG, "The Role of the Advisor," ms, n.d., and Maj Nguyen Thanh Tri, "Vietnamese Advisor," Marine Corps Gazette, Dec68, pp. 29-32 (MarAdvU File).

Naval Advisory Group, Naval Advisory Units

1 Capt Robert H. Whitlow, *U.S. Marines in Vietnam, 1954–1964: The Advisory and Combat Assistance Era* (Washington, D.C., Hist&MusDiv, HQMC, 1977), p. 142, hereafter Whitlow, *Marines in Vietnam 1954–1964*.

The Rung Sat Special Zone

2 Maj Ronald S. Neubauer intvw, dtd 26Jun75, Tape 6025 (Oral HistColl, MCHC, Washington, D.C.).

3 JO1 Bob Williams, "Rung Sat," *Leatherneck*, Oct71, pp. 83-84.

The Mekong Delta Tactical Zone

4 MACV, ComdHist 1971, vol. II, p. p-E-12. Also, CinCPac ComdHist71, vol. 1, p. 313.

5 Maj Donald R. Gardner ltr to LtCol Arnold dtd 30Oct75; MajGen Donald R. Gardner, comments on draft ms, dtd 23Jan90 (Vietnam Comment File).

Naval Advisory Group, Marine Advisory Unit

6 Col Victor J. Croizat comments to Maj Melson dtd 28Sep87; Whitlow, *Marines in Vietnam 1954–1964*, p. 16; Command Histories and Historical Sketches of RVNAF Divisions, dtd 6Feb73.

7 Col Joshua W. Dorsey III intvw dtd 21May75, Tape 6023 (OralHistColl, MCHC, Washington, D.C.); Senior Marine Advisor, Senior Officer Debriefing Report dtd 23Jan73, hereafter SMA debrief; and Award Recommendation, Dorsey III, Joshua Worthington, dtd 26Feb73 (MarAdvU File).

'Trusted Friends'

8 Capt Ray L. Smith intvw dtd 9Mar75, Tape 6020 (OralHistColl, MCHC, Washington, D.C.). Also, Maj Theodore L. Gatchel & Maj Donald L. Price, Advisor Presentation to the Company of Military Historians, 4May74, hereafter CMH Presentation (Vietnam Comment File).

Winding Down

9 MarAdvU ComdC, Jul71, Aug71

10 SMA Briefing Folder, Tab I, Marine Base Concept, 11Dec71; Engineer Advisor Folder, Tab C, Base Camp Brief (MarAdvU File).

11 Turnover dtd 15Nov71, Tab V, Training Advisor Folder (MarAdvU File).

12 MRC62/MRC63 Radio Relay Equipment, p.1, Tab-7, Training Folder (MarAdvU File); MarAdvU ComdC, Sept71.

13 Dorsey intvw; MAU Goals and Objectives FY72 dtd 4Oct71, Senior Marine Advisors Goals, p. 4, SMA Briefing Folder (MarAdvU File).

Along the DMZ

14 MACV Advisory Team 155 records (Boxes 111 to 114, AccNo. 334-74-146, WRNC, Suitland, Md.); also Col Donald J. Metcalf, USA, intvw by MACV dtd 15Sep72; Tm 155 AAR dtd 30Mar-1May72; and "Why the Defense of Quang Tri Province, SVN, Collapsed," AWC study dtd 23Oct72 (Vietnam Comment File). Also, Howard C.W. Feng, "The Road to the 'Ben Hai' Division: An Analysis of the Events Leading to the Formation of the 3d ARVN Infantry Division in October 1971," MA thesis dtd Aug87 (University of Hawaii), Aug87.

15 Capt Walter E. Boomer intvw dtd 9Mar75, Tape 6020 (OralHistColl, MCHC, Washington, D.C.).

16 MarAdvU ComdC, Nov71.

17 Dorsey intvw.

18 MarAdvU ComdC, Dec71.

19 Col Donald L. Price, comments on draft ms, dtd 7Feb90 (Vietnam Comment File)

20 LtCol Robert H. Sheridan intvw dtd 21Mar75, Tape 6022 (OralHistColl, MCHC, Washington, D.C.); LtCol Robert H. Sheridan, comments on draft ms, dtd 20Mar90 (Vietnam Comment File).

21 Col William C. Camper, USA, comments on draft ms, dtd 19Jan90 (Vietnam Comment File).

22 Gen Westmoreland msg to JCS dtd 1Feg72 (Vietnam Comment File).

23 ComUSMACV msg to 7AF, USARV, NAVFORV, XXIVCORPS, SRAG, TRAC, DRAC dtd 1Feb72 (Vietnam Comment File).

24 MarAdvU ComdC, Jan72.

25 Sheridan intvw; MarAdvU ComdC, Feb72.

26 CNA Hue & QuangTri, p. A-7.

27 XXIV Corps, Periodic Intelligence Report 5-72 dtd 5Mar72, pp. 11-13; LtGen Welborn G. Dolvin, USA, Senior Officer Debriefing Report dtd 20Mar72, p. 3; MajGen Frederick J. Kroesen, USA, Quang Tri, hereafter Kroesen (ms, MHRC, Carlisle Barracks, 1974), pp. 3-4; MACV, The Nguyen Hue Offensive, study dtd Jan73, hereafter MACV Nguyen Hue study; Besch comments. Also, Col Peter F.C. Armstrong, "Capabilities and Intentions," *Marine Corps Gazette*, Sept86, pp. 38–47 (Vietnam Comment File).

28 MajGen Walter E. Boomer, Comments on draft ms, 28Dec89 (Vietnam Comment File).

29 Manh Nhieu, "With a Shock Unit," *Vietnam*, No. 168, 1972, pp. 14–16.

PART II

THE SPRING OFFENSIVE

CHAPTER THREE
THE RING OF STEEL

*Turley with Team 155 • The Opening Round • Team 155 under Fire • The Outposts Fall • At the
Combat Base at Ai Tu • VNMC Brigade 258 Reinforces • Enemy in the Wire, 31 March 1972 • Fire
Support Base Sarge Holds On • The Collapse of the Ring of Steel*

Turley with Team 155

Recently assigned as Assistant Senior Marine Advisor (ASMA) with the Naval
Advisory Group, Vietnam, Lieutenant Colonel Gerald H. "Gerry" Turley was eager
to get to Quang Tri Province to pay a visit to the two VNMC brigades, 147 and 258,
under the operational control of the 3d ARVN Division. After two weeks of
orientation in Saigon, Turley arrived at the Ai Tu Combat Base on 29 March 1972
by helicopter, drove out to the Mai Loc Combat Base, and spent the night with
VNMC Brigade 147. The brigade, with Major Jim R. Joy as senior advisor, was
responsible for the western segment of the 3d ARVN Division's area of operations.
Lieutenant Colonel Nguyen Nang Bao, brigade commander, told Lieutenant
Colonel Turley that Mai Loc had not received any incoming artillery for almost two
years. It was a particularly peaceful night and a pleasant change of pace from
garrison duty in Saigon.[1]

The next morning Lieutenant Colonel Turley was unable to go by helicopter to the
brigade's outposts because of poor flying weather and returned to the 3d ARVN Division
command post at Ai Tu, accompanied by Major Joy. During the course of the morning
Turley received briefings from MACV Advisory Team 155 on the disposition of forces,
the state of readiness of division units, and American support available — although
practically all American combat units had been withdrawn from Vietnam. The Army
briefing revealed that the 3d ARVN Division was a newly constituted and untested
organization. It had been in existence for less than six months and did not represent a
significant increase of combat power to I Corps. The division, activated on 1 November
1971, had completed the organization of its infantry regiments only the month before.
One of its three infantry regiments manning the northern front had been operating as a
unit for only the last three weeks. Short of equipment and not fully organized or trained,

the 3d ARVN Division was unready for combat. Even so, Brigadier General Vu Van Giai's aggressiveness, professionalism, and depth of combat experience had won him the respect of the U.S. Marine advisors and had created a sense of confidence and self-assurance among his soldiers.

The division, with the 2d, 56th, and 57th ARVN Regiments, had its headquarters at Ai Tu, between Dong Ha and Quang Tri City. In fact, at the very moment of Lieutenant Colonel Turley's briefing, the 56th and the 2d ARVN Regiments were administratively exchanging areas of operations.[2] The 56th was replacing the 2d at Camp Carroll, Khe Gio, and Fire Support Base Fuller while the 2d simultaneously relieved the 56th at Alpha 4, Charlie 2, and Charlie 3. At Camp Carroll was a composite artillery group of 26 pieces ranging from 105mm howitzers to 175mm self-propelled guns. Included in this group was a battery of VNMC 105mm howitzers. The 57th Regiment's area of operations covered the rest of the northern front extending from Dong Ha, northward to the DMZ. Fire support bases included in its area were Alpha 1, Alpha 2, and Alpha 3, with regimental headquarters at Charlie 1. The area to the east of QL-1 to the Gulf of Tonkin, was nominally under the control of the Quang Tri Province chief and his local forces.

In the VNMC Brigade 147 area were outposts at Nui Ba Ho and Sarge held by the 4th VNMC Battalion, along with two companies of the 8th VNMC Battalion operating in the vicinity of Fire Support Base Holcomb, forming the western flank of the defensive arc. All three positions were on dominant terrain features overlooking the natural avenues of approach from the Laotian border. Sarge and Nui Ba Ho overlooked Highway 9, the east-west route which the French had built and the U.S. forces had improved during their stay. Fire Support Base Holcomb overlooked the beautiful Ba Long Valley through which the Thach Han River flows. The other brigade, VNMC Brigade 258, was at Fire Support Bases Nancy and Barbara to the south.[3] General Lam, commanding I Corps, which encompassed the five northernmost provinces of South Vietnam, had called the disposition of the 3d ARVN Division on fixed combat bases his "ring of steel."[4]

Other familiarization briefings for Lieutenant Colonel Turley included sensor placements and reporting, special radio and intelligence networks, and the combat support available from the U.S. Navy and U.S. Air Force. They were good briefings; Turley was to realize their value a few hours later. He was anxious to return to Saigon, but the briefings and poor flying weather had taken up the morning. His return would have to wait until after lunch at the well-appointed Team 155 dining facility.

The Opening Round

Combat outposts Sarge and Nui Ba Ho, occupied by the 4th VNMC Battalion, stood astride the historic invasion routes into Quang Tri Province and Hue City. Major Walt Boomer was with the battalion commander, Major Tran Xuan Quang, and the "Alpha" group on Sarge and Captain Ray Smith was on Nui Ba Ho with the "Bravo" group of the battalion.[A] Outpost Nui Ba Ho was actually two positions, Nui Ba Ho and Ba Ho East. The formidable hill mass rose abruptly from the valley floor and its slopes were so steep that, as Captain Smith recalled, "no one ever climbed to the top just for the fun of it." The top of the hill was so small that a UH1E helicopter could barely land, while larger helicopters could not land there at all. At approximately 1030 on 30 March 1972, a platoon patrol from the 1st VNMC Company on Ba Ho East made contact with an enemy platoon 1,000 meters northwest of Nui Ba Ho. Moments later, the 8th VNMC Battalion, operating in the vicinity of Holcomb, also reported making contact with the enemy. As these engagements progressed, NVA 120 and 130mm artillery firing from positions to the west struck Mai Loc and Camp Carroll. The fire was so intense that the South Vietnamese were unable to man their guns and provide counter-battery or supporting fires. Under this protective umbrella, the NVA infantry boldly advanced on the Marine positions.

Shortly after 1100, Captain Smith saw three company-sized NVA units advancing on the base of Nui Ba Ho. They were "marching in mass formation, right across Highway 9, at sling arms." These units were acutely vulnerable to friendly artillery fires but none were then available. Heavy cloud cover and accompanying low visibility along the entire DMZ also prevented use of close air support, although airborne forward air controllers were on station.[5] Smith, who was one of few advisors fluent in Vietnamese, was listening to the enemy artillery fire direction net. Smith determined that the NVA were shooting destruction missions with adjustments to within five meters, some very precise shooting. Since all South Vietnamese locations were well known to the enemy, devastating fire now fell on all positions and particularly on the fire support bases.

Team 155 under Fire

During his noon meal, Lieutenant Colonel Turley sat with Major James E. Smock, USA, the senior U.S. Army advisor to the 20th ARVN Tank Battalion of the 1st ARVN Armored Brigade. This was the only operational ARVN battalion equipped with U.S. M48 tanks in South Vietnam. The 20th Tank Battalion had just completed training and had not yet fired a shot in anger.[6]

(A) It was common practice for the Vietnamese Marines to divide their infantry battalions into two command groups, each controlling two reinforced rifle companies. The battalion commander, with the senior advisor headed the Alpha group, while the executive officer, with the assistant advisor was with the Bravo group.

Coming out of the dining hall at noon on 30 March 1972, Lieutenant Colonel Turley heard the all-too-familiar swishing-sound of incoming artillery rounds followed by the impact in their Ai Tu perimeter. Although he did not realize it at the time, it became evident that the North Vietnamese had launched a well-coordinated, well-planned, three-pronged infantry attack across the entire Quang Tri frontier. More than 12,000 rounds of enemy rocket, mortar, and artillery fire prepared the way for the largest NVA offensive into South Vietnam. Supported by Soviet and Chinese-built tanks and artillery, some 25,000 North Vietnamese infantry attacked across the Demilitarized Zone with such rapidity and shock that the men facing the onslaught were stunned. Every outpost and fire support base along the DMZ under the command of the 3d ARVN Division was taken under accurate and devastating fire. Perhaps it was, as higher headquarters put it "only a feint," but the quiet period was over and the "feint" was to continue unabated for the next six days. Realizing that he would be unable to return Saigon with the airfield under fire, Lieutenant Colonel Turley, with Captain John D. Murray — an advisor with VNMC Brigade 147, left behind when Major Joy made his way back to Mai Loc with the opening rounds, ran to the tactical operations center to keep abreast of the situation and to assist Team 155, as they could.

The artillery preparation, which had begun precisely at noon, was followed by infantry attacks by units of the *304th, 308th*, and *324B NVA Divisions,* five infantry regiments of the *B5 Front*, three artillery regiments, two tank regiments, and several sapper battalions.[B] [7] The fledgling 3d ARVN Division met this onslaught with five regiments of infantry, including two VNMC brigades, nine battalions of artillery, armor, and ranger forces. The enemy had a numerical advantage of over three to one and overwhelmed the ill-trained and equipped defenders.

Although the intelligence agencies of the military commanders, both U.S. and ARVN, had expected a major confrontation during 1972, the bold and sudden thrust directly across the DMZ was neither predicted nor expected.[C] In fact, when a speculative question of a possible NVA attack directly across the DMZ was posed to General Lam, he replied, "They cannot!" His reply was not one of arrogance, but was based on past experience. This had been, and was, a war of guerrilla activity and attrition, with major confrontations, such as Tet in 1968, occurring only after months of intensive preparation and stockpiling. Besides, it would be illogical for the enemy to

---

(B) *B5 Front*: 27th Infantry Regiment; 31st Infantry Regiment; 126th Infantry Regiment; 246th Infantry Regiment; 270th Infantry Regiment; 38th Artillery Regiment; 84th Artillery Regiment; 164th Artillery Regiment; 202d Armor Regiment; 203d Armor Regiment. *304th NVA Division*: 9th Infantry Regiment; 24th Infantry Regiment; 66th Infantry Regiment; 68th Artillery Regiment. *308th NVA Division*: 36th Infantry Regiment; 88th Infantry Regiment; 102d Infantry Regiment. *324B NVA Division*: 29th Infantry Regiment; 803d Infantry Regiment; 812th Infantry Regiment.

(C) The use of the *304th NVA Division* and *308th NVA Division* to cross the DMZ indicated a major effort. Both commands had fought at Dien Bien Phu against the French in 1954, and were considered "Iron Divisions." A recent North Vietnamese publication stated "Quang Tri – Thua Thien was chosen to be the main focus of the offensive" Tap So Do Cac Tran Danh, p. 18, as translated by Robert J. Destatte. (Hanoi, Ministry of Defense, 1986). (Vietnam Comment File)

attack openly across a coastal, piedmont region, fully exposed to friendly air power, long-range artillery, and the all-weather American naval guns. In addition, the South Vietnamese forces in that area were firmly entrenched on the critical terrain facing the classic avenues of invasion. In the minds of both the ARVN and U.S. commanders a massive attack by the NVA across the entire DMZ, and especially its eastern portion, was unthinkable.[8]

It did seem feasible that an attack, an end run, could come from the west. The allies had long detected enemy movements in western Quang Tri Province and patrols west of the Rockpile often heard mechanized activity. Additionally, enemy unit movements were covered by an appreciable buildup of supporting antiaircraft guns. On this basis, intelligence evaluators had predicted a limited attack and infiltration from the west and had suggested February 1972 as the likely month. But the allies had no plan to defend against a conventional combined arms invasion and had not fortified their static positions against such an assault. Knowledge of the enemy's past performance and capabilities simply did not point toward such an eventuality. The fixed outposts and fire support bases, although deteriorating to some extent, had served satisfactorily both the U.S. Marines and U.S. Army over the past five years and appeared well placed to counter enemy infiltration and harassing tactics from the north and west. All this analysis became academic. As the thunder of massed artillery smothered the now exposed division headquarters, it also hindered the hasty preparations of the South Vietnamese and American advisors to counter the new threat to MR 1.[9]

The Outposts Fall

While Nui Ba Ho was under attack by the *9th NVA Regiment*, the Alpha command group on Sarge, only 2,000 meters to the south, began receiving a heavy artillery barrage. Over 500 rounds of accurate fire killed 15 Vietnamese Marines the first day. Major Boomer continuously moved along the exposed face of the mountain top trying to locate the enemy guns firing from across Highway 9 to the northwest. In spite of the heavy fire hitting Camp Carroll and Mai Loc, he was able to call in some counterbattery missions which he credited with the destruction of several enemy gun positions. The adverse weather kept U.S. Air Force fighter-bombers at Da Nang and carrierbased aircraft in the South China Sea from responding in support of the Marines on the battered hilltop.

A direct hit destroyed the bunker housing special equipment for monitoring enemy radio nets. At the command bunker, losing contact with the two U.S. Army operators,

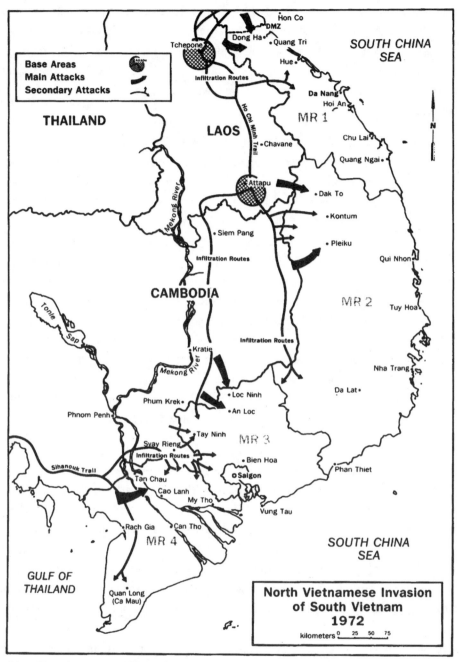

Adapted from Government of Vietnam Material

Major Boomer moved outside the command bunker to discover that the radio facility had collapsed and was burning. He approached the inferno in a vain attempt to rescue the men, but quickly realized there were no survivors.[10]

Because of the small size of the hilltop on Nui Ba Ho, the enemy's larger caliber guns had difficulty zeroing in on the Marine position. By the middle of the afternoon, however, 82mm mortars had been moved into firing positions by the NVA infantry and were doing heavy damage. The only counterbattery fire came from the battalion's sole 60mm mortar on the position. While engaged in serving this weapon, every member of the Marine mortar crew was either killed or wounded.

At 1700, a platoon outpost 600 meters to the north of Nui Ba Ho came under intense small arms and rocket-propelled grenades. The Marine defenders repelled three "human wave" ground attacks with small arms, M79 grenade launchers, and hand grenades. Simultaneously, the enemy assaulted the squad outpost on the south side of Nui Ba Ho. A 106mm recoilless rifle on Nui Ba Ho fired a flechette round in support of the southern squad, but the weapon malfunctioned before a second round could be fired.[D] As darkness fell, the enemy having failed to dislodge the defenders, pulled back and harassed the Marines with resumed artillery bombardment. During the night the enemy continued to maneuver into position for an attack the following morning.

At the Combat Base at Ai Tu

Lieutenant Colonel Turley and Captain Murray, anxious to learn the fate of the Marine held positions under attack on 30 March 1972, had remained at the 3d ARVN Division tactical operations center. The operations center, jointly manned by ARVN personnel and MACV Advisory Team 155 members, was receiving reports of enemy contact throughout its entire area of operations. Naval Gunfire Team "1-2," with First Lieutenant Joel B. Eisenstein in charge, and a U.S. Air Force tactical air control liaison team were situated within the TOC. They also provided command and control communications links to the maneuver units, but the artillery fire that slashed through the TOC "antenna farm" rendered the ARVN Communications System ineffective.

As Lieutenant Colonel Turley and Captain Murray became more involved in the TOC, coordination problems became evident. Looking forward to a weekend with his family in the Philippines, Colonel Donald J. Metcalf, the senior advisor, had left for Saigon as the initial rounds fell upon Ai Tu. Murray recalled that no contingency plans were implemented, administrative radio messages cut out tactical nets, logs and journals were not maintained, no coordinating efforts were made between Team 155

(D) Flechette rounds were anti-personnel projectiles which discharged thousands of tiny steel darts. The flechettes looked like finishing nails with four fins stamped on their bases. They were deadly when used against "human wave" attacks.

and its ARVN counterparts, and the senior MACV Advisory Team 155 officer present, Major Jimmy Davis, was collapsing from fatigue.[11] Turley and Murray, neither in the ARVN or MACV chain-of-command, but both eager to get involved in the war, moved to help the Assistant G3 Advisor, Major Davis. The Marine officers noted that by evening on the 30 March, U.S. Army support personnel of Team 155 were openly packing their belongings, preparing for departure.

VNMC Brigade 258 Reinforces

At 1400, 30 March 1972, General Giai ordered Vietnamese Marine Brigade 258, with Major Jon T. Easley as the senior advisor, to displace its 3d, 6th, 7th Infantry, and artillery battalions northward from Fire Support Bases Nancy and Barbara along the My Chanh River. The Marine battalions were moved to reinforce the northern defensive line and to assume overall security for the Dong Ha area and the Highway 9 and Highway 1 road junction. This shift left the division's southwest flank exposed to possible enemy action. Just at dusk, the brigade command group, the 3d VNMC Infantry Battalion, and the 3d VNMC Artillery Battalion headed north up QL-1, unaware of the tactical situation. As they drove through the night, they passed elements of the 20th ARVN Tank Battalion all along the road. The tankers had just completed a command post field exercise and were considered qualified for combat. It was reassuring for the brigade's Marines to move past the newly acquired American-built M48 battle tanks.[12]

On the morning of 31 March, Colonel Metcalf arrived back at the 3d Division TOC. He asked Lieutenant Colonel Turley to assume the duties of senior American advisor within the operations center, in place of the exhausted Major Davis. Colonel Metcalf wanted to stay with General Giai and that Lieutenant Colonel Normand Heon, USA, the Team 155 assistant senior advisor, was required to select and prepare a less exposed command post south of the Thach Han River in Quang Tri City. In addition, Turley had already been helping and was abreast of the tactical situation.

Turley initially balked at this request. He realized that he was from a different service advisory chain-of-command, and that his visit had placed him in the Ai Tu TOC strictly as an interested, but detached, observer. Then considering the urgency for continuity in such a rapidly changing and confusing period, he complied with Metcalf's requests. Turley's priorities at the moment were to stop the enemy attack and stabilize a badly deteriorated situation. Consequently, he directed that the TOC query all U.S. combat support units with which it had communications with as to possible assistance. Insistent calls went out to the First Regional Assistance

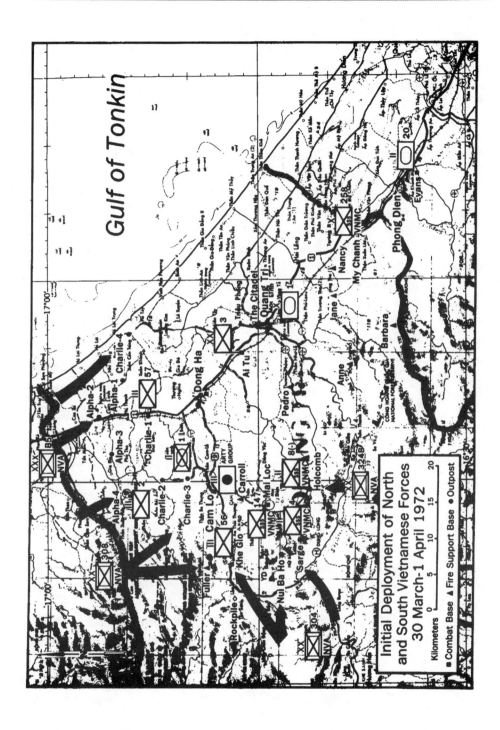

Initial Deployment of North
and South Vietnamese Forces
30 March-1 April 1972

Kilometers
0   5   10   15   20

■ Combat Base   ▲ Fire Support Base   ● Outpost

Command in Da Nang, and to U.S. naval gunfire support ships offshore. Turley also opened a journal to include the events occurring within the 3d ARVN Division's operations area.[E]

Enemy in the Wire, 31 March 1972

At first light, 31 March, the enemy made a mass assault on the north section of Nui Ba Ho. A Marine 106mm recoilless rifle on the northern slope, firing flechette rounds into the formation, was instrumental in stopping the enemy at the perimeter. The NVA withdrew, leaving an estimated 100 dead on the wire. At 1000, having stopped three more ground probes, the Marines on Nui Ba Ho were hit by 130mm artillery rounds. This time the fire was more accurate. Trench lines and bunkers began to collapse. At approximately 1500 the determined enemy unleashed a massive ground attack up the northern slope from the saddle between Nui Ba Ho and Ba Ho East. The integrity and mutual support of the two positions were destroyed, but not without a price; the outer band of barbed wire was completely hidden by NVA bodies. Meanwhile, 75mm recoilless rifles, brought up by the enemy during the previous evening, systematically began to reduce South Vietnamese defensive positions.

The battalion executive officer in charge of the Bravo group was finally able to establish communications with the VNMC 105mm howitzer battalion. He urgently radioed, "We are going to die if we don't get some support." One platoon of two guns responded to this desperate request even though the gunners had to pull their lanyards while lying prone under the intense enemy counterbattery fire. Their valiant effort was credited with killing many enemy soldiers and knocking out two of the recoilless rifles on the northern slope.

At 1730, Captain Smith saw an enemy company moving up the southern slope, hauling a "large wheeled gun." At precisely that moment the weather cleared and a flight of U. S. Air Force McDonnell Douglas F4 Phantoms provided the sole air strike in support of Nui Ba Ho, knocking out the gun and dispersing the force to the south. At darkness on 31 March, the NVA resumed the attack on the northern slope, tenaciously assaulting the pinnacle. Fewer than four squads now defended the position. At about 2130, a U.S. Air Force Lockheed AC130 Spectre gunship came on station to support the defenders but could not acquire targets anywhere in the area. The aircraft was unable to fire its Gatling guns but did drop flares. One of the flares, breaking through the haze and casting an eerie glow, revealed the grim fact that the NVA had completely inundated the position. At 2205, one of the surviving command post troops, calling from the perimeter, reported that he had been captured but had escaped. He said the enemy force had control of the hill mass and suggested it was time to evacuate the position.

(E) A version of this was used to establish the chronology for the events described.

Smith, grabbing a PRC25 radio and an M16 rifle, was the last to clear the command bunker. As he emerged he did not see anyone he knew, but he did see five NVA about three meters in front of the bunker. He recounted, "The NVA were as confused as I by then, I ran right by them without being detected." At the back side of the hill Smith heard some familiar voices calling names he recognized. He approached the group of survivors huddled against the southeast corner of the wire:

> I realized they were afraid to go through the wire because of the booby traps. By this time it was obvious that the position was lost. So my counterpart and I began directing the 26 survivors single file through a gap in the first band of wire. As we were doing this, an NVA began firing over our heads no more than five feet to my right rear. I turned and fired, knocking him down."[13]

Realizing that the shot would bring more NVA to their position, Captain Smith moved quickly to the head of the column, which was held up at the outer perimeter of concertina wire. Unhesitatingly, he threw himself backwards on top of the booby-trap-infested wire. Recalling this later he said that he had foolishly thought that the radio on his back would absorb the blast had he tripped a mine. Quickly the Marines scrambled over the American's body, passing over the wire. With severe cuts on his arms and legs, Captain Smith crawled off the wire leaving most of his clothes entangled behind him.

Having cleared the outer perimeter of the wire, practically naked and bleeding profusely, Smith assisted the executive officer in rallying the Marines and moved toward Mai Loc. Evading the NVA along the eastern slope, he continued to call for artillery fire on top of the hill while the harried survivors, chilled by the cold wind and rain, moved into the darkness. Nui Ba Ho, the first position lost to the enemy, fell at 2140 on 31 March 72. The Communist offensive was less than two days old.[14]

Fire Support Base Sarge Holds on

On 31 March 1972, Fire Support Base Sarge continued to be hit with massive fire and infantry assaults by the *66th NVA Regiment*. Major Boomer was in radio contact with Captain Smith on Nui Ba Ho. Although Smith's voice was steady throughout the day, that night, as the two were talking, Boomer knew the situation was bad when Smith's voice broke a little as he said, "If we make it, it'll just be luck." Major Boomer knew that Nui Ba Ho had to be manned if Sarge was to be held, since Nui Ba Ho dominated the approaches to its southern neighbor. He was dismayed when, at 2150, he heard Smith calling for artillery fire on top of the position which the Bravo group was supposed to be occupying. He was unable to communicate with Smith, apparently because of Smith's evasion tactics. The two Marine officers were close friends and Boomer believed that a last ditch effort to stop the NVA at Nui Ba Ho had failed and that Smith had been killed.

Enemy ground attacks on Sarge persisted through the night of 31 March. By 0200 on 1 April 1972, the NVA had overrun all of the squad outposts to the north, east, and south and penetrated the defensive perimeter. The bad weather continued unabated, but a B-52 Arc Light struck likely enemy staging areas west of Highway 9. Despite the efforts of the Vietnamese Marines, the NVA launched wave after wave of infantry attacks against the hill.

"The enemy is thrown into confusion and his resistance is weakening," reported an NVA cameraman with the attacking *Long Chau Unit*.[15] At 0345, during a deluge of rain and intense enemy fire, what remained of the Alpha command group evacuated Sarge. Moving off the hill between two enemy units, Boomer radioed Joy at Mai Loc, "... we're moving." Shortly thereafter Boomer lost all radio contact with brigade. It was as if the entire 4th VNMC Battalion had been swallowed up into the night.

At dawn, a "Victory" banner was brandished over Sarge's command post by the NVA, with "enemy [South Vietnamese] Marines emerging from their bunkers," while "PLAF men pursue those fleeing southward." Escape from the encircling enemy brought the Marines no respite from chilling rains or from the fatigue brought on by two days of fighting without food and sleep. All through the day of 1 April the survivors of Sarge followed a tortuous route through the jungle, evading a seemingly ubiquitous enemy.

During this period, higher headquarters ordered B-52 strikes into Laos and Khe Sanh against the enemy's resupply and staging areas. MACV and the RVN Joint General Staff, nevertheless, believed that the NVA would not cross the DMZ with more than a feint and any main NVA attack would be at MR 2. Thus they concentrated the air effort in the Kontum area in order to prevent the NVA from seizing Pleiku.

The NVA's sudden shift from guerrilla harassing tactics to mobile conventional warfare caught both General Giai and the commander of I Corps, General Lam, by complete surprise. Never before had the North Vietnamese struck either military or civilian areas with such a concentration of artillery fire. During the first 48 hours a hail of artillery and rocket rounds struck each of the combat bases and the surrounding civilian areas along the entire buffer zone. In the face of this unprecedented attack, civilians began gathering their belongings and fled south to Dong Ha.[16]

By midday of 1 April 1972, members of the 57th ARVN Regiment on Alpha 2, at Gio Linh, abandoned their exposed positions on the perimeter and sought protection in bunkers in the southern portion of the fire base. ARVN artillerymen refused to leave their bunkers to fire counter battery missions. Naval gunfire from the USS *Buchanan* (DDG 14) and the USS *Joseph P. Strauss* (DDG 16), directed by a five-man ANGLICO spot team at Alpha 2, suppressed enemy supporting arms fire and impeded the advance of the NVA infantry, allowing the ARVN forces to withdraw.

Corporal James F. "Diamond Jim" Worth was a field radio operator with First Lieutenant David C. Bruggeman's ANGLICO spot team with the ARVN 57th Infantry Regiment at Alpha 2. The 20-year-old Worth, from Chicago, Illinois, had been in Vietnam with Sub Unit One since the previous year. According to Lieutenant Colonel D'Wayne Gray, Worth had requested mast to get back into the "field," rather than the relative safety of Saigon. Gray described Worth as "an Irish charmer and not at all above conning his CO."[17] The outpost had been hit with heavy artillery, rocket, and mortar fire when the North Vietnamese attacked. For two days Corporal Worth and the other members of his team called for suppression, interdiction, and counterbattery fire during the critical initial stages of the attack while the 3d ARVN Division had lost most of its artillery and the weather prevented close air support. Communist ground forces had probed Alpha 2 and cut the position off from friendly support. The situation now reached a climax as the enemy launched its final assault supported by artillery. As the fight went against the South Vietnamese that morning, Lieutenant Bruggeman requested helicopter evacuation for his team through Lieutenant Eisenstein at the division tactical operations center.[18]

From his position on the Alpha 2 observation tower, Corporal Worth watched the soldiers of the ARVN 57th Regiment abandon their fighting holes on the outpost's forward slope. As he looked to the rear he saw the ARVN 105mm howitzers also abandoned as NVA infantry closed from three sides of fire base. An evacuation helicopter was on its way if the Marines could make the relative safety of Alpha 2's southeastern corner.

After some delay, Worth and the other Marines spotted an Army UH-1. The U.S. Army UH-1 helicopter, piloted by Warrant Officers Ben Nielsen and Robert Sheridan, flew in low and landed. Sheridan, a door gunner, and Lieutenant Eisenstein, quickly jumped out to assist the Marines. With their weapons and gear, Worth and the other Marines prepared to board the helicopter. That instant, mortar rounds struck the landing zone, mortally injuring Lieutenant Bruggeman and dispersing his men. As the Marines scrambled on board the helicopter, Worth was not with them. As Warrant Officer Sheridan glanced about him, he saw a few shell-shocked Vietnamese soldiers, but all the rest of the ARVN force had left.

The aircraft took off, flew to the Ai Tu Combat Base to pick up ANGLICO's HM1 Thomas "Doc" Williamson, USN, who attempted life-saving measures on Bruggeman. With the corpsman on board, Sheridan then headed for Da Nang. Lieutenant Bruggeman died of wounds halfway back to the medical facility. Corporal James Worth was never seen again after the fall of Alpha 2. He joined the ranks of the missing Americans, who were either dead or captured at the war's end.[F] [19]

As Alpha 4, Alpha 2, Fuller, Khe Gio, and Holcomb were lost, General Giai moved his division headquarters to the rear. With the departure of the bulk of Team 155 south of the Thach Han River, VNMC Brigade 258 headquarters was ordered to leave its 3d VNMC Battalion at Dong Ha and to move to Ai Tu to assume overall control of the division forward command post during the displacement. As Lieutenant Colonel Ngo Van Dinh and his staff arrived at Ai Tu around 1500, along with the 6th VNMC Battalion which had come up from FSB Barbara, a barrage of more than 800 rounds of artillery greeted them.[20]

The Collapse of the Ring of Steel

At 1620, 1 April, Lieutenant Colonel Normand Heon, assistant senior advisor, Team 155, had recommended the withdrawal of all the remaining U.S. personnel at Ai Tu. The U.S. Marine advisors, not subject to this order, stayed with their Vietnamese counterparts. Two U.S. Army advisors also voluntarily remained with the 56th ARVN Regiment at Camp Carroll. The forward command post at Ai Tu, manned by 30 Americans, both officers and enlisted men, represented the U.S. Marine Corps, Army, and Air Force. Now under Lieutenant Colonel Turley, each man volunteered to remain to operate the division-level combined arms coordination center, the only command and control center north of Da Nang with working communications.[21]

By 1700, Charlie 1 and Charlie 2 were abandoned. As the fire support bases below the DMZ fell and were evacuated, soldiers and civilians thronged southward and were infiltrated by NVA forward observers. Refugees moving east along Highway 9 reported that the *27th NVA Regiment* was at Cam Lo. Refugees and ARVN stragglers came across the Dong Ha bridge in an unbroken stream. ARVN units were fragmented and ineffective. No kind of identification of rank or unit was in evidence. Approximately one out of three "fatigue-clad persons" carried a weapon. Press reports called it a "3d Infantry Division debacle ... as government troops panicked."

Colonel Metcalf, observed later that it took a great deal of expertise to withdraw correctly in combat, "in the sense of being able to deploy yourself by echelon down a highway or out of an area." With the hasty retreat of the ARVN forces, Metcalf learned

(F) He was listed missing in action and declared dead by the Secretary of the Navy under Title 37, U.S. Code, Section 555 on 17 December 1976.

that you "can't sit down as the senior advisor with the division commander or the senior advisor with the regimental commander and say well, this is the way the book says."[22] By darkness on 1 April every ARVN combat base north of the Cam Lo River had fallen.[23] The northern "ring of steel" had taken a mere 48 hours to crush. At best, the retreating ARVN had served to slow the NVA because the enemy had deployed into battlefield formations.

At 1900, on 1 April 1972, Colonel Metcalf left Ai Tu Combat Base with General Giai for the new command post location at the Citadel in Quang Tri City. Since the main 3d ARVN Division command post displaced to Quang Tri City without maintaining the normal duplicate command and communications radio channels, Turley and his small staff were the only facility which had the capability of controlling all U.S. supporting arms. During the initial critical days of the invasion, this small band of Americans operated around the clock to recommended B-52 Arc Light strikes, directing tactical air support, adjusting Vietnamese artillery and naval gunfire support. All the fire support coordination in Quang Tri Province for the next few days was carried out by 30 men in one bunker north of the Thach Han.

Although good communications were maintained with FRAC's operations center in Da Nang as well as with the 3d ARVN Division main command post at Quang Tri City, at no time did Turley receive any major tactical guidance from these higher headquarters. General Frederick J. Kroesen's newly organized FRAC headquarters had replaced the Army's XXIVth Corp, which only 10 days earlier had departed for Japan. The advisory command, recalled General Kroesen, was "heavily weighted to provide administrative assistance and logistical advice," with only a token intelligence and operations section. It was neither manned nor equipped to monitor the combat activity or to provide tactical guidance.[24]

Turley continued to operate in his own fashion relying on his previous experience and Marine Corps training.[G] Brigadier General Thomas W. Bowen, USA, the deputy FRAC commander, authorized him the use of B-52 Arc Light bombing to halt the attack. An unidentified Air Force "general" called directly from Saigon and told Turley to give him the center of impact for desired targets and that he would provided them as requested. Turley requested strikes on areas that earlier sensor "readings" indicated were assembly areas or likely enemy avenues of approach. The U.S. Air Force flew 64 B-52 strikes called by Turley on these targets. Despite these strikes the enemy closed on the ARVN defenses south of the Cam Lo, Mian Giang, and Qua Viet Rivers. The situation was critical.[25]

(G) Lieutenant Colonel Turley was awarded a Legion of Merit Medal, in part for his advisory actions that were credited with the delay of the multidivision attack in MR 1 that allowed I Corps units to organize a defense in Quang Tri Province.

CHAPTER THREE ENDNOTES

Unless otherwise noted, material in this chapter is derived from: MarAdvUComdC, Mar, Apr72; Lt Gen Ngo Quang Troung, The Easter Invasion (Washington, D.C., U.S. Army Center of Military History, 1979), hereafter Troung, Invasion; Lt Gen Le Nguyen Khang intvw dtd 30Sept75; Operations Evaluation Group, Defense of Hue and Quang Tri City, ONR report CNS 1035 dtd May72 (CNA, Washington, D.C.), hereafter CNA Hue&QuangTri; HqPacAF, "The 1972 Invasion of Military Region 1: Fall of Quang Tri and Defense of Hue," Project CHECO report dtd 15Mar73, hereafter CHECO Invasion72. Also, LtCol Gerald H. Turley & Capt Marshall R. Wells, "Easter Invasion 1972," Marine Corps Gazette, Mar73, pp. 18-29; and Jeffrey J. Clarke, Advice and Support: The Final Year (Washington, D.C., U.S. Army Center of Military History, 1988).

Turley with Team 155

1 Maj Jim R. Joy, memo dtd 10Apr72 (MarAdvU File); LtCol Gerald H. Turley intvw dtd 17Jan74, Tape 6029, intvw dtd 31Jul75, Tape 6027 (OralHistColl, MCHC, Washington, D.C.).

2 Camper comments.

3 Gen Frederick J. Kroesen, USA, comments on draft ms, dtd 3Jan90 (Vietnam Comment File).

4 MarAdvU ComdC, Mar72; Kroesen, p. 7.

The Opening Round

5 Smith intvw.

Team 155 under Fire

6 Maj James E. Smock, USA, "Organization and Training of the ARVN 20th Tank Squadron," ms dtd 1976; LtCol Louis P. Wagner, USA, "Comments of the 1st Armored Brigade Senior Advisor," AAR dtd 1972 (Vietnam Comment File).

7 MACV, PerIntRep dtd May72; MACV Nguyen Hue study; and XXIV Corps, PerIntRep 5-72.

8 Kroesen, p. 4.

9 App A, Brig 147, pp. 1-12, FRAC, Narrative Description of Vietnamese Marine Division Operations dtd 1Oct72, hereafter FRAC/VNMCOpns (MarAdvU File).

The Outposts Fall

10 MajGen Walter E. Boomer, comments on draft ms, dtd 28Dec89 (Vietnam Comment File).

At the Combat Base at Ai Tu

11 Capt John D. Murray, etal, USNA Advisor Presention dtd 28Feb73, Tape 3060 (OralHistColl, MCHC, Washington, D.C.), hereafter USNA presentation; Intel/Recon Advisor recommendations dtd 25Apr72, p. 2, SMA, Advisor's Personal Evaluation of the NVA Easter 72 Offensive Folder, hereafter SMA evaluation (MarAdvU File).

VNMC Brigade 258 Reinforces

[12] Maj Jon T. Easley, etal., USNA presentation; Maj Regan R. Wright intvw dtd 23Apr72, Tape 5089 (OralHistColl, MCHC, Washington, D.C.); Intelligence Tab, p. 2, SMA evaluation (MarAdvU File).

Enemy in the Wire, 31 March 1972

[13] Smith intvw.

[14] Capt Ray L. Smith, et al, USNA presentation.

Fire Support Base Sarge Holds on

[15] Manh Nhieu, "With a Shock Unit," *Vietnam* No. 168, 1972, pp. 14-16.

[16] Kroesen ms, p. 7.

[17] Gray comments.

[18] 1stLt Joel B. Eisenstein intvw by Col Gerald H. Turley; SU1, OIC Naval Gunfire Liaison Spot Team 1-2 AAR dtd 30Apr72 (Vietnam Comment File).

[19] SU1 ComdC, Apr72, p. 6; HQMC Report of Casualty #364-72 and #364A-72.

[20] App B, pp. 1-2, FRAC/VNMCOpns; Easley, USNA presentation; Capt William D. Wischmeyer intvw dtd 16Apr72, Tape 5094 (OralHistColl, MCHC, Washington, D.C.); Maj William R. Warren intvw dated 16Apr72, Tape 5095 (OralHistColl, MCHC, Washington, D.C.).

The Collapse of the Ring of Steel

[21] CNA Hue & Quang Tri p. 118.

[22] Metcalf intvw, p. 2.

[23] Turley intvw; Metcalf intvw; Battreall intvw.

[24] Kroesen comments.

[25] Col Gerald H. Turley, Comments on draft ms, 15Dec89; Maj David A. Brookbank, USAF, Special Report Air Liaison Officer, 31 Jul72, hereafter Brookbank report (Vietnam Comment File).

CHAPTER FOUR
THE DEFENSE OF DONG HA

The Easter Sunday Crisis • The Dong Ha Bridge • Action at the Bridge • Reaction at Saigon •
Camp Carroll Surrenders • Mai Loc Exposed • The Dong Ha Bridge Destroyed •
Callsign Bat-21 • Mai Loc Evacuated

The Easter Sunday Crisis

Easter Sunday, 2 April 1972, proved to be a fateful day for all the defenders of northern Quang Tri Province. Sunday morning things looked grim at Mai Loc, where VNMC Brigade 147 remained under constant enemy artillery fire. Extremely bad weather limited the effectiveness of the airborne forward air controllers and air support. The 155mm guns at the combat base had depleted their ammunition in largely futile counterfire. After almost three days of constant bombardment and no radio contact with the battalion at Sarge or the two companies on Holcomb, no supporting B-52 strikes, and rapidly depleting supplies, Major Jim R. Joy, the brigade advisor, made a desperate request for support from the 3d ARVN Division. Major Joy called for resupply of small arms ammunition, artillery rounds, and food.[1]

The survivors from Sarge and Nui Ba Ho started to reappear after a long night on the run. Major Tran Xuan Quang, the 4th VNMC Battalion commander, and Major Walter E. Boomer, had decided at daybreak to stop evading and struck out for friendly lines at Mai Loc combat base. Just as the group of survivors left the jungle going into a cleared, hilly area, an NVA unit attacked. The exhausted Marines, with little ammunition and some without weapons, broke and ran, leaving their wounded comrades. Major Boomer realized they had become completely disorganized and covered the retreat with his own fire. His delaying action allowed the dispirited troops to withdraw to the east. Boomer, who was no longer with the battalion commander, guided eight other Vietnamese Marines to the comparative safety of Mai Loc.

Lieutenant Colonel Gerald Turley's position at Ai Tu as an involved visitor had become one of grave responsibility and direct involvement. The only optimistic note was a report from a naval gunfire ship which informed him that the 31st MAU was present on Seventh Fleet amphibious assault ships within sight of the beach. At 0915,

Colonel Metcalf telephoned Lieutenant Colonel Turley from the newly established 3d ARVN Division command post in the Citadel of Quang Tri City, and told him, "You are directed to take over as senior American advisor to the 3d ARVN Division, Forward by order of the Commanding General, FRAC."[2]

The battered and disorganized 57th ARVN Regiment, which almost 24 hours earlier had evacuated its command post at Charlie 1, radioed Ai Tu around 1015 and reported NVA armor on QL-1 in the vicinity of Alpha 2. The radio message reported the vehicles as 20 Soviet-built PT-76 and T-54 tanks. When asked if they could stop the tanks north of the Mieu Giang River, the unidentified voice indicated that they could not. Turley passed this information to FRAC headquarters, as it appeared that the road to Dong Ha was wide open to a rapidly moving enemy armored force.

Now Communist T-54 main battle tanks, PT-76 amphibious tanks and BTR-50 armored personnel carriers drove across the DMZ creating panic among the confused refugees.[A][3] As "tank panic" took hold, soldiers of the 3d ARVN Division threw their weapons and equipment away and joined the civilian exodus. General Giai, while hastily formulating a defensive plan, personally attempted to stem the wholesale desertions of the DMZ defensive positions by his soldiers, but all order had been lost. Whatever General Giai's faults, he was not a coward, recalled an Army advisor at the time.[4]

As soldiers of the 57th ARVN Regiment streamed across the Dong Ha Bridge, Giai grabbed them and demanded to know why they were running and was told "tanks, tanks!" Giai replied "Show me a tank and I will go with you, and we will destroy it together." Personal example was to no avail.

The Dong Ha Bridge

Outside of Dong Ha was the 3d VNMC Battalion, with Captain John W. Ripley as its advisor. This meager blocking force had to gain enough time for the 3d ARVN Division to organize a new defensive line along the Mieu Giang River. With the report of advancing NVA armor, Lieutenant Colonel Ngo Van Dinh, Marine Brigade 258 commander at Ai Tu, immediately ordered Major Le Ba Binh, 3d Battalion commander, to defend Dong Ha and its bridges "at all costs." Dinh also sent four of the 6th VNMC Battalion's jeep-mounted 106mm recoilless rifles north to provide antitank

---

(A) The North Vietnamese had always had armored units and some vehicles had been used in the south in the past. More recent experience was available with the NVA use of armor during the 1971 Lam Son 719 incursion into Laos and in their attack on the Plain of Jars. The two armored units committed — the *202d and 203d NVA Armored Regiments*, as well as the infantry divisions, used a variety of armored vehicles, differing in nomenclature and technical details. After action analysis revealed the vehicles to be a mix of Soviet and Chinese manufactured equipment, for example: the Soviet T-54 or the Chinese Type 59, the Soviet PT-76 amphibious tank or the similar Chinese Type 63, the Soviet BTR-50 armored personnel carrier or the Chinese Model 1967, and the Soviet M46 130mm gun or the Chinese Type 59. For simplicity in the narrative, the terms used are those found in the contemporary records. (Besch comments)

support. At Quang Tri, Colonel Ngo Van Chung, deputy commander of the 3d ARVN Division, in the absence of General Giai, committed the freshly painted and newly received M48 battle tanks of the 20th ARVN Tank Battalion, also to meet this threat.[5]

Major Binh had very little intelligence on the situation he now faced. A North Vietnamese red and gold flag was seen flying from the girders of the old railway bridge over the Mieu Giang River. When Major Binh heard a spurious radio report of the fall of Dong Ha, he turned to Captain Ripley and said, "If you please, I am going to send a message on my command net." He sent over both Vietnamese and American channels the message that there were "Vietnamese Marines in Dong Ha" and "as long as one Marine draws a breath of life, Dong Ha will belong to us."[6]

Major Easley, Senior Advisor to Brigade 258, had called Captain Ripley and told him to expect the worst and that reinforcements were not anticipated. Easley said that radio contact with the 57th ARVN had been lost, NVA tanks were on the move southward, refugees were streaming across the Dong Ha Bridge, and that the brigade headquarters had to remain at Ai Tu Combat Base to maintain perimeter security for the forward command post of the division.

At approximately 1100, the Marines were joined by elements of the 20th ARVN Tank Battalion, under the command of Lieutenant Colonel Ton Ta Ly with U.S. Army Major James E. Smock as his counterpart. General Giai designated Lieutenant Colonel Ly, who was senior in rank to Major Binh, as overall area commander. As control was passed, the two unit command posts were consolidated in an M113 armored personnel carrier (APC). By 1115, forward elements of one company of the 3d Battalion were just short of the Dong Ha Bridge waiting for the rest of their unit to join them.

As two rifle companies of the 3d Battalion moved into Dong Ha from the west to establish a defensive position on either side of the bridge, a third company was extended westward along Highway 9 to cover the railroad bridge. The position was in full view of the NVA on the north bank, particularly the NVA soldiers at the railroad bridge. As the battalion command group, now mounted on tanks, moved past the outskirts of Dong Ha, a devastating artillery barrage hit it. All troop movements south of the river stopped. Ripley described it as an "absolute fire storm." Shells blew buildings and defensive structures apart. The enemy artillery took their toll of civilian refugees fleeing the battle. The march to the bridge had to loop to the south to enter Dong Ha from a less exposed direction.

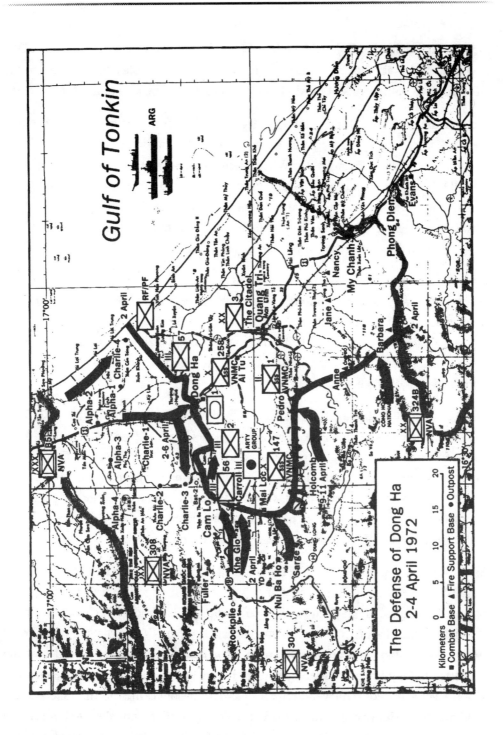

The Defense of Dong Ha
2–4 April 1972

At one point, a large group clad in ARVN uniforms passed the Marines, "not a civilian refugee among them, just a huge glob of men — moving south, neatly dressed and covered but with no rank or insignia. About every third man was armed." It was more than Major Binh could take. He leaped off his tank, grabbed one of the fleeing soldiers and screamed at him, "Where are you going?" The startled soldier replied that it was "no use, no use." Major Binh drew his pistol and killed the soldier on the spot, but the retreating horde continued southward unimpeded. No one even took notice of the incident as they skirted the fallen soldier and continued southward.

The *36th NVA Regiment* attempted to cross both the partially destroyed railroad bridge. When the NVA infantrymen gained a foothold on the south side of the railroad bridge, Captain Ripley called for a continuous naval gunfire mission. His request went directly to the fire support coordinators at the Ai Tu tactical operations center. First Lieutenant Eisenstein, in charge of the ANGLICO liaison team, contacted Commander William J. Thearle, USN, commanding officer of the USS *Buchanan* (DDG 14). The *Buchanan*, a guided missile destroyer, was the flagship of Naval Gunfire Support Task Unit 70.8.9. The task unit included the destroyers *Buchanan*, *Strauss* (DDG 16), *Waddell* (DDG 24), *Hamner* (DD 718), and *Anderson* (DD 786). Ripley called for interdiction fire in the vicinity of the railroad bridge, 300 meters to the right and left of the bridge. There was almost instant response. The ANGLICO team, consisting of Lieutenant Eisenstein and Sergeant Joe D. Swift, also worked up a number of defensive fire plans in the vicinity of QL-1 and called for fire on unobserved targets. Four columns of black smoke indicated that the ships' automatic 5-inch guns had found their targets.

For more than an hour continuous naval gunfire interdicted the approaches to both bridges. Ripley requested that fire support boxes of approximately 1,000 x 2,000 meters be shifted between the bridges.[B] It was a very effective and responsive system. No fire commands, no map checks, no adjustments — just a request for more fire at the railroad bridge. Upon hearing tanks on the north bank about 200 meters up QL-1, Ripley called for another fire mission which bracketed the area.

The 3d VNMC Battalion continued to deploy under the protective fire of U.S. Navy ships. Shortly, two companies of Marines and the 3d Troop of the 20th ARVN Tank Battalion moved forward and occupied Dong Ha and established defensive positions on the south side of the bridge. The 1st Troop and Headquarters' Tank Section occupied the high ground southwest of the village, a position which provided good observation of QL-1 north of the Mieu Giang River. Upon seeing four enemy PT-76 tanks traveling along the banks of the river just east of Dong Ha, Ripley shifted the

---

(B) Boxes are rectangular areas in which naval gunfire projectiles impact.

naval gunfire. With responsive and accurate fire, the gunfire ships destroyed all four tanks. Ripley was watching from a vantage point. He recalled the incident:

> We could see them burning clearly. My counterpart, the Marine
> Battalion commander and the tank battalion commander were both
> observing this superb display of naval gunfire. When the tanks were hit
> and burning, both were surprised and elated in seeing the potential of
> NGF. I was to receive many requests for NGF by the Vietnamese after
> this attack.[7]

At 1200, an NVA tank column came into view moving south along QL-1 from Charlie 1 toward Dong Ha. Although the range was in excess of 2,500 meters, the tanks of 1st Troop on the high ground immediately took the column under fire and knocked out six enemy vehicles. The NVA unit commander was stunned. His monitored radio message to his higher headquarters reported the loss of six tanks to direct fire weapons, but he indicated that he had no idea where the fire had come from. The 20th's executive officer, Major Kieu, in command of his own tank claimed two of the T-54s, spotting his cannon shots through the use of machine-gun rounds viewed through his rangefinder at a range of 3,000 meters. The South Vietnamese tankers had learned their lessons well.[8]

The *308th NVA Division's* thrust from the DMZ to the south had gained momentum as each ARVN outpost and fire support base fell. After more than three days of continuous artillery attacks and tank-infantry assaults, it now appeared that the North Vietnamese were making their main attack along the axis of QL-1. At this time Camp Carroll and Mai Loc to the west were still in friendly hands, but all resistance to the north of the Cam Lo and the Cua Viet River had crumbled. By noon on Easter Sunday nothing was between the enemy and the coveted Quang Tri City — except a river, a bridge, and a battalion of Vietnamese Marines and ARVN tanks.

At about 1215, as the first NVA tank nosed out toward the north side of the bridge, Vietnamese Marine Sergeant Huynh Van Luom, a veteran of many years fighting, took two M72 Light Antitank Weapons (LAW), simple shoulder-fired, single-shot rockets, and walked up to the south side of the bridge. Although he was an assault team section leader, he had elected to move forward alone. As he reached the planking of the bridge he took two ammunition boxes filled with dirt and one strand of concertina wire and placed them in front of him. It was a ludicrous situation, the 90-pound Marine crouched in the firing position to do battle with the 40-ton behemoth bearing down on his meager fortification. Luom coolly extended both his LAWs as the tank started across the bridge.

The tank stopped, perhaps the tank commander could not believe his eyes, but he stopped dead in his tracks as he watched the lone Marine take aim. Luom fired. The round went high and to the right. The tank started to ease forward. Luom picked up the second rocket, aimed and fired. The rocket ricocheted off the front armor, detonated on the turret ring, and caused the turret to jam.

The whole incident took only a few seconds. The slightly damaged tank backed off onto the north side of the bridge. Sergeant Luom grinned. The whole front breathed easier. In his assessment of the situation, Captain Ripley gave Sergeant Luom credit for single-handedly stopping the momentum of the entire enemy attack. Ripley called Sergeant Luom's initial decisive action at the bridge the "bravest single act of heroism I've ever heard of, witnessed, or experienced." The enemy tank commander, in backing off the bridge, had made the worst possible decision he could have made, for all at once the Marines along the river realized that an enemy tank could be stopped. While Sergeant Luom's heroic stand had temporarily stopped the NVA, Captain Ripley knew that they would try again in overwhelming force and that the outnumbered Marines might not be able to hold. Both he and Army Major Smock, with 20th Tanks, radioed the Ai Tu TOC and requested permission to destroy the bridge.[9]

Lieutenant Colonel Turley conferred with VNMC Brigade 258's Colonel Dinh. The two professional soldiers knew bridges are not arbitrarily blown in combat. A local commander must consider all aspects before destroying a bridge that, only hours later, could be beneficial to him. General Giai wanted armor to cross over and secure a bridgehead on the north bank for a counterattack and his Chief of Staff, Colonel Chung, would not give permission to destroy it. Ripley, the man on the spot, persisted, "you can't deny me permission, we only have one company at the bridge ... you've got to permit me to blow it!" Turley shot back a "Wait, out," which is radio procedure indicating a reply is forthcoming after a moment of consultation.

The moments dragged as Turley deliberated what to do. He was the senior American north of the Thach Han River, but his role was that of an advisor. Colonel Dinh said that he could not make the decision, this would have to come from I Corps. The operations center became very quiet as the Americans there and two Americans at the bridge waited for a decision. If the bridge were not blown, it would only be a matter of hours before the North Vietnamese armor would be rolling into Quang Tri or even Hue. Turley fidgeted as he waited for his counterpart to take action. He felt, due to Major Smock and Ripley's insistent, on-site, appraisal of the situation, that it had become an operational necessity to blow the bridge. Turley called the FRAC G-3 and presented the plight, but the FRAC tactical operations center could not permit the bridge to be destroyed. Based on a MACV standing operational procedure, FRAC denied permission to destroy the span; permission would have to come from Saigon

At 1245, Turley took matters in his own hands. He radioed Smock and Ripley to blow the Dong Ha Bridge immediately. Turley indicated that, if necessary, additional demolitions would be sent up and that FRAC had been informed of the decision. Ripley replied, almost gleefully, that he had always wanted to blow a bridge.[10]

As Turley consolidated available support, fragmentary information sent out by the forward command post over the radio was confused by Destroyer Squadron 3, which sent a message to the Amphibious Ready Group and 31st MAU requesting immediate withdrawal of U.S. personnel from Ai Tu and the possible landing of the landing force.[C] The squadron commander, Captain Roger D. Johnson, went on to state that "NVA and ARVN tanks engaged at Quang Tri airfield," while the NVA armor was still north of the Cam Lo-Mieu Giang-Cua Viet River. Information copies of the message were sent to FRAC, NavForV, MACV, and had entered the national military command system. Lieutenant Colonel D'Wayne Gray, commanding Sub Unit One, who was at FRAC headquarters in Da Nang to coordinate ANGLICO support, was in radio communications with Brigadier General William H. Lanagan, Jr., at MACV in Saigon and the ANGLICO team at Ai Tu. Lanagan thought Turley "had gone crazy," as the garbled message traffic arrived at MACV with "Turley Sends," and wanted to know what a Marine was doing with an army unit.[11] Lieutenant Colonel Turley had more immediate concerns at the time.

Action at the Bridge

Captain Ripley, a U.S. Naval Academy graduate, had commanded a rifle company in Vietnam in 1966, earning a Silver Star Medal. He had gained extensive experience with demolitions attending the U.S. Army Ranger School and while serving with British Royal Marines. As Ripley walked forward toward the bridge, Major Smock drove up on an ARVN tank, yelled to him, "Hey Marine, climb aboard and let's go blow a bridge."

The two Americans with two ARVN tanks moved forward to within 100 meters of the bridge to the junction of highways 9 and 1, known as "The Triangle." The tanks, being in total defilade, stopped at this point. Ripley and Smock dismounted and, shielded from enemy view by an old, heavily constructed Dye Marker[D] bunker, moved behind the bunker. From the bunker to the bridge was open space and enemy artillery and small-arms fire was sweeping the area. The sun was bright, the weather had cleared, but there were no aircraft overhead and no naval gunfire coming in.

(C) ComDesRon 3 msg to CTG76.4 dtd 020510Apr72. This "landing force" message was used to recall Turley to Saigon to explain to Rear Admiral Robert S. Salzer, commander of U.S. Naval Forces Vietnam, his reasons for sending the message.

(D) "Dye Marker" was the code name given to the McNamara Line which was constructed along the trace of the DMZ in 1967–1968.

The two men ran forward across the open space and found a small group of ARVN engineers desperately trying to emplace demolition charges. The engineers had about 500 pounds of TNT block and C4 plastic explosive positioned at the juncture of the bridge and the approach ramp. The Dong Ha Bridge was a two-lane, 60-ton, American-built bridge made of concrete and steel girders, with a wooden roadway approximately 505 feet long. The ARVN engineers, however, had placed the explosives in such a position that upon detonation, the bridge might have merely "flapped" in place and would not have torqued and dropped.

Ripley realized that all of the explosives, C4 and TNT blocks in about 25–30 wooden artillery ammunition boxes, would have to be transported onto the bridge and placed in a staggered alignment underneath the girders. A high chain-link fence topped by concertina "German-steel-tape" wire prevented easy access to the underpinnings of the bridge. After a quick conference with Smock, it was agreed that once Ripley cleared the fence, Smock would push the TNT over the fence and Ripley, in turn, would place it underneath the spans.

Swinging his body up and over the fence, Ripley barely cleared the concertina as he slashed his uniform on the barbed-wire. Clearing this obstacle, with a satchel charge and some blasting caps, the Marine started crawling hand-over-hand above the water along the first "I" beam girder. From underneath, the bridge "looked like a battleship" in size and appearance. Halfway out the span over the swiftly flowing stream, he tried to swing himself up into the steel girders by hooking his heels on either side of the "I" beam. It was then that he realized that he still had on his personal combat equipment and that his CAR15 rifle was slung over his shoulders.[E] All at once the weight was oppressive. As he was hanging by his hands, laden with explosives, web gear, and weapons, and with the NVA soldiers on the north bank watching, Ripley made an effort to secure a foothold on the beam. His arms ached with pain, his finger grasp felt insecure, and he could not hang there indefinitely. After several attempts to swing his body, he lodged his heels on the "I" beam. Working his way up into the steel of the bridge, he discovered that the support girders were separated by practically the width of the artillery ammunition crates in which the explosives had been packed.

Crawling back and forth between the beams, Ripley placed the demolitions in a staggered alignment between the six beams. Major Smock, remaining at the fence, muscled the 50-pound boxes near the five channels created by the six beams by climbing the fence each time and placing them within reach. As each channel was armed, it was necessary for Ripley to drop down from one beam and swing over the next, very similar to a high wire act in a circus.

(E) The CAR15 was a shortened and modified version of the M16 service rifle, not standard issue to the Marine Corps, but available through other sources. It was also known as the XM177 Colt Commando.

As the Marine laboriously dragged each crate of explosive charges down the chute formed by the legs of each of the "I" beam, Major Smock became impatient with Ripley's meticulous manner. He called, "Hey, you dumb jar-head, that isn't necessary ... What are you doing that for? Work faster!" Ripley replied, "This is the way the Army taught me, you tankers don't know anything![12] Ripley assured Smock that the charges had to be placed diagonally in order to torque the span from its abutment. Smock insisted that there was enough power to blow that bridge and "three more like it." Despite the "interservice" rivalry, the bridge had to blow on the first try. There would be no time for a second attempt. After lifting all the demolition boxes to Ripley, Smock, exhausted, sat down and lit a cigarette while Ripley relaxed amidst the steel girders.[13]

Reaction at Saigon

While these events were underway, Lieutenant Colonel Turley received a response from Saigon, but not the one he expected. During the first few days of the offensive, the situation in northern MR 1 was viewed by MACV with concern, if "not with alarm." With Colonel Metcalf at Quang Tri City, Turley was the senior advisor for the ARVN units with direct contact with the major elements of three NVA Divisions. He was constantly on the radio with higher headquarters at Da Nang and Saigon in an effort to convince them that the attack that "could not happen," was, in fact, underway. MACV and Vietnamese Joint General Staff lulled into complacency by reports of the success of the Vietnamization effort and by the intelligence community's forecasts, were very skeptical of these reports, despite the evidence that now faced them. Earlier in the day, the senior Marine advisor, Colonel Dorsey, had tried to get Turley out of Ai Tu. By this time, General Abrams was even more exasperated by the spurious request for Seventh Fleet Marines. Colonel Dorsey again ordered Turley to return to Saigon as soon as possible in a message passed by ANGLICO's Lieutenant Colonel Gray, at Da Nang, who had voice radio communications with the Ai Tu operations center.[14] This would be overtaken by other battlefield events.

Camp Carroll Surrenders

At 1520 Sunday afternoon, the forward division tactical operations center received a radio call from U.S. Army Lieutenant Colonel William C. Camper, senior advisor to the 56th ARVN Regiment at Camp Carroll.[15] Camper reported that white flags were going up all over the place, the Vietnamese were surrendering, and that he requested to be evacuated immediately. At that moment an Army Boeing CH-47 Chinook, callsign "Coachman 005," appeared over Mai Loc, dropped an external load of artillery ammunition at the position, made an abrupt turn and headed for Camp Carroll, with two escorting gunships. Apparently the pilot had monitored the conversation.

The fall of Camp Carroll was a significant blow to the overall defense of Quang Tri Province, and has yet to be fully explained. Team 155 contemporary after-action reports indicated that the fate of the 56th Regiment "remains unknown," after it had been told the division and corps had no more reserves to support it and that the commander should act as he thought proper. Personnel of the regiment had made radio contact with the NVA to negotiate terms of capitulation, or as the Communists would call it, a "collective combat refusal."[F] Camper had advised the ARVN commander, Lieutenant Colonel Pham Van Dinh, to break out with available armored vehicles and those soldiers willing to fight. When Dinh refused, Camper requested evacuation of the Americans.

Men of the *24th NVA Regiment* were coming through the camp gate as the helicopter landed at Carroll to get Camper, Major Joseph Brown, Jr., USA, and their ARVN radio operators. Camper loaded another 30 ARVN soldiers who had kept their weapons and "were willing to fight on." Battery B, 1st VNMC Artillery Battalion, continued to resist until overrun at dusk. In the confusion caused by this surrender, none of the artillery pieces were destroyed. By the time the South Vietnamese called an air strike on the base, the NVA had moved the self-propelled guns. Eventually 1,000 soldiers of the 2,200 man regiment regained friendly lines.[16]

Mai Loc Exposed

Because of their mutually supporting missions, the fall of Camp Carroll left Mai Loc open to enemy ground attack without supporting artillery fire. The Marine advisors at Mai Loc had been without rest for more than 96 hours. During this period Captains Earl A. Kruger, David S. Randall, and Clark D. Embrey time and again had moved between the brigade operations center and battalion command posts across fire-swept terrain to erect fallen AN/RC292 radio antennas in order to maintain communications with the 3d ARVN Division. Major Joy realized that the tactical situation had become untenable and briefed his advisory personnel on the withdrawal plan, at the same time he directed the destruction of all equipment which could not be carried. Stragglers from the 8th VNMC Battalion from Holcomb and elements of the 4th VNMC Battalion from Sarge and Nui Ba Ho, as well as remnants of the 56th ARVN Regiment from Carroll, began consolidating at Mai Loc with the battalion of regional forces located there.[17]

At this time, Major Boomer and his small band arrived at Mai Loc as the rest of the Alpha command group straggled in. The 4th VNMC Battalion, which had been 632 strong, could muster only 285 of its Marines, including the wounded who had been

---

(F) On 3 April 1972, the 56th ARVN Regiment commander made a broadcast on Radio Hanoi asking other South Vietnamese units to surrender.

able to walk. In recalling the incident, Major Boomer said that the NVA ground attack on Sarge and Nui Ba Ho had been carried out flawlessly, that enemy artillery was deadly, accurate, and intense; and that he had the distinct impression that the 3d ARVN Division headquarters was not convinced of the urgency of the situation.[18] Boomer and Captain Ray Smith, both believing the other to be dead, were reunited outside of Mai Loc. They remained outside the base perimeter with the survivors of their battalion "watching it receive a great deal of accurate enemy artillery fire," but were not attacked themselves. Joy briefed them by radio about the plans to pull out. Smith and Boomer's exodus was not over.[19]

The Dong Ha Bridge Destroyed

While Ripley completed preparations at the highway bridge, Major Smock and the ARVN engineers went to complete the demolition of the railroad bridge upstream. Finally, with all the explosives in place, Ripley took electric blasting caps from his pocket and crimped them to communications wire and ran this from the charges. As a precaution he had also prepared 30 to 45 minutes of time fuse before attempting an electrical detonation. Clearing the fence, he ran the wire to a nearby M151 utility truck, a Jeep which had been hit by shell fire and was still burning. Ripley touched the communication wire to either terminal, but the bridge did not blow. Now it seemed the fate of South Vietnam's northern provinces rested on a burning fuse sputtering its way toward 500 pounds of high explosive. After what seemed an eternity, the time fuse was nearing its end. The tell-tale smoke trail was now out of view and Ripley "waited and hoped."

At this point in time, the command group of the 1st ARVN Armor Brigade reached Dong Ha and the unit's commander and his advisor, Lieutenant Colonel Lewis C. Wagner, Jr., moved to The Triangle to see the bridge their unit was supposed to cross and to assume command of the Dong Ha area. Colonel Nguyen Trong Luat and Lieutenant Colonel Wagner felt that the bridge should not be destroyed until the situation was clearer. At this time the only enemy action was sporadic small arms and mortar fire met by friendly air and naval gunfire. Suddenly, the bridge blew! The span, curling in the predicted twisting manner, was severed from the abutment and "settled into the river." The open-space between the north and south banks was a sight to see and the wooden roadway was to continue to burn for several days. Ripley reported to Turley that both Dong Ha bridges had been destroyed at 1630.[(G) 20]

Other enemy tanks, however, appeared on the horizon, raising "rooster tails" of mud and dust as they barreled down QL-1 toward the main Dong Ha Bridge. When the tanks were within 1,000 meters of the bridge, the weather cleared, and Vietnamese

---

(G) Team 155's Colonel Metcalf stated "a great amount of confusion" existed about the blowing of the Dong Ha bridges. Eventually credit was given to the 57th ARVN Regiment, 20th Tanks, and the 3d VNMC Battalion. (Metcalf intvw)

A-1 Douglas Skyraider aircraft, orbiting overhead, dived through the cloud opening and bombed and strafed the fast-moving tanks. The VNAF pilots destroyed 11 tanks, but one pilot was forced to bail out of his burning aircraft. The violent and savage noise of battle strangely quieted as opposing elements stopped firing and looked skyward as the pilot's parachute blossomed and he drifted slowly toward imminent capture on the north side of the river.

The cleared skies permitted the Vietnamese A-1s to stop the tanks momentarily, but others continued the thrust southward. Although the NVA tanks across the river were moving in defilade, Ripley could hear them and see the dust raised by their tracks. An observation aircraft orbiting overhead kept the command center at Ai Tu informed of the tanks' movement. At Ai Tu, Turley and Dinh anxiously monitored the positioning of the thin line of defense along the river line.

Now all the firing had stopped and there was a calm for a few moments. Then, on the north side, armor noise was evident once more as the NVA medium tanks shifted their positions to make room for the amphibious tanks to come forward to the river's edge. The enemy seemed determined to cross. Ripley saw four of them ready to cross and immediately called a naval gunfire mission. The *Buchanan* sailed within the five fathom curve, a minimum safe depth, to get within effective range and let go with a salvo. All four tanks were destroyed on the river bank. Ripley later remarked that it probably was one of the few ships in the Navy that rated four enemy tanks painted on her stacks. Subsequently, a B-52 strike, which had earlier been scheduled for that area, silenced the tank activity to the east of Dong Ha, for the time being at least.[21]

With their armored thrusts thwarted at the Dong Ha and mouth of the Cua Viet River, the determined enemy exerted pressure in the western portion of the battle area. The Cam Lo Bridge, directly south of the abandoned combat base at Charlie 3 was the next objective. The 1st ARVN Armored Brigade's advisor called for airstrikes to destroy the bridge and naval gunfire support was called for by the Ai Tu forward command post and the fire from the guns of the *Buchanan, Strauss,* and *Waddell* squelched the enemy movement. All night long, hundreds of naval projectiles were called in upon the enemy. It was not uncommon to call in "danger close" missions, that is firing upon targets that were within 300 meters of friendly forces.

Callsign BAT-21

At 1800 on 2 April, a U.S. Air Force Douglas EB-66 electronic warfare aircraft was hit by a Communist missile over the DMZ while covering a B-52 strike. The aircraft radio callsign was "BAT-21" and the recovery of its sole survivor, also known as BAT-21, began to take shape.[22] Air Force Captain David K. Mann, with the Pacific Air Force Headquarters Operations Analysis directorate concluded that the mission "was possibly the most extensive SAR effort ever attempted." In mounting the largest scale rescue operation of the war, Seventh Air Force, acting for MACV, assumed control of all American supporting arms within the operating area of the 3d ARVN Division for the next 11 days. A no-fire zone was place around the American airmen to protect them from "friendly fire." The authority to request and control air, naval gunfire, and artillery was preempted by the I Direct Air Support Center (I DASC) at Da Nang. This sent ANGLICO'S Lieutenant Colonel Gray into a rage that drove him "absolutely up the wall. I could not convince the Air Force colonel in Da Nang to change his position. Neither could I get his U.S. Army seniors to even try to change his position." That there were other Americans and South Vietnamese at risk had no weight.[23]

According to Major General Frederick J. Kroesen, at FRAC, this rescue mission and the absolute fire control vested in the Air Force "was a peacetime system imposed on a wartime situation for which it was totally anachronistic." Remembered Lieutenant Colonel Turley, then at the Ai Tu Combat Base, the "unilateral rear area arrangement of giving the USAF control of all TAC air, naval gunfire, and artillery fire probably seemed like a rational decision to officers 80 kilometers from the battle lines. However, it was a tragic decision for the 3rd ARVN Division."[24] But, concluded General Kroesen, "no commander in MR 1 could change it and no command authority in Saigon could be convinced of the need to change it."[25]

The 3rd ARVN Division continued to fire organic artillery despite the no-fire zones and rescue force aircraft did attack North Vietnamese forces, but the enemy was not met with the kind of concentrated defensive fires needed at a critical period. Colonel Turley cites this as one reason that the then critical Cam Lo River Bridge was not destroyed prior to its capture by the Communist forces. To the surprise and frustration of the American and Vietnamese fighting for their lives to hold collapsing positions south of the DMZ, this MACV operation took on a life of its own, seemingly out of proportion with the defense of Quang Tri Province.[26]

Mai Loc Evacuated

Low on ammunition and without resupply, Colonel Bao, the 147th brigade commander recommended that Mai Loc be evacuated. General Giai concurred and the evacuation plan went into effect. All equipment that could not be carried was destroyed.[27] The Bravo command group of the 4th VNMC Battalion, which had reorganized at the village of Mai Loc, led the column eastward toward Dong Ha. Earlier the executive officer of this battalion had watched a U.S. Army CH-47

Chinook helicopter come in on a resupply run. He noticed that the helicopter had flown low to the ground and had not been fired upon during its approach. Taking an azimuth on its route, just as night was falling, he then put the stragglers in column and charted the way to Dong Ha. Brigade 147 was evacuating Mai Loc, but it was leaving as an organized fighting unit, with a point, flank security, a rear guard, and with all of its wounded.[28]

Left as the rear echelon of the withdrawing brigade was the recently attached 7th VNMC battalion, from VNMC Brigade 258. Major Andrew D. DeBona and Captain Ronald R. Rice were present at 1815 when the order to pullout arrived. They would later recall the "monumental" effort for the battalion to disengage, as two of three rifle companies were fighting the 66th NVA Regiment. As darkness fell, the battalion was separated into disorganized groups mingling with the Brigade 147 column or preceding on their own towards Ai Tu. The battalion command group started across country on a compass azimuth, with two companies and an assortment of civilian refugees. The 20-kilometer, cross-country march did not end until 1000 the next day. For the two Marine advisors it proved to be a long, dark, wet, and anxiety-ridden ordeal.[29]

The 3d ARVN Division had failed to hold its main defensive positions in Quang Tri Province.

CHAPTER FOUR ENDNOTES

Unless otherwise noted, material in this chapter is derived from: SMA ComdC, Mar72, Apr72; Brig 258 Tab, SMA Evaluation; Capt John W. Ripley memo to SMA dtd 14Jan73 (MarAdvU File). Also, Gerald H. Turley, The Easter Offensive (Novato, Presidio Press, 1985); John G. Miller, The Bridge (Annapolis, Naval Institute Press, 1989); and Vicki Vanden Bout, "Ripley at the Bridge," Leatherneck, Feb86, pp. 16-19.

The Easter Sunday Crisis

1 Capt David S. Randall, Jr., intvw, Mar72, Tape 5093 (OralHistColl, MCHC, Washington, D.C.); Randall, et al., USNA presentation.

2 Order of battle worksheets (Besch comments)

3 Col Raymond R. Battreall, USA, intvw by MACV, 14Jan73, p.12 (Vietnam Comment File).

4 Turley intvw.

The Dong Ha Bridge

5 FRAC/VNMCOps App B, Brig 258, pp. 1-3; Easley, et al., USNA presentation

6 Maj John W. Ripley intvw, 23Apr72, Tape 5089 and 21Aug75, Tape 6032 (OralHistColl, MCHC).

7 Col John W. Ripley, Comments on draft ms, 29May90 (Vietnam Comment File); Ripley intvw.

8 Maj James E. Smock, USA, ltrs to LtCol Arnold, dtd 19Mar76 and 23Mar76 (Vietnam Comment File).

9 Ripley comments.

10 Ripley comments and intvw.

11 LtCol Gerald H. Turley ltr to CdrNavForV, dtd 6Apr72, SMA evaluation (MarAdvU File); Gray comments.

Action at the Bridge

12 Ripley comments.

13 Ripley comments and intvw.

Reaction at Saigon

14 Gray comment.

Camp Carroll Surrenders

15 Camper comments.

16 LtCol William C. Camper, USA, intvw by Col Gerald H. Turley dtd 18Jun83; LtCol George Philip III, comments on the draft ms, dtd 21Dec89 (Vietnam Comment File); Randall intvw; Kroesen, p. 8; LtCol Pham Van Dinh, ARVN, broadcast transcript, dtd 3Apr72; "Contacts with Saigon Mutineer Officer," Vietnam, 169/1972, pp. 6-7.

Mai Loc Exposed

[17] Boomer intvw.

[18] Boomer intvw.

[19] Boomer comments.

The Dong Ha Bridge Destroyed

[20] Ripley comments; Turley intvw; MACV TM 155 AAR, Annex F, Execution; LtCol Louis C. Wagner, Jr., USA, Senior Advisor After Action Report, 1st Armor Brigade, dtd 1Apr-2May72, p. 5, hereafter Wagner report (Vietnam Comment File).

[21] Ripley comments; Capt John W. Ripley Navy Cross award citation (RefSec, MCHC, Washington, D.C.. Also, Peter Braestrup, "Destruction of Bridge Halted Communist Push at Dong Ha," *The Washington Post*, 26Apr72, p. 19 (Vietnam Comment File).

Callsign BAT-21

[22] LtCol Andrew E. Andersen, Jr., comments on draft ms, dtd 1Dec89; LtCol Andrew E. Andersen, Jr. intvw by FMFPac dtd 4May72, Tape 5040 (OralHistColl, MCHC, Washington, D.C.).

[23] Gray comments.

[24] Turley, *The Easter Offensive*, p. 201.

[25] Kroesen comments.

[26] Turley intvw; Brookbank report. See also William R. Anderson, *Bat-21* (Englewood Cliffs: Prentice-Hall, Inc., 1980).

Mai Loc Evacuated

[27] Troung, Invasion, p. 30.

[28] App B, pp. 9-11, FRAC/VNMCOps; Capt David S. Randall, Jr., memo dtd 18Apr72, Brig 258 Tab, SMA evaluation (MarAdvU File).

[29] LtCol Andrew D. DeBona, comments on draft ms, dtd 12Dec89; Maj Andrew D. DeBona intvw by Col Gerald H. Turley, pp. 8-14 (Vietnam Comment File).

CHAPTER FIVE
BATTERED QUANG TRI HOLDS

The Fighting Continues • At Dong Ha • Developments in the West • The Fight for Pedro •
Bright Lights • The NVA Mount a Third Attack in MR 1

The Fighting Continues

On 3 April 1972, I Corps' Lieutenant General Lam, now convinced that the action in north was the predicted Communist offensive, requested reinforcements for the Quang Tri area. After three days of continuous and brutal fighting, the ARVN tanks and Marines had held their ground against greatly superior North Vietnamese forces. The destruction of the bridge at Dong Ha had broken the impetus of the NVA attack across the DMZ.[1] Infantry, armor, and naval gunfire had won this fight, since, during these days, heavy cloud cover and NVA air defenses had precluded effective close air support and had prevented assessment of the results of the B-52 strikes flown each day against suspected enemy concentrations and staging areas.[2] The situation was still tenuous, but General Lam wanted to launch a counterattack as soon as weather permitted the use of close air support.

During his return south on 3 April, Lieutenant Colonel Turley slept for the first time since the invasion began. The responsibility for assisting with the defense of Dong Ha was left to the U.S. Marine advisors and ANGLICO Marines with VNMC Brigade 258 at Ai Tu. In Saigon that afternoon, an anxious Turley met Rear Admiral Robert S. Salzer, Commander Naval Forces Vietnam, and briefed the admiral on the situation along the DMZ, using maps and log entries. Salzer directed Turley to return back to MR 1 with Colonel Joshua W. Dorsey and the VNMC Division.[3] That same day, Lieutenant Colonel Camper had arrived at Da Nang and reported to General Kroesen for debriefing. Camper reported that the enemy had launched a massive invasion in the north and that civilians and ARVN troops were fleeing southward in panic and confusion. The 56th ARVN Regiment had surrendered Camp Carroll to the NVA without attempting to destroy its artillery, ammunition, or facilities. Camper's report confirmed Turley's assessment of the situation in MR 1 that had only begun to filter through I Corps and MACV.[4]

During the week after Easter, the headquarters of the VNMC Marine Division and VNMC Brigade 369, which had been Joint General Staff reserve in Saigon, moved by air transport to the Phu Bai Airfield. The division headquarters and its supporting elements established themselves in the Citadel at Hue, under the command of Lieutenant General Le Nguyen Khang, who was put in command of the Hue City defenses. The subordinate brigades of Khang's division were under the tactical control of General Giai at Quang Tri City. Brigade 147, consisting of the 4th and 8th battalions, was at Hue City to refit and act as the corps' reserve. Brigade 369 took charge of a large and critical area north of the My Chanh River.

Besides the additional Marine brigade, the arrival of the ARVN Ranger Command, which consisted of three groups of three battalions each, supplemented by another Ranger Group from Quang Nam, bolstered the troops of the 3d ARVN Division and seemingly ensured the successful defense of the northern provinces. The presence of these reinforcements strengthened General Lam's resolve to regain lost territory.[5]

Brigade 369, commanded by Colonel Pham Van Chung, was given an area of operations bordered on the east by the South China Sea, on the north by the Nhung River, and on the west by the jungles of Hai Lang District. The brigade's 5th VNMC Battalion, the Black Dragons, arrived by truck from Phu Bai and were dropped off on QL-1 about five kilometers north of the My Chanh River. Colonel Chung ordered the battalion westward to occupy Fire Support Base Jane. Enroute, the battalion advisor, Major Donald L. Price, observed a VNAF helicopter gunship circling low over the units route. Suddenly he saw a smoking contrail streak towards the helicopter. Price first thought an NVA gunner had fired an RPG (rocket propelled grenade) antitank rocket, "a dumb mistake for the gunner in view of the gunship's firepower." Then Price realized the rocket had changed course as the helicopter banked hard to avoid it. As the battalion continued on to Jane, they captured a young NVA soldier, who was dazed by the gunship's attack. On questioning, he admitted the Communists had a small surface-to-air missile that one man could fire, that will "chase the fire in the airplane," the heat-seeking SA-7. Major Price reported this information to his senior advisor at brigade, Major Robert F. Sheridan. They recalled that the conduct and effectiveness of airborne control and close air support significantly changed from that time onward.[6]

At Dong Ha

While reinforcements were hurriedly being shuttled northward, the 3d VNMC Battalion and 20th ARVN Tank Battalion repulsed repeated enemy attempts to capture the now-ruined town of Dong Ha. The enemy's artillery and mortar fire continued unabated and each night, using small craft, he attempted to infiltrate platoon-size units across the river on either side of the blown bridges. Initially, the 20th Tank Battalion's crews illuminated these attempted probes with their tank-mounted searchlights. The searchlights quickly became targets for NVA artillery and mortar fire and after two or three nights were no longer effective. During daylight, intermittent sniper fire came from the north side of the river. A steady rain cloaked the battle area and allowed enemy troops to make small, undetected forays along the south bank. In spite of numerous minor penetrations of the thin defense line, from 3 to 8 April 1972, the small combined force prevented the NVA from establishing a major bridgehead. The gunfire support ships which delivered planned fires and responded to urgent requests from the field fully supported the defenders. Although the tank units shifted regularly to alternate positions, the battalion advisor, Army Major Jim Smock, felt that the blocking mission assigned to the tank battalion nullified the tanks' mobility, fire power, and shock effect. Additionally, lack of aggressive leadership and the reluctance of the ARVN tank commander to visit forward positions increased the problems of the tankers' morale and desertion rate. With the only information regarding the friendly situation being the sight of the local forces withdrawing through their defensive positions, the individual tankers assumed that they had been abandoned to a last-ditch effort to hold Dong Ha.

Nearly 20,000 civilian refugees had already fled south, but there were an estimated 28,000 more to come.[7] It would be inviting disaster to allow them to move, in unbroken pace, through the Dong Ha area defensive positions; they would have to bypass to the east. To reduce the problem of enemy infiltration, 3d battalion's Major Binh blocked refugees from coming into Dong Ha Village. Brigadier General Thomas W. Bowen, Jr., deputy commander of FRAC, had notified Ai Tu that "all restrictions are off on air."[8] Arc Light operations continued north of the Cua Viet River irrespective of civilian presence, "accepted and endorsed as a military necessity ..." by the American and South Vietnamese authorities.[9]

With Dong Ha devoid of civilians, looting of the destroyed houses and household possessions occurred by soldiers in search of food and other belongings. At Hue, General Khang heard about the looting and took immediate steps to stop any misconduct by his service. Khang issued instructions by printed proclamation which was distributed over the battlefield from helicopters. The letter cited the achievements and the fighting spirit of the Vietnamese Marines against overwhelmingly superior enemy forces. He acknowledged that their accomplishments had given a new spirit to the will of the Vietnamese populace and congratulated his warriors for their valiant deeds. Then in no uncertain terms he stated that due to the current tactical situation, the conduct of operations in densely populated and built-up areas was necessary, but that all "... fighting men are instructed to assist the people in every way possible to protect lives and property. Marine unit commanders are ordered to kill on sight any Marine who is caught red-handed robbing!" The looting ceased immediately.[10]

A group of 250 men, comprising the 57th ARVN Regiment, arrived at Dong Ha, to give some relief to the 3d VNMC Battalion and the 20th ARVN tanks. This battalion-size regiment was assigned an area from Highway 9 to the naval base boat ramp on the Cua Viet River. The still-rattled ARVN unit permitted the enemy to gain a foothold on the south side shortly after they arrived, though the 20th's tanks provided support by fire. Major Binh, disgusted with the 57th ARVN, requested that another Marine battalion be sent forward to reinforce his battalion.

Developments in the West

Before the invasion, the 1st VNMC Battalion, operating from Fire Support Base Pedro, had encountered a company-size NVA patrol and had killed 32 enemy soldiers. One of the dead had a map indicating every fire support base and trail in the vicinity. It was evident that the enemy had more than a passing interest in the area, so the Brigade 258 commander, Lieutenant Colonel Dinh, decided to strengthen his western flank with mines. By now, the 1st Battalion, with Major Robert C. Cockell as senior Marine advisor and Captain Lawrence H. Livingston as his assistant, had laid approximately 5,000 mines along the forward edge of the western perimeter of Ai Tu out to Pedro except for the road leading into the fire support base itself. On 4 April 1972, the Bravo group with Captain Livingston, was hit by a "sapper" attack during the early morning hours. The attack was stopped short when the NVA were caught in the crossfire between the Alpha and Bravo groups.[11] The question the advisors now asked was when will the enemy attack next?

On 5 April 1972, General Giai had alerted the 6th VNMC Battalion at Ai Tu to prepare to move to the vicinity of Dong Ha at first light the next day. Major Do Hu Tung, the battalion commander, after a reconnaissance to Dong Ha, began briefing his unit on the move north. Assisting in this were his advisors, Major William R. Warren and Captain William D. Wischmeyer. By 1300, however, the plans had been changed; the 6th VNMC Battalion was going to Pedro instead and the 1st VNMC Battalion moved back to Ai Tu to assume a portion of the perimeter defense.

Further south, by now, VNMC Brigade 369 was to the west of Hai Lang and had the mission of keeping open this highway, QL-1, the main supply route from Hue to the battle area. The brigade's battalions occupied a series of old and abandoned U.S.

Army fire support bases in open, rolling, terrain. They included FSBs Barbara, Sally, Nancy, and Jane, which blocked the approaches into southern Quang Tri Province from the Ba Long River Valley and the Hai Lang national forest.[12]

On the morning of 6 April, some unexpected visitors arrived at Dong Ha in a rented Citroen automobile. They were news reporters and television cameramen intent on getting the story of the Dong Ha standoff first-hand. The news contingent reached the mobile command posts of the 3d VNMC Battalion and the 20th Tank Battalion as an enemy force approached through a wood line a scant 50 meters to the north. Although Captain Ripley was concerned with the pressing tactical situation, the ring of correspondents closed on the American Marine. As microphones were thrust into his face, and cameras whirred away, the clucking sound of mortar rounds being dropped into their tubes was distinctly heard.

Ripley yelled for everyone to take cover as an incoming mortar round detonation rent the air. The explosion sent bodies flying in all directions. Ripley, ringed in by the newsmen, was unhurt but, the shell had killed Ripley's radioman and all seven of the correspondents were wounded. As the thumping of mortar rounds increased, Ripley ran back across the field where the group had initially been taken under fire. He was attempting to find a radio antenna to replace the one that had been destroyed when his operator had been killed. He wanted to get the radio operating in order to call for a medical evacuation helicopter. The tempo of the mortar attack increased. Ripley yelled to Major Jim Smock, "They've bracketed us!" Smock, himself wounded, quickly assisted the other wounded in boarding an armored personnel carrier. A nearby explosion sent the tank advisor sprawling into a ditch with a painful back wound. Unaccountably, Ripley remained unscratched as he moved through the dense fire.

The armored vehicles pulled back from the impact area on orders from their commander. Ripley flagged down a withdrawing M113 and helped some of the wounded climb aboard. The APC pulled off, however, leaving other newsmen in the ditch. With the persuasion of his leveled CAR15 rifle, Ripley convinced the commander of the last tank departing the battlefield to stop. As he helped Smock and the rest of the wounded Americans onto the superstructure of the tank, the enemy seemed to be concentrating his fire on them. The tank departed abruptly, leaving Ripley amid exploding mortar rounds. Later, Major Smock was to credit Ripley for displaying "the only resemblance of command and control on the battlefield," in that he had remained calm and had immediately organized a blocking force that had enabled the evacuation of all the wounded.

As Ripley stooped to lift the body of his radio operator, he realized he was all alone on the battlefield. He saw a squad of NVA infantrymen moving across Highway 9 and into the cemetery to the northwest. Although they were less than 50 meters away, the enemy simply watched as the American Marine captain shouldered his dead radio operator and, without glancing back, started walking toward friendly lines. He expected to be shot in the back at any moment as he walked down the road to relative safety. Only when the NVA saw that Major Binh and his two "cowboys"[A] had returned to search for their advisor did they open fire. The small group made its way to friendly lines through a maze of burning buildings with the NVA in hot pursuit.[13] Suddenly, a large rocket shot from ground level in the northwest sector and headed toward an airborne FAC spotter aircraft. Ripley, who had never before seen a surface-to-air missile (SAM), said "it looked like a telephone pole lumbering skyward." The SAM missed, perhaps due to the low altitude of the OV-10, but the enemy's threat to allied air took on a new meaning.

This enemy antiaircraft capability, now at the forward edge of the battle area, severely hampered search and rescue operations as well as restricted use of those AC-130s specially equipped for suppressive fire support north of Ai Tu Combat Base. Overhead was Sergeant J. Pritchard, an ANGLICO spotter in an OV-10 Bronco, who had been monitoring Ripley's radio messages and relaying them to the Ai Tu COC. Pritchard was flying in one of the four Air Force Rockwell International OV-10 Bronco's that had recently been flown north at the urging of Lieutenant Colonel Gray who, with Major Edward J. Dyer, was now supervising the ANGLICO effort for MR 1.

The battered 3d VNMC Battalion was withdrawn from Dong Ha on 7 April, the town was now defended by the 1st ARVN Armored Brigade, the 4th and 5th Ranger Groups, and the understrength 57th ARVN Regiment. The 1st and 3d Troops of the 20th Tank Battalion remained in support of the Ranger Groups, while the 2d Troop moved to Ai Tu Combat Base as a local reserve. The 3d VNMC Battalion rejoined its sister battalions, the 1st and the 6th, as VNMC Brigade 258 consolidated its perimeter security at Ai Tu Combat Base and defended the western portion of the 3d ARVN Division's area. With the 20th ARVN Tank Battalion, these Marines had stopped a reinforced NVA division at the river's edge at a place where, according to later intelligence reports, the NVA had foreseen little opposition. For the 3d VNMC Battalion, the cost had been high, of 700 Marines who had been ordered to Dong Ha on 30 March, only 200 walked back to Ai Tu eight days later.[14]

The Fight for Pedro

In Brigade 369's area of operations, the 5th VNMC Battalion commander, Lieutenant Colonel Ho Quang Lich, had his executive officer, Major Tran Ba, take two companies

---

(A) The combination bodyguard-personal servants who accompanied Vietnamese officers and their advisors.

1,200 meters west of Fire Support Base Jane to see if contact could be made with the enemy. Upon entering the Hai Lang Forest on 8 April 1972, the South Vietnamese found a well dug-in NVA force with mortars and machine guns. Ba and his command group were cut down at the outset and Captain Marshal N. Wells, the American advisor, assisted the now leaderless Marines back to Jane. Major Price recalled that as this group broke cover from the treeline, artillery and machine gun fire had to be used to shake off the pursuing NVA. The death of Ba, a well respected combat officer and personality, caused brigade commander, Colonel Pham Van Chung, to focus on the danger from the west to QL-1, and the NVA concentrated there. A threat that FSB Jane was in position to meet.[15]

To the northwest, on the morning of 8 April 1972, the 6th Battalion command group arrived at Fire Support Base Pedro, but fortunately, Major Tung elected not to position his command post inside the base. Instead, he moved his remaining three companies to the north and northeast of Pedro and formed them into a crescent perimeter which intersected a dirt road used to resupply Pedro from Ai Tu. Intelligence reports indicated that enemy armor would soon would attack from the west along the axis of Route 557.

On 9 April, the battalion commander's judgment was vindicated. Following their established pattern of preceding a ground assault with intense artillery preparation, the NVA opened fire on Ai Tu with 130mm guns shortly after midnight. The heavy barrages continued throughout the night. At first light, enemy tanks could be seen through the haze to the west, rolling up Route 557 and across the open piedmont countryside. By 0645, it was clear that 16 tanks and two battalions of enemy infantry were in the attack.

The lead tanks, moving at an estimated 20 miles per hour, outstripped their supporting infantry and breached Pedro's perimeter at approximately 0715. They easily rolled over the two protecting bands of concertina wire and collapsed the decrepit bunkers. An entire platoon outpost was overrun and annihilated either by gunfire or the churning tank tracks. The Marines inside Pedro crouched in their holes while firing their small arms. The tank rolled over the entire area, killing some of the defenders in their positions and taking those who had fled toward Ai Tu under fire with their main guns. While two T-54s were thoroughly churning up Pedro's defensive positions, the other tanks without waiting for their infantry protection started moving across the mine field. Nine tanks were lost in the process.

Although there was a 1,000-foot ceiling that prevented close air support, horizontal visibility was good. Upon seeing the first two T-54s, Major Warren called Major

Easley at brigade on the advisor's radio net. He requested reinforcement by the troop of the 20th Tank Battalion which was in reserve at Ai Tu and also called for a heavy artillery concentration to be fired on the enemy infantry which followed in trace one-half mile behind the assaulting tanks. As he was talking to Easley, he reported, "the NVA tanks are flying red over white, swallow-tail pennants from their radio antennas." Almost immediately, all the pennants disappeared. Obviously the NVA were not only employing fluent English-speaking operators on their radios but also were coordinated and tied together with radio communications since all the tanks reacted simultaneously.[16]

As reports of the enemy tank attack came into VNMC Brigade 258's headquarters over both the Vietnamese tactical and U.S. advisor nets, Lieutenant Colonel Dinh began assembling a reaction force. Within 30 minutes, two infantry companies of the 1st VNMC Battalion accompanied by Captain Livingston as advisor, and an armored force of eight M48 tanks and 12 M113 armored personnel carriers from 2d Troop, 20th ARVN Tank Battalion were moving quickly to reinforce the 6th VNMC Battalion. At the same time Vietnamese Marine 105mm howitzer fire, augmented by two barrages from ships just offshore, forced the NVA infantry to withdraw from the battlefield and seek refuge in the Ba Long Valley.

Meanwhile, a hole had opened up in the overcast, allowing four Vietnamese A-1 Skyraiders to attack the tanks threatening the 6th VNMC Battalion's command post. The bombs knocked out five tanks that were maneuvering toward the slight knoll on which the command group was located. Although the Communist-built tanks were within easy striking distance of the battalion's command post, inexplicably they did not fire their main guns before the air strikes came in.

The break in the weather and its attendant air support had provided the time necessary for the reaction force to arrive on the scene. A brief tank battle occurred as the leading ARVN M48s moved into position around the 6th VNMC Battalion's command post, with the M48 proving more than a match for the Communist-built T-54s. The ARVN tank crews achieved first or second round hits on T-54s at ranges up to 1,500 meters. The NVA tanks' fire control system seemed to be not as effective since the T-54 tank crews appeared to try to bracket their targets. When the smoke had cleared the ARVN tanks had destroyed five T-54s without losing any of their tanks. Major Nguyen Dang Hoa had organized the counterattack with his own 1st VNMC Battalion and the Bravo command group of the battalion. The Marines, mounted on tanks and APCs, quickly retook Pedro. Bravo Group, with Captain Livingston, moved through the fire support base and swept south for about 1,000 meters. The sweep accounted for some 100 enemy dead and one captured tank.

Captain Livingston, later recalling the incident, stated that the enemy employed poor tactics: their artillery, tanks, and infantry were used in an uncoordinated manner. He said that the Vietnamese Marines were terrified when first confronted by the armor and reacted in an "uncontrolled state of panic," but once they realized that their LAWs could knock out a T-54, they reacted with confidence. In fact, some of the Vietnamese Marines crouched in their holes and let the tanks run over them and then hit the tank in the rear with a LAW. The 1st VNMC Battalion, over six months, was credited with destroying more than 60 enemy tanks with the LAW. A fellow advisor said that Livingston probably had "more experience with nose-on-nose tank battles than any other U.S. Marine" during this period.

Within two hours after Major Hoa's force had begun its counterattack, 13 of the 16 T-54 tanks had been destroyed by mines, tank fire, air strikes, or infantry weapons. One tank escaped, but the remaining two were captured. One of the tanks was captured in a most unorthodox manner. An unnamed VNMC private in an outpost position held fast in his hole as one of the T-54s came clanking up a slight incline. The angle of the tank's bow, as it climbed the hill, obstructed the driver's view; he could not see the private's position. Suddenly the Marine leaped up with his M16 rifle and motioned for the driver and the crew, who had their hatches open, to dismount. The NVA, looking somewhat sheepish, cleared the tank, turning it over to the Vietnamese Marines. This tank, along with the other captured one, was driven back to the Ai Tu Combat Base. There, the tanks were adorned with huge Vietnamese Marine Corps emblems and later sent to Saigon as war trophies.

On 10 and 11 April 1972, additional attacks were beaten back by the Pedro defenders with the NVA leaving 211 dead behind. On 12 April, the Bravo command group of the 1st VNMC Battalion, with Captain Livingston, was ambushed by an estimated two battalions of NVA which had infiltrated during the previous night and had dug in astride the dirt road leading back to Ai Tu. The enemy had recoilless rifles and antiaircraft guns in the fighting holes with them. Major Tung, 6th VNMC Battalion commander, deployed his units and, after a reconnaissance by fire, ordered an assault led by his executive officer, who was killed during the attack. Captain Livingston rallied the Marines, then led the armor assault force until the senior company commander was able to direct the action. The shock effect of the armor, immediately followed by the supporting infantry proved to be too much for the disciplined enemy. Although some withdrew, most fought and died in their holes. Captain Livingston received the Silver Star Medal for his courage and leadership while under fire.[17]

An enemy prisoner and some captured documents revealed that the NVA's effort against the Marines' western front had consisted of an infantry regiment and a tank battalion. Had the enemy been successful in his attack, he would have destroyed the combat effectiveness of the 3d ARVN Division's forces north of the Thach Han River. The enemy, however, had not been successful and the Vietnamese Marine Corps proved that individuals could indeed destroy enemy armor with their own antitank weapons. The M72 LAW had been thoroughly tested against armor in a wide variety of controlled situations during its development and had been carried by U.S. Marines for years in Vietnam. The NVA offensive, however, provided its first battlefield test against enemy armor. Its success in this role bolstered the morale of the South Vietnamese forces. While it was reassuring for the Marines to know they could stop the mighty T-54 main battle tank with their LAWs, it was the Communist 130mm gun that was the real problem. The incessant pounding of the "130s" indicated that, despite setbacks, the North Vietnamese intended to continue their attack toward Quang Tri and toward their final objective — the ancient imperial capital of Hue.

In the week following the battles at Pedro, numerous enemy attempts to break the stabilized 3d ARVN Division defense lines were turned back. I Corps headquarters repeatedly reported that South Vietnamese infantry, tanks, and artillery, augmented by U.S. naval gunfire, caused the attacking enemy to break and withdraw in disorder. Continued bad weather, however, precluded the use of VNAF or U.S. tactical air power. General Lam, commanding I Corps, continued to plan for a counteroffensive as soon as the weather lifted and his air support could be employed. Another factor noted by General Kroesen was that General Lam's horoscope was favorable for such a move.[18]

Bright Lights

Concurrent with these events, the BAT-21 incident still continued just south of the DMZ. By this time in the war, political pressure would not permit any more Americans to be captured, the South Vietnamese not withstanding.[19] Marine Lieutenant Colonel Andrew E. Andersen was the officer-in-charge of the MACV-SOG Joint Personnel Recovery Center (JPRC) tasked with the location and recovery of Americans evaders and prisoners in Southeast Asia.[B] His "Bright Light" teams provided for the recovery of Americans after the search and rescue efforts had ended. He was nearing the end of his tour in 1972 when the Spring Invasion began and was sent to MR 1 to direct the recovery of airmen and any advisors who were behind

---

(B) MACV's 2,000-man Studies and Observation Group, commonly know as "SOG," conducted special warfare tasks throughout Southeast Asia. By definition, special warfare consisted of the three interrelated tasks of counterinsurgency, unconventional warfare, and psychological warfare. Unconventional warfare included guerrilla operations, resistance operations, and escape and evasion operations. MACV-SOG was composed of units from the Army, Navy, and Air Force and some 8,000 local irregulars. Marine Corps units were not assigned to the task force, but direct support was provided throughout the war and individual Marines were assigned to fill various billets within the command.

enemy lines. Prior to this, two Air Force OV-10s and an HH-53 had been shot down, additionally two Army helicopters were lost, before the recovery effort was turned over to the JPRC.

Arriving at the 3d ARVN Division headquarters at Quang Tri City, Lieutenant Colonel Andersen and a team of two American and six Vietnamese special forces from the SOG-Maritime Operations Branch moved west out Highway 9 to an ARVN blocking position at the Cam Lo Bridge. From this location it was possible for his men, dressed as civilians, to cross the Cam Lo River and recover the evaders.[C] Andersen established the no-fire "boxes" around the American evaders and felt that the 3d ARVN Division "had quit by this time!" As many as 90 air strikes a day were run in direct support of the rescue effort. By 13 April, two American airmen were recovered alive by the JPRC teams of Lieutenant Colonel Andersen. Andersen wrote later that there "were no friendly forces forward of our recovery position ... Khe Sanh to our west was lost and a major enemy thrust to cross at Dong Ha was expected at any moment."[20]

The month's first two weeks also witnessed the arrival of III Marine Amphibious Force units responding to direction from Seventh Fleet, CincPac, and JCS. In addition to forces afloat off the DMZ, two Marine fighter squadrons flew in from Iwakuni, Japan, with their mount-out supplies, and set up at Da Nang Air Base. Highly sophisticated electronic sensor aircraft were deployed to bolster the overall air effort. ANGLICO's Sub Unit One expanded from 89 to 191 personnel. On 13 April, air observers from the Okinawa-based 3d Marine Division reported to Sub Unit One in Da Nang. On 14 April, more air observers, newly arrived from Camp Pendleton, California, were briefed at Saigon before departing for MR 1 and MR 4 for spotting duty from USAF and VNAF aircraft. Major Glen Golden, a naval air observer and artillery officer, reported to the 3d ARVN Division at the Quang Tri Citadel with the assignment as Naval Gunfire Officer for MR 1. ANGLICO's Lieutenant Colonel D'Wayne Gray regarded Golden as an expert practitioner of fire support coordination and a "rock of stability during a time when stability was hard to find." Available naval gunfire support now included 27 destroyers, 2 light cruisers, and a heavy cruiser.[21]

Since the beginning of the offensive, General Giai, responding to the continuous enemy pressure, had persistently requested reinforcements from the corps commander. General Lam reluctantly committed the reinforcements which, in keeping with the principle of unity of command, were attached to the 3d ARVN Division. Now, the unwieldy command structure of the division was breaking down in its efforts to control of two ARVN infantry regiments, two VNMC brigades, four Ranger groups, and one armor brigade, as well as the Regional and Popular Forces in Quang Tri Province.[22]

(C) This exploit earned Lieutenant Thomas R. Norris, USNR, the Medal of Honor.

The Ranger groups and Marine brigades, under the operational control of the 3d ARVN Division at Quang Tri City, continued to report to their parent organizations for support. The reason for this was two-fold. Loyalty to their units played a part, of course, but, more importantly, at no time was the 3d Division headquarters' communications system or logistic base expanded to provide adequately for the command or support of the attached units. Attached Rangers and Marines were forced to use their own command channels in order to have their needs met. In retrospect, it was evident that the commanders of I Corps and the 3d ARVN Division could not properly accommodate the rapid buildup of forces. As an example, a request by General Khang, supported by General Kroesen, to assume control of his three brigades was dismissed as unnecessary by General Lam.[23]

The NVA Mount a Third Attack in MR 1

The invading NVA, thwarted at Pedro, continued to push men and armor toward Quang Tri City, crossing the Cam Lo and Mieu Giang River barrier by the still standing Cam Lo Bridge. After more than two weeks of rain and dense cloud cover, the weather broke allowing a massive air effort to hit every suspected enemy position and staging area. Increased numbers of B-52 "Arc Light" strikes as well as hundreds of tactical air strikes were flown each day in support of ARVN ground forces.[24]

On 14 April, Fire Support Base Bastogne, southwest of Hue City, fell to units of the *324B NVA Division*, giving General Lam worries other than retaking lost ground. The *324B* was now in position to attack Hue City, considered by the Vietnamese and MACV to be "the focal point of history and culture" for central Vietnam. Critical fighting occurred with the 1st ARVN Division for control of the Bastogne and Birmingham fire support bases. In spite of the concentrated allied air offensive, the enemy moved his units into position, ready for the attack. This put an end to General Lam's optimistic desire for a counteroffensive.

On 16 April, Fire Support Base Jane was attacked by infantry and artillery, catching the 5th VNMC Battalion out of position. The battalion's Bravo group was surrounded and had to fight its way to the base under the cover of air strikes controlled by Major Price from Jane. As had happened a week earlier, Captain Wells was with the cutoff unit, having a radio shot off his back and collapsing from exhaustion. Major Price played an important role in getting the survivors back to the fire support base, earning a Silver Star Medal for his actions. After dark, Wells and the other serious casualties were evacuated by helicopter. Jane held, but the battalion had suffered and Colonel Chung, the brigade commander, relieved them the next day with the 7th VNMC Battalion. The enemy began to pressure the

Marines of Brigade 369 on their hills as North Vietnamese gunners "blew the tops off the bases" with artillery fire.

On 18 April at 1830, *304th NVA Division* struck all along the western front moving toward Quang Tri City. At the same time another NVA force of the *308th NVA Division* moved south passing through Camp Carroll and Mai Loc towards Dong Ha. The 5th Ranger Group, with the 20th ARVN Tank Battalion in support, confronted an enemy regiment southwest of Dong Ha along the Vinh Phouc River. As the intensity of the battle increased, desperate ground forces, naval gunfire, along with diverted B-52 and tactical air strikes, stopped the NVA forces. VNMC Brigade 258, with a troop of 20th Tank Battalion tanks, experienced a strong enemy attack along its western front. The ARVN tanks, although they were continuously sniped at by enemy antitank teams, enjoyed excellent results. Bravo group of the 1st VNMC Battalion took heavy casualties, but by midnight all was quiet again.

As the enemy withdrew, the 6th VNMC Battalion captured a tank and a prisoner. The tank was practically new and the prisoner had a fresh haircut, new uniform, good equipment, and an extra pair of shoes. It was believed that the enemy had placed a high priority on first hitting Ai Tu combat base, but had shifted his emphasis to the attrition of South Vietnamese troop units. These fresh troops and supplies indicated to Major Warren and Captain Wischmeyer, with the 6th VNMC Battalion, that the enemy felt the tactical situation was worth the investment of additional men and material.[25]

CHAPTER FIVE ENDNOTES

Unless otherwise noted, material in this chapter is derived from MarAdvU ComdC, Apr72, May72; App A and B, FRAC/VNMCOps (MarAdvU File).

The Fighting Continues
1 MACV Nguyen Hue study, p. 6.

2 CGFRAC msg to ComUSMACV dtd 8Apr72 (Vietnam Comment File).

3 Col Dorsey memo to BGen Lanagan dtd 12Apr72, MarAdvU Turnover Folder (MarAdvU File).

4 Turley intvw.

5 Kroesen ms, p. 12.

6 Col Donald L. Price, Comments on draft ms, dtd 10Oct90 (Vietnam Comment File).

At Dong Ha
7 RVN Ministry of Land Development and Hamlet Building, Emergency Reconstruction War Victim Resettlement and Rehabilitation (Saigon, 1973), pp. 82-86.

8 LtCol Gerald H. Turley memo to ComNavForV dtd 6Apr72, MarAdvUnit Turnover Folder (MarAdvU File).

9 CGFRAC msg to ComUSMACV dtd 8Apr72 (Vietnam Comment File).

10 Ripley intvw; Maj Jim R. Joy memo to SMA dtd 3May72 (MarAdvU File).

Developments in the West
11 Maj Robert C. Cockell intvw dtd Apr72, Tape 5092; Capt Lawrence H. Livingston, et al., USNA presentation; Capt Allen D. Nettleingham intvw, Tape 5085 (OralHistColl, MCHC, Washington, D.C.).

12 Price comments.

13 Smock ltrs; Ripley intvw; Holger Jensen, Associated Press, ltr to BGen Thomas W. Bowen, USA, dtd 19Apr72 (Vietnam Comment File).

14 Ripley intvw.

The Fight for Pedro
15 Price comments.

16 Maj William R. Warren intvw dtd 11Apr72, Tape 5095; Warren, et al., USNA presentation; and Capt William D. Wischmeyer intvw dtd 11Apr72, Tape 5094 (OralHistColl, MCHC, Washington, D.C.).

17 Maj Lawrence H. Livingston Silver Star award citation (RefSec, MCHC, Washington, D.C.).

18 CGFRAC msg to ComUSMACV dtd 13Apr72 (Vietnam Comment File).

Bright Lights
19 Andersen comments; CHECO 72, Invasion, p. 22.

20 Andersen comments.

21 Maj Glen Golden intvw dtd 3Jul75, Tape 6026 (OralHistColl, MCHC, Washington, D.C.); SU1 memo to CMC dtd 12Nov72 (LtCol George E. Jones, comments on draft ms, dtd 10Jan90 (Vietnam Comment File).

22 MarAdvU CmdC, May72.

23 Kroesen, p. 10; Kroesen comments.

The NVA Mount a Third Attack in MR 1
24 Kroesen, p. 14.

25 MarAdvU CmdC, May72.

CHAPTER SIX
EXODUS FROM QUANG TRI

Drive from the West • Confusion at Quang Tri • Team 155 and General Giai Depart • VNMC Brigade 147 on Its Own

Drive from the West

While the ARVN defenders held the Dong Ha positions, the emphasis of the battle, both offensively and defensively, had shifted to the western approaches of the Ai Tu and Quang Tri areas. Thwarted at Dong Ha, the enemy continued to advance from the west along Highway 9 and had crossed over the river at Cam Lo. This maneuver rendered the defenders of Dong Ha vulnerable to enemy moves to sever QL-1 between them and Quang Tri City.

On 22 April 1972, VNMC Brigade 147, which had been at Hue City for a period of rest and refurbishing, sent its 8th Battalion north to relieve the 3d VNMC Battalion at Ai Tu. The next day, the remainder of VNMC Brigade 147 relieved VNMC Brigade 258 there. Under 147's operational control were the 1st, 4th, and 8th VNMC Battalions and the 2d VNMC Artillery Battalion. The brigade headquarters, the artillery battalion, and the reconnaissance company set up within the Ai Tu Combat Base with the 4th VNMC Battalion responsible for perimeter defense. The 1st VNMC Battalion was deployed approximately 3,000 meters to the southwest between Ai Tu and FSB Pedro. The 8th VNMC Battalion was positioned one kilometer to the northwest of Ai Tu.[1]

The 1st ARVN Armored Brigade was responsible for the area from QL-1 to five kilometers to the west, bounded by the Cam Lo River on the north and the Ai Tu Combat Base on the south. The brigade, in addition to its organic units, controlled the 57th ARVN Regiment and the 4th and 5th Ranger Groups. The 2d ARVN Regiment had the area south of Ai Tu to the Thach Han River. The 1st Ranger Group was located south of the Thach Han River, VNMC Brigade 369 was still further south near Hai Lang, and the 3d ARVN Division's headquarters was at the Quang Tri Citadel.[2]

During the period 23 to 26 April, on orders from the 3d ARVN Division, VNMC Brigade 147 conducted operations to the west searching for enemy units. Several times, the Marines spotted the enemy and called artillery fire. The 8th VNMC Battalion spotted two tanks, and turned them away with artillery fire.[3] For the first time AT-3 Sagger wire-guided antitank missiles were used against M48 tank crews along Highway 9 west of Dong Ha. The ARVN tankers "seemed fascinated by their flight and would stare at them, rather than firing the readily identifiable firing positions or moving."[4] U.S. Army advisor Lieutenant Colonel Louis P. Wagner reported that the forward deployed M48s were particularly vulnerable to NVA teams armed with the Saggers and B-40 rocket-propelled grenades.[5]

At 0630 on the morning of 27 April, the *304th NVA Division* launched an attack on the Ai Tu area from the southwest. The enemy, supported by 130mm artillery fire, attacked VNMC Brigade 147 and the 1st ARVN Armored Brigade to the north of the Marines. In VNMC Brigade 147's area, the 1st VNMC Battalion, with Major Robert C. Cockell and Captain Lawrence H. Livingston, made the first contact. Although hit with more than 500 rounds of 82mm mortar fire within the first two hours, as well as artillery fire, the battalion stopped two ground attacks while suffering only minimal casualties.[6] During the late afternoon, Communist tank and infantry forces attacked both the 1st and 8th VNMC Battalions. Artillery and the ARVN M48s, in direct support of the Marines, destroyed 15 enemy tanks and drove back the infantry. By nightfall, the two outlying battalions were pulled in closer to the Ai Tu perimeter. However, enemy 130mm fire struck the base ammunition dump and destroyed most of the brigade's ammunition stockpile.

At the 3d ARVN Division headquarters in Quang Tri, ANGLICO's HM1 Thomas E. Williamson was manning an improvised dispensary that had been established with Lieutenant John M. Lapoint, HMC Donovan R. Leavitt, HM2 Francis C. Brown, and HM3 James Riddle, from the Naval Advisory Unit in Da Nang. They had been able to provide treatment to ARVN wounded who were unable to be cared for at the swamped province military hospital where the main South Vietnamese medical effort was concentrated. They had also assisted with injured Americans, including the "BAT-21" airmen. As the situation deteriorated on 27 April, Williamson heard that a seriously wounded American advisor with the 2d ARVN Regiment was cut off from air and road evacuation. "Doc" Williamson loaded a medical bag and with a U.S. Army sergeant, Roger Shoemaker, obtained an ARVN armored personnel carrier to take them north of the Thach Han River through small arms and artillery fire. They were able to evacuate the seriously injured Lieutenant Colonel William C. Camper, saving his life.[7]

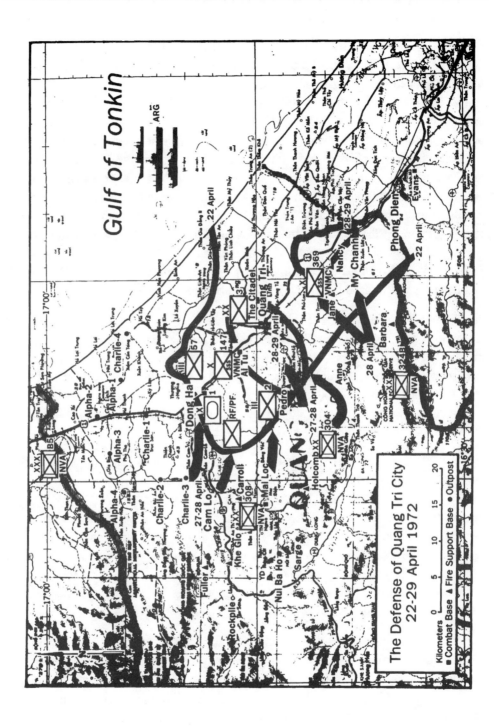

The Defense of Quang Tri City
22-29 April 1972

Kilometers

■ Combat Base ▲ Fire Support Base ● Outpost

This pressure on Ai Tu from the west led indirectly to the collapse of the South Vietnamese lines at Dong Ha by 28 April. Responding to a penetration from the west which threatened to cut logistical support from Ai Tu Combat Base, the 1st ARVN Armor Brigade commander recalled the 20th ARVN Tank Battalion from its supporting positions in Dong Ha and along the Cua Viet River and sent the unit southward to deal with the threat. The 57th ARVN Regiment, seeing the tanks pulling out, broke from its defensive positions and retreated in disorder toward Quang Tri City. That morning, a massive traffic jam quickly occurred at the northern gate of Ai Tu. The Marines refused to let the panic-stricken forces through the gate. Finally, brigade commander, Lieutenant Colonel Bao, after talking with the officers of the retreating units, let them through rather than have a milling mob destroy the tactical integrity of the northern perimeter. That afternoon, Joy sent all his advisors, except Major Emmett S. Huff and Captain Earl A. "Skip" Kruger, to Quang Tri City to establish a new command post to support a possible withdrawal.[8]

The 3d ARVN Division sent the 369th brigade's 7th VNMC Battalion north to reinforce Brigade 147, leaving Fire Support Base Jane unoccupied. Enroute to Quang Tri, the battalion made heavy contact with the enemy, and only two companies succeeded in breaking through to Quang Tri City, arriving at Ai Tu shortly before dark. After dark, 10 M48 tanks that had previously been sent to the south of the river to reopen QL-1, returned to Ai Tu led by the 20th ARVN Tank Battalion commander. The tanks were back in direct support of the Marines.[9]

At 0200, 29 April, the NVA launched a tank and infantry assault along the 2d ARVN Regiment's front and the Thach Han River, securing the north end of the bridge leading into Quang Tri City. Forward air controllers operating under flare-light, brought in strike after strike on the enemy's position. Three of the five enemy tanks were destroyed northwest of the bridge, but the enemy still controlled the north end. At first light, Brigade 147 assigned the two companies of the 7th VNMC Battalion the mission of opening the bridge to Quang Tri City. Supported by the tanks from the 20th Battalion, the Marines routed the NVA from the bridge's defensive bunkers, killing 12 enemy soldiers and taking two prisoners.

The 4th and 5th Ranger Groups, which were supposed to secure the re-established bridgehead, had crossed over to the Quang Tri City side of the bridge and kept going. Finally, Lieutenant Colonel Bao, unable to find any ARVN, and no longer confident in the division's ability to keep it open, assigned the 7th Battalion units responsibility for holding the bridge. As this occurred, the defensive positions north of Ai Tu, which had held against the enemy for almost a month, continued to crumble. The ARVN infantry broke from their positions in an unauthorized withdrawal and flowed south in disorder across the Thach Han Bridge. Late in the afternoon of 29 April, NVA artillery again hit the Ai Tu ammunition dump. Fires and explosions raged among the remaining ammunition stocks until the morning of 30 April, reducing the Marines to less than 1,000 rounds of ammunition for their howitzers. It had become evident to Major Jim R. Joy, the senior brigade advisor, in view of the mass withdrawal from the north, that Ai Tu was no longer defensible.

Early Sunday morning, 30 April 1972, an ARVN soldier, who had been captured at Camp Carroll by the NVA and had escaped, made his way into the 8th VNMC Battalion. He reported that a regimental-size enemy force supported by 20 tanks was in assembly areas southwest of Ai Tu. Up to this point, artillery and tanks had stopped the attacks, but now, ammunition supply was critical and the 20th ARVN Tanks had been ordered south of the Quang Tri River to establish a defense around Quang Tri City. Naval gunfire could not be used against the staging area designated by the ARVN noncommissioned officer as it was near maximum range and the friendly forces were on the gun-target line.[A] The Marines called in tactical air with sorties striking so close to the front lines that the enemy troops fled into the defensive wire in an effort to escape the napalm and bombs.

At first light on 30 April, Colonel Chung of VNMC Brigade 369, sent his 5th Battalion north up QL-1 to open the road to Quang Tri. The battalion was mounted on M48 tanks and M113 personnel carriers. Just south of the O Khe River Bridge, the battalion was hit by heavy automatic weapon and recoilless rifle fire. "The Marines continued to advance on foot, driving the enemy skirmishers back," recounted the battalion advisor, Major Donald L. Price. As the battalion commander, and Major Price moved forward for a better view of the bridge, they heard the sound of an NVA tank engine starting up on the north bank of the river. With the possibility of a tank ambush, Major Price began what he called a "duel between forward observers."

Major Price on the south side of the O Khe, called for naval gunfire, concentrating on the vicinity of the tank engine noise. Meanwhile, the NVA on the north side of the river called in 122mm and 130mm artillery fire apparently on the roadway to the south. This duel went on for over an hour until Major Price was able to prevail with a series of accurate airstrikes that resulted in secondary fires and explosions from the enemy position. The 5th battalion then remounted the armored vehicles and attacked across the bridge with the M48's in the lead, firing rapidly into suspected ambush locations along the road.

Another bottleneck was reached between the bridge and Hai Lang, where the NVA had installed themselves in former ARVN outposts alongside the highway. Major

---

(A) A "gun-target line" is drawn between the weapon and the target and is used in fire control to make corrections to impacting rounds. The possibility of error is greatest along the axis of this line at extreme range, in some case rendering supporting fire impractical due to the risk of hitting friendly forces.

Price called in air, including an AC-130 gunship, "to blow the target away." As the 20mm Gatling guns and the 105mm howitzer of the Specter opened up, tactical aircraft arrived on station and followed the AC-130 attack with devastating accuracy on the now-smoking target. Hit by a lethal combination of MK82 high-explosive bombs and napalm fire bombs, surviving NVA infantry attempted to escape in all directions, "most being shot down by 5th Battalion Marines." With the destruction of this enemy force, down QL-1 "came an exodus of refugees fleeing south." Despite this, the battalion's prospects of linking up with units in Quang Tri City faded. They were now overextended, low on ammunition, and were unable to move up the road into the flow of refugees. Colonel Chung ordered the battalion back to the O Khe Bridge and to hold it open for a breakout of units from the north.[10]

Confusion at Quang Tri

Even heavy air attacks could not save the untenable salient north of the Thach Han River. At noon, on the 30 April 1972, the 3d ARVN Division's commander, Brigadier General Giai, made the decision to withdraw the Marines from Ai Tu Combat Base and to bring VNMC Brigade 147 to Quang Tri City to provide a defensive force and to concentrate on securing his line of communications to the south. Lacking secure communications to all his subordinate commands, General Giai called all his unit commanders to a meeting at the Citadel. Here he explained his rationale for retirement south of the Thach Han River: the expectation of a renewed enemy offensive; shortages of fuel and ammunition; concern for artillery pieces being captured; the real possibility of being cut off by enemy action; and constant enemy fire at helicopter flights into Quang Tri and Ai Tu. Under this closely held plan, the security of Quang Tri City would be maintained by VNMC Brigade 147, the only tactical unit remaining in any condition to hold the northern approach to Quang Tri City. General Giai's senior American advisor, Colonel Metcalf, felt "It would be our last ditch defense" against the attacking *304th NVA Division*.[11] The remaining ARVN and Ranger forces would form a defensive line on the south bank of the Thach Han. The armor and armored cavalry would be committed to open the highway to the south toward Hue.[12] Colonel Bao, along with Major Joy, attended the meeting at the Quang Tri Citadel. When they received the order to pull back, Bao and Joy tried to telephone Lieutenant Colonel Nguyen Xuan Phuc, the deputy brigade commander, who was at Ai Tu with Major Huff, and inform him of the decision. Secure voice communications could not be established, so the deputy commander was ordered to report to Quang Tri for a briefing. While awaiting his arrival, Colonel Bao and Major Joy conducted a reconnaissance of the city.

Upon the arrival of Phuc, Bao briefed him on the division withdrawal plan. Although Joy had attempted to persuade the brigade commander to return to Ai Tu to personally oversee the withdrawal, Bao felt he could exercise better control from his new command post in the position formerly occupied by MACV Advisory Team 19, the U.S. Army advisory team for Quang Tri Province.[13] While the brigade deputy was enroute back to Ai Tu, 3d ARVN Division received intelligence that indicated the NVA planned a division-size attack on Quang Tri City that night and ordered Ai Tu to commence the evacuation immediately. The plan had already been explained to the subordinate commanders north of the river and began smoothly as the Marine brigade headquarters and its artillery battalion departed first. The 1st VNMC Battalion comprised the main body, followed by the 8th VNMC Battalion in trace, covering the western flank. The 4th VNMC Battalion closed the column as the rear guard.

Prior to leaving, Major Huff and Captain Earl A. Kruger destroyed the secure voice radio equipment and other classified material. The American advisors, having finished their destruction duties, joined the 4th VNMC Battalion just as it was clearing the southeastern perimeter of the Ai Tu Combat Base. Captain Kruger, later awarded the Silver Star Medal for his actions, effectively directed and controlled tactical air strikes, and artillery and naval gunfire missions, slowing the pursuing NVA and permitting the brigade's orderly and covered withdrawal.

As VNMC Brigade 147 moved south from Ai Tu, Major Huff made requests for fire to ANGLICO's Major Glen Golden, who, in turn, relayed the requests to the ships. At that time there were 16 naval gunfire ships responding to Golden's requests. These ships included the 8-inch cruiser USS *Newport News*, three 6-inch cruisers, and 12 5-inch destroyers. Golden attempted to keep gunfire between the brigade and the NVA, to provide some form of continuing fire support. In the existing situation, he was concerned that he might have to walk out of Quang Tri City on a pair of arthritic knees.[14] The withdrawal was going as planned until the Marine column, approaching Quang Tri City, discovered that ARVN engineers had destroyed both bridges across the Thach Han River. The Marines tried to tow their artillery across a ford, but the swift current and soft bottom frustrated their efforts, forcing them to destroy 18 howitzers and 22 vehicles. Fortunately, 16 of the 18 remaining tanks of the 20th ARVN Tank Battalion were able to ford the river one kilometer north of the bridges. Two tanks were lost, one to a mine and the other to recoilless rifle fire. Marine infantry swam and waded the river at the bridge site and moved directly into their defensive positions. While wading the river, Captain Kruger narrowly escaped drowning as a Vietnamese Marine, losing his footing, panicked and grabbed Kruger's arm. Twice the advisor went under, but he maintained his hold on the radio floating on an air mattress. Major Huff pushed the air mattress toward Kruger, who then pulled himself to safety.[15]

By dark, the brigade had occupied its planned defensive positions in Quang Tri City. The 1st VNMC Battalion had an area west of the city; the 4th VNMC Battalion guarded the eastern and southern approaches; and the 8th VNMC Battalion defended the north. The headquarters and the remaining units occupied a location inside the Citadel compound.[16]

Team 155 and General Giai Depart

The 3d ARVN Division command post, within the Citadel, was having a difficult time coordinating the maneuver elements of the division. Command integrity had completely dissolved. Infantry units along the river, seeing the tanks continuing to move south, abandoned their positions. All types of vehicles began to run out of fuel and were abandoned. Major Golden, the MR-1 Naval Gunfire Officer, who had arrived at the 3d ARVN Division command post a week earlier, found little cohesion between the ARVN staff and their U.S. Army counterparts. According to Golden, two bunkers inside the Citadel served as the control center of the division. One bunker housed the combat operations center (COC) of the ARVN division; the other, 50 yards away, contained the command center of MACV Team 155. The only interchange that existed was at the highest level between Brigadier General Giai and Colonel Metcalf. Other counterparts did not talk to each other and the 27 maneuver battalions reported, if they reported at all, as individual units.

On his own initiative, Golden installed a direct telephone line between the ARVN artillery officer in the ARVN combat operations center bunker and himself in the advisor bunker. As he received fire requests from Marine advisors withdrawing with their units, or from ANGLICO aerial observers flying in U.S. Air Force OV-10s, he was able to fire several massed time-on-targets with ARVN artillery and American naval gunfire. There was no formal fire planning, but air, artillery, and naval gunfire managed to keep pressure on the enemy. Golden received his first and only guidance from Colonel Metcalf, who pointed to a map and said, "everything outside this circle around the Citadel is a free fire zone." Although Golden fired thousands of naval gunfire rounds in support of the withdrawal, he later stated "the only thing that saved the entire situation, the only thing that slowed the NVA down, was American tactical air....We had so much of it."[17]

The enemy, however, had routed the South Vietnamese in the north and wanted to maintain their pressure on the city. On 1 May, General Giai decided that further defense of Quang Tri City would be fruitless and to protect "the lives of all of you," he decided to pull all units back to a defense line at My Chanh.[18] Intelligence reports indicated that the city would be hit by a 10,000 round artillery attack beginning at 1700. At 1215, the 3d ARVN Division's chief of staff walked into Advisory Team 155's bunker and, using American radio circuits, called all the subordinate commanders and their advisors and said "General Giai has released all commanders to fight their way to the My Chanh River!" This came as a complete surprise to all Americans in the tactical operations center. Within 30 minutes, the I Corps commander, Lieutenant General Lam, or his deputy, issued a counterorder to "stand and die." This directive was from Saigon as Lam was reporting directly to President Thieu.[19]

At this point, General Giai's subordinates refused to obey and said he could withdraw with them or be left at the Citadel, "a threat they proceeded to carry out."[20] All across the northern salient, commanders had already begun their withdrawal and a mass exodus had begun. Unit commanders did not acknowledge the change in orders or openly refused to deviate from the original command. Within hours the entire area was in chaos and confusion reigned.[21]

No orderly withdrawal plan was promulgated or even suggested. It was every battalion for itself. Any identifiable sense of unity crumbled. The confusion of orders, combined with a month of constant bombardment and combat, destroyed the last trace of cohesion among the ARVN troops and advisors. A frightened mob poured out like a "tidal wave on to Highway 1" and fled southward toward Hue. Only Marine Brigade 147 remained under control. Shortly afterwards, Colonel Metcalf called brigade headquarters via secure radio and said, "the ARVN are pulling out; advisors may stay with their units or join me" for evacuation. Major Joy responded that the Brigade 147 advisors would remain with their units.[22]

Brigade 147 withdrew from Quang Tri, destroying excess equipment in the process. This orderly destruction also included large amounts of communications gear left by advisory teams which previously occupied the position. A little after 1300, the brigade headquarters and artillery battalion headquarters moved to a point southwest of the Citadel where they expected to be joined by the 3d ARVN Division commander and staff and then to push on to the south to link up with VNMC Brigade 369 at My Chanh.[23] In a letter home, a U.S. Army captain who was serving as an advisor with the ARVN, praised VNMC Brigade 147 for its coolness:

> As bad as I hate to say it, thank God for the Marines. The ARVN
> regulars, rangers, and militia ran, and I do mean ran, away from the
> NVA. However, one brigade of Marines not only stood and fought but
> damned if they didn't launch a counterattack while everyone else ran
> away. Without doubt they saved us ....[24]

General Giai had loaded his remaining staff officers on three armored personnel carriers and had roared out of the Citadel in an attempt to breakout with his retreating men. The departing M113's left behind about 80 Americans and Vietnamese of the advisory compound. Colonel Metcalf called General Kroesen for rescue helicopters in accordance with pre-arranged plans with FRAC and said, "now is the time."[25]

General Giai and his staff, unable to break through the encircling enemy and link up with VNMC Brigade 147, came roaring back into the Citadel, adding at least 40 more personnel to be evacuated by helicopter. By 1500 the helicopters had not arrived. Golden had lost radio contact with VNMC Brigade 147 as it moved out of range. At this time, as he was destroying all radio equipment and weapons, the telephone rang, the commercial telephone circuit to Hue continued to function.[B] In spite of the urgency of the moment, with flames leaping around the burning war material, Golden answered the call in the precise military manner that professionals use in telephone conversation. All at once it felt good to do something normal. The feeling, however, did not last long, for the voice on the other end, the naval gunfire officer at Hue, casually asked as to how everything was going up there. Infuriated by the "social" call, Golden ripped the telephone from the wall and hurled it into the raging fire.

At 1635, U.S. Air Force search and rescue helicopters arrived to remove the 118 persons inside the Citadel. U.S. Army gunships escorted the helicopters and U.S. Marine and Air Force fighters provided air cover. The first helicopter landed and quickly loaded 40 people, including General Giai. The second helicopter landed in trace, and after taking on about 40 more people, flew away. Sixteen Americans remained in the Citadel in addition to the remaining 3rd ARVN Division staff. After a seemingly interminable wait, a third HH-53 came in low and settled into the landing zone. Hurriedly, the remaining survivors clambered onboard. Colonel Metcalf and Major Golden were the last Americans on the ground at the Citadel. As this helicopter lifted off, a lone enemy rifleman entered the compound and fired several rapid shots at the aircraft. The hazardous rescue mission had been completed with no time to spare.[C] [26]

VNMC Brigade 147 on Its Own

To the south, Brigade 147 had been waiting for Giai and his staff to arrive for the move to the My Chanh River. Major Joy had been talking with Colonel Metcalf earlier in the afternoon to coordinate the effort. After being unable to break through and join the brigade, Metcalf radioed Joy that the linkup could not be made and that the advisors with the brigade should resort to their own devices. In what had to be taken as a

---

(B) One item of equipment lost at this time was the naval gunfire beacon, a transponder that allowed the naval gunfire ships to compute accurate firing data, especially important considering the lack of landmarks along the coast of MR 1.

(C) Appendix N provides additional informational analysis of these events.

gesture, Metcalf again reiterated that the Marine advisors, who included Majors Huff, Charles J. Goode, and Thomas E. Gnibus, and Captains Kruger and Marshall R. Wells, could rejoin him for the helicopter lift out. Major Joy declined the invitation, saying the advisors would remain with their units. The departing Team 155 senior advisor replied, "Good Luck." Major Joy saw the "Jolly Green Giant" helicopters going into the Citadel. He then realized that there was only enemy to the north.

Brigade 147 proceeded east for approximately 2,000 meters and then turned south. After making several difficult stream crossings, the column arrived at the Hai Lang area, ten kilometers south of Quang Tri City. The enemy had engaged the fleeing ARVN forces just west of the Hai Lang District Headquarters, halting all movement to the south. An NVA Corporal with a mortar unit reported, "the people were moving on bicycles, motorbikes, and buses .... No one was able to escape.[27] The interdiction of the road by the artillery and infantry weapons earned it the title of the "Highway of Horror" for the estimated 2,000 civilian and military left dead along this three-quarters-of-a-mile stretch. "A solid wall of military and civilian rolling stock of every description, bumper to bumper and three vehicles abreast." Personal effects, equipment, and bodies occupied the vehicles and were along the road and to the east where individuals attempted to flee to safety.[28]

Colonel Bao, the 147 commander, after a long and heated discussion with his battalion commanders, decided to establish a tight perimeter for the night and resume the march the next day. In the course of the conference it was ascertained that all units in the brigade were still well organized and combat effective. Ten M48s, however, had been lost in the vicinity of the Nhung River. Four were destroyed by enemy recoilless rifle fire, while six had been lost trying to ford rivers. Only six tanks remained of the original 42 that had arrived at Dong Ha on Easter Sunday. Major Huff, assisting the brigade operations officer, prepared the night defensive fires and requested that a forward air controller, one of whom had been in contact with the column since it had departed Quang Tri City, remain on station throughout the night. An AC-130 gunship was also made immediately available by 1 DASC should any contact be made during the night. Major Joy, on VNMC Brigade 369's tactical net, contacted Major Robert F. Sheridan, that brigade's senior advisor. Major Sheridan had followed his fellow advisors' radio traffic closely in the days preceding the mass exodus. Sheridan gave Joy a thorough briefing on the situation and the area that VNMC Brigade 147 was moving to.

Major Sheridan had advised Colonel Chung to keep Brigade 369 moving, including his 105mm howitzers. The constant shifting of positions, never spending two nights on the same piece of terrain, served to keep the NVA artillery and infantry off balance. Captain George Philip, with the artillery battalion, felt the brigade was in the "Bull's Eye" for the NVA artillery. "A favorite target was the VNMC 105mm batteries which were woefully outranged and usually easily observed" by the NVA from their elevated positions to the west. The Marine batteries had to displace four to five times a day to survive, saved by the "extremely slow" time it took the NVA observers to get a bracket.[29] It was still a helpless and frustrating experience. Recalled Major Andrew D. DeBona, "we were continually on the move, rarely staying over one day in the same spot." He did note that the digging of new fighting positions did not suffer, as "nothing enhances your ability to dig like incoming."[30]

Without the battalion at Jane, the brigade had been unsuccessful in its attempts to keep open the road between Quang Tri and Hue, it had inflicted exceptionally heavy losses on the enemy in close combat.[31] It was estimated that at least a reinforced NVA regiment held QL-1 at Hai Lang. The horde of intermingled civilian and ARVN stragglers prevented maneuver on the highway.

Brigade 369's efforts were now directed at keeping the bridges over the O Khe and My Chanh open to the withdrawing troops and civilians. With Quang Tri City lost, Colonel Pham Van Chung decided that VNMC Brigade 369 would be hit by the NVA the next day at first light. In planning for the defense of the O Khe and My Chanh River lines, recalled Sheridan, "he ordered antitank mines be emplaced immediately along Highway 1, that naval gunfire and artillery be registered" and that battalion blocking positions be established along the highway.[32]

At dawn on 2 May, VNMC Brigade 369's "whole world came apart" as it was subjected throughout its area to artillery fire. Major Sheridan stated that "we all just got deeper in our holes and called NGF on the suspected routes of advance." The brigade's two forward battalions, advised by Major Donald L. Price and Major James D. Beans, were hit by tanks and infantry and had to fight their way to the My Chanh River a mile or so to the south, "destroying NVA troops along the way." At the My Chanh River, the brigade dug in astride QL-1 to hold the bridges at My Chanh. As Sheridan watched, thousands of civilian refugees, interspersed with troops passed over the bridges.[33] Major Price recalled, there was great concern that NVA armor would pursue VNMC Brigade 147. This concern was focused on the large highway bridge, adjacent to the long-destroyed railway bridge, across the My Chanh River.

Further to the north, early on the morning of 2 May, after an uneventful night, VNMC Brigade 147 prepared to move out as planned. At 0500, tank noises were reported to the west, near the 1st VNMC Battalion's area. Brigade headquarters placed the entire perimeter on 100-percent alert. By 0600, no tanks had appeared from the west, but the 8th VNMC Battalion reported tank rumblings due south, in the direction the brigade was heading to cross the O Khe River. At 0715, units began receiving small arms fire from the northwest, followed by a heavy volume of small arms fire from the vicinity of Hai Lang to the east. The brigade and its remaining 20th ARVN Tank Battalion armor, with assorted ARVN and civilian stragglers interspersed, was surrounded.

Simultaneously, enemy armor supported by infantry and 57mm and 75mm recoilless rifle fire came from the north, west, and east. The ARVN tank and APC drivers panicked and fled in their vehicles to avoid enemy contact. They broke without returning a single shot. None of the remaining M48 tanks reached the My Chanh River; all were believed to have become casualties of the terrain. With the bolting of the armored task force, effective command and control of VNMC Brigade 147 evaporated as anxiety gave way to hysteria.

Majors Joy and Huff jumped off the command APC as it broke from the column. Joy yelled for the other advisors, riding on the following vehicle, to jump also. An American civilian evacuee, Jerry Dunn, a communications technician from the provincial CORDS advisory team, joined the six Marines. Two U.S. Army advisors remained on the APC and were swallowed up in the dust and confusion. The Marine advisors, moving at the end of the column, continued to call air strikes on the Hai Lang area where the attack had originated. It was soon apparent that the advisors were hopelessly separated from their counterparts, who had remained on the APCs. While on the move, Major Joy told Major Huff to contact the forward air controller flying overhead and to request an emergency helicopter evacuation. The air controller acknowledged the request and then reported that there were enemy tanks moving toward the advisors from the east and south. It appeared that in less than ten minutes the NVA tanks would be on top of them.

At 0945, the advisors heard a helicopter overhead. Major Huff gave it a bearing and, as the pilot started a downward spiral, Major Joy popped a smoke grenade and stood up to guide the helicopter into the landing zone. The helicopter landed in a deluge of artillery, mortar, small arms, and recoilless rifle fire. The instant before touch-down, the aircraft commander, Captain Stanley A. Daugherty, USA, shifted his approach 90 degrees, thus turning the port side toward the senior advisor, but denying the remaining members of the group easy access to the hatch.

Under fire from all sides, the advisors scrambled by panicked ARVN stragglers who were grabbing onto the helicopter. The helicopter unexpectedly lifted off with Major Huff astraddle one of the skids, holding on to Captain Kruger with one hand and onto the aircraft with the other. At about 50 feet altitude, the pilot, seeing Kruger dangling below his aircraft, set back down in a hail of fire, permitting the two Marines to board.

With rotors turning furiously, the pilot attempted to take off once more. Finally, after kicking all but four ARVN soldiers from the skids, the aircraft gained some altitude, only to go into a 45-degree plummet toward the earth. At tree top level, the now-smoking helicopter pulled out of the steep dive and picked up speed. As they skimmed south over the My Chanh River, the Marines discovered that they had been rescued by FRAC's Brigadier General Thomas W. Bowen, Jr., USA. Bowen, who had been flying in the area, had ordered his pilot to make the courageous rescue attempt. Six Marines, one civilian, and four ARVN soldiers had literally been plucked from imminent capture or death.[34]

After a desperate march south, most of VNMC Brigade 147 eventually straggled into the lines of VNMC Brigade 369. Once across the My Chanh River, VNMC Brigade 147 reassembled at the Hue Citadel to regroup once more.[35] As the day ended, the flood of refugees across the bridges became a trickle and oncoming units were directed to cross on the coast to the east.

On orders from Colonel Chung, Major Price destroyed the My Chanh River Bridge. A squad of Marine engineers attempted to render the bridge impassable. With only a limited amount of explosives, they set off a charge under the center span, but succeeded in only destroying a few wooden cross members and dislodging others. Realizing that this could be easily repaired by the enemy, Major Price had the engineers siphon fuel from the tanks of their vehicles. Forming a "bucket brigade" with the engineers, using their helmets to hold the fuel, they soaked the wooden road bed and supports in gasoline and diesel fuel. Major Price set the bridge on fire with signal flares. Commented Sheridan, "although not as spectacular as our friend John Ripley's Dong Ha Bridge, it nevertheless had the same result." Chung's VNMC Brigade 369 held the key terrain and he stated "no Communist will cross the river and live." Prisoners captured that day confessed to be surprised by the resistance they met, they had been told the road to Hue City was open.[(D) 36]

VNMC Brigade 369 now had access to the vast array of American firepower from the air and at sea. That evening Sheridan was trying to coordinate fire missions on the visible NVA tanks and infantry north of the My Chanh River, and was frustrated by an air controller who wouldn't clear air strikes because the FAC could not see the

---

(D) Marine Division casualties through May were 764 killed, 1,595 wounded, and 285 missing.

targets. Chung did not care, so long as the air support continued north of the river. As Sheridan called Lieutenant Colonel Turley at the Marine division command post for help in resolving this impasse, he recalled "I was knocked to the ground and bounced around for what seemed to be an eternity." Six B-52s dropped their bomb loads just on the other side of the river. When the concussions ended, a disheveled Colonel Chung got out of his collapsed bunker and said with a smile, "that was very good. Do it again.[37]

CHAPTER SIX ENDNOTES

Unless otherwise noted, material in this chapter is derived from: MarAdvU ComdC, May72, and MarAdvU HistSum72.

Drive from the West

1 Maj Jim R. Joy memo, dtd 3May72, Brig 147 Tab, p. 16, SMA Evaluation (MarAdvU File); Col Charles J. Goode and LtCol Marshall R. Wells intvw, dtd 19Jan84 (Vietnam Comment File).

2 MarAdvU HistSum, May72.

3 Maj Thomas E. Gnibus intvw dtd Jul72, Tape 5087 (OralHistColl, MCHC, Washington, D.C.).

4 Wagner report (Vietnam Comment File).

5 Maj Michael J. Hatcher, USA, Comments of Advisor, dtd 8 Apr-2 May72 (Vietnam Comment File).

6 Ibid.

7 LCdr Francis C. Brown, comments on draft ms, dtd 24May90; "Vietnam Heroism Earns Corpsman a Silver Star," Hawaii Marine, 23Mar73, p. 1.

8 Wagner report, pp. 12-14; Troung, *Invasion*, pp. 41-44; Kroesen ms, pp. 15-16; and Metcalf intvw, 21-23.

9 Turley intvw.

10 Price comments.

Confusion at Quang Tri

11 Metcalf intvw, p. 8.

12 Kroesen ms comments; Kroesen, p. 17; Metcalf intvw; Brookbank report, p. 20.

13 MarAdvU ComdC, May72.

14 Gray comments.

15 Turley intvw.

16 Brig 147 Tab, p. 14, SMA Evaluation.

Team 155 and General Giai Depart

17 Maj Glen Golden intvw dtd 3Jul75, Tape 6026 (OralHistColl, MCHC, Washington, D.C.); LtCol Glen Golden, comments on draft ms, dtd 12Dec89 (Vietnam Comment File).

18 CG3dARVNDiv msg dtd 30May72 (Wagner report).

19 Kroesen comments.

20 MajGen Kroesen msg to Gen Abrams dtd 2May72 (Vietnam Comment File).

21 Ibid.

22 Metcalf intvw, p. 9; Kroesen, p.19; Joy, op. cit., p. 17.

23 Joy, op. cit., pp. 11-12.

24 Ltr to Col James T. Breckinridge dtd 26May72 (Vietnam Comment File).

25 Brookbank report, pp. 20-21.

26 Metcalf intvw, p. 14.; Golden comments.

VNMC Brigade 147 on Its Own
27 RVN Ministry of Foreign Affairs, The Communist Policy of Terror (Saigon, 1972), pp. 41-42; See also RVN Ministry of Information, La Route De L'Horreur (Saigon, 1972).

28 Maj Anthony P. Shepard, comments on draft ms, dtd 11Jan90 (Vietnam Comment File).

29 Philip comments.

30 DeBona comments.

31 Maj William T. Sweeney memo dtd 8May72, Brig 369 TAB, SMA Evaluation (MarAdvU File).

32 LtCol Robert F. Sheridan, comments on draft ms, dtd 20Mar90 (Vietnam Comment File).

33 Sheridan comments; Price comments.

34 Joy, op. cit., pp 19-23; Brig 147 TAB, pp. 20-21, SMA Evaluation.

35 Maj Robert F. Sheridan, et al., USNA presentation; App C, Brig 369, p. 1, VNMC/FRACOpns.

36 Price comments; Sheridan comments.

37 Sheridan comments.

PART III

THE CEASEFIRE CAMPAIGN

CHAPTER SEVEN
THE DEFENSE OF HUE CITY

Holding the My Chanh Line • Fleet Marine Force Support • Truong Takes Charge •
The Vietnamese Marine Division • The Marines Attack • The North Vietnamese React •
Operation Song Than 6-72 • In the Balance

Holding the My Chanh Line

South Vietnam reeled from the setbacks of the past month. By 2 May 1972, the entire province of Quang Tri, including Quang Tri City, had fallen to the NVA. Elsewhere in MR 1, the invaders threatened Hue City by occupying Fire Support Base Bastogne. The populace of Hue was in a "near state of panic."[1] In MR 3, just northwest of Saigon, NVA tanks rolled into An Loc and were held there only by the bitter fighting on the part of the South Vietnamese forces. The South Vietnamese and American governments had to react to a critical situation and, within less than a week after Nui Ba Ho had fallen, the Americans responded with a rapid build-up of air power within South Vietnam and with forces offshore. ARVN unit equipment losses were staggering, but American trucks, tanks, howitzers, aircraft, and additional advisors began arriving at Da Nang.[2]

Fleet Marine Force Support

In response to General Creighton W. Abram's desire for direct American support, CinCPac and Seventh Fleet deployed elements of the Marine Amphibious Force (MAF) into the combat area. Marine Aircraft Group (MAG) 15, with two fixed-wing squadrons, operated from Da Nang in defense of Hue City. The 9th Military Amphibious Brigade (MAB), as the landing forces component of the Seventh Fleet, had also responded rapidly to the invasion. Elements of the fleet's amphibious forces were in the Gulf of Tonkin.[3] The initial tasks of the fleet's amphibious forces had been to provide MACV security and emergency evacuation for U.S. forces should the need arise. By the time MACV and the South Vietnamese recognized the extent of the invasion, the U.S. had four amphibious ready groups off Vietnam, totaling 16 ships under the command of Rear Admiral Walter D. Gaddis in the USS *Blue Ridge* (LCC 19).

After the loss of Quang Tri City, ANGLICO's Sub Unit One regrouped its shore fire control parties in MR 1 and established new arrangements for air observations teams at Phu Bai, Da Nang, and Chu Lai. By now, liaison/spot teams were deployed in three of the South Vietnamese military regions. On 2 May, Lieutenant Colonel D'Wayne Gray, of ANGLICO, sent a message to FMFPac requesting additional naval gunfire officers, air observers, and enlisted communicators. Within 48 hours, more than 200 Marines had reported to MACV headquarters in Saigon. These specially trained Marines were from FMFPac units in California, Okinawa, Hawaii, and Japan. Lieutenant Colonel Gray formed the incoming personnel into naval gunfire spot teams and deployed them with the ARVN Airborne and Marine Divisions. For Gray, this response for help was "heartwarming."[4]

Lieutenant Colonel Gray had more serious misgivings, however, about the handling of supporting arms during the previous month in MR 1 after receiving reports and listening to the needs of the commanders of the 1st ARVN Division and the Vietnamese Marine Division.[A] He informed Brigadier General William H. Lanagan, with MACV J-3, that the defense of Hue City required "an effective commander for I Corps," who could command the respect of his division commanders. Moreover, the Americans needed to replace the South Vietnamese artillery and tank losses. He strongly argued that priority of American firepower must by given to the defense of Hue. Gray believed that effective targeting and coordination centers for the total fire support effort needed to be established and this "will require strong American action; the Vietnamese do not know how to do it." This could only happen if General Abrams personally intervened at once with the senior U.S. Army advisor and the Air Force commander. General Lanagan forwarded these concerns to the MACV chief of staff, stating that the crux of the problem was obvious, "the almost total disconnect between the air war and the ground war ...."[5] The Americans had to get their house in order before they could hope to help the Vietnamese.[B]

Truong Takes Charge

Abrupt changes in the MR 1 and FRAC command structures strengthened the organizational unity of the South Vietnamese forces. On 4 May, the South Vietnamese Joint General Staff replaced General Lam with Lieutenant General Ngo Quang Truong. Truong moved to his main command post to the Hue Citadel, a move that

---

(A) Gray had maintained a continuing relationship with the Vietnamese Marines from a previous advisory tour and from Vietnamese classmates in Marine Corps Schools at Quantico, Virginia.

(B) In 1975 the Center for Naval Analyses studied this period, concluding that the presence of moderately sophisticated antiaircraft weapons hampered U.S. abilities to provide close and direct air support, adverse weather during April 1972 severely degraded what close air support was available, naval gunfire played a vital role in compensating for air support, and trained and experienced fire support personnel were essential to coordinate these supporting arms. (CNA, Hue & Quang Tri, pp. 1–2)

reflected a change in purpose and focus for operations in MR 1.[C] His immediate task was to stabilize his forces and to make effective use of available American support through FRAC. Major General Frederick J. Kroesen, the FRAC commander, recalled that General Truong's first actions and concerns were "consolidation of the defense of Hue." He had to restore the ARVN command structure and organize a reliable logistics system to his front-line units.[6] Truong's available forces included the Marine and ARVN Airborne divisions responsible for the north and northwest of Thua Thien Province, the 1st ARVN Division south and southwest of Hue City, and the 2d ARVN Division in MR 1's southern provinces.

On the same date, command changes also affected the Vietnamese Marine Corps, while visiting Marine division headquarters at Hue, President Nguyen Van Thieu announced that the Marine Commandant, Lieutenant General Le Nguyen Khang, had been promoted to Chairman of the Joint General Staff for Operations. The President named General Khang's deputy, Colonel Bui The Lan, as interim VNMC Commandant. Thieu's order of the day was that the My Chanh Line would hold; there would be no further withdrawals.[7]

The Vietnamese Marine Division

For the first time since the Spring Offensive had begun, the VNMC Division had its own tactical area of responsibility.[D] Its battle line extended from the Gulf of Tonkin, westward across QL-1, and on into the foothills of the Annamite Cordillera. The division forward command post moved from Hue City to the village of Huong Dien near the coast north of Hue. Colonel Joshua Dorsey's Marine Advisory Unit found itself fully committed to field operations with the VNMC Division, establishing a combat operations center, a fire support coordination center, and a communications center, in the village school house. Colonel Dorsey abolished the battalion advisory billets and increased the brigade advisory teams to six officers, including a fire support coordinator. Frequent task organizing of the brigade teams still provided advisors to the battalions when required.[8]

In order to support the division, elements of the Amphibious Support Battalion were deployed to MR 1 from Saigon to operate with the ARVN 1st Area Logistics Command at Hue with the rear headquarters of the Marine division. To control the infusion of American supporting arms, the division needed critical support in the form

---

(C) Previously, General Lam operated from both Hue and Da Nang.

(D) The creation of a division-sized force of Vietnamese Marines was the advisory units major goal for a number of years. Designated a division in 1968, the personnel strength was not attained until September 1970, and specialized support and service units were still lacking in 1971. In March 1971 during Lam Son 719 a division command post deployed to control VNMC brigades involved in the incursion into Laos with mixed results. By 1972 the desire to field the VNMC Division as a unit was high on the list of advisor priorities.

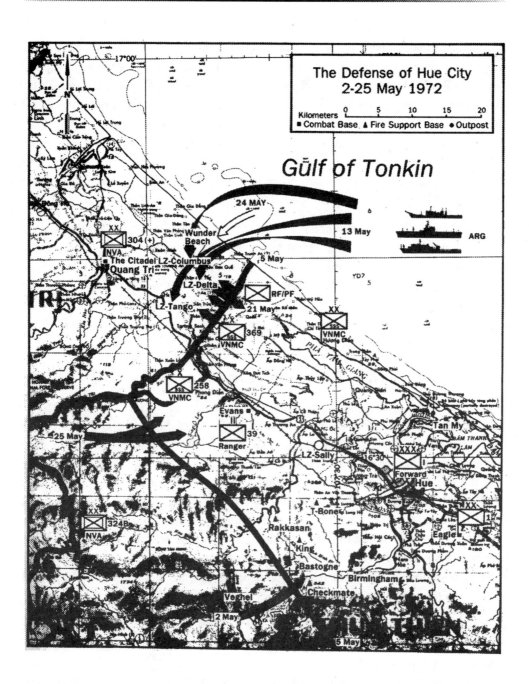

The Defense of Hue City
2-25 May 1972

of communications equipment, operators, and fire support coordination personnel drawn from ANGLICO, 1st Radio Battalion, the Air Force's 20th Tactical Air Support Squadron (TASS), and the Army's 14th Signal Company.[9] As the NVA offensive halted at the My Chanh River, everything to the north was declared a free fire zone. The First Regional Advisory Command believed that the Communist forces were capable of launching a new offensive in Thua Thien Province. The *304th, 308th* and *324B NVA Divisions*, the *202d* and *203d NVA Armored Regiments*, and supporting units were all available to the enemy. The NVA could also hold Quang Tri Province with two divisions, supported by artillery and armor.[10] From 5 to 25 May, the NVA probed the river-edge defenses. Losses sustained in previous weeks did not permit full-scale offensive actions, but the enemy's intentions were clear. Hue was the target and a major assault of the My Chanh Line was imminent.

On 5 May, VNMC Brigade 258 displaced its headquarters north from Hue to Phong Dien on QL-1 to relieve the headquarters of VNMC Brigade 369. It was a shift of headquarters only, as the respective battalions remained in place and the 39th ARVN Rangers assumed control of Camp Evans. Brigade commander, Lieutenant Colonel Ngo Van Dinh, concentrated his 2d VNMC Battalion at the junction of QL-1 and the My Chanh River in order to prevent any reconstruction of the bridge by the enemy. Dinh heavily reinforced his western flank as he anticipated the all-out attack of Hue to originate in the nearby foothills. The area to the west, due to thick canopy and rolling hills, was well concealed from aerial observation. The Marines of Brigade 258 were thinly spread over a large area, but Dinh was confident. He kept his units moving, effectively employing the principle of economy of force by concentrating his forces only as enemy threats developed. Static defensive positions did not suit him; he was anxious to push north. He told his advisors, "give me 20 tanks and a diversionary attack from the east, and we will be in Quang Tri City in two days."[11]

VNMC Brigade 369 assumed operational control of the eastern half of the division's area of the My Chanh Line, including the regional and popular force units responsible for the area near the coast. This reduced VNMC Brigade 369's area of responsibility drastically and the My Chanh Line was stronger than ever. Colonel Pham Van Chung, who commanded Brigade 369 during the withdrawal of South Vietnamese forces from Quang Tri City and to My Chanh River, became division chief of staff (forward). Lieutenant Colonel Nguyen The Luong then assumed command of the brigade.

VNMC Brigade 147 remained at Hue with the 4th and 8th VNMC Battalions, replacing personnel and making up supply losses directly from U.S. Marine Corps stocks. Lieutenant Colonel Turley assisted Colonel Dorsey in these supply efforts. New antitank weapons arrived to augment the Vietnamese Marine capabilities to defeat armor on the ground.[12]

North Vietnamese 130mm guns, however, continued to trouble the Marine defenders along the My Chanh River. The ARVN 175mm guns, which outranged the enemy artillery, were back in action. The reorganized Marine division fire support coordination center (FSCC) at Hue made every effort to provide lucrative enemy targets for the 175s. Heavy NVA artillery was extremely well deployed, making it difficult for the air observers to get a fix on firing positions. Due to the SA-7 antiaircraft threat, airborne forward air controllers, forced to fly above 9,500 feet, could not readily spot enemy gun flashes. The enemy guns had no more than two platoons (two to four guns) in any one position. These were spread all over the northwest portion of Quang Tri Province. As FACs flew over suspected enemy gun positions, the guns obviously would cease firing and another platoon would open up from a different sector, linked by an apparently efficient communications network.[13]

The Marines Attack

Using his Marine and airborne units in MR 1, General Truong conducted a series of limited objective attacks and raids. These were a combination of heliborne and amphibious assaults together with ground attacks that provided the South Vietnamese time to prepare for their counteroffensive and succeeded in keeping the NVA off balance. The South Vietnamese gave the code name Song Than (Tidal Wave) to these operations.[14] With two usable bridges and available air, naval gunfire, and artillery support under his control, Colonel Lan began planning for operations within his area. Colonel Dorsey suggested a heliborne assault into the Hai Lang District. The commanding general of MR 1, General Truong, fully concurred with the Marine recommendation and asked General Abrams for Seventh Fleet support from the 9th MAB. Under the guidance of their commander, the Vietnamese Marines began planning a helicopter raid. Within 72 hours of final approval, the raid, named Song Than 5-72, was underway.

During darkness on 12 May, the first Marines to go north since the NVA invasion clandestinely crossed the My Chanh River. Captain Luc of Brigade 369's reconnaissance company, First Lieutenant Thu Xuan, the communications officer of the 9th VNMC Battalion, and a small group of other Marines swam the river to establish a communications site in order to facilitate the command and control of the operation the next morning.[15]

With the first instance of direct support from the 9th MAB, CH-46s and CH-53s from HMM-164 lifted 1,138 Vietnamese Marines into attack positions. To move the two battalions, 60 Vietnamese Marines were carried by each U.S. Marine CH-53 and 20 by each CH-46 in two sequential waves. Lieutenant Colonel Edward C. "Ed" Hertberg of HMM-164 planned to provide the maximum possible lift capability in each wave and to reduce possible losses. Operations officer, Major Donald C. Brodie explained the "helicopter assault routes were flown at 'nap-of-the-earth' height," contrary to then current practice. The CH-46s were to be 30 to 40 feet off the deck (above ground) and the CH-53s only slightly higher.[16] A single wave of helicopters was used for each of two landing zones, reducing the exposure time to NVA antiaircraft fire.

Major Frank S. Bells' maintenance crews on the USS *Okinawa* (LPH 3) made the aircraft ready for launch and began their long wait for recovery. The first helicopter launch from the offshore amphibious ready group went at 0800, 13 May, and within 40 minutes all helicopters were in the air and enroute to Fire Support Base Sally to load the 3d and 8th VNMC Battalions, the assault force from Lieutenant Colonel Luong's 369th Brigade.

Six AH-1Gs, two OH-6As, and a UH-1 of the Army's Troop F, 4th Cavalry (Air Cavalry) flying from Hue/Phu Bai provided armed escort. Brodie commented that the transport helicopters were free to employ whatever evasive maneuvers they felt the terrain and enemy threat presented: "Troop F would adjust their flight paths as necessary to avoid us and attack the targets or areas of potential threat. With our 'jinxing' flight and their escort service, I always thought it looked like snakes crawling through a kettle of spaghetti."[17]

The two landing zones received devastating fire from the air and sea. As a result, touchdown in Landing Zone Tango occurred at 0930 without opposition in a cloud of dust and smoke. The Marine helicopters returned to the ships for fuel then flew back to Fire Support Base Sally for the second wave at 1055. As the lead aircraft touched down in Landing Zone Delta at 1136, Major David J. Moore, the squadron executive officer, radioed the "LZ is hot from here on in" as moderate small-arms fire was received. Immediately, the Army commander of the escorting gunships shifted the landing to the southern portion of the zone. "Troop wave continue ..." was the order passed to the flight.[18] The enemy hit three CH-46s and Marine airmen left one CH-53 in the zone with a damaged tail rotor. The crew of the downed Sea Stallion returned to the ship with the other helicopters, having had to destroy the aircraft to prevent its capture. Colonel Sumner A. Vale, the 9th MAB chief of staff recalled, "We received the report that one was down due to mechanical problems and it was known what the problem was .... the squadron wanted to go in to repair it or lift it out." General Miller denied the request because of the tactical situation.[19]

During the day's fighting, U.S. Marine helicopters flew 18 wounded Vietnamese Marines to Hue and also delivered supplies from FSB Evans. The 9th MAB's naval gunfire spot element of Detachment Bravo, HML-367, flew support for the landing from the USS *Denver* (LPD 9). By 1250, the assault was complete and the 9th MAB Marines were back on ship. One brigade helicopter was lost, another crashed at sea, and a single squadron Marine was wounded by enemy fire.[20]

Once on the ground, the two VNMC battalions swept south and attacked toward the My Chanh River. Shortly thereafter, the 9th VNMC Battalion crossed the My Chanh and attacked north toward its two sister battalions. The *66th NVA Regiment* was caught completely by surprise. Captain Richard W. Hodory, assistant battalion advisor to the 3d VNMC Battalion, landed with one of the assault companies. As the Marines debarked from their helicopter the enemy brought heavy automatic weapons fire upon them. Captain Hodory moved with the Marines as they assaulted across 400 meters of open rice paddies toward an entrenched enemy. This aggressive action drove the NVA from their positions, but as the Marines consolidated, heavy enemy mortar, automatic weapons, and small-arms fire began raking the area. Captain Hodory immediately called for and controlled supporting artillery fire. In the face of this fire the enemy broke as the Marines counterattacked. Hodory then called for air strikes and naval gunfire, inflicting severe casualties on the withdrawing forces, and earning himself a Bronze Star Medal.[21] As the battalion then marched south to link up with the 9th VNMC Battalion, it uncovered large quantities of combat equipment and freed more than 150 civilians who had been detained by the enemy.

Although the operation lasted only one day, Song Than 5-72 worked. The Marines owed much of this success to the element of surprise and to the heavy fire support available. Elements of the division FSCC had displaced to the brigade command post at Phong Dien to support the attack. The U.S. Air Force representative directed tactical air support from the main division FSCC. Major Golden, MR 1 naval gunfire officer, flying over the battle area, and three ANGLICO spot teams moving with the ground elements, controlled naval gunfire and ARVN artillery. The joint efforts resulted in reports of 240 NVA soldiers killed, three enemy tanks destroyed, and two 130mm guns put out of action.

The North Vietnamese React

Stunned by this attack on their rear, the NVA quickly rallied and, on 21 May, mounted a full-scale armor and infantry attack on the My Chanh Line. Contrary to what Colonel Lan and his staff had expected, the NVA attacked due south down the coastal highway, Route 555, moved across the My Chanh River, and penetrated Brigade 369's defensive area. The Regional Force troops fell back, exposing the flanks of the 3d and 9th VNMC Battalions. Vulnerable to the overwhelming armor threat, both battalions withdrew. After an all-day fight, however, the two battalions, assisted by close air strikes and ARVN armored cavalry, began pushing the enemy back towards the My Chanh River. The Marines had suffered heavy casualties, but nightfall had restored the line. The enemy remained determined to gain a foothold on the south bank of the river.

At 0100, 22 May, the NVA launched a tank-infantry attack against the 3d VNMC Battalion. They had the initiative and could "smell blood," reported one American advisor.[22] The numerically superior force, supported by 25 tanks, overran the forward battalion, but not before the Marines had destroyed eight tanks with M72 LAWs and direct fire from 105mm howitzers. Continuing their attack through the early morning darkness, the enemy penetrated deeply into friendly territory, hitting VNMC Brigade 369's command post at first light. Inside the command bunker was Major Robert D. Shoptaw, an advisor with the division staff, who recalled Major Regan R. Wright, the brigade artillery advisor, "getting a crash course on how to fire the LAW from a young Vietnamese Marine." The brigade advisor, Major Robert E. Sheridan, directed Major Donald L. Price to see if the newly arrived antitank weapons could be used. A U.S. Army sergeant fired the TOW (tube-launched, optically-tracked, wire-guided) missile system from atop the command and control center bunker. Vietnamese Marines cheered as a PT-76 burst into flames and then as a second missile demolished a heavy machine gun nest. This action marked the first time the ground TOW system had been fired in combat.[E][23] Five enemy armored vehicles came within 400 meters of the command post before being destroyed. By 0930, a total of 10 tanks and armored personnel carriers had been destroyed. As the 8th VNMC Battalion counterattacked, the enemy fled the battlefield, leaving their dead and wounded. The NVA had paid a heavy price and gained nothing; the My Chanh Line was intact.[24]

Operation Song Than 6-72

The VNMC's next offensive action, a spoiling attack, took place using the 4th, 6th, and 7th Battalions of VNMC Brigade 147. This time, the Marines used both surface and vertical assaults. From planning to execution, the amphibious assault took less then 36 hours. On 23 May, the 7th VNMC Battalion and its advisors moved by truck to the Tan My naval base where it boarded landing craft for the short trip to the ships of the U.S. amphibious force — the *Schenectady* (LST 1185), *Manitowoc* (LST 1180), *Cayuga* (LST 1186), and the *Duluth* (LPD 6).

(E) G-4 advisor Major Robert D. Shoptaw noted, "Since the TOW was large and the Vietnamese were small, they didn't favor it. This was the same attitude they harbored about carrying 81mm mortars. Despite the field advisors pleas ...." efforts were made to obtain vehicle-mounted systems.

The VNMC G-3 operations officer, Lieutenant Colonel Do Ky, and a small division staff went on board the *Blue Ridge* with Colonel Lan to coordinate the assault. The amphibious assault, known as Operation Song Than 6-72, was conducted with VNMC Brigade 147 Headquarters serving as landing force headquarters. Detailed planning and close coordination were required with Brigadier General Edward J. Miller and his 9th MAB, the U.S. Navy amphibious ships of ARGs Bravo and Charlie, the American B-52 Arc Light strikes, and the largest collection of naval gunfire support ships in the Vietnam War. Early on the next morning, the VNMC Division's combined surface-helicopter assault took place at Wunder Beach — the former "Street Without Joy" area, a few miles southeast of Quang Tri City.

On the *Cayuga* and the *Duluth*, the Vietnamese Marines were assigned boat teams and lined up on on deck in that order. The Vietnamese Marines stayed in place until called away to load the amphibian tractors. Final coordination and briefings were completed by the Vietnamese and American assault units. Major Walter E. Boomer, with the 7th, recalled that most of the Vietnamese Marines had never made an amphibious landing before and spent the night on the open flight decks of the landing ships.[25]

As the Vietnamese stretched out along the deck and ate their evening meal, curious U.S. Marines came over and struck up conversations in halting phrases. Some advisors, Vietnamese Marines, and American Marines of the landing force had served together previously. As old acquaintances were renewed, the Vietnamese invited the Americans to come along with them for the assault: "Together they would kill many Communists! Sat Cong!" Ritual landing preparations continued throughout the amphibious task force, undertaken with the routine of an exercise, creating a feeling of life imitating art for those not actively involved in the landing. Yet previous enemy artillery hits on naval gunfire ships and resistance to the first helicopter landing showed the Communists could and would inflict damage offshore.

The landing began the next morning, 24 May, with artillery, air, and naval gunfire strikes on Red Beach and Landing Zone Columbus. Lifting off the *Okinawa* at 0750, the helicopters of HMM-164 headed towards Tan My to pick up the VNMC assault troops. Elements of the 4th and 6th VNMC Battalions met Lieutenant Colonel Hertberg's aircraft on a highway which served as the pick-up zone. Loading some 550 Vietnamese Marines, the helicopters took off for their objective.

The LSTs launched 20 amphibian tractors, with Marine crews and VNMC assault troops, from a release point 3,600 yards off Wunder Beach. Watching from the *Cayuga* was company First Sergeant Robert S. Ynacay, who commented "It was a beautiful day for a landing, nice and clear ...."[26] The LVTs formed into two waves, the first consisting of First Lieutenant John T. Paparone's LVT Platoon, BLT 1/4, and the second by First Lieutenant Robert L. William's LVT Platoon, BLT 1/9. As the "Amtracs" closed within 2,000 yards of Red Beach a final B-52 Arc Light placed a string of bombs down the length of the beach in a curtain of fire and dust. The tractors hit the beach at 0832 and were met by scattered NVA infantry and artillery fire. Lieutenant Williams commented:

> We approached the beach as the first mortar rounds went off. As soon as
> they hit, a Vietnamese Marine tried to crawl up my leg and out the hatch.
> We beached, dropped the ramp, and literally threw Marines out the hatch.[27]

As the Vietnamese Marines consolidated and moved off the beach behind continuing air support and naval gunfire, the U.S. Marines turned their amphibian tractors into the water and returned to the ships. It was the first combat experience for nine out of every 10 Americans involved.[F] While launching the surface assault, the *Duluth* and the *Cayuga* were fired upon by an NVA artillery battery. The destroyer USS *Hanson* (DD 832) immediately joined the other gunfire support ships in returning fire and silenced the NVA battery.[28] On the *Duluth*, BLT 3/4's Lieutenant Colonel William R. Von Harten remembered the ship "made black smoke and we got the hell out of shore fire range."[29]

Initial reports from the landing force indicated that the 7th VNMC Battalion had secured its immediate objectives, killing at least 50 Communist troops in the process. As they quickly moved over the sand dunes to the south, the Marines encountered only token resistance from the surprised enemy. Later field messages reported large amounts of enemy weapons, ammunition, and food caches captured.

At 0940, 18 CH-46 and CH-53 helicopters from HMM-164 lifted elements of the 4th and 6th VNMC Battalions into Landing Zone Columbus near Quang Tri City at the road junction of Routes 555 and 602. Artillery smoke was laid west of LZ Columbus to screen the helicopter movement from enemy artillery fire and the Army air-cavalry gunships marked the zone with suppressive fires. No enemy fire was encountered by the Marine helicopters as the Vietnamese Marines unloaded. Soon after landing, however, both battalions made heavy contact with elements of the *18th NVA Regiment, 325th NVA Division*.[G] Two enemy soldiers captured by the Marines stated that their regiment had just arrived in the area in preparation for an attack on the My Chanh Line.

(F) A combat cargo officer had initially refused to issue contingency ammunition (L Form) to the "Amtrackers" until overruled by the BLT 1/9 commander of troops on the ship, Captain Dennis R. Kendig, who cited the authority of "common sense." (Kendig Comments)

(G) *325th NVA Division*: 18th Infantry Regiment; 95th Infantry Regiment; and 101st Infantry Regiment.

All the battalions of Brigade 147 returned to the My Chanh position, terminating the second offensive action by the VNMC. For the second time in 11 days, Vietnamese Marines supported by the 9th MAB and Task Force 76 effectively countered the Communist threat to Hue. In addition to the two prisoners of war, more than 369 enemy were killed, three tanks were destroyed, and over 1,000 civilians rescued from Communist control.[30]

While VNMC Brigade 147 was engaged on the coast, the NVA executed an attack of its own.[31] One day after the landing, at 0530, 25 May, a numerically superior NVA tank-infantry force hit Brigade 258 in the western portion of the VMNC division's large area of responsibility. The regimental-size enemy force made a stubborn attempt to break the My Chanh Line. Although enemy armor was employed in unprecedented numbers, the NVA committed its infantry prematurely, exposing it to heavy supporting arms fire. Water from the many small tributaries of the My Chanh River became undrinkable due to the hundreds of enemy dead polluting these streams. The countryside was covered with burned-out hulks of enemy vehicles.

One of the biggest advantages the Vietnamese Marines enjoyed during their defense of the My Chanh River was the combat information provided by air observers and forward air controllers. "They were faceless, but every advisor knew them intimately by their callsigns," wrote Major Sheridan who had been with VNMC Brigade 369. "They were our link with the outside world." Captain George Philip, also with 369 recalled, "The observers were on station 24 hours a day and Spectres [AC-130s] were up every night."[32]

One Marine advisor, Captain Allen D. Nettleingham with VNMC Brigade 258, said the USAF FACs did an outstanding job in spite of the restrictions placed upon them:

> ... no way we can praise them enough. In fact we were extremely
> fortunate in that most of the FACs who came up to fly for us just
> happened to have 'faulty' altimeters and that helped us considerably. The
> FACs, flying much lower than the prescribed ceiling, would trace tank
> tracks right into the hootches with the tanks sitting inside. They would
> then call in an airstrike and blow the tanks away. Other FACs flying at
> night picked up a couple of convoys just north of the bridge and called in
> an "artillery raid" — a massive TOT[(H)] — and destroyed the trucks.[33]

As air observers and FACs uncovered road and trail networks or spotted troop movements and vehicles, they would report them to the Marine defenders along the My Chanh. As trails, supply points, and troop sightings were plotted and connected, a pattern soon developed showing lines of communications mainly from the Ba Long Valley toward Camp Evans. With the arrival of the *325th NVA Division* in Quang Tri Province, the Communists had three divisions with which to attack the My Chanh Line.[34]

(H) TOT, Time-on-target, is a procedure by which artillery fire from several different locations is directed at a single target and is scheduled to arrive on time.

Early on the morning of 26 May, a reinforced enemy battalion launched a savage attack against Brigade 258's western flank. Captain Robert K. Redlin, an artillery officer who had been assigned on an emergency basis as an infantry advisor, was present as one element of the enemy force made the 9th VNMC Battalion pull back over 1,000 meters in order to consolidate. Redlin directed heavy air strikes and naval gunfire on the enemy who finally broke contact leaving their dead where they had fallen. The 1st VNMC Battalion, with Captain Lawrence H. Livingston, also was heavily hit by the enemy's fierce attack. Two NVA battalions from the *88th NVA Regiment*, supported by tanks, mortars, recoilless rifles, and artillery fire, threatened to overrun the 1st VNMC Battalion's position. Livingston quickly called air strikes on the enemy, inflicting many casualties. Again the South Vietnamese had stopped the enemy drive to Hue. As the NVA withdrew from the VNMC Brigade 258 area, they left more than 200 corpses on the battlefield.

May had been a bad month for the NVA along the My Chanh River. They had suffered more than 2,900 soldiers killed, 1,080 weapons captured, and 64 armored vehicles destroyed or captured. The Communists had failed to fulfill their plans to capture Hue. The My Chanh Line had held and it was a good month for the Vietnamese Marines. On 28 May 1972, on the Emperor's Walkway, in front of the Imperial Palace at Hue, President Thieu personally promoted Colonel Lan to brigadier general. During the month more than 15,000 Vietnamese Marines had joined the defenders of MR 1 and practically every able-bodied Marine was now in the northern provinces.

In the Balance

The first part of June 1972 was characterized by limited South Vietnamese offensive thrusts north across the My Chanh River, but by the end of the month a major effort had been launched to recapture Quang Tri City. Major General Howard H. Cooksey, USA, replaced General Kroesen as the senior American in MR 1, and as such, he continued the American support to General Truong in the defense of Hue and the counteroffensive to regain Quang Tri Province. This month also witnessed the departure of General Creighton W. Abrams and his replacement by General Frederick C. Weyand, USA, as MACV commander.

With its maneuver battalions up to combat strength and fire support agencies consolidated in the VNMC Division's FSCC, the Vietnamese Marines took the initiative on 8 June and launched a spoiling attack named Song Than 8-72. All three VNMC brigades were committed in a four-battalion attack across the river. The Marines moved forward under the cover of a closely coordinated and well-executed fire support plan which included B-52 strikes, tactical air, artillery, and naval gunfire. The American-established FSCC at division headquarters permitted supporting arms to be fired in concert, a technique heretofore fraught with problems of execution. According to Lieutenant Colonel Duncan M. Jones, the division artillery advisor who had helped set up the fire support coordination center, "there were still many problems, but none that could not be overcome."[35]

As the battalions crossed the My Chanh River, the heaviest resistance was encountered along the coastal areas, particularly along Route 555, familiarly known to the Americans as the "Triple Nickel." The enemy was well entrenched, but friendly casualties were light with nine men killed in action. The NVA took a heavy beating, with the successful Marine operation accounting for 230 enemy killed, 7 tanks destroyed, and 102 weapons, including several SA-7 surface-to-air missiles captured or destroyed. At the conclusion of the operation the Marines were north of the My Chanh River, once again in Quang Tri Province, and anxious to continue north.[36]

In order to consolidate the Marines' captured territory, ARVN engineers built pontoon bridges across the My Chanh River to give tanks, artillery, and trucks access to Quang Tri Province. Plans were already being made to send the Marine brigades back into the offensive. Such plans culminated in Song Than 8A-72. This operation was another spoiling attack which began on 18 June. Once again all three VNMC brigades were involved. Marine Brigade 147 struck north along Route 555, into the notorious "Street Without Joy" coastal area. VNMC Brigade 369 held the center position as it attacked across open rice paddies flanked to the west by VNMC Brigade 258, moving along QL-1. The NVA forces were defending in depth along QL-1 and Route 555, reinforced by armor, artillery, and antiaircraft units. Stream and canal networks between the two roads were laced with trenches and fortified positions. Further to the west lay rolling hills and the enemy's 130mm guns.

As the 6th VNMC Battalion with VNMC Brigade 147 moved north along Route 555, it was met by an enemy counterattack. During darkness on 20 June, a reinforced enemy infantry battalion supported by tanks and artillery hit the 6th battalion's defensive positions. The NVA tanks were not coordinated with the infantry maneuver and VNMC artillery quickly responded to each tank sighting with massed fire.[37] Despite the heavy artillery fire, at least 40 NVA soldiers were able to break through the 6th Battalion's perimeter and attack the battalion command post, fragmenting the command group.

Major James M. Tully and the attached ANGLICO naval gunfire spot team became separated from the Vietnamese Marines. Locating the battalion commander, Tully, with the aid of the spot team, assisted in calling for supporting fires.[38] For the next eight hours the battle raged. Both tactical aircraft and naval gunfire supported the battalion as Lieutenant Colonel Do Huu Tung rallied his battered Marines for a tank and infantry counterattack. Backed by B-52 strikes and other supporting arms, the 6th VNMC Battalion pushed the enemy from the penetrated position.[I] The enemy responded with heavy artillery and mortar fire throughout the entire zone of action. While the 6th VNMC Battalion was fighting for its life, the 1st and 5th VNMC Battalions also repulsed large armored counterattacks.

By 27 June, the VNMC had successfully established a new defensive line four kilometers north of the My Chanh River. The operation had netted 761 enemy killed, eight tanks destroyed, and freed several hundred captive villagers.[39] The liberated Vietnamese from a hamlet in Hai Lang District described their life under the Communists as being full of terror and forced labor. More than two-thirds of the population had fled south in the face of the Communist invasion; those who had stayed behind in hope of harvesting some of their rice crop found life miserable. According to one of the escapees, a young farmer named Le Thi, the NVA told the villagers that those who had fled to Hue with the ARVN forces would starve and that if any of those who had remained tried to escape they would be shot. Another said that the invaders forced the people to carry supplies, harvest rice, dig weapons caches, and build field fortifications. The attacks by the South Vietnamese Marines had made escape from the NVA occupation possible for more than 2,000 people. The villagers were sent south to the My Chanh River where boats picked them up at the river's edge and took them to Hue. Trucks eventually transported them from Hue to Da Nang refugee camps.[40]

(I) Major Tully was instrumental in helping organize the effort to repulse the enemy and later was awarded the Silver Star Medal.

CHAPTER SEVEN ENDNOTES

Unless otherwise noted, material in this chapter is derived from: MarAdvU HistSum72; MarAdvU ComdC, May72, Jun72; MarAdvU G3 TOC Duty Log, 1May72–20Jun72 (MarAdvU File); Truong, *Invasion*; and FMFPac MarOpsSEA.

Holding the My Chanh Line

1 LtCol Gray memo to BGen Lanagan dtd 4May72 (Vietnam Comment File).

2 MGen Kroesen msg to Gen Abrams dtd 2May72 (Vietnam Comment File); SMA ltr to FRAC dtd 8May72, VNMC Confirmed Losses dtd 3May72, Logistics Tab, SMA Evaluation (MarAdvU File).

Fleet Marine Force Support

3 BrigGen William H. Lanagan, Jr., intvw dtd 31May72, Tape 5036 (OralHistColl, MCHC, Washington, D.C.).

4 Sub Unit1, 1stANGLICO ComdC, May72; SU1 memo dtd 26Jul72 (Vietnam Comment File).

5 BGen Lanagan memo to MACV C/S dtd 5May72 (Vietnam Comment File).

Truong Takes Charge

6 Truong, *Invasion*, p. 48; Kroesen comments.

7 Truong, *Invasion*, pp. 48-57; LtGen Le Nguyen Khang intvw, dtd 30Sept75 (OralHistColl, MCHC, Washington, D.C.); App C, pp. 1-2, FRAC/VNMCOps.

The Vietnamese Marine Division

8 MarAdvU ComC, May72, Encl 12.

9 SMA debrief, pp. 16-17; Capt Thomas Zalewski memo dtd 8Jan73, Tab 2, Operational Communications Folder; Status of Amphibious Support Battalion During Current Operations dtd 22Oct72, MarAdvU Turnover Folder (MarAdvU File).

10 FRAC IntSum 125-72 dtd 3May72 (Vietnam Comment File).

11 Capt Allen D. Nettleingham intvw dtd 11Jun72, Tape 5085, (OralHistColl, MCHC, Washington, D.C.).

12 Col Joshua W. Dorsey III summary of action dtd 26Feb73, MarAdvU Turnover Folder (MarAdvU File).

13 MarAdvU ComdC, May72; Philip comments.

The Marines Attack

14 Major General Howard H. Cooksey, USA, Senior Officer Debriefing Report dtd 25Jan73, p. 5, hereafter Cooksey debrief (Vietnam Comment File); Truong, *Invasion*, pp. 56-60.

15 Dorsey, op. cit.

16 Maj Donald C. Brodie, comments on draft ms, dtd 5Feb90 (Vietnam Comment File).

17 Brodie comments.

18 LtCol David J. Moore, comments on draft ms, dtd 12Dec89 (Vietnam Comment File).

19 Col Sumner A. Vale, comments on draft ms, dtd 11Jan90 (Vietnam Comment File).

20 FMFPac MarOpsSEA, pp. 2-14 to 2-16; CNA MarActySEA, pp. 52-56.

21 Capt Richard W. Hodory Bronze Star award citation (RefSec, MCHC, Washington, D.C.).

The North Vietnamese React
22 Maj Emmett S. Huff memo to SMA dtd 17May72 (MarAdvU File).

23 LtCol Robert D. Shoptaw, comments on draft ms, dtd 27Dec90 (Vietnam Comment File).

24 Turley intvw; CWO James E. Hill ltr to USAIC, Ft. Benning, Ga., dtd 23Aug72, Ordnance/Maintenance Turnover Folder (MarAdvU File).

Operation Song Thanh 6-72
25 Boomer comments.

26 SgtMaj Robert S. Ynacay, comments on draft ms, dtd 20Dec89 (Vietnam Comment File).

27 1stLt Robert L. Williams intvw, Tape 5076; 1stLt John T. Paparone intvw, Tape 5077 (OralHistColl, MCHC, Washington, D.C.).

28 Golden intvw.

29 LtCol William R. Von Harten, comments on draft ms, dtd 11Jan90 (Vietnam Comment File).

30 CG9thMAB debrief to CMC dtd 15Feb73, Tape 5035 (OralHistColl, MCHC, Washington, D.C.); 9thMAB PAO news release dtd 24May72 (Vietnam Comment File).

31 Brig 147 Tab, SMA Evaluation; FMFPac MarOpsSEA, pp. 2-16 to 2-17; CNA MarActySEA, pp. 53-54.

32 Sheridan comment; Philip comment.

33 Nettleingham intvw.

34 FRAC IntSum 152-72 dtd 30May72 (Vietnam Comment File).

In the Balance
35 LtCol Duncan H. Jones intvw by LtCol Arnold dtd 21Aug75 (Vietnam Comment File).

36 App D, pp. 1-2, FRAC/VNMCOps; Song Than 8-72 Folder (MarAdvU File).

37 LtCol Peter S. Morosoff, "Coordinating Defensive Fire Support," *Marine Corps Gazette*, Jun87, pp. 19-20.

38 Sub Unit One memo; "Augmentation Personnel," SU1 memo dtd 26Jul72; Golden intvw (Vietnam Comment File).

39 App D, Brig 147, pp. 3-5, FRAC/VNMCOps; Song Than 8A-72 Folder (MarAdvU File). 40 *Covan*, 1Jul72 (MarAdvU files).

CHAPTER EIGHT
QUANG TRI CITY REGAINED

Truong's Counteroffensive • The Battle for Quang Tri City • Taking the Citadel • The Final Assault

Truong's Counteroffensive

With a firm hold on the southern portion of Quang Tri Province and daily attacking the enemy supply lines, the South Vietnamese planned in earnest for the recapture of lost territory to the north. I Corps' Lieutenant General Ngo Quang Truong wanted to defend Hue against threats from the west while conducting offensive operations from positions along the My Chanh River to regain the Quang Tri-Dong Ha area. Troung wrote, the "limited offensive operations had brought us enough time to prepare for the long-awaited big push northward."[1] FRAC's Major General Howard H. Cooksey reported that the objective was to recapture Quang Tri Province, but that the destruction of enemy forces and material was an important secondary task and the South Vietnamese decided, at first, to bypass Quang Tri City.[2]

Teams from ANGLICO were in all four military regions to meet the increased demands for fire support coordination. In response to Lieutenant Colonel D'Wayne Gray's urgings, the American command organized its fire support assets, including ANGLICO, to support offensive as well as defensive operations in MR 1. FRAC integrated air, artillery, and naval gunfire for maximum effect in support of the ground fighting. Major Glen Golden was with the liaison team with FRAC in Hue; liaison/spot teams were with the VNMC Division, the Airborne Division, 1st ARVN Division, 2d ARVN Division; and naval gunfire air spot teams were flying out of Phu Bai and Da Nang.[3]

Phase one of Lam Son or Total Victory 72, the multi-division I Corps counteroffensive, began after six days of extensive preparatory fires by all available supporting arms and an amphibious feint at the mouth of the Cua Viet River.[A] The

---

(A) Known as Song Than 9-72 to the VNMC.

operational concept was for the Vietnamese Airborne Division and the Marine Division to attack abreast to the northwest employing both surface and helicopter assaults to seize a line along the Thach Han River. The Marines' axis of advance was along Route 555, taking in the area from the coast to QL-1. The Airborne Division's area included QL-1 on the right to the foothills on the left, with Quang Tri City in their zone of action.

A 9th MAB amphibious demonstration on "D-1" preceded the counteroffensive. A special amphibious task group was activated by Task Force 76 to simulate the preparation and conduct of an amphibious assault. VNMC units were taken on board ship from Tam My to add credence to the northern feint. On 27 June 1972, the American amphibious forces moved to the objective area and by 0800 landing craft and amphibian tractors carrying South Vietnamese Marines were near their turnaway point. Helicopters from HMM-165, commanded by Lieutenant Colonel Charles H. F. "Doc" Egger, launched from the USS *Tripoli* (LPH 10) and headed for the beach. At 0806, the surface force — simultaneously with the helicopter force — reversed direction 5,000 yards from the shore.

Intelligence estimates by the 1st Regional Assistance Command later indicated confusion and relocation of some NVA units in response to the demonstration, contributing to the initial success of Lam Son 72. It was also noted that the North Vietnamese reacted quickly, firing artillery at the amphibious ships from the mainland and offshore islands.[4] Colonel Sumner A. Vale, the 9th MAB chief of staff, witnessed the NVA shore fire "landing in the wake of the *Blue Ridge* and a ship to the starboard of her." Second Lieutenant Stephen C. Fogleman, a rifle platoon commander with BLT 1/9, recalled:

> ... We were on the *Schenectady* and were heading out from the beach.
> Tiger Island was passing on our port side. It was flat and green and
> fairly low in the water. We saw white flashes from the foliage, then saw
> the shellbursts walking towards us, both in the air and on the surface.
> The Marines passing ammunition on the aft gun-mount didn't flinch and
> continued to pass ammunition to the 3"50s which banged away. The
> cruiser [*USS Newport News*] came in and opened up, after which the
> guns on Tiger Island remained silent. It was more fire than we had
> received during Song Than 6-72.[5]

On 28 June, the Marine Division's portion of the overall I Corps effort began. The 3d, 5th, 7th, and 8th VNMC Battalions pushed north and immediately encountered stiff resistance. The enemy was well dug in and showed no inclination to withdraw. General Lan launched a helicopter-borne assault behind the enemy lines to relieve the pressure on the attacking Marine battalions. On 29 June, the 1st and 4th VNMC Battalions, supported by the 9th MAB, conducted a helicopter assault and secured key objectives along Route 555 and the coastline in the vicinity of Wunder Beach. For a third time, U.S. Marine CH-46 and CH-53 helicopters had lifted Vietnamese Marines into enemy-held positions.

A helicopter pilot with HMM-165 described his first combat flight:

> The first wave lifted off and the second wave of 46s were pulled out of the stack and spotted. Within seconds they were turning and launched. We were spotted on two and three. We unfolded our blades and the crewchief went topside to check the locking pins. As soon as we were turning, tower cleared us to launch.[6]

Helicopters from the USS *Tripoli* and *Okinawa* loaded the two VNMC battalions at Tan My, flew them north, and put them down in Landing Zones Flamingo and Hawk. After intensive shore, sea, and air bombardment — including B-52 Arc Lights — had blasted the enemy, the helicopters landed and were met by small arms fire. Only scattered enemy forces opposed and the 1,450 Vietnamese Marines landing with precision. The helicopters from HMM-164 and HMM-165 returned to the ships with minor damage and no casualties. ANGLICO's 1st Lieutenant Stephen G. Biddulph recalled, with the 1st Battalion, recalled that after the assault "the enemy on several occasions tried to rush tanks and armored personnel carriers down the surf to envelop us." The NVA did not succeed because of the direct fire from naval gunfire ships positioned 4,000 meters offshore.[7]

The start of Lam Son 72 was a complete success as the vertical envelopment relieved the pressure to the south and facilitated a rapid advance and recapture of lost territory.[8] As June ended, the NVA had given up more ground as they were pushed further back into Quang Tri Province. The South Vietnamese daily captured artillery, tanks, and armored personnel carriers. During the month, the allies killed 1,515 enemy and destroyed 18 armored vehicles. The Marines took 15 enemy soldiers prisoner.

Flying in support of these operations were airborne air controllers and naval gunfire spotters with 20th TASS out of Da Nang. As part of this continuous coverage on 29 June, Captain Steven L. Bennett, USAF, and an ANGLICO air observer, Captain Michael B. Brown, USMC, flew one such sortie in an OV-10. After operating for three hours over the battle area, Captains Bennett and Brown received an urgent request from a South Vietnamese unit under attack by a larger NVA force. With no air support in the immediate area and the combatants too close for gunfire, Bennett rolled in to strafe the enemy. After the aircraft pulled out of its fifth run, an SA-7 missile struck

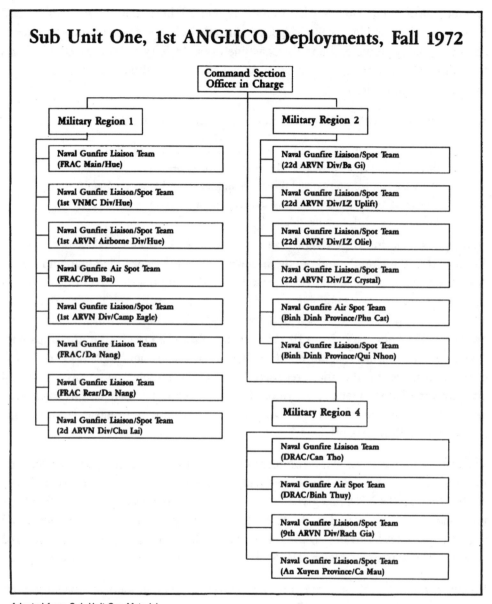

Sub Unit One, 1st ANGLICO Deployments, Fall 1972

**Command Section
Officer in Charge**

Military Region 1

Naval Gunfire Liaison Team
(FRAC Main/Hue)

Naval Gunfire Liaison/Spot Team
(1st VNMC Div/Hue)

Naval Gunfire Liaison/Spot Team
(1st ARVN Airborne Div/Hue)

Naval Gunfire Air Spot Team
(FRAC/Phu Bai)

Naval Gunfire Liaison/Spot Team
(1st ARVN Div/Camp Eagle)

Naval Gunfire Liaison Team
(FRAC/Da Nang)

Naval Gunfire Liaison Team
(FRAC Rear/Da Nang)

Naval Gunfire Liaison/Spot Team
(2d ARVN Div/Chu Lai)

Military Region 2

Naval Gunfire Liaison/Spot Team
(22d ARVN Div/Ba Gi)

Naval Gunfire Liaison/Spot Team
(22d ARVN Div/LZ Uplift)

Naval Gunfire Liaison/Spot Team
(22d ARVN Div/LZ Olie)

Naval Gunfire Liaison/Spot Team
(22d ARVN Div/LZ Crystal)

Naval Gunfire Air Spot Team
(Binh Dinh Province/Phu Cat)

Naval Gunfire Liaison/Spot Team
(Binh Dinh Province/Qui Nhon)

Military Region 4

Naval Gunfire Liaison Team
(DRAC/Can Tho)

Naval Gunfire Air Spot Team
(DRAC/Binh Thuy)

Naval Gunfire Liaison/Spot Team
(9th ARVN Div/Rach Gia)

Naval Gunfire Liaison/Spot Team
(An Xuyen Province/Ca Mau)

Adapted from Sub Unit One Material

its left engine, setting it on fire, dropping the landing gear, and piercing the canopy with fragments. Bennett turned south and he and Brown prepared to eject. At this point Brown reported "my ejection system was severely damaged" and would not work. With this, Captain Bennett chose to ditch the aircraft in the Gulf of Tonkin, an unheard of procedure for the OV-10 and one from which no crew had previously survived. The aircraft cartwheeled repeatedly on impact with the water. As Brown swam clear, Bennett sank with the wreckage, giving his life for his crewmember.[B]

On 30 June 1972, President Thieu went out to the USS *Blue Ridge* to express his personal appreciation for the American assistance during these operations. That same day fighting continued on the ARVN Airborne Division's portion of the Quang Tri battlefield. Corporal John E. Parton was attached to the 3d ARVN Airborne Battalion as an ANGLICO naval gunfire spotter. The battalion was engaged by a well-entrenched Communist unit and unable to move forward. Corporal Parton took a LAW antitank rocket and moved forward in an attempt to locate the machine gun position to his unit's front. Exposing himself to fire, he located the machine gun and launched the rocket at it, destroying the gun while receiving mortal wounds in the process.[C] The airborne soldiers then assaulted the enemy position and continued forward. American support was not limited to advice and material alone.

Other ANGLICO Marines with the Airborne Division were among the first to reach the outskirts of Quang Tri City. First Lieutenant Anthony P. Shepard's spot team was assigned to the 2d ARVN Airborne Brigade. At 2300 on 4 July, the spot team accompanied the brigade reconnaissance company through friendly lines to a position southeast of the city. The 90-man company lead by Captain Tran Ut, with Army 1st Lieutenant Terry Griswold as an advisor, split into three groups and moved to within 300 meters of the Quang Tri Citadel walls. From this location Shepard and Lance Corporal Michael Jurak directed numerous air and artillery strikes on the Citadel and surrounding NVA positions.[9]

The Battle for Quang Tri City

By 7 July, the Airborne Division, in its offensive to the west, was trying to keep abreast of the Marines to its right and had reached positions just south of Quang Tri City and the Vinh Dinh River. The airborne troops had run head on into a strongly entrenched enemy force determined to hold the city. By 10 July, the forward Marine units consisting of the VNMC 1st, 3d, 5th, 7th, and VNMC 8th Battalions were on a line that ran generally from the bend in Route 555 as it turned west toward Quang Tri City, eastward to the coast. With the ARVN Airborne Division stalled on the outskirts

---

(B) For his action, Captain Bennett was awarded a posthumous Medal of Honor.

(C) For his actions, Corporal Parton was awarded a posthumous Silver Star Medal.

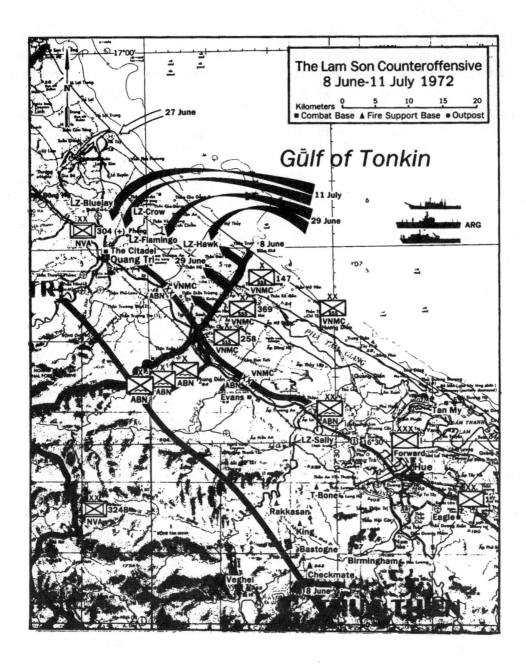

of the city, General Lan was reluctant to expose an unprotected flank as his division continued northward.[10] To break the impasse, Lan decided to move one battalion by helicopter across the Vinh Dinh River to a position just northeast of the city while two battalions would assault enemy positions from east to west. The mission of the Marines was to block Route 560 and to prevent the enemy from resupplying his forces in the city itself.

Supporting fires for the helicopter move began at 0600, 11 July, and the final Arc Light hit 15 minutes prior to landing at approximately 1200, "L-Hour." Thirty-four American helicopters from HMM-164 off the Okinawa and HMM-165 off the *Tripoli* carried 840 Marines of the 1st VNMC Battalion with 12,000 pounds of ammunition and rations into the attack. Six U.S. Army air cavalry gunships led the troop-laden helicopters into landing zones Blue Jay and Crow, 2,000 meters north of Quang Tri City. The six hours of heavy preparatory fires had not blunted the enemy's ability to fight.

Throughout the eight-mile flight to the objective, SA-7 surface-to-air missile firings caused the helicopters to fly the contour of the earth at the highest possible speed. Within 10 minutes of landing the helicopters had disembarked the Vietnamese and had lifted off. One pilot had been surprised when he landed practically on top of an NVA T-54 tank. Quick reaction by a Bell AH-1 Cobra gunship knocked out the tank with a TOW antitank missile before it could respond. Another helicopter had landed on top of an NVA command post. Twenty-eight of the helicopters entering the landing zones were hit by small arms fire. In spite of evasive flying, one CH-53 carrying 55 Vietnamese Marines was hit by a SA-7, burst into flames, and went down with heavy loss of life. Five U.S. Marine crewmen of a downed CH-46 were extracted from the zone by U.S. Army crews of Troop F, 4th Air Cavalry who braved withering fire to effect the rescue. Five of the Army's six helicopters were shot up during the assault.[11] Losses by the 9th MAB were a CH-53 and two CH-46s (both recovered), two Marines killed, and seven wounded. The four survivors from the CH-53 Sea Stallion were recovered later.

The CH-53 carried 50 Vietnamese Marines, an American crew of five, and a combat photographer from BLT 1/9. It was struck on its approach to the landing zone while 100 feet above the ground. The detonation of the SA-7's 5.5 pound warhead in the helicopter's right power plant sent engine-turbine fragments down and forward into the passenger compartment. The pilot autorotated the flaming aircraft to the ground in a hopeful, controlled "crash and burn" procedure. Two crewmembers were killed outright and a third seriously injured. Of the Vietnamese Marines on board, most were killed, with only seven returning to friendly lines. The helicopter was completely destroyed by fire and the detonation of ammunition carried by the Vietnamese. The surviving Americans took shelter in a nearby bomb crater and "hunkered-down" as the wreckage cooled and NVA soldiers poked through the remains. At dusk a VNMC patrol located them and brought them to friendly lines and American Army helicopters then returned them to their ship.[12]

Despite the helicopter losses and damage, the American-supported Vietnamese attack had been executed with precision and superb coordination. Lieutenant Colonel Gerald Turley commented, "The execution was beautiful; lift off, staging, coordination, control, communications, prep fires — everything went on schedule — never looked more beautiful." Since the beginning of July, with the arrival of Lieutenant Colonel Walter D. Fillmore as the new assistant Marine advisor, Turley concentrated on the recapture of Quang Tri City as the G-3 advisor to the Vietnamese Marine Division.[13]

The 1st VNMC Battalion, commanded by Major Nguyen Dang Hoa, encountered unexpectedly heavy fire while disembarking in the landing zone and the Marines began taking heavy casualties as they engaged elements of the *320B NVA Division.*[(D)] After landing and consolidating, Major Hoa personally led his men against the dug-in enemy. Two trench lines had to be overrun before the landing zone perimeter was secure. Despite severe losses, the Marines fought off the enemy and expanded their positions. By consolidating and defending the landing zones, the South Vietnamese killed 126 Communists, captured six, secured large quantities of material, and flanked the NVA position.[14]

The naval gunfire spot team officer, First Lieutenant Stephen G. Biddulph, was hit in the legs shortly after leaving his helicopter. Captain Lawrence H. Livingston, the 1st VNMC Battalion advisor, moved through intense small arms fire to carry the wounded lieutenant to safety. He "came sliding in beside me like a man stealing second base," recalled Biddulph.[15] At the same time, Corporal Jose F. Hernandez of ANGLICO, braved enemy fire and helped wounded Vietnamese Marines find protection in a nearby depression. He then called in naval gunfire in an attempt to halt onrushing NVA reinforcements. The wounded Vietnamese and American Marines, although requiring urgent medical attention, could not be evacuated as the enemy kept the landing zones saturated with artillery, mortar, and antiaircraft fire.

Despite the expansion of the perimeter, the Marines were still in a tenuous position as heavy fire continued to come from one of the initial objectives, an enemy trench network in a tree line approximately 50 meters away. Captain Livingston formed the Vietnamese into an assault force. Although blown off his feet by an exploding round in the early stage of the assault, Livingston led the casualty-riddled force to the edge of the trench fortifications. The enemy soldiers rushed from their entrenchments and

---

(D) *320B NVA Division:* 48th Infantry Regiment (only element encountered); 52d Infantry Regiment; and 64th Infantry Regiment.

engaged the Marines hand-to-hand, but were defeated in the savage fight. After seizing the objective, Livingston moved back through hostile fire to ensure the wounded Lieutenant Biddulph whom he had earlier pulled from danger was still safe.[E] Fighting continued for nearly three days in the 1st VNMC Battalion's area. Not only did the Marines seize and hold their initial objectives, but in doing so they forced the NVA to withdraw to the west toward Quang Tri City. During this same three-day period, the 7th VNMC Battalion, as it moved against the enemy, overran an armored regiment's command post. The action resulted in numerous enemy tracked vehicles and trucks being destroyed or captured.

Realizing the need to facilitate resupply — particularly ammunition — to the Marines in their extended position, General Cooksey requested that Vice Admiral James L. Holloway III provide a five-section causeway pier at Wunder Beach, now under South Vietnamese control. The pier provided a much-needed alternative line of communication to the battered QL-1 and other constricted coastal routes. Seventh Fleet furnished the USS *Alamo* (LSD 33), an underwater demolition team, and tugboat for support. On the morning of 13 July, naval construction personnel, "Seabees," began installation. By 1300 they had completed the job. Once the causeway was rigged and operating, U.S. Marine shore party and naval beachmaster personnel went ashore to instruct and supervise the Vietnamese units responsible for beach operations.[16]

By 14 July, the Vietnamese had cut the enemy's main supply route, Route 560, into Quang Tri City resulting in diminished fighting. Only then could the first "medevac" helicopters clear the wounded from the combat area.[17] Among those flown to Hue City by the Army aircraft was ANGLICO's Lieutenant Biddulph, who "lay on the floor near the left hatch with my M16 rifle stuck out the door to the ready. He remembered, "A litter patient lay squarely across my wounded legs and I held another patient around the body to prevent him from falling out ... we still had to make it over the heads of the enemy to get back."[18]

On 17 July, the Marine Advisory Unit received needed replacements when nine officers from the 1st Marine Division at Camp Pendleton, California, arrived in Saigon. By the middle of July, the VNMC was at its peak combat strength and its prestige was such that volunteers had to be turned away. By 20 July, the VNMC Division had consolidated its position northeast of Quang Tri City, as the Airborne Division continued its efforts to take the city. Heavy fighting was continuous, but little progress could be made beyond the city's outskirts. The NVA commented "the liberation forces again hashed up its best" forces.[19]

(E) For his actions, Captain Livingston was awarded the Navy Cross; First Lieutenant Biddulph and Corporal Hernandez received Silver Star Medals.

For General Troung, the determination of the NVA to hold Quang Tri City at all costs caused problems. He recalled, that although the city had not been a primary objective, "it had become a symbol and a major challenge."[20] In response to pressure from President Thieu, General Cooksey observed that General Troung "played a crucial role, both in planning and execution in the battle of the Citadel."[21]

Realizing that the NVA were concentrating on defending the Citadel of Quang Tri, the Marines seized another opportunity to exploit the enemy weakness along the coast by enveloping his left flank and severing his lines of communications south of the Cua Viet River. General Lan assigned this task to VNMC Brigade 147, with three battalions. The plan called for two battalions supported by tanks to attack north from their positions and link up with a third battalion that would be landed by helicopter approximately four kilometers to the north. After joining, all three battalions would attack to the southeast, seizing a critical road junction. This would either drive the enemy across the Thach Han River or force him north toward the Cua Viet River.

On 22 July 1972, the amphibious task force's USS *Okinawa*, *St. Louis* (LKA 116), *Manitowoc* (LST 1180), and *Point Defiance* (LSD 31) moved into position to launch Lieutenant Colonel Hertberg's helicopters. The USS *Denver* was also assigned to provide deck space. Air, artillery, and naval gunfire softened up the enemy position for three and a half hours. Arc Lights struck the landing zones just prior to HMM-164's arrival; the 5th VNMC Battalion assaulted with two waves totaling 688 men. Gunship escorts of Troop F shot-up both zones, reporting enemy fire from Landing Zone Lima, but none in Victor. Landing occurred at 0938 in Lima and at 1004 in Victor with initial objectives secured, the supporting arms plan had worked well. With moderate contact in the landing zones, the 5th VNMC Battalion moved out rapidly and linked up with the two surface assault battalions. The 2d VNMC Battalion, however, ran into stiff resistance as it maneuvered to cut the enemy's supply route along Route 560. U.S. close air strikes hit the NVA bunkers, enabling the Marine battalion to move through the fortified area and complete the link up. Once consolidated, the brigade secured its initial objective against relatively light opposition. Throughout the remainder of the two-day operation, enemy contact was light to moderate. The operation ended on 24 July. It netted 133 Communist soldiers killed, three enemy tanks destroyed and two armored command vehicles captured, a 100-bed hospital overrun, as well as numerous weapons captured or destroyed. No losses were sustained by the supporting American Marines.

By the end of July it was apparent that the Airborne Division, its combat effectiveness weakened by previous battles in the Central Highlands, could not overcome the hardcore NVA defenders of the Quang Tri Citadel. The paratroopers, although only 200 meters from the Citadel's wall, stood down as the Marine Division was given this mission. Lieutenant Colonel Turley briefed the advisors that changes would be required in the type of operations to attack and destroy the enemy entrenched in the city itself.[22]

During darkness on 27 July, VNMC Brigade 258 relieved the ARVN airborne troops in place. The next four days saw heavy ground contact and massive artillery duels between the Marines and the NVA. The enemy fired over 1,000 mortar and artillery rounds daily against the Marines, who responded in kind. Captain David D. Harris, an advisor with VNMC Brigade 147, had to be evacuated to the United States with severe leg and back wounds. Killed alongside him was ANGLICO's First Lieutenant Edward G. Hayen II.

The Communists were defending the city with the *325th NVA Division,* reinforced by elements of the *308th*, and *320B NVA Divisions* and supporting forces in southeastern Quang Tri and Thua Thien Provinces.[(F)] During the month of July, these units had paid a heavy price for their persistence in holding on to Quang Tri City: more than 1,880 enemy dead and 51 armored vehicles, 7 antiaircraft guns, 4 artillery pieces, a 20-ton ammunition dump, and 1,200 individual weapons had been captured or destroyed.[23] In other areas of MR 1 there were continued concerns about NVA threats from the west, as Que Son and FSB Ross were hit in August by 130mm guns and ground attacks by the *711th NVA Division*.[(G)] This threat to Da Nang would continue through the following month.[24]

As August 1972 began, most of Quang Tri City remained in Communist hands. The territory north and west of the Thach Han River, particularly around the Ai Tu combat base, was dotted with NVA artillery units.[25] The enemy maintained a seemingly ceaseless artillery and mortar barrage on the South Vietnamese, who now burrowed into the ground "like gophers."[26] This was a busy time, for Sub Unit One, 1st ANGLICO. Lieutenant Colonel George E. "Ed" Jones, commanding Sub Unit One since the previous month, recalled that in addition to controlling naval gunfire and air strikes, ANGLICO radios and operators provided an extensive and "very solid backup system for the operational South Vietnamese units as well as the U.S. Marine and U.S. Army Advisors."[27] Air observers from ANGLICO continued "dawn to dusk" coverage from American and Vietnamese Air Force aircraft, providing the primary "eyes" over areas considered no-man's land.

The brigades of the Marine Division were well placed to deny the enemy resupply and to make a final lunge into the heart of the city, the Citadel, but were held by the well-concealed defenders. Enemy fire and the congestion of friendly units in the area

---

(F) Enemy order of battle was based on a number of sources in MR 1. Most timely were the VNMC units in contact, as verified by FRAC and the military intelligence chain.

(G) *711th NVA Division*: 31st Infantry Regiment; 38th Infantry Regiment; and 270th Infantry Regiment.

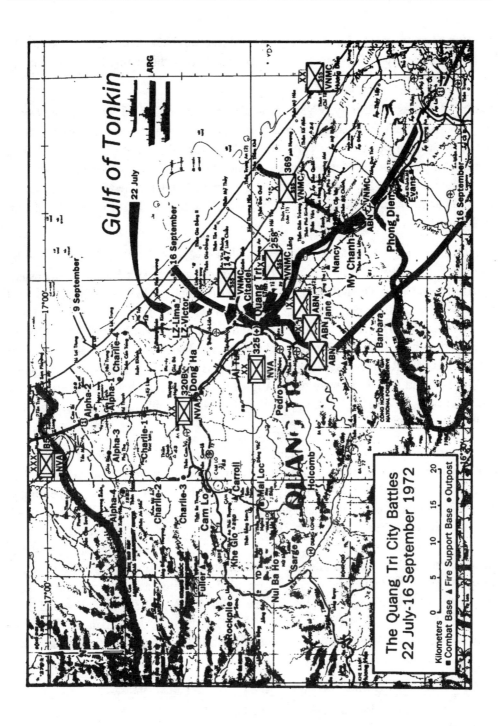

The Quang Tri City Battles
22 July-16 September 1972

severely hampered maneuver by the Marines. Marine Brigade 147, operating northeast of Quang Tri City, began receiving heavy pressure from the enemy, but had thwarted several attempts by the numerically superior enemy to reopen Route 560 northeast of the city. The Marines' supply blockade began to take its toll on the NVA's ammunition stockpiles. All enemy supplies making their way into the city had to be ferried across the Thach Han River.[28] To the south, VNMC Brigade 258, with four maneuver battalions under its operational control, was in heavy house-to-house fighting around the Citadel. The 3d VNMC Battalion attacked from the northeast, with the 6th and 9th VNMC Battalions closing in from the southwest. Each day, VNMC Brigade 258 moved slowly forward tightening its grasp on the enemy forces still in the Citadel. This slow progress made General Lan realize that he would have to reinforce his maneuver forces if they were to overpower the three NVA regiments holding the Citadel.[H] Lan continued to keep VNMC Brigade 369 in division reserve.[29]

Taking the Citadel

On 22 August, an unusual, but significant, contact was made by the 8th VNMC Battalion as it confronted a sizable enemy force attempting to break out from the Citadel. Preceding the attack, the enemy artillery provided a curtain of fire. The NVA infantry advanced behind the cover of tanks. The Marines, surprised at such an action, quickly rallied and drove the NVA back into the Citadel. During the remainder of the month, the desperate enemy increased the number of his night attacks in an effort to rupture the tight circle the Marines had drawn. By this time in the invasion and the Lam Son counteroffensive, the VNMC had suffered 1,358 men killed and 5,522 wounded. The Corps estimated it had killed 10,285 Communists during this same five-month period.[30]

As September began, Marine units had been in constant street fighting inside the city for 35 days under some of the heaviest enemy artillery shelling since the invasion in March. The forward maneuver battalions had been under daily counterattacks by enemy units of the *308th NVA Division*. In the city, the VNMC 1st, 3d, 5th, 6th, and 8th Battalions attacked through the rubble to reach the Citadel and the QL-1 highway bridge over the Thach Han River.

On 5 September, Major Richard B. Rothwell, with the 5th VNMC Battalion, helped blunt a local counterattack by the enemy inside the Citadel. As the enemy attacked the 5th VNMC Battalion's command post just at dusk, Rothwell rushed to a balcony on the second floor of a building to gain a better view of the enemy disposition. Although wounded in both the head and face from an exploding mortar round, he called for supporting fire. Despite his painful wounds, he kept calling and adjusting artillery fire

---

(H) It was determined later that the NVA rotated units in and out of Quang Tri City to maintain fresh defenders.

and directing air strikes. At 2130 the enemy withdrew in confusion having left behind more than 50 individual and crew-served weapons.[I]

A battalion from VNMC Brigade 147 had taken up positions at the An Tiem Bridge where Route 560 crossed the Vinh Dinh River. All enemy supply and infiltration routes and lines of communications to the north were effectively blocked. The Communists were feeling the bite of supply and ammunition shortages. On 8 September, the three battalions of the 1st Ranger Group relieved VNMC Brigade 147 of its blocking mission north of the city. General Lan now had two brigades he could commit in the pincer movement which would begin the all-out assault on the city. Marine Brigade 258 continued its attack along the southern front with four battalions while VNMC Brigade 147 attacked from the northeast with the 3d and 7th VNMC Battalions.[31]

Generals Truong and Lan also requested an amphibious demonstration by Seventh Fleet to draw the enemy away from the Vietnamese Marines attacking the Citadel. The U.S. amphibious forces agreed to carry out the feint, except for an actual landing. Virtually all aspects of an assault were conducted, including an operation order, increased radio traffic, and covert missions which discreetly left evidence in the vicinity of the landing beaches. The USS *Juneau* (LPD 10) loaded 400 ARVN rangers from Tan My for the supposed surface assault.

The Final Assault

On 9 September, the final assault on Quang Tri City began with intensive artillery fire and air strikes on the Citadel. On the same day, Task Force 76 and the 9th MAB carried out an amphibious diversion north of the Cua Viet River. As the Vietnamese Marines launched their attack to recapture Quang Tri City, a B-52 strike, naval gunfire, and tactical air opened up in the diversionary objective area.[32] The 9th MAB saw the heaviest volume of supporting arms fire yet, which reached a peak at H-Hour minus 3 through H-Hour. Lieutenant Colonel Robert W. Kirby, observing from the primary control ship, remembered that the "firepower brought to bear on that beach was enormous."[33] As these fires ceased, B-52s bombed the landing beaches while the task force concentrated for the landing. Surface and helicopter forces approached their turnarounds as naval gunfire stopped. Surface forces turned back at 10,000 yards and the helicopters of HMM-165 at 5,000 yards. Upon retiring from the beach, the amphibious forces returned to holding areas and the Rangers returned to Tan My.

The NVA reacted by hastily shifting major forces and artillery north of the Cua Viet River to counter this apparent amphibious assault, thus markedly reducing the level of artillery and antiaircraft fires at Quang Tri City. The diversionary action enabled the

---

(I) For his actions, Major Rothwell was awarded the Bronze Star Medal.

Marine Division to advance rapidly. An additional bonus to the deception became evident immediately following the B-52 strikes. As the bombers departed, the NVA emerged from the tree line to defend against the anticipated assault from the sea. Naval gunfire inflicted casualties on these troops in the open.[34]

At Quang Tri City an imaginary line drawn across the middle of the Citadel became the boundary between the two Marine brigades. VNMC Brigade 258 continued its attack in the southern portion while VNMC Brigade 147 attacked in the northern half. The 3d VNMC Battalion, now attached to VNMC Brigade 147 and closest to the northern wall of the Citadel, stood fast while the 7th VNMC Battalion deployed to its north. Near the southeast corner of the Citadel, Lieutenant Colonel Do Huu Tung, commanding officer of the 6th VNMC Battalion with VNMC Brigade 258, set up a forward command post and moved within striking distance of the 18th century walls of the Citadel, which were 30 inches thick and 15 feet high. A lot of this wall had already been reduced to rubble, but unsurprisingly much of it still stood. Progress toward the wall was slow because the enemy had tunneled an intricate and interlocking defense system throughout the entire fortress. On the night of 9 September, a squad of Marines from the 6th VNMC Battalion managed to slip in and out of the Citadel.

At 2100 on 10 September, Lieutenant Colonel Tung launched a night attack against the enemy on the southeast corner and was successful in gaining a lodgement on top of the wall. Early on 11 September, a platoon moved over this section of the wall, and in spite of stubborn enemy resistance, expanded to occupy company-size position within a few hours.

While the fighting for the Citadel was going on, the 1st VNMC Battalion had secured the bridgehead where QL-1 crossed the Thach Han River and held it despite several fierce NVA counterattacks. From 11 to 15 September 1, the 2d VNMC Battalion reached the Thach Han River, closing the gap between the 1st and 6th VNMC Battalions. The VNMC 3d and 7th Battalions fought their way through the northern part of the city and reached the fortress wall on the morning of 15 September. At 1015 that same day, the 3d VNMC Battalion entered the north side of the Citadel. That afternoon the enemy stiffened his resistance and called in a massive artillery barrage to stop the 3d and 6th VNMC Battalions as they advanced toward the west wall. By 1700 on 15 September, the Marines had gained complete control of the Citadel.

The NVA withdrew, stating that with "modern technology and weapons and a maximum of firepower, the U.S. had schemed to level this area and turn Quang Tri town into a land of death with no place for the revolutionary forces."[35] At 1245 the next day, the red and yellow flag of the Republic of South Vietnam was raised over its west gate by members of the 6th VNMC Battalion. The ceremony marked the end of 138 days of NVA occupation of Quang Tri City.

President Nguyen Van Thieu visited the frontline positions of the Vietnamese Marine Division on 20 September to congratulate General Lan and the officers and men of the Vietnamese Marine Corps. The President then flew by helicopter to the command post of VNMC Brigade 147, after which he drove to the 6th VNMC Battalion's command post. There he personally congratulated Lieutenant Colonel Tung and his Marines on their success inside the Citadel. The recapture of Quang Tri was probably the most significant South Vietnamese victory of the spring invasion.[J] [36] During the seven-week battle to recapture Quang Tri City, the VNMC had suffered 3,658 casualties of the more than 5,000 casualties sustained since June 1972 — about 25 percent of the entire Corps.[K] [37] The Vietnamese Marine Division, with its victory at Quang Tri City, had come of age as a fighting unit.[38]

(J) This prompted General Cooksey, the FRAC commander, to recommend the Vietnamese Marine Division for a United States Presidential Unit Citation.

(K) Edwin W. Besch, in Saigon, observed later that an "Inchon-style" landing in North Vietnam by Vietnamese or American forces might have been less costly.

CHAPTER EIGHT ENDNOTES

Unless otherwise noted, material in this chapter is derived from: MarAdvU HistSum72; MarAdvU ComdC, Jul, Aug72; MarAdvU Daily OpSum Folder, Jul, Aug, Sept72; FMFPac MarOpsSEA; and LtCol Gerald H. Turley and Capt Marshall R. Wells, "Easter Invasion, 1972," *Marine Corps Gazette*, Mar73, pp. 18-29, hereafter Turley & Wells.

Truong's Counteroffensive

1 Truong, *Invasion*, p. 64.

2 Troung, *Invasion*, pp. 64-66; Cooksey debrief, pp. 5-6.

3 SU1 memo to CMC dtd 12Nov72 (Vietnam Comment File).

4 Vale comments; FMFPac MarOpsSEA, pp. 3-1 to 3-3; CNA MarActySEA, pp. 51-52.

5 Capt Stephen C. Fogleman intvw by Maj Melson dtd 9Mar87 (Vietnam Comment File).

6 Laurence W. Rush, *Nickles, Dimes, Rubberbands and Glue* (New York, Carlton Press, 1979), p. 82.

7 FLt Stephen G. Biddulph, comments on draft ms, dtd 2Nov89 (Vietnam Comment File).

8 App D, pp. 1-2, FRAC/VNMCOps.

9 Shepard comments.

The Battle for Quang Tri City

10 App E, pp. 1-2, FRAC/VNMCOpns; Turley & Wells, p. 28.

11 Turley intvw; 9thMAB debrief.

12 Cpl Steven C. Lively debrief dtd Jul72, Kue Army Hospital, Okinawa; LtCol Michael L. Powell, comments on draft ms, dtd 14Jun90 (Vietnam Comment File).

13 Turley intvw.

14 FMFPac MarOpsSEA, pp. 3-1 to 3-6; G-3 memo dtd 12Jul72, Song Than 9-72 Folder (MarAdvU File).

15 Biddulph comments.

16 9thMAB debrief.

17 Song Than 9-72 Folder (MarAdvU File).

18 Biddulph comments.

19 "Quang Tri: An Immortal Epic," *Vietnam*, 172/192, pp. 2-4 (Besch comments).

20 Truong, Invasion, p. 67.

[21] LtGen Howard H. Cooksey comments on draft ms, dtd 9Jan90 (Vietnam Comment File).

[22] G-3 Advisor's Planning Guidance in Preparation for the Recapture of Quang Tri City, SVN, dtd 25Jul72, Song Than 9-72 Folder; App E, Brig 147 Tab, p. 4, FRAC/VNMCOpns.

[23] App E, Brig 258 Tab, p. 4, FRAC/VNMCOpns.

[24] MACV Nguyen Hue study, pp. 15-16.

[25] FRAC IntSum 228-72 dtd 14Aug72 (Vietnam Comment File).

[26] LtCol Richard B. Rothwell, "Leadership and Tactical Reflections on the Battle for Quang Tri," *Marine Corps Gazette*, Sept79, p. 39.

[27] Jones comments.

[28] App F, pp. 1-2, FRAC/VNMCOpns.

[29] App F, Brig 258 Tab, p. 2, FRAC/VNMCOps.

Taking the Citadel
[30] App F, Encl a, b, FRAC/VNMCOps; also MarAdvU HistSum72, App B, C, D.

[31] Turley & Wells, p. 28.

The Final Assault
[32] 9thMAB debrief.

[33] Col Robert W. Kirby, comments on draft ms, dtd 20Dec89 (Vietnam Comment File).

[34] Col Charles T. Williamson, comments on draft ms, dtd 13Mar90; FMFPac MarOpsSEA, pp. 4-4 to 4-9; CNA MarActySEA, pp. 51-52.

[35] "Quang Tri: An Immortal Epic," *Vietnam*, 172/1972, pp. 2-4 (Besch comments).

[36] CGFRAC ltr to ComUSMACV dtd 1Oct72 (MarAdvU File).

[37] App G, p. 2, FRAC/VNMCOps; SMA debrief.

[38] SMA debrief; Cooksey debrief, pp. 9-10.

CHAPTER NINE
RETURNING NORTH

Consolidation • Push to the North • Reorganization • The Eleventh Hour • Ceasefire

Consolidation

On 25 September 1972, VNMC Brigade 369 opened a new command post at Hai Lang Village and assumed operational control of the battalions at Quang Tri City, and VNMC Brigade 147 assumed defensive positions along the coast and the division's right flank. VNMC Brigade 258 reverted to division reserve. Major Gordon W. Keiser took over as senior advisor for Brigade 258 from Major Robert D. Kelly.[1] For the Americans of ANGLICO and the advisors there was a sense of accomplishment. For the South Vietnamese, however, the battle was not over.

The Vietnamese Marine Division had used tactical air almost daily since the NVA invasion in March 1972. Between June and September, there had been 3,381 American and 775 Vietnamese air tactical sorties, and 525 B-52 strikes flown in support of the VNMC. From 26 to 28 September, 18 VNMC officers, two from each of the infantry battalions, underwent instruction on close air support and naval gunfire spotter techniques, followed by an immediate practical application with U.S. Marine advisors. Most of the Vietnamese officers became fully competent in coordinating U.S. air strikes through an airborne FAC and controlling naval gunfire. This added capability further reduced the necessity for ANGLICO and advisor involvement in the control of U.S. supporting arms.[2]

With the capture of the Quang Tri Citadel and the establishment of Marine blocking positions at the approaches to the city, the VNMC Marine Division, with its forward headquarters at Huong Dien, was in a position to push north. General Lan was anxious to reoccupy all of the territory lost during the NVA invasion prior to any kind of ceasefire negotiations. Since the beginning of the Easter Invasion, when President Nixon outlined the conditions for such a ceasefire, President Thieu had been concerned that all lost South Vietnamese ground be regained prior to an in-place settlement. Enemy activity had dropped sharply after the taking of Quang Tri City, but it was evident that the NVA was still present in strength just outside the city. The identification of the presence of a unit from the *312th NVA Division* raised the enemy presence to six divisions in Quang Tri Province, as reported by the First Regional Assistance Command.[A] The enemy artillery fire from the northwest which daily showered Vietnamese Marine positions; occasionally was followed by nighttime probing attacks.[3]

Heavy monsoon rains began to fall in October and would continue until the end of December. The area to the east of the city was low-lying coastal marshlands, criss-crossed with rivers, and were difficult enough to move across in good weather. The torrential rains would make passage impossible in some areas. Experience had shown that during the monsoon a 200-meter-wide river could become a two-kilometer wide bay overnight, a vital consideration when moving armor, artillery, and foot troops. With growing concern about the peace negotiations in Paris, General Lan recommended that an attempt to take the offensive should be made immediately, taking full advantage of the lull in enemy operations and the continued presence of 9th MAB support. Route 560, north of Quang Tri, was the only improved line of communications east of QL-1 leading to the Cua Viet River. This was the obvious axis of attack and Lan hoped to attempt to move north by some other route and to do so before the monsoon, restricting his options. He ordered Colonel Nguyen Nang Bao's VNMC Brigade 147 to attack north along Route 560 to push the enemy beyond mortar range of Quang Tri City and to capture Trien Phong District Headquarters. Accomplishment of this mission would also serve to cut a major NVA supply line.[4]

On 7 October, prior to H-Hour, the division's fire support coordination center arranged for heavy artillery, naval gunfire, and close air support. General Cooksey's headquarters in Hue coordinated the American fixed-wing aircraft and helicopters. U.S. Army helicopters provided armed reconnaissance forward of the axis of attack and eastward to the beach. Flights were composed of two U.S. Army light observation helicopters with ANGLICO air observers on board, providing excellent naval gunfire coverage on targets up to 5,000 meters inland. This capability was particularly valuable during inclement weather when aircraft could not operate because of limited visibility.

Push to the North

At H-Hour, the 8th VNMC Battalion moved out in the attack under difficult circumstances along Route 560. The highway ran through marshlands between the Thach Han River and the Vinh Dinh River, where thick groves of bamboo and hedgerows permitted enemy snipers to fire point-blank at the advancing Marines. The

---

(A) *312th NVA Division:* 141st Infantry Regiment; 165th Infantry Regiment (only element encountered); and 209th Infantry Regiment.

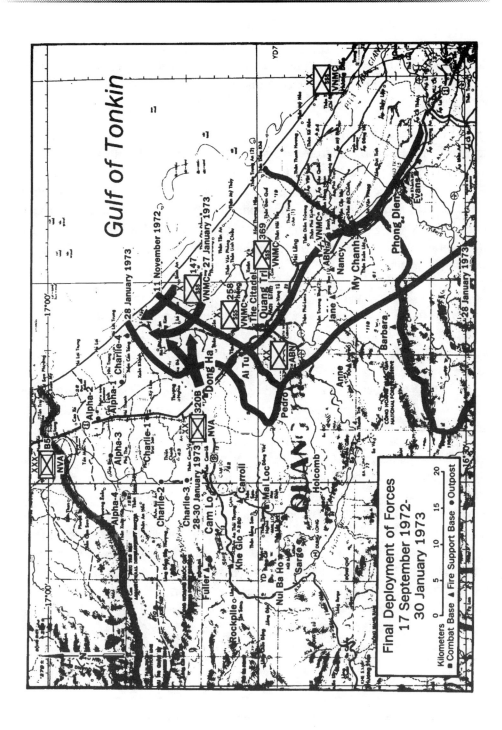

Final Deployment of Forces
17 September 1972-
30 January 1973

Kilometers

0   5   10   15   20

■ Combat Base ▲ Fire Support Base ● Outpost

attack continued for three days against heavy enemy resistance. On 10 October, with the front lines extended to the desired distance, Colonel Bao, commander of Brigade 147, moved his other three battalions on line and awaited further orders. The operation had resulted in 111 enemy killed and 55 weapons captured.

On 20 October, General Lan ordered Bao to conduct a second operation along the eastern flank of the brigade front. The attack, conducted by the 9th VNMC Battalion supported by armor, was designed to extend the friendly lines north toward the Cua Viet River. The river was critical to the defense of Quang Tri City; whoever controlled the Cua Viet controlled the economic lifeline to Quang Tri Province. The river was sufficiently deep and wide to accommodate landing-craft inland all the way to Dong Ha and into Quang Tri City. It was essential that this artery be in South Vietnamese hands prior to any settlement.

The 9th VNMC Battalion encountered stiff resistance as it moved north. The eastern portion of the two-prong attack reached its objectives, but the western portion was held up by a heavy 122mm rocket attack. U.S. Army armed helicopter "Pink Teams" were called in to suppress the rocket positions. Captain George Philip III, a U.S. Marine advisor flying in the command and control helicoter, served as the liaison between the VNMC units on the ground and these American helicopters. With the fire suppressed, the western prong moved on line with the eastern force on an axis about six kilometers from the Cua Viet River, still short of its south bank.[5]

VNMC Brigade 369, commanded by Lieutenant Colonel Nguyen The Luong, held the western portion of the division front against an enemy ground attack the first week of October, but the rest of the month was relatively quiet with the exception of daily enemy bombardments. The brigade conducted limited patrolling to its front and improved defensive positions in Quang Tri City. During the month several reconnaissance patrols crossed the Thac Han River to try to determine the enemy's intentions. VNMC Brigade 258, with Colonel Ngo Van Dinh in command, remained the division reserve. By October's end, the Marine front lines had stabilized along a line that could permit subsequent efforts to establish a foothold on the Cua Viet outlet to the sea. Morale and discipline remained high for all VNMC units as they improved positions and replacements filled the depleted ranks.

Reorganization

Due to the preponderant number of recent recruits that had reported to MR1 to fill the ranks of his battalions, General Lan directed that, commensurate with military operations, all elements of the division undergo troop inspections. Battalions rotated out of the line and positioned themselves on the hard sandy beaches near Wunder Beach. The U.S. Marine advisors were amazed at the detailed inspections. Inspecting officers meticulously went over each item of equipment laid out in parade-ground fashion on the beach. Individual weapons were inspected by these officers with the thoroughness of a drill instructor. Basic skills and knowledge were demonstrated in an area which was only four miles behind the front lines.

On 1 November, orders came from Saigon for the Marines to cross the Thach Han River west of Quang Tri in an effort to expand the division's area of control. Under the cover of early morning darkness, VNMC Brigade 369 sent 600 Marines led by the 6th VNMC Battalion across the Thach Han River directly opposite the Citadel. The crossing, using sampans, small boats, and barges, was not without difficulties. Some Marines drowned as sampans overturned and guide ropes broke. By dawn on 2 November, however, nearly 200 Marines were established on the western side, followed shortly by 200 more. As the Marines moved inland they were vigorously opposed by the enemy. The forward elements bogged down 500 meters from the river line in the face of heavy enemy automatic weapons and mortar fire. The NVA counterattacked the Marine foothold with a regiment supported by mortars and artillery. The massive counterattack reflected the enemy's firm intention to maintain positions west of Quang Tri City and to deny the southern forces access to the Ai Tu area. Later in the day as the Marines moved north along QL-1, between a small canal and the Thach Han River, they came under intense small arms fire from concealment in the dense foliage. All of the company commanders were killed and more than 40 Marines were reported missing. Despite the employment of every available supporting arm, the Marines could not make headway. During the hours of darkness of 2 and 3 November, the 6th VNMC Battalion withdrew east of the Thach Han River, leaving only a reconnaissance team on the west bank. The 6th VNMC Battalion operation was the Marines' last effort to cross the Thach Han River prior to the ceasefire in January 1973.[6]

The Eleventh Hour

On 11 November, the day after the U.S. Marines had celebrated their 197th birthday, the VNMC began an operation to extend its control to the northwest. As Lieutenant Colonel Tran Xuan Quang's 4th VNMC Battalion attacked, it was stopped by intense artillery and mortar fire and localized ground counterattacks. The NVA appeared determined that the Marines would not reach the Cua Viet River. In spite of severe resupply problems, the NVA expended five times more ordnance during November than they had in October.[7]

The monsoon rains heavily curtailed both enemy and friendly movement. Transporting supplies was difficult for both sides, and living conditions were equally oppressive. The two sides could see each other occasionally, but neither seemed inclined to fire; they shared a miserable lot. Routes previously used to resupply were flooded. Route 555 itself was nearly obliterated by rising water and rendered unusable.[8]

The Communists expended every effort to keep forward units close to the Marine positions and thus hopefully to make tactical air and naval gunfire support impossible. On one occasion, however, the tactic did not work. A B-52 strike was conducted in support of the 4th VNMC Battalion which was operating just south of the Cua Viet River near the beach. Six prominent hill masses were the only logical positions for the enemy to occupy, above the flooded lowlands. Previously, B-52s had dropped their bombs with such devastating effect that it was unnecessary to rebomb the same position. On this occasion, however, three of the six hill masses were programmed for an additional strike six minutes after the first. As the second flight struck, the NVA that had survived the first attack had moved back into their battered positions. Vietnamese and U.S. Marines 3,000 meters away bore witness to the devastating effectiveness of strategic bombers in a tactical role.[9]

December 1972 was marked by the ever-present possibility that the continued negotiations between American National Security Advisor Henry Kissinger and North Vietnam's Le Duc Tho would result in a ceasefire agreement and that truce accords would go into effect. Generally the frontlines remained static with the VNMC no closer than three and a half miles from the Cua Viet River. During the first part of the month the NVA initiated nothing larger than company-size attacks. However, at dawn on 17 December, the enemy launched a battalion-size attack on the 7th VNMC Battalion located west of the Vinh Dinh Canal. The NVA, in two separate attacks, lost 37 dead on 18 December, and 132 were killed the next day, and gained no ground. Documents found on enemy dead and prisoners revealed that at least three regiments opposed the VNMC efforts to move north. The *27th NVA Regiment*, the *48th NVA Regiment*, and the *101st NVA Regiment* were making every effort to fix the Marines in place.

Lieutenant Colonel George E. Jones' Sub Unit One continued to support South Vietnamese forces in MR 1 and throughout the rest of the country. During the last quarter of 1972, American ships, their fire coordinated and controlled by ANGLICO personnel, fired 211,700 rounds in direct support of the Armed Forces of South Vietnam. U.S. naval gunfire enabled South Vietnamese artillery to move inland and provide support for areas further to the west. Due to heavy rain curtailing airborne air controllers and tactical air support, almost twice as many naval rounds were fired during November and December in MR 1 as were fired by South Vietnamese 155mm howitzers. An NVA soldier captured by the ARVN Airborne Division, which was positioned west of the VNMC Division, reported that naval gunfire was extremely effective along the Thach Han River and that he, and others, had surrendered due to the heavy pounding.

By the year's end, naval gunfire spotter instruction had been given to Vietnamese artillery forward observers who then applied their new skills upon returning to the field.[10] On Christmas Day 1972, Sub Unit One suffered its last death in action when a Marine air observer in a Vietnamese air force Cessna 0-1 Bird Dog aircraft flew along the Cua Viet River to inspect the NVA positions to the north. First Lieutenant Dwight G. Rickman left Phu Bai that day to confirm that the Communist forces were complying with the truce. He never returned.[11]

There was very light contact between the two forces as 1973 began. Both sides made probes and counterprobes. On 14 January, the frontline battalions of VNMC Brigades 147 and 258 had heavy contact with the enemy all along the front. With a ceasefire likely, the 9th MAB became involved in coordinating plans to take all U.S. personnel out of MR 1. General Miller requested that MACV make it clear to CinCPac that the amphibious forces were the only available resources capable of the task and that they not be used for clearing mines in North Vietnamese waters.[12] On 15 January, under orders from Saigon, General Lan began planning for a final effort to gain the Cua Viet River prior to the now-certain ceasefire. The attack was to be made by an infantry and tank force with enough power to reach and cross the Cua Viet River. Task Force Tango was organized with the mission to seize the former U.S. naval base and LST ramp at the mouth of the river.

At 0655 on 26 January, as the main VNMC attack began, every available supporting arm was brought to bear on the NVA. The ground attack, led by Colonel Nguyen Thanh Tri, the deputy commandant of the VNMC, advanced in two mechanized columns. Major James R. Sweeney, as the senior U.S. Marine advisor with Task Force Tango, moved forward with Colonel Tri. One column moved north along the coastal sand dunes while the other took advantage of a woodline which ran roughly three kilometers inland from the beach to move north by a parallel axis. Within three hours, the Marines had seized the intermediate objectives despite determined resistance from the NVA.

As the 4th VNMC Battalion under Lieutenant Colonel Nguyen Dang Tong, with Major William M. Keys as advisor, proceeded towards the final objective, the South Vietnamese armor came under fire by wire-guided AT-3 missiles. During the next 18 hours, 26 M48 tanks and M113 armored personnel carriers were lost to the

Communist missile teams employed in groups of two and three. During this time, SA-7 surface-to-air missiles destroyed two allied aircraft flying close air support. The NVA resisted fiercely as the left-hand column closed on its fortified positions.[13] At 0145, 28 January, the column along the beach, with only three tanks in support of a mixed force of 3d, 4th, and 5th VNMC Battalion Marines, made a final assault. At 0700, 300 Vietnamese Marines broke through the Communist lines and hoisted a red and yellow South Vietnamese flag at the Cua Viet River. A radio message to the task force command post reported the lead company had secured the LST ramp on the south bank of the Cua Viet River and they were standing knee-deep in the river. Colonel Tri radioed back "... go deeper!"[14]

Ceasefire

At 0745, the USS *Turner Joy* (DD 951) fired the last U.S. naval gunfire support in the Vietnam War and pulled off the gun line. Lieutenant Colonel Gerald H. Turley noted this action in the advisors' operational log. This was a fitting climax as the *Turner Joy* had been involved in the Gulf of Tonkin since 1964. At the same time, the U.S. withdrew all support to Task Force Tango, anticipating the ceasefire that would go into effect at 0800. Beginning around 0600, all artillery north and south of the front began firing, gradually increasing in rate. Both sides had been stockpiling artillery ammunition for the final moments of the war. Neither side wanted the other to be able to make any last minute gains of ground.[15]

The final enemy shelling produced some surprises, at least for Major Nguyen Dang Hoa's 1st VNMC Battalion east of Quang Tri City. During the previous few weeks the battalion command group, which was located in an abandoned village a short distance to the rear of its forward companies, had experienced only desultory harassing fire. As the area was quite flat and the enemy possessed no vantage spot from which to adjust artillery fire, it was assumed that the command group's location was not known to the NVA. This assumption proved to be wishful thinking.

After a few ranging shots of high-explosive, point-detonating rounds, the enemy switched to shells armed with hitherto rarely used delay fuzes. While the well-built South Vietnamese bunkers provided a more-than-adequate defense against the former rounds, they were no match for the delay-fuzed variety. Although the area was saturated with delay rounds, none hit any of the crowded bunkers. With low-hanging clouds precluding any friendly air support and the U.S. Navy pulling off the gun line, there was little else to do but wait for the ceasefire. At 0800, all firing stopped. While the Americans and the South Vietnamese in good faith observed the truce accords, the NVA prepared for a new offensive.[16] Recalled Lieutenant Colonel Turley, who had served through to the end, "all U.S. Marine advisors were formally relieved of their duties with Vietnamese battalions." They returned to the division command post at Huong Dien where General Lan assembled the Marine Advisory Unit for a final formation. The next morning, all but five remaining advisors returned to Saigon for rotation back to the United States.[17]

For Task Force Tango along the Cua Viet River, the fighting continued. That evening the NVA launched a counterattack against VNMC forces at the naval base. Other NVA units proceeded to cut across the rear of both columns in an effort to cut them off from support, succeeding in this by 30 January. At this point, a company-size force from 4th Battalion was encircled at the Cua Viet River outposts. Efforts to resupply the Marines from across the beach resulted in the loss of a mechanized landing craft, (LCM). The VNMC units attempted to break out south along the beach on 31 January, rather than be isolated by the NVA. "All contact with beleaguered Marines was lost and the outpost overrun," was the terse wording of the division operations summary as of 0935 that morning. The South Vietnamese suffered 40 casualties and lost 20 armored vehicles in this post-ceasefire incident.[18]

CHAPTER NINE ENDNOTES

Unless otherwise noted, material in this chapter is derived from: MarAdvU HistSum72; MarAdvU ComdC, Oct,Nov,Dec72; MarAdvU Daily OpSum Folder, Oct,Nov,Dec72,Jan73; SU1 ComdC, Oct, Nov, Dec72; FMFPac MarOpsSEA.

Consolidation

1 FRAC/VNMCOpns; Covan, 1Oct72 (MarAdvU Files).

2 SU1 memo to CMC dtd 12Nov72 (Jones comments).

3 *Public Papers of the Presidents of the United States, Richard Nixon, 1972*, (Washington, D.C.: National Archives and Records Service, 1974), pp. 583-587; FRAC IntSum 266-72 dtd 21Sept72; Turley intvw.

4 MarAdvU ComdC, Oct72.

Push to the North

5 Philip intvw.

Reorganization

6 MarAdvU Daily OpSum Folder, Nov72 (MarAdvU File).

The Eleventh Hour

7 Ibid.

8 Turley intvw.

9 Ibid.

10 SMA memo dtd 26Dec72, MarAdvU Turnover Folder; MarAdvU Daily OpSum Folder, Dec72 (MarAdvU File).

11 SU1 ComdC, Dec72; Jones comments.

12 9thMAB debrief.

13 LtCol Gerald H. Turley, "Time of Change in Modern Warfare," *Marine Corps Gazette*, Dec74, pp. 18-19.

14 Turley intvw.

Ceasefire

15 SMA msg to FRAC dtd 30Jan73 (MarAdvU File).

16 MarAdvU Daily OpSum Folder, Jan73 (MarAdvU File).

17 Turley comments.

18 SMA to FRAC msg dtd 1Feb73 (MarAdvU File).

PART IV

THE MARINES WERE THERE

CHAPTER TEN
A TRACT OF TIME

*9th MAB and the Naval Campaign • Support to the Fleet • Evacuations • Search and Rescue •
NGF Airborne Spotters, Fast and Slow Raids and Demonstrations • Redeyes at Sea •
Support to Military Region 1 • Fleet Support Continues •
Across the Beach: The Lam Son Landings • Turnaway at Quang Tri*

9th MAB and the Naval Campaign

Separate from the advisory effort with the Vietnamese Marine Corps in MR 1, III Marine Amphibious Force aviation and ground units participated with the Seventh Fleet and the Seventh Air Force in reacting to the enemy's Spring Offensive. The North Vietnamese attack of 30 March 1972 had found III MAF forces deployed for rapid response to the unfolding and confused situation. Brigadier General Edward J. Miller's 9th Marine Amphibious Brigade (MAB) Headquarters was on the USS *Blue Ridge* at White Beach, Okinawa; Colonel Walter C. Kelly's 31st Marine Amphibious Unit (MAU) had just departed the U.S. Naval Base Subic Bay, Philippines, for the South China Sea on Amphibious Ready Group (ARG) Alpha ships; Lieutenant Colonel Phillip B. Friedrichs' Battalion Landing Team 1/9 (BLT Bravo) with ARG Bravo had left Hong Kong for the East China Sea.[A] [1] On the morning of 2 April, the 31st MAU and BLT Bravo were already off the Vietnamese coast awaiting developments in MR 1. Admiral William P. Mack, the Seventh Fleet commander, had diverted ARGs Alpha and Bravo to positions 15 nautical miles east of the Demilitarized Zone (DMZ) for possible evacuation of Americans from Dong Ha. On the *Tripoli*, Colonel Kelly and Lieutenant Colonel William R. Von Harten, commanding BLT 3/4, monitored radio traffic sent by Lieutenant Colonel Turley from the Ai Tu Combat Base, as he "attempted to bring order from chaos."[B] [2]

(A) ARG A: 31st MAU, BLT 3/4, HMM-165, and Logistic Support Unit Alpha on the *Tripoli, Anchorage, Duluth,* and *Schenectady*. ARG B: BLT 1/9 on the *Denver, Tuscaloosa,* and *Mobile*.

(B) Later it was found that General Cao Van Vien of the South Vietnamese Joint General Staff and General Abrams were still assessing the situation in MR 1 and had not sent or approved the initial calls for assistance to the Seventh Fleet, requests that had been generated from the confused situation in MR 1. See Chapter 4 for details.

Admiral John S. McCain, Jr., CinCPac, canceled Exercise Golden Dragon on 3 April, and III MAF's commander, Lieutenant General Louis Metzger, ordered General Miller and the 9th MAB staff to remain on the USS *Blue Ridge* for combat or evacuation operations. The *Blue Ridge*, with the Task Force 76 commander, Rear Admiral Walter D. Gaddis, and General Miller, sailed for Vietnam on 5 April. Admiral Mack returned ARG Bravo to White Beach, Okinawa, to replace defective amphibian tractors and to load additional supplies and personnel. These orders were passed through the operational chain of command to the "action agency" — III MAF in General Metzger's case. He recalled that Seventh Fleet was saturated with message traffic at this point in time. Aviation deployments with "tight" time schedules required Metzger to move his forces and to notify Seventh Fleet that unless otherwise directed he would do so "in accordance with orders from higher authority.[3]

With the forward deployment of amphibious forces to holding areas off the DMZ, Admiral Mack directed units to conduct "ready operations," a term that included both contingency and support activities. The 9th MAB had various contingency plans which were based on its task-organized character. After the initial attacks, the amphibious brigade turned its attention from emergency evacuations to a buildup of forces. During the next 10 months there were over nine changes in task organization as amphibious ready groups and Marine units rotated. Changes occurred because of ship availability, contingency requirements, and the long intervals at sea.[C][4]

Marine units at sea for operations on 9 April were the 9th MAB headquarters, 31st MAU, and BLT Bravo. Upon arriving in the Tonkin Gulf, the brigade organized itself into a regimental landing team and a composite helicopter squadron.[D][5] Admiral Mack kept Amphibious Squadron 5 (Phibron) in the Western Pacific as the ARGs Alpha and Bravo, despite its planned return to the United States. On 11 April, the newly arrived Amphibious Squadron 7 formed Amphibious Ready Groups Charlie and Delta.[E] General Metzger formed an additional MAU and BLT to provide landing forces for Charlie and Delta. The 33d MAU was activated under Colonel Robert J. Perrich, then

---

(C) There were three general arrangements: first, the preinvasion ready force of an embarked Marine amphibious unit and an additional battalion landing team; next, the expansion of contingency forces to two MAUs and two BLTs; finally, the retention of two MAUs as the probability of intervention lessened in late summer 1972.

(D) Initial task organization on 9 April 1972: 9th MAB (TG 79.1), H&S Co, 9th MAB (TU 79.1.0), Det, 1st RadBn (TE 79.1.0.1),RLT 4 (TU 79.1.2), Hq, 31st MAU (TE 79.1.2.0), BLT 3/4 (TE 79.1.2.1), BLT 1/9 (TE 79.1.2.2), Det B, HML-367 (TE 79.1.2.2.1), Det A, HML-367 (TU 79.1.3); BLSG (TU 79.1.4), LFSP (TU 79.1.5); HMM-165 (TU 79.1.6).

(E) Phibron 5: USS *Tripoli* (LPH 10), *Duluth* (LPD 6), *Denver* (LPD 9), *Mt. Vernon* (LSD 39), *Anchorage* (LSD 36), *Mobile* (LKA 115), *Tuscaloosa* (LST 1187), and *Schenectady* (LST 1185). Phibron 7: USS *Okinawa* (LPH 3), *Juneau* (LPD 10), *Pt. Defiance* (LSD 31), *Alamo* (LSD 33), *St. Louis* (LKA 116), *Manitowoc* (LST 1180), *Sumter* (LST 1181), *Cayuga* (LST 1186), *Barbour County* (LST 1195), and *Bristol County* (LST 1198).

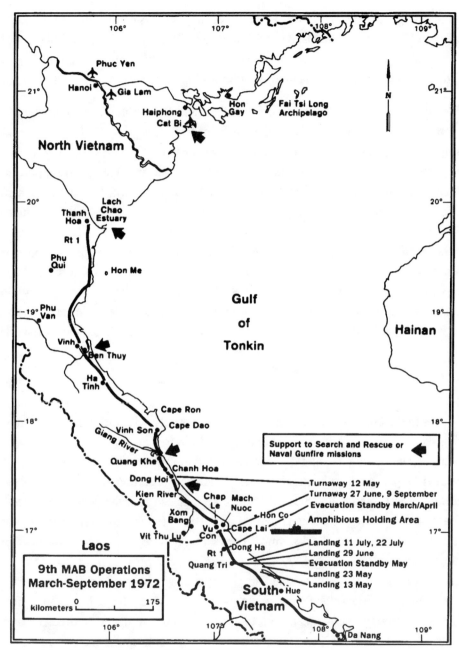

**9th MAB Operations
March-September 1972**

kilometers 0 ——————— 175

Support to Search and Rescue or
Naval Gunfire missions

Turnaway 12 May
Turnaway 27 June, 9 September
Evacuation Standby March/April
Amphibious Holding Area

Landing 11 July, 22 July
Landing 29 June
Evacuation Standby May
Landing 23 May
Landing 13 May

Adapted from Naval Historical Center Material

commanding 4th Marines. This amphibious unit consisted of Lieutenant Colonel Edward C. Hertberg's HMM-164 and Lieutenant Colonel Clyde D. Dean's BLT 1/4. Embarkation on amphibious ships was followed by landing exercises in the Philippines, and then deployment to amphibious holding areas off the coast of Vietnam.

When the USS *Blue Ridge* arrived off the DMZ with Task Force 76 and the 9th MAB, Admiral Gaddis and General Miller were ordered by Seventh Fleet to conduct "amphibious operations as directed." Five possible courses of action arose: evacuations, landings, demonstrations, support to the Seventh Fleet, and support to the South Vietnamese. Prompted by Admiral Mack's and Admiral McCain's need for a variety of alternatives during April, Admiral Gaddis and General Miller conducted a wide-ranging and at times frenzied planning effort simultaneously with ongoing operations.[F][6] The Marines of the 9th MAB were soon involved in the tasks other than their amphibious assault mission. This dictated separation from task force and parent units to meet commitments that were not anticipated in existing contingency plans. Most assignments were parallel at various times with ready operations and support to the Republic of Vietnam.[7] "They were interesting times," concluded General Miller.[8]

Support to the Fleet

The Seventh Fleet amphibious ships soon found that the demands of 24-hour combat watches in the Gulf of Tonkin could not be met entirely with the ship's crew, most of whom were standing both regular and general-quarter duties at such points as gun positions, watch stations, and damage control stations. Battalion and squadron staffs manned shipboard coordination centers for operations, logistics, and fire support during general quarters (particularly when Vietnamese Marines were embarked and Task Force 76 provided command and control facilities).[G] To counter the threat of Communist small-boat attacks, ships' crews manned deck-mounted machine guns. When sailors assigned to fire .50 caliber machine guns proved unskilled in their use, Marine armored vehicle crews and truck drivers who were trained to use the M2 Browning and M60 machine guns were pressed into service to conduct training for the sailors. As landing operations began, the ships' captains assigned Marines to landing crafts to operate machine guns. Embarked Marines continued these shipboard duties throughout the crisis in the gulf.

(F) The 9th MAB operations officer, Lieutenant Colonel James L. Shanahan, recalled this description as "possibly not extreme enough." (Shanahan comments)

(G) Marines onboard ship were commanded by the senior Marine present, the "commanding officer of troops,"who answered to the vessel's captain for their discipline and welfare. Under normal circumstances, requirements for mess, maintenance, and police functions to support the ship came from a "ship's platoon" from which the Marine's share of housekeeping duties was met.

Seventh Fleet used Admiral Gaddis' ships, with General Miller's Marines on board, to augment other fleet units such as the carrier and naval gunfire groups, for naval gunfire spotting, antiaircraft defense, and electronic support measures. These tasks were concurrent with ready operations but required independent steaming and sent Marines the length and breadth of the Tonkin Gulf's area of operations. In one instance, the departure of fleet hospital ships from Seventh Fleet had left Admiral Mack without medical facilities closer than the naval hospital at Subic Bay, Philippines. At the start of the Spring Offensive, surgical teams were established on the USS *Tripoli* and *Okinawa*, and these ships were positioned to provide medical coverage for carrier and gunfire strikes. These same facilities treated Vietnamese Marines wounded during assault landings.[9] Other amphibious ships were diverted at various times to provide search and rescue platforms, helicopter gunship support, disaster relief operations, and mine clearing — taking their embarked troops with them. These final events were conducted after the combat crisis in MR 1 had passed in mid-1972. The flexibility of the amphibious task force was one of its greatest assets, but had to be employed discreetly. The use of Marines for numerous essential and unexpected duties caused enough concern at Headquarters Marine Corps for staff to observe in a study:

> ... Some of the functions performed by the 9th Marine Amphibious
> Brigade during the period reported on normally are not assigned to the
> landing force; for example: mine sweeping missions supported by
> Marine assets; augmenting ship AA defenses with landing force surface
> to air missiles; dedicating amphibious lift assets to SAR functions. The
> Marine Corps position is that landing force assets will not be assigned to
> perform these functions except in an emergency when other assets
> cannot be made available.[10]

Evacuations

The uncertainty of the military situation in MR 1 made the evacuation of Americans from MR 1 the most probable mission. General Creighton W. Abrams requested Admiral Mack to support possible withdrawals from Hue, Phu Bai, and Da Nang. Major General Frederick J. Kroesen, Jr., USA, commanding 1st Regional Assistance Command, planned for the evacuation of 2,240 Americans and U.S. employees and 65,000 pounds of cargo. If movement by USAF aircraft was not possible, this would be accomplished by Task Force 76 and the 9th MAB. Admiral Mack allocated a single Marine amphibious unit — a reinforced infantry battalion and a composite helicopter squadron — to carry out these plans, on the assumption that withdrawals would be sequential. The Da Nang plan required an additional helicopter squadron.

Simultaneous withdrawals from Da Nang and Phu Bai would need an additional Marine amphibious unit and naval amphibious ready group.

Existing operation plans dealt with administration, logistics, reporting, and standardized amphibious landings rather than with any specific contingencies. As a result, units had to draw up evacuation plans from scratch.[11] Responsibility for contingencies rotated with 9th MAB units on "Yankee Station"[H] and were the subject of continuing coordination with the FRAC through July 1972, even as the North Vietnamese threat to MR 1 diminished.[12] Of major concern was the 8th Radio Research Field Station (RRFS) at Hue/Phu Bai and its 1,000 special intelligence personnel and their equipment. Plans called for 9th MAB to secure landing sites, provide security, and to withdraw the evacuees by helicopter or amphibian tractor. Marines went ashore to coordinate and conduct required reconnaissance of Hue/Phu Bai for this possible mission. After his reconnaissance, Lieutenant Colonel Von Harten told the 31st MAU commander, Colonel Kelly, that defenses ashore were virtually nonexistent and that an evacuation under enemy attack was doubtful. On another visit, a BLT 1/9 helicopter was not allowed to land at the 8th RRFS helicopter landing pad because it did not have the proper clearance to enter a "sensitive" area.[13]

Search and Rescue

Amphibious ships from Task Force 76, at one time including both helicopter carriers, were used as search and rescue (SAR) stations in support of Task Force 77 carrier air-attacks. These vessels deployed to positions off North Vietnam rather than remain in the amphibious holding area near the DMZ. The "Big Mothers" of TF 77's Helicopter Combat Support Squadron (HC 7), flying Sikorsky SH-3 Sea King helicopters from TF 76 amphibious ships positioned in the Tonkin Gulf were the primary SAR aircraft to recover Air Force and naval crews who went "feet wet." With a motto of "you fall, we haul," Navy SAR crews picked up others from under the guns of shore-based North Vietnamese forces. Marine helicopters and crews stood by to assist. To support recovery attempts, Admiral Mack had ordered General Miller to have a 300-man helicopter reaction force available on 48-hour standby to rescue downed air crews or escaping prisoners from shore.[14]

On 14 April, the brigade received a reminder that being offshore was still within the combat zone. The Navy's helicopter direction center (HDC) on the *Tripoli* dispatched an unarmed Marine HMM-165 helicopter to assist in the search for a missing Marine Intruder EA-6A pilot off the coast of North Vietnam. The CH-46, flown by First Lieutenants Lawrence J. "Hal" Paglioni and Michael L. Powell flew a lazy search pattern in the humid air of the Tonkin Gulf in response to vectors from the ship's

---

(H) "Yankee" and "Dixie" were naval terms for specific locations of carrier task force operations in the Gulf of Tonkin and the South China Sea. In 1972, Yankee Station was used in a more generic sense for any ship location in the Gulf of Tonkin.

HDC. As the aircraft reached Tiger Island (Hon Co), North Vietnamese antiaircraft gunners opened up on the helicopter flying at 500 feet. A single 14.5mm round passed through the front of the aircraft, between Powell's legs, ripping diagonally through the front and out the side of the armored seat, exploding and wounding him in the face. As they made their way back to the *Tripoli*, the two pilots berated the HDC for the error and pointedly observed that there was "still a war going on."[15]

One Marine pilot who flew search and rescue off North Vietnam, First Lieutenant Laurence W. Rush, recalled these operations at general quarters:

> ... Everyone was sleeping fully clothed and with life vests on. The air strike was due to start at three. The air was tense with expectation .... We expected to be busy in a very short time .... Dawn came and a new dimension was added. We could actually see our planes diving in and the smoke trails of the missiles coming up to meet them. We could see the shore line and the ship was ordered to proceed to a new holding area just beyond sight of shore.[16]

The Marine and Navy helicopters rescued several American aircrews shot down during the intensified air war over North Vietnam. One Thailand-based Air Force F-4 crew was recovered during an April 1972 strike at Thanh Hoa. They where floating off the coast, when a SH-3 SAR "bird" located them; the downed airmen first thought it was a North Vietnamese helicopter! Despite this misconception, the SH-3 picked them up and ferried them to the LPD USS *Denver*. In another instance, Lieutenant Randall H. Cunningham and Lieutenant (jg) William P. Driscoll were picked up by Navy SAR helicopters after shooting down their fifth MIG and becoming the Navy's leading air aces. A Marine CH-46 from the USS *Okinawa* carried Cunningham and Driscoll to their own ship, the *Constellation*.

NGF Airborne Spotters, Fast and Slow

Admiral Mack requested General Metzger to provide aircraft and Marines to support Task Group 77.1 engaged in naval gunfire strikes north of the DMZ. General Metzger, himself an air observer, proposed using McDonnell Douglas TA-4F Skyhawk dual-seat jets flying out of Da Nang as "Fast FACs" because the threat of enemy antiaircraft fire over the DMZ and North Vietnam prevented the effective use of anything but jet aircraft. He also proposed UH-1E helicopters off amphibious ships as spotting platforms. Trained personnel to support this were in two naval gunfire spot teams already with General Miller, in an additional team at Subic Bay, and among 16 more air observers rushed out from Okinawa and Hawaii. Additional air observers were with the infantry and artillery units of the brigade.

On 18 April, the USS *Denver* departed the amphibious holding area off the DMZ to join Task Group 77.1 for naval gunfire operations. General Miller established a naval gunfire support element on board the *Denver* using two UH-1E helicopters of Detachment Bravo, HML-367, and two UH-1Es from HMM-165 from the USS *Tripoli*. The element was initially under Major Harrison A. Makeever, but Captain Stephen D. Hill was the officer in charge during most of its existence. This detachment included five naval gunfire spotters and support personnel. On 19 April, a conference was held on the USS *Chicago* (CG 11) to organize the participants. Airborne spotters were used off Vinh on 20 April and then off Hon Mat, Thanh Hoa, and Dong Hoi on succeeding days. Mission effectiveness was marginal and conferences on board the USS *Denver* on 23 April and the USS *Long Beach* (CGN 9) on 27 April were unable to resolve the difficulties encountered in providing effective spotting. Admiral Mack suspended spot missions at the end of the month and directed the *Denver* to rejoin Task Force 76.

In retrospect, the enemy situation did not allow this concept to succeed. As naval gunfire strikes were conducted in daylight, the UH-1E spotting aircraft could not fly over land and still avoid the SAM and AAA threat. The spotters encountered problems in lack of coordination from communications procedures to tactics. The naval gunfire ships, outgunned by shore batteries, made their runs at the coastline in column, turning in line to fire while parallel with the coast, then back to column for withdrawal. They could not wait for subsequent corrections from the spotters. As the threat of North Vietnamese countermeasures increased, the ships conducted their fires at night which made air spotting difficult, if not impossible. These missions also hampered Lieutenant Colonel Friedrich, who found his efforts to prepare BLT 1/9 for contingencies because of the 180-mile separation of his staff and units from the rest of the brigade for a two-week period in support of such operations.[17]

Raids and Demonstrations

American planners had long considered the possibility of an amphibious landing at Vinh to cut the Vietnamese panhandle north of the DMZ. The Marine Corps Schools, Quantico, Virginia, had presented such a landing as a planning exercise to students in the past. Lieutenant General William K. Jones, commanding general of Fleet Marine Force Pacific, remembered suggesting this option to General William C. Westmoreland in 1965 while Jones was a brigadier general in charge of the MACV operations center. In practice, Seventh Fleet conducted feints north of the DMZ in 1968 and 1971.[18] The availability of the U.S. forces and the vulnerabilities of the North Vietnamese to this course of action were never greater than in the spring of

1972 as authorities in Washington and CinCPac considered the feasibility of raids and demonstrations by amphibious forces. A Central Intelligence Agency analyst on Ambassador Ellsworth Bunker's staff in Saigon, Edwin W. Besch, observed that an amphibious landing in North Vietnam to the rear of NVA forces would have had a greater operational effect than the tactical landings conducted in South Vietnam.[19]

Early on, Seventh Fleet's Admiral Mack proposed an amphibious assault directly at the North Vietnamese mainland, or at least a feint or demonstration.[(l)] Soon after arriving in the Tonkin Gulf, Admiral Gaddis issued an order for a Task Force 76 demonstration against the Dong Hoi-Quang Khe areas. Admiral McCain, CinCPac, then directed a demonstration just south of the DMZ. The 1st Regional Advisory Command's General Kroesen objected and did not want the amphibious task force to operate away from its northern holding area. He was concerned that the *325th NVA Division* would move into MR 1; he believed that the amphibious task force off the DMZ prevented this by posing a threat to the rear and supply lines of the *NVA B-5 Front*. Both operations were canceled prior to a proposed D-Day of 24 April 1972.[20]

By late April, planning focused on more specific contingencies. Prompted by the need to relieve pressure on South Vietnamese forces in MR 1 and by the possibilities of having to rescue stranded aircrews, General Miller and Admiral Gaddis developed plans to land Marines by surface and air assault on several points in North Vietnam. Lieutenant Colonel James L. Shananhan, the 9th MAB operations officer, commented that there "was scarcely a single square inch of the North Vietnamese coastal littoral of any value whatsoever which was not the subject of a least one plan."[21] Lieutenant Colonel George B. Crist as brigade plans officer considered Vinh, Dong Hoi, Quang Khe, and Hon Matt island as logical targets. Courses of action included a two BLT demonstration at Dong Hoi, a two-BLT raid at Quang Khe, a one-BLT raid on Hon Mat, a two-BLT demonstration at Vinh, and a raid or a feint at Quang Khe with up to two BLTs. Brigade proposals called for the transportation and support of Vietnamese forces to conduct these same missions using TF 76. General Miller emphasized throughout the planning process the requirement for absolute local superiority in supporting arms.[22]

Colonel Robert J. Perrich's 33d MAU joined 9th MAB in the Tonkin Gulf on 28 April. On Okinawa, Major General Joseph C. Fegan, Jr., the 3d Marine Division commander, assigned Lieutenant Colonel John C. Gonzales' 2/9 as BLT Delta, the division's air contingency unit. On 1 May, ready forces went on two-hour standby for evacuation

---

(l) Amphibious demonstrations were operations conducted as a deception to cause North Vietnamese forces to redeploy or remain inactive in order to deal with a perceived threat. The full range of preparation was conducted to include troop movement, communications, and preparatory and supporting fires. The assault was executed as an actual attack with surface and airborne forces turning away at the last moment prior to landing.

operations in support of FRAC. Marines and sailors of the 31st MAU, BLT Bravo, and the 33d MAU manned battle stations until MACV Advisory Team 155 withdrew from Quang Tri City in USAF HH-53 "Jolly Green Giant" helicopters. The majority of U.S. Marine advisors remained with their Vietnamese units as they retreated south from Quang Tri towards Hue. With the dissolution of the 3d ARVN Division[J] and the South Vietnamese withdrawals to the My Chanh River, the situation in MR 1 was critical.[23] American combat forces in MR 1 were reduced to the 11th Aviation Group, the 196th Infantry Brigade, and USAF base defense forces at Da Nang as incremental redeployments continued.[K] [24]

By 7 May, ARVN units, backed by American firepower, formed a defensive line along the My Chanh River. Lieutenant General Ngo Quang Truong took command of I Corps from Lieutenant General Hoang Xuan Lam and moved into forward headquarters in the Citadel in Hue.[L] General Truong's immediate task was to defend Hue and stabilize his forces. Supported by MACV's 1st Regional Assistance Command, General Truong moved swiftly to establish his chain of command, designate reserves, and enhance his control of supporting arms. This set the stage for 9th MAB's direct support of FRAC and the VNMC Division in the defense of Hue and the I Corps counteroffensive that followed.[25]

Redeyes at Sea

Admiral Mack had been concerned since mid-April that the North Vietnamese would try to attack one of his carriers as operations intensified in the Tonkin Gulf. Whether the Communists could tell the difference between an aircraft or helicopter carrier was not known and academic to Marines who found themselves going to general quarters on both. At this time, a North Vietnamese MiG-17, Mikoyan-Gurevich Fresco, bombed the USS *Higbee* (DD 806) while engaged in a surface attack on Dong Hoi, highlighting the vulnerability of Seventh Fleet ships to North Vietnamese air attack.[M] Because of the lack of effective point air defense weapons[N] on some ships, Admiral Mack asked the Marine Corps to provide "Redeye" missiles and forward air defense teams for protection. General Jones, FMFPac, authorized the deployment of missile

---

(J) The "Ben Hai Flyers" to the Marines afloat, although this was unjust considering the relative strengths of the forces involved.

(K) By 30 April 1972, actual American troop-strength in South Vietnam was at 68,100 — compared to the authorized goal of 49,000.

(L) General Metzger held Truong in high esteem from the period of close work between the 1st ARVN Division and the 3d Marine Division in 1967, considering him "an exceedingly competent and able combat commander." (Metzger comments)

(M) This was on 19 April 1972. The MiG was shot down by the USS *Sterett* (CG 31) with a Terrier missile.

(N) Available 3"/50 and 5"/54 guns were not designed for use against high-performance aircraft.

teams on 7 May after an evaluation by First Fleet showed the feasibility of the concept of employing shoulder-fired missiles on board ship. On 8 May, First Lieutenant James B. Dowling's 3d Redeye Platoon, 3d Marine Aircraft Wing, departed MCAS El Toro, California. The platoon of 42 men took 44 missile systems, six night viewing devices, and associated support equipment. Arriving in the Western Pacific they were assigned to General Miller for support of the Seventh Fleet. This allowed naval gunfire ships to continue to fire against targets in North Vietnam without diverting carrier aircraft to combat air patrols.

While an American "Thunder Curtain" of supporting naval gunfire, tactical air, and B-52 Arc Lights protected the South Vietnamese in MR 1, Admiral Mack again moved north, issuing an initiating directive for Operation Heroic Action, a raid to seize the Dong Hoi ferry crossings south of Vinh. General Miller said the purpose was "to go into North Vietnam and a whole bunch of other things."[26] Wrote a young battalion-staff officer, First Lieutenant Charles D. Melson:

> ... One morning in May 1972 aboard the USS *Denver* (LPD 9), I was sorting incoming message traffic when I came to an operations order. I turned to the battalion operations officer and said, "This looks like the real thing." He looked at the message and headed for the commanding officer's stateroom muttering about "going to war."[27]

A week of intense planning followed; orders, maps, and aerial photos were issued to the rifle companies and attached units. The Marines on ship in newly issued camouflage "utility" uniforms focused on cleaning weapons, packing combat equipment, and a series of detailed inspections. Seventh Fleet assigned four destroyers for naval gunfire, two destroyers for escort, and two aircraft carriers for support. Rehearsal and communication exercises began on 11 May off Dong Hoi. On 13 May, Admiral Thomas R. Moorer, Chairman of the Joint Chiefs of Staff, postponed the operation indefinitely, because he wanted amphibious forces to remain in position to back-up MR 1.[28] Admiral McCain, CinCPac, then ordered a demonstration for the next day, but canceled it when he concluded that the absence of both helicopter carriers, supporting other operations, would defeat the purpose the maneuver. General Miller was called off "at the last minute."

A 9th MAB message to General Metzger described Heroic Action as a turnaway landing. General Jones, then FMFPac, remembered the raid "as a fact," but agreed with Admiral McCain's final decision. Records from Seventh Fleet and Fleet Marine Force Pacific indicated it was to be a raid, while records from the Pacific Command and JCS stated for political reasons it was never more than a deception plan. The possibility of landing was valid considering the availability of forces and a situation that lent itself to success, and this was what the North Vietnamese were to believe.

Seventh Fleet amphibious forces were now totally committed to the support of American and Vietnamese units in South Vietnam.

Support to Military Region 1

To this point, 9th MAB and TF 76 operations had been unilateral Seventh Fleet actions. This condition changed to meet General Creighton W. Abram's need for direct support to FRAC and the South Vietnamese in MR 1. General Miller observed that, "... political constraints precluded the reintroduction of U.S. Marine Corps troops into South Vietnam in a land warfare role. Still, there were other alternatives to simply landing U.S. Marines.[29] The flexibility and availability to General Miller and Task Force 76 provided the Seventh Fleet with a wide variety of options to support MR 1. The close relation between the Vietnamese and American Marines, built up over the years, provided for excellent coordination. Direct support to the Vietnamese Marine Corps Division included command and control, staff planning, fire support, assault support, and logistics. Lieutenant Colonel Gerald H. Turley, the G-3 Advisor to the VNMC Division, referred to the amphibious sailors and Marines as "our brothers off shore" for the subsequent contributions by the amphibious forces to the defense and counterattack in MR 1 from May through September 1972.[30]

General Truong and FRAC's General Kroesen met with the 9th MAB staff for the ongoing defense of Hue City. This broadened to planning with MACV for amphibious support of General Truong's efforts to regain Quang Tri City. General Abrams forwarded General Truong's request for Seventh Fleet support to Admiral McCain, and subsequent planning conferences in Hue ironed out the planning details and allowed for coordination of supporting arms and communications. Initial plans called for offensive operations in the Hai Lang Forest area.

Early on 13 May, Marines of 33d MAU's HMM-164 and BLT 1/4 "stood to" in anticipation of the day's activities. The USS *Okinawa, Mobile, Cayuga, Manitowoc, Point Defiance*, and *St. Louis* moved into a holding area 30 miles from the coastline. To allow for simultaneous launch, helicopters were positioned on all available deck space.[(0)] Marines augmented the ships' crews manning battle stations: guns, medical, deck, damage control, and search-and-rescue. The success of this first combined operation began the series of landings used to contain and later to defeat the Communist forces in MR 1.

Fleet Support Continues

The first Redeye missile teams deployed the day after arriving at Subic Bay, Philippines. By 19 May 1972, 10 teams of four men each were on naval gunfire ships in the Tonkin

---

(0) Twenty-two aircraft from six ships.

Gulf. The initial assignments found Lieutenant Dowling and a team on the USS *Providence* (CLG 6), with others on the USS *Mullinnix* (DD 944), *Everett F. Larson* (DD 830), *Benjamin Stoddert* (DDG 22), *Eversole* (DD 789), *Berkley* (DDG 15), *Hanson* (DD 832), *Hull* (DD 945), *Buchanan* (DDG 14), and *Dennis J. Buckley* (DD 808). Lieutenant Dowling's missile teams rotated on board additional ships depending on their proximity to the North Vietnamese shore defenses. Eighteen two-man teams were organized by the middle of the year to provide additional coverage. Training of navy gunners began at Subic Bay and Twenty Nine Palms, California, allowing the Navy to take over missile defense from the Marines.[P] The effectiveness of this expedient antiaircraft defense was never put to the test. The U.S. soon conducted naval gunfire attacks at night and American aircraft bombed the airfields that posed a threat to the Seventh Fleet.[31]

BLT Delta (BLT 2/9) boarded ARG ships and arrived off MR 1 on 22 May. This brought the 9th MAB to its maximum strength during 1972. The Brigade consisted of the 31st MAU (Provisional Marine Aircraft Group 10) and 33d MAU (Regimental Landing Team 4), with 6,042 men and 46 aircraft, a brigade in strength as well as name. This was the largest concentration of amphibious forces during the Vietnam War, and the largest wartime amphibious force since the Inchon and Wonsan landings of the Korean War. The size of this force alone gave the North Vietnamese some concern about U.S. intentions.[32]

With the success of Song Thanh 5-72, the VNMC Division launched Song Thanh 6-72. The operation was in the same general location as the first, but closer to the coast where the NVA were using small boats to supply their forward units. Again the object was to disrupt North Vietnamese forces and to relieve pressure on the My Chanh Line. The landing plan used a mix of brigade units under the 33d MAU's Colonel Perrich and HMM-164, ARG Bravo, and ARG Charlie supporting the Vietnamese assault force.[33] On 23 May, the 7th VNMC Battalion loaded on the *Cayuga* and *Duluth* in preparation for landing. Helicopters from HMM-164 filled available deck space for a single wave launch.[Q] As they had in the previous assault, the Vietnamese Marines carried out this operation successfully. Helicopters brought Vietnamese casualties to the ships, demonstrating the reality of war to the Americans offshore.

On 17 June, General Robert E. Cushman, Jr., Commandant of the Marine Corps, visited with III MAF commanders as part of his Western Pacific inspection trip, which included Vietnam.[34] Major David J. Moore, executive officer for HMM-164, flew

---

(P) By 31 July 1972, training and turnover was completed and the 3d Redeye Platoon returned to the United States.

(Q) Twenty aircraft and 20 LVT5s from nine ships. USS *Duluth, Cayuga, Okinawa, Schenectady, Sumter, Juneau, St. Louis, Mobile,* and *Manitowoc*.

General Miller into Da Nang, where they met General Cushman and took him to Hue City and later to the *Okinawa*. Recalled Moore, "Because of the SA-7 threat, our trip to Hue was a bit more exciting than General Cushman expected."[35] By then, the South Vietnamese in MR 1 had regained the initiative over the Communists. Lam Son 72 was General Truong's plan to recapture portions of MR 1 lost at the beginning of the Easter Offensive and he directed the Vietnamese Airborne and Marine Divisions to attack north from the My Chanh River to seize a line along Route 602 from Hai Lang to Wunder Beach.

Across the Beach: The Lam Son Landings

In support of Lam Son 72, Admiral Gaddis and General Miller assembled ARG Charlie with the 31st MAU and ARG Alpha with the 33d MAU in a staging area for preparations for a demonstration just north of the Cua Viet River.[R] While in the staging area, the amphibious forces conducted a command post exercise, and, at the same time attacked selected targets in the objective area with naval gunfire and tactical air strikes. The main enemy threat to this operation was from coastal artillery from Hon (Tiger) Island. On 26 June, the amphibious task group was activated by Task Force 76 and a second rehearsal was conducted, surface and air attacks continued in the objective area, and South Vietnamese Navy landing craft loaded Vietnamese Marines at Tan My to join the task force.

Following the amphibious demonstration of 27 June, the 9th MAB prepared to continue with Operation Lam Son 72 with a two VNMC battalion helicopter assault into landing zones behind Communist lines on 29 June. At the same time, the remainder of the Vietnamese Marine Division launched a frontal attack from the My Chanh. American amphibious support to this phase of Lam Son 72 allowed the rapid advance of South Vietnamese forces to the outskirts of Quang Tri City. On 30 June, the President of South Vietnam, Nguyen Van Thieu, visited the USS *Blue Ridge* to convey his personal thanks to the sailors and Marines of the amphibious forces for "the preservation of Peace and Freedom" in South Vietnam."[36]

Another opportunity for a helicopter assault on the exposed Communist seaward flank occurred when strong NVA forces entrenched in the outskirts of Quang Tri City and to the south and east along the Vinh Dinh River stalled the South Vietnamese attack. General Troung and a new FRAC commander, Major General Howard H. Cooksey, decided on a two-battalion ground movement from the east supported by a heliborne assault from the west across the Vinh Dinh River to turn the NVA defenses. General Miller, and the new task force commander, Rear Admiral Wycliffe D. Toole, Jr., used combined brigade helicopter assets and Task Force 76 ships for a maximum buildup

---

(R) 31st MAU: BLT 1/4, HMM-164: 33d MAU: BLT 1/9, HMM-165.

of combat power. The 31st MAU of Colonel Donald E. Newton and the 33d MAU of Colonel Robert J. Perrich carried out the new assignment with the experienced HMM-164 on the *Okinawa* and HMM-165 from the *Tripoli*. At the planning conference for this operation at the VNMC division command post, Colonel Perrich pointed out that the use of a single helicopter squadron would require two separate lifts to complete and that a delay was in order until both squadrons were available on 11 July. In the wake of this hard-won assault, General Cooksey requested Seventh Fleet's Vice Admiral James L. Holloway III to provide an alternate means to resupply VNMC units along the coast. The solution was the installation of a five-section causeway at Wunder Beach by the USS *Alamo* (LSD 33) by navy beachmasters and Marine shore party.

On 14 July, the VNMC continued its attacks on Quang Tri City in support of the ARVN Airborne Division. On 22 July, Brigadier General Lan conducted a two-battalion ground movement, supported by tanks and artillery, attacking up the coast and linking up with a third battalion making a heliborne assault 4,000 meters to the north. General Miller and Admiral Toole used the 31st MAU and ARG Charlie ships to support this, and Admiral Mack even ordered the USS *Denver* from operations with Task Force 77 to provide additional deck space for helicopter staging.[S] After this operation, General Lan said that the 9th MAB and Task Force 76 support enabled the offensive to be launched with success, citing the devastatingly accurate preparation fires by naval gunfire. According to Lan, the 9th MAB supported the multi-battalion heliborne assaults with professional skill, courageous performance, and a timeliness "which allowed the VNMC forces to aggressively attack.[37]

A typhoon in the Philippines in July caused Admiral McCain to direct Admiral Holloway to provide relief to America's longtime Asian ally. The USS *Blue Ridge*, *Tripoli*, *Juneau*, *Alamo*, and *Cayuga* diverted from combat operations in Vietnam to humanitarian service in the Philippines from 22 July through 13 August 1972. The 33d MAU remained on 120-hour recall to MR 1 while conducting relief activities.[T] The MAU commander commented that the Marines of Lieutenant Colonel Charles H. F. Egger's HMM-165 flew "their helicopters in near-zero visibility to deliver emergency food supplies to people stranded in villages that were cut off .... BLT 2/4 Marines worked under equally miserable conditions to provide assistance."[38] After a short period of training and an amphibious exercise, the 33d MAU, now commanded by Colonel Charles T. Williamson, and the ARG Alpha ships proceeded to the Gulf of Tonkin to relieve the 31st MAU and ARG Charlie on 24 August.[39]

(S) See Chapter 13.

(T) The 33d MAU and subordinate units were awarded the Philippine Presidential Unit Citation for their efforts.

General Miller and the 9th MAB staff remained off the coast on the USS *Paul Revere* (LPA 248) while the South Vietnamese engaged in heavy fighting to retake Quang Tri City. Contingency and support planning continued through the month. Lieutenant Colonel Robert W. "Rip" Kirby, commanding BLT 2/4, made a liaison visit to the VNMC Division command post, in part a reunion with an Amphibious Warfare School classmate — General Lan. Kirby asked Lan about the tactical situation during the tough fighting at Quang Tri City, and the Vietnamese Marine general replied without pause, "I'm still using the yellows," referring to the doctrinal "school solutions" used by Marine Corps Schools at Quantico, Virginia.[40]

Turnaway at Quang Tri

More specific planning began in August 1972 at the request of General Abrams and FRAC's General Cooksey. The object was to draw NVA units away from Quang Tri City and to the northeast. General Truong believed an amphibious demonstration on, or about, 1 September would accomplish this. When this was not approved in time by CinCPac, another amphibious demonstration was requested to take place between the Cua Viet River and the DMZ for the following week. As with deceptions, the fact the landing was to be a demonstration was kept from both American and South Vietnamese participating forces.

On 6 September, Admiral Toole and General Miller using ARG transports with the 33d MAU[U] occupied the amphibious holding area off the DMZ. They conducted communication tests, fired naval gunfire, and began tactical air attacks in the objective area, including Tiger Island and Cap Lay. On 7 September, Vietnamese ships and the USS *Juneau* (LPD 10) embarked 400 ARVN Rangers from Tan My for the surface assault. Naval gunfire and tactical air continued hitting the objective area. On 8 September the amphibious task group was activated and rehearsals began. Air Force B-52s and naval gunfire struck enemy targets; South Vietnamese field artillery reinforced the American fires. The turnaway was completed on 9 September without incident and the amphibious forces returned to the off-shore holding areas.

Marine and naval officers continued liaison with I Corps, FRAC, and MACV, but the task force provided no further direct combat support after October 1972. Both the North and South Vietnamese units juggled for tactical ground and political bargaining positions during the continuing Paris Peace Talks, while 9th MAB and Task Force 76 remained off the coast. The 9th MAB's backing of the VNMC and FRAC helped to recapture Quang Tri City and denied North Vietnamese military and political objectives in MR 1. Throughout, the Marines and sailors of the 9th Marine Amphibious Brigade, seabased with Task Force 76, contributed their full share to the

(U) BLT 2/4 and HMM-165.

total naval options available to the Seventh Fleet in response to the North Vietnamese offensive. The Seventh Fleet commander stated the response of all ships and units to the surge in Seventh Fleet operations caused by the invasion of the Republic of Vietnam had been noteworthy in every sense of the word.[41] Added were the comments of General Cushman, CMC, that "I am happy to see that in each instance Marines met the challenges head-on in an outstanding manner."[42]

CHAPTER TEN ENDNOTES

Unless otherwise noted, material in this chapter is derived from: FMFPac MarOpsSEA; SeventhFlt ComdHist72; Marine Corps Operations and Analysis Group, "Documentation and Analysis of U.S. Marine Corps Activity in Southeast Asia," ONR study CNA 1016, dtd July 1973 (CNA, Washington, D.C.), hereafter CNA MarActySEA; and 9thMAB ComdC, Apr-Dec72. See also MajGen Edward J. Miller and RAdm Wycliffe D. Toole, Jr., "Amphibious Forces: The Turning Point," *Naval Institute Proceedings*, Nov74, pp. 26-32, hereafter Miller & Toole.

9th MAB and the Naval Campaign

1 FMFPac MarOpsSea, pp. 1-16 to 1-17.

2 LtCol William R. Von Harten, comments on draft ms, dtd 11Jan90 (Vietnam Comment File).

3 LtGen Louis Metzger, comments on draft ms, dtd 8Dec89 (Vietnam Comment File).

4 For specific composition see FMFPac MarOpsSEA, pp. 2-7 to 2-11, 3-10 to 3-12, 4-3, 5-2; CNA MarActySEA, pp. 29-37.

5 A Brief History of the 9th Marine Amphibious Brigade dtd 28Sept78; Lineage of the 9th Marine Amphibious Brigade dtd 22May85 (RefSec, MCHC, Washington, D.C.).

6 Col James L. Shanahan, comments on draft ms, dtd 8Jan90 (Vietnam Comment File).

7 CNA MarActySEA, pp. 58-59.

8 LtGen Edward J. Miller intvw dtd 6Feb86 (OralHistColl, MCHC, Washington, D.C.).

Support to the Fleet

9 Metzger comments.

10 CMC ltr dtd 28Feb74 (CNA MarActySEA).

Evacuations

11 In 1972, JCSPub 1 defined special operations as supporting or secondary operations for which no single service was assigned primary responsibility.

12 FMFPac MarOpsSEA, pp. 2-11 to 2-13; CNA MarActySEA, p. 52.

13 Von Harten comments.

Search and Rescue

14 CNA MarActySEA, pp. 5, 13, 20, 50.

15 Powell comments.

16 Rush, op. cit., pp. 116-117.

NGF Airborne Spotters, Fast and Slow

17 CNA MarActySEA, pp. 17-18; Maj Melson notes as S3A, BLT 1/9 (Vietnam Comment File).

Raids and Demonstrations

18 LtGen William K. Jones, comments on draft ms, dtd 22Nov89 (Vietnam Comment File); Graham A. Cosmas and LtCol Terrence P. Murray, *U.S. Marines in Vietnam, 1970–1971* (Washington, D.C., Hist & Mus Div, HQMC, 1986), pp. 386-387.

19 Edwin W. Besch, "Amphibious Operation at Vinh," *Marine Corps Gazette*, Dec82, pp. 54-60; Miller & Toole, pp. 27-32.

20 CNA MarActySEA, p. 64.

21 Shanahan comments.

22 CNA MarActySEA, p. 51.

23 Feng, op. cit.

24 MACV ComdHist72-73, pp. F-56 to F-60.

25 Truong, *Invasion*, p. 48.

Redeyes at Sea

26 Miller intvw.

27 Maj Melson ltr to the *Marine Corps Gazette*, Dec82, pp. 10-11.

28 Jones comments; FMFPac MarOpsSEA, pp. 51, 61; CNA MarActySEA, p. 2-13.

Support to Military Region 1

29 Miller & Toole, p. 28.

30 Marine Corps Command and Staff College, The Easter Offensive Symposium dtd 4Dec86 (OralHistColl, MCHC, Washington, D.C.), hereafter CSC symposium.

Fleet Support Continues

31 FMFPac MarOpsSEA, pp. 2-28 to 2-29, 3-24, 4-2; CNA MarActySEA, pp. 109-111.

32 MCHC, Status of Forces dtd 23May72.

33 CNA MarActySEA, p. 55.

34 Gen Robert E. Cushman, Jr. intvw dtd 1Nov-9Dec 1982 (OralHistCol, MCHC, Washington, D.C.).

35 Moore comments.

Across the Beach: The Lam Son Landings

36 FMFPac MarOpsSEA, pp. 3-1 to 3-4; RVNAF Official Order #042/TTM/CL/NQ dtd 14Apr73 (JGS Archives Center).

37 FMFPac MarOpsSEA, pp. 3-8 to 3-9.

38 Williamson comments.

39 FMFPac MarOpsSEA, pp. 3-9 to 3-10, 4-1 to 4-2. CNA MarActySEA, pp. 119-120.

40 Kirby comments.

Turnaway at Quang Tri
41 ComSeventhFlt msg to SeventhFlt dtd 13Apr72 (Vietnam Comment File).

42 CMC msg to ALMAR/54 dtd 2Jun72 (Vietnam Comment File).

Long-range air transport was provided by Lockheed KC-130 Hercules, as this aircraft from VMGR-152, indicated by the "QD" call-letters on the vertical stabilizer. These aircraft moved both supplies and fuel as an essential element of the forward deployment.

The location of the Marine units at Nam Phong was a remote shipping point for both personnel and material. As an expeditionary base, everything needed to power it had to be produced on the spot. Logistics Support Group Delta ("Miracles Done Immediately") fulfilled these needs. This power plant dispensed electricity to run the base service facilities.

Air traffic control communications and electronic support was by Marine Air Traffic Control Unit 62. This backing included the control tower, precision radar, surveillance radar, and the associated navigational aids required for around-the-clock air operations.

Americans were still present in Military Region 1, but with a less active role than during the previous year's fighting. These 9th MAB Marines are examining captured Communist weapons in front of the Vietnamese Marine Division command post at Huong Dien.

As active combat ended, the ready forces of the Seventh Fleet remained for a variety of contingencies. With the departure of the USS *Blue Ridge*, the amphibious and landing force headquarters was on the USS *Paul Revere*, here for joint training new Tan My.

Air bases in South Vietnam remained the target of Communist attacks. Smoke rises as a group of rockets hits at Da Nang in this period. These were followed by ground assaults.

Security concerns continued for Task Force Delta. But Nam Phong's distant location provided the best defense. A sapper demonstration team is used to show task force personnel how terrorists attacks could be conducted through the base's defensive perimeter.

Conditions in confinement varied with location. In North Vietnam, prisons were administered by the Interior Ministry, with the prisoners exploited by the Army. This wartime picture shows two unidentified Americans working under guard in the north.

Heavy fighting took place at the walls of the Citadel as massive artillery duels occurred. Despite serious losses, the Communists held onto the position through August 1972.

Firepower from both sides reduced Quang Tri City to a uniform level of destruction. This is the view along Quang Tri Street after the South Vietnamese retook the city.

Marines of the 9th Battalion consolidate their gains. Here a TOW antitank missile team installs a launcher. At right, LtCol Nguyen Kim De, the battalion commander, and Maj Paul L. Carlson, an advisor, supervise the emplacement of this weapon system.

Some U.S. Marines worked .50 caliber heavy machine guns during landing operations by the South Vietnamese armed forces. Shown here are South Vietnamese Rangers loading landing craft at Tan My for movement to amphibious assault ships located offshore.

Glad to be back, Navy Lt Randall H. Cunningham and Lt (jg) William P. Driscoll arrive on the USS *Constellation* after being rescued in the Gulf of Tonkin. They got three MiGs before going down. The CH-46 that brought them back is from HMM-164.

Not all hazards to flight were from the enemy. Mechanical failure claimed this UH-1 from the USS *Okinawa*. The crew was recovered, but the aircraft was lost at sea.

McDonnell Douglas F-4B Phantom fighter-bombers of VMFA-115 were among the initial aircraft from MAG-15 to arrive in Da Nang after III MAF air power was committed in response to the Communist Spring Offensive. A workhorse aircraft, it was used by Marine, Air Force, and Navy squadrons. The tail letters "VE" indicate its squadron.

The value of good relations with the local people was a lesson brought back to Vietnam by the returning Marines. SSgt Frank H. Peace of MAG-12 fills the fuel tank of a generator that supplied electricity to the Ke-Sat Orphanage near Bien Hoa. The generator had been reconditioned by the Marines as a good-will project.

Division and front-heavy artillery units prepared the way for the Communist offensive by disrupting the South Vietnamese defenses and command structure. North Vietnamese Army gunners prepare to shoot 122mm field guns that fire as far as 23,900 meters.

An infantry attack in a "combat" photograph by the North Vietnamese. The soldier to the left of the tower waves a red and blue National Liberation Front banner, despite this being a NVA unit.

South Vietnamese troop movement was hampered by large numbers of refugees on the roads, including military stragglers.

Despite reliance on armor and motorized forces, the North Vietnamese Army's infantry displayed a greater degree of cross-country mobility than their opponents. An NVA infantry unit crosses a stream carrying individual and unit equipment with it.

This diorama depicts the situation Capt John W. Ripley faced in placing demolition charges underneath the Dong Ha Bridge. The boxes containing explosives were slid down the bridge framework.

Communist soldier pursued South Vietnamese and American stragglers after the fall of the defensive positions. This was often a confused situation that saw the fragmentation of units on both sides as one moved to escape and the other moved to destroy them.

Special forces such as these MACV Special Operations Group maritime commandos at Da Nang were used to recover the American airmen evading capture north of the Cam Lo River. Though wearing South Vietnamese uniforms, most of the weapons they carry are of Communist origin. The two submachine guns, however, are Swedish Karl Gustavs.

Once again civilian and military refugees fled from the fighting. These civilians, walking along National Highway 1 and south of Quang Tri City near Hai Lang, blocked the road south.

The deployment and conduct of operations by the entire Marine Division required command and control facilities near the front lines. The location of the division forward command post was the small coastal village of Huong Dien within the local school building. The building housed the combat operations and fire support coordination centers.

The Marine leadership for the defense of Hue included, from left, BGen Edward J. Miller of the 9th Marine Amphibious Brigade; Col Joshua Dorsey, Senior Marine Advisor; and BGen Bui The Lan, commanding the Vietnamese Marine Corps. Gen Lan's use of the nametape "Laan" was as an aid for pronunciation for the benefit of the Americans.

U.S. Marine direct support arrived from the 9th MAB for the defense of Hue. Here Vietnamese Marines board a Boeing CH-46 Sea Knight from HMM-164 for the first of a number of helicopter assaults behind enemy lines flown by the Americans in the spring of 1972.

Other American support arrived in town in the form of new weapons to counter the armor threat. Here a Vietnamese Marine commander and American advisor supervise the installation of the TOW wire-guided antitank missile launcher. Though effective to 3,000 meters, the system was considered too heavy to be man-packed by the individual Vietnamese.

A landing craft approaches the open stern of an amphibious transport dock (LPD) where South Vietnamese forces will embark for the Wunder Beach landing. The well deck can accommodate a number and variety of landing craft and allows the transfer of ground combat forces with the more time-consuming and dangerous use of nets and ladders.

The surface assault for Song Than 6-72 moves toward Wunder Beach. The amphibian tractors (LVTs) are in two parallel platoon columns as the cross behind the USS *Duluth*.

The heavy cruiser USS *Newport News* shelled the beach as the landing was completed and the LVT platoons returned to the amphibious group. In the background is the flat coastal plain which made reference points for naval gunfire hard to locate from the sea.

U.S. Marine helicopters turn away from the Vietnamese coast during the amphibious demonstration by the 9th MAB for the Lam Son counteroffensive. Both the air and surface assaults were aimed at the North Vietnamese rear positions along the Cua Viet River.

The instrument of forward deployment was the Marine landing forces and the amphibious assault ship (LPH) and two amphibious transports (LPDs) underway in the Western Pacific in the 1970s.

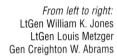

From left to right:
LtGen William K. Jones
LtGen Louis Metzger
Gen Creighton W. Abrams

The senior Vietnamese and American Marine leaders, in late 1971 are, from left, LtGen Le Nguyen Khang, Commander of the Vietnamese Marine Corps; Col Joshua W. Dorsey III, Senior Marine Advisor; and RAdm Robert S. Salzer, Commander Naval Forces Vietnam and the Naval Advisory Group.

Another focus of the advisory effect was on equipment and maintenance training. A lance corporal from the 3d Marine Division instructs a Marine from the VNMC Signal Battalion in the use of communications equipment.

The main threat to the South Vietnamese and the Americans came from the full-time soldiers of the North Vietnamese Army. This mortar unit's haircuts, uniforms, and training were those of a conventional force.

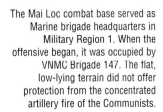

The Mai Loc combat base served as Marine brigade headquarters in Military Region 1. When the offensive began, it was occupied by VNMC Brigade 147. The flat, low-lying terrain did not offer protection from the concentrated artillery fire of the Communists.

Within a short time, this tent city was erected to become the billeting area for Headquarters and Maintenance Squadron 15 and Marine Air Base Squadron 15. Looking south, in the foreground are supplies and material being stored in the open for lack of adequate warehousing. The jungle terrain surrounding the base appears to stretch to the horizon.

The fighter-attack group was joined by VMA(AW)-533 and its all-weather attack Grumman A-62 Intruders. The Intruders' bomb-carrying capacity and flight time were impressive.

An essential element of the air effort was the continued upkeep of aircraft systems. The Wonder Arch shelters allowed the 24-hour-a-day support needed to keep planes flying.

A Grumman EA-6A of VMAQ-2 prepares to launch from a carrier deck. The squadron is identified by the "Playboy" logo and aircraft call-letters "CY" on the vertical stabilizer.

South Vietnamese Marines head north once more as the Lam Son counteroffensive returns them to Quang Tri Province. Helicopters from HMM-164 and HMM-165 pick up waiting helo-teams from the 1st and the 4th VNMC Battalions, using a road as a pickup zone.

"Like a school of sharks," was one description of the low-level flight pattern used by the Marines to evade enemy antiaircraft fire enroute to Landing Zones Flamingo and Hawk. Army escort gunships and supporting arms were also used to reduce the enemy threat.

Helicopters from the 9th Marine Amphibious Brigade were used to place Vietnamese Marines in position around Quang Tri City on 11 July 1972. Here HMM-165 aircraft from the USS *Tripoli* arrive to pick up Marines of the 1st VNMC Battalion behind friendly lines.

Air photographs were used in the planning of operations led by the allied forces. This shows one of the landing zones in which every heavy resistance was met on 11 July 1972. The annotations were keyed to suspected enemy dispositions and weapons emplacements.

Meals in the north were lacking in basic vitamins and protein, but most were at routinely issued. In the south, this depended entirely upon what the local Communists had available for food themselves. If they did not eat, the prisoners also starved.

American prisoners were put on display for visiting delegations, for example when American actress Jane Fonda arrived in Hanoi on 8 July 1972. Along with meeting the prisoners, touring bombed areas, and making radio broadcasts, Fonda visited with NVA antiaircraft crews where this photograph was taken.

The returnees maintained their composure until it was clear that they were again safe under American control. No one was silent as this Air Force C-141 Starlifter left the runway in Hanoi. The photographer, TSgt Robert N. Denham, USAF, observed, "You could hear the shouts and cheers all over the aircraft" on this 28 March 1973 flight.

"Welcome home, Marine!" heard from the Commandant of the Marine Corps. At Camp Pendleton, California, Gen Robert E. Cushman, Jr., promotes CW03 William E. Thomas, Jr., in front of other returnees. In most cases, promotions waited several years to be presented, making some Marines several ranks senior to what they were when they were captured.

An AH-1J Sea Cobra from HMA-369 in this case flies the call-letters of HMM-165 while part of a composite squadron. It is armed with 20mm cannon and Zuni rocket pods.

Combat flights over North Vietnam, and Route Package 6 in particular, were subject to the full range of enemy weapons. Antiaircraft artillery included these S-60 57mm antiaircraft guns, used in conjunction with the "Flap Wheel" radar, in batteries of six guns.

An "illegal assembly" as defined by the military law and leadership, is represented by this gathering of Marines at Camp Schwab, Okinawa, in January 1972 on Dr. Martin Luther King, Junior's birthday. The group included outsiders from other facilities and services.

Training had functional and institutional aspects in readiness and discipline. Inspections on ship served as a measure of both physical and psychological preparedness, sharpened by the proximity of the fighting.

The Nam Phong base of Task Force Delta was nicknamed the "Rose Garden" from this recruiting poster and slogans used by the Marines.

CHAPTER ELEVEN
ANY TIME, ANY PLACE

The Storm Breaks – Marine Air Responds • Support to the Air Force, MAG-15 Operations • Support to the Air Force, MAG-12 Operations • Task Force Delta • The Rose Garden Grows

The Storm Breaks – Marine Air Responds

While the 30 March 1972 offensive affected all Marines in Southeast Asia, especially those with Seventh Fleet, it directly triggered the movement of major Marine air units back into Vietnam to reinforce the Seventh Air Force. Major General Robert G. Owens, Jr.'s 1st Marine Aircraft Wing (1st MAW) provided critical attack, fighter, electronic warfare, and support aircraft needed to augment U.S. air in South Vietnam and Thailand. Marine helicopter and fixed wing units of the Seventh Fleet were already off the coast of Vietnam as other units from the 1st MAW moved into action. The wing first organized a large and potent force from its bases in Japan and on Okinawa.[1] The 3 April dispatch of a detachment from Marine Composite Reconnaissance Squadron (VMCJ) 1 to the Naval Air Station, Cubi Point, Philippines, marked the beginning of the reentry of Marine high-performance aircraft to combat in Vietnam.

At FMFPac, Lieutenant General William K. Jones reasoned that while it was unlikely that American ground troops would be recommitted to the fighting, an immediate buildup of tactical air would occur. General Jones, with the CinCPac staff, believed the best response to MACV and South Vietnam's need for more air support could be met by the dual-mission, extended-range McDonnell Douglas F-4 Phantom jets of the 1st MAW. The Phantom was used by both the Navy and the Air Force, which made logistic support of these planes easier than other Marine aircraft types, but as Marine Fighter Attack Squadron (VMFA) 212's Lieutenant Colonel Richard D. Revie observed, they had "very few compatible parts" and even flew different model aircraft in his squadron's case.[2] On 5 April, General Owens received a warning from III MAF's Lieutenant General Louis Metzger to deploy, on order from JCS and CinCPac, two Phantom squadrons to Vietnam to support the Seventh Air Force. General Owens directed VMFA-115 and VMFA-232 to deploy for "training" to Cubi Point; from there they were in position to respond rapidly to the developing situation in South Vietnam.[3]

Overseeing the whole air campaign was Admiral John S. McCain, Jr., and his staff. Previous air operations against North Vietnam were part of CinCPac's Operation Rolling Thunder, which had begun in 1965 and continued until the bombing halt of 1968. After this date, U.S. aircraft operations over North Vietnam were limited to armed reconnaissance, combat air patrols, and protective-reaction sorties. Air attacks continued on Laos, Cambodia, and South Vietnam with increased intensity through the 1972 fighting. Marine air was fitted into existing Navy and Air Force command and control structures that had evolved over the long course of the war. The Southeast Asia Tactical Data System allowed the Air Force's Airborne Tactical Data System and the Navy's Tactical Data System to exchange information throughout Southeast Asia and the Tonkin Gulf. This enabled tactical commanders to control airspace to rendezvous and refuel, and to coordinate with surface and air units.

Together with the interface of aircraft, the Air Force and Navy organized common control measures with the region divided into tactical control areas or route "packages." General John W. Vogt, Jr.'s Seventh Air Force was responsible to General Abrams' MACV for operations in South Vietnam and into Route Package (RP) 1.[A] General Vogt reported to Pacific Air Force's General Lucius D. Clay for Route Packages 5 and 6a. On the Navy side, Vice Admiral Damon W. Cooper of TF 77 answered to Admiral William P. Mack for Seventh Fleet's Route Packages 2, 3, 4, and 6b. A further division existed between the daytime bombing of point targets by the Navy and Air Force and night area bombing by Strategic Air Command B-52s from Guam and Thailand.

Support to the Air Force, MAG-15 Operations

Reinforcement of Seventh Air Force by 1st MAW began with the movement of air units to Cubi Point and ended with an eventual commitment of an estimated total of 4,895 Marines and 120 aircraft. The staging of 12 F-4Bs and 15 F-4Js allowed the 1st MAW commander to deploy his units at short notice.[4] The lead aircraft touched down at Da Nang on 6 April within hours of the orders from 1st MAW. This rapid arrival in Vietnam drew the praise of The White House, the surprise of the Air Force, and the vexation of the Japanese government for supposedly departing for Vietnam from Japanese bases without prior notification.[B][5]

(A) General Vogt was "double-hatted" in April 1972 as Deputy Commander for Air Operations, MACV. In June 1972 he also became Deputy Commander, MACV, as well as Commanding General, Seventh Air Force.

(B) General Metzger takes exception to FMFPac records of Japanese vexation, commenting that all deployments from Japanese bases were to areas other than Vietnam. Once underway, or after arrival at intermediate bases, unit movement was then approved to Vietnam. American commanders in Japan "were well aware of this concern and were careful to comply with this policy" of Japan not being involved in U.S. operations in Vietnam. (Metzger Comments)

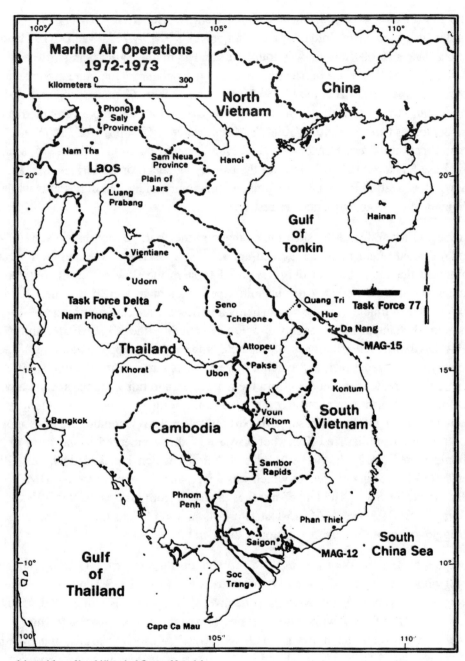

Marine Air Operations
1972-1973

kilometers 0 ——————— 300

Adapted from Naval Historical Center Material

The first Phantoms of Lieutenant Colonel Kent A. McFerren's VMFA-115 "Silver Eagles" and Lieutenant Colonel Joe L. Gregorcyck's VMFA-232 "Red Devils" landed on Da Nang's 10,000-foot runway four hours and 55 minutes after being ordered from the Philippines. The airlift of necessary support personnel and equipment took another four days for a total of 26 aircraft, 984 Marines, and 2,099,702 pounds of cargo. While reinforcing Air Force wings in South Vietnam, the Marine squadrons remained under the control of Colonel Keith O'Keefe's Marine Aircraft Group (MAG) 15 (Forward). Subordinate units were Headquarters and Maintenance Squadron (H&MS) 15, Marine Air Base Squadron (MABS) 15, and the two flying squadrons. Marines in MAG-15 met Vietnamization troop levels by being in temporary additional duty status while in Vietnam, thus avoiding manpower restrictions.

Colonel O'Keefe found the situation changed in the short 10 months since MAG-15 had departed Vietnam under agreed-upon troop reductions. Weather and terrain remained the same, but the flying required to stem the flow of North Vietnamese forces was quite different. After an initial period of maneuver, battle lines became fixed and identifiable from the air as enemy and friendly areas. In northern MR 1 were the mixed elements of the enemy *B-5 Front*, including the *304th, 308th,* and *324B NVA Divisions*, and a number of separate infantry and sapper battalions.[5] These heavily concentrated men and machines were "troops in the open" targets, but also presented a greater risk to flyers from the massed antiaircraft weapons accompanying them. The North Vietnamese employed antiaircraft weapons in quantity to compensate for a lack of air support. Not only were heavy antiaircraft guns moved south of the Demilitarized Zone, but also a new threat emerged in the form of the shoulder-fired SA-7, the Soviet-produced "Grail," which knocked down 27 allied aircraft in 1972, but only one of which was a jet plane.[C] Aircraft near the DMZ were also targets for SA-2 "Guideline" missiles launched from just inside North Vietnam.[7] Flying from Da Nang, MAG-15 lost two F-4s and a TA-4 to these defenses in the struggle to regain lost territory in South Vietnam.[8]

Despite the desperate situation in MR 1, combat operations for MAG-15 did not start until pilots had received in-country indoctrination from the Seventh Air Force in compliance with General Abrams' directives.[D] Preparations completed, combat flights began on 9 April with close air support missions in MR 1 to defend Hue. In the transition between the northeast and southwest monsoon seasons, the weather hampered the Marine missions. Even so, Marine aircraft flew both close and general support in MR 1 near Dong Ha, Quang Tri, and Hue, and in MR 2 near Pleiku,

---

(C) The missile was also known by the Soviet designation "Strella" or arrow. Basically, this threat required helicopters to fly lower and fixed wing aircraft to fly higher than before. Some 27 allied aircraft were downed, compared to a reported 351 SA-7 missile launchings during this period.

(D) Indoctrination included learning rules of engagement, communications procedures, and escape and evasion plans, and receiving friendly and enemy situation briefs.

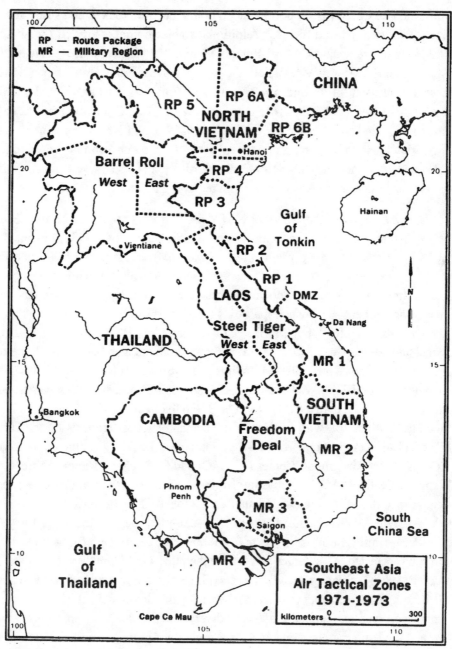

RP — Route Package
MR — Military Region

100
105
110

CHINA

RP 5   RP 6A
NORTH
VIETNAM   RP 6B

Hanoi

Barrel Roll

West   East

RP 4

RP 3

20

20

Gulf
of
Tonkin

Hainan

Vientiane

RP 2

RP 1

LAOS   DMZ

Steel Tiger   Da Nang

West   East

THAILAND

15

MR 1

15

Bangkok

CAMBODIA

SOUTH
VIETNAM

Freedom
Deal

MR 2

Phnom
Penh

MR 3

Saigon

South
China Sea

Gulf
of
Thailand

MR 4

Southeast Asia
Air Tactical Zones
1971-1973

10

10

kilometers 0   300

Cape Ca Mau

100
105
110

N

Adapted from Task Force Delta Material

Kontum, and Phu Cat.[9] This support included bomb, napalm, rocket, and strafe attacks within 200 yards of ground forces.[E] Additional fighter-bombers arrived on 14 April with 12 F-4Js of Lieutenant Colonel Revie's VMFA-212 "Lancers" from Hawaii. On 16 April, five H&MS-15 McDonnell Douglas TA-4Fs came from Japan. These Skyhawks were used for air and naval gunfire spotting missions north of the DMZ. Known as "Fast FACs," the TA-4 detachment flew ANGLICO air observers as naval gunfire spotters and forward air controllers over MR 1 and North Vietnam in areas denied to slower aircraft by antiaircraft fire. Fast-FAC missions soon increased to four each day and continued at that rate until the North Vietnamese shore-based defenses caused the naval gunfire strikes to be conducted at night.[10(F)]

The NVA invasion found the allied air effort in a period of transition from U.S. Air Force to Vietnamese Air Force control. The Tactical Air Control System and Air Ground Operations System operated at reduced levels from the peak of the American involvement, reflecting differences between American and Vietnamese resources. While the direct air support centers and corps-level tactical operations centers were adequate, the tactical air control parties at division and lower unit levels were "generally unsatisfactory by Marine Corps standards."[11] Available ANGLICO personnel and advisors were spread thin on the ground and also had to fulfill the role of forward air controllers. Mission fragging authority resided with MACV's air commander, General John W. Vogt, Jr., of Seventh Air Force, who also was MACV Deputy Commander for Air Operations. The 366th Tactical Fighter Wing at Da Nang provided tactical control, with terminal guidance and support requests by the USAF 20th Tactical Air Control Squadron and the Vietnamese 1st Air Division, collocated in the I Corps Direct Air Support Center (I DASC) and Control and Reporting Center at Da Nang. Typically, MAG-15 would inform the Air Force of the number of sorties it expected to fly the following day. Lieutenant Colonel Revie of VMFA-212 recalled that the Air Force then scheduled targets and take-off times, as they had for years "with little flexibility." Following normal briefings and aircraft preflight procedures, the aircraft proceeded to the target area where the pilot would "link up" with the FAC who controlled the strike on specific targets. Greater use was made of Air Force and ANGLICO airborne controllers to compensate for the deficiency in ground control. For unplanned requirements, aircraft were diverted from scheduled missions. Under this system the sortie rate remained constant regardless of the ground situation.

A study of this air employment by the Marine Corps Operations Analysis Group of the Center for Naval Analyses in 1973 concluded "that Marine Corps tactical air was not

---

(E) "More like *50 meters*," observed Lieutenant General Leslie E. Brown. (Brown Comments)

(F) FMFPac records 87 sorties flown; CNA lists 90. By 3 May 1972, Seventh Fleet and TF 77 felt there was a lack of effective employment to justify the continued use of the TA-4s. Problems encountered were similar to those of helicopter NGF spotting attempts described in Chapter 10.

used as effectively as it might have been had the Marines been fully supported with its own command and control system," especially in the close air support role.[12] The Marines felt there was a better way to do business. Colonel O'Keefe believed that close air support target assignments of 1,500 meters from friendly units were being used out of ignorance of Marine capability to hit safely closer to friendly forces. Another difference under the Air Force system, was that final control remained with the pilot in the aircraft while the Marines placed it with the commander on the ground. All this was compounded by language difficulties when Vietnamese forces were supported.

At Da Nang, base defense was the responsibility of the South Vietnamese and U.S. Air Force Security Police "ground defense forces." Already, 11 Communist attacks by fire had been launched against four South Vietnamese air bases, inflicting 97 casualties and damaging 17 aircraft. Seven of these attacks were against the Da Nang Air Base.[13] MAG-15 was vulnerable to the "standoff" attacks and sapper raids by NVA or VC units. Internal security was MAG-15's responsibility, but the air and ground crews were working around-the-clock with flight operations. Colonel O'Keefe requested additional support to facilitate the mission. Concerned with MAG-15 and the eventual security of MAG-12, General Metzger ordered Major General Joseph C. Fegan's 3d Marine Division to provide security forces from the division's alert units or from the 9th MAB. The task of providing combat forces to the air groups in Vietnam was assigned to 3d Battalion, 9th Marines, which was III MAF's Air Contingency Battalion, then on 24-hour standby on Okinawa. Forces were provided on a "temporary" basis to accommodate personnel ceilings and because "it would be good training."[G][14] Lieutenant Colonel Ronald A. Clark's battalion had been "chaffing at the bit" about being in the rear during the 9th MAB buildup. This new assignment was referred to cryptically as "the mission." The 3d Battalion was going to Vietnam.

Meanwhile, Major General Leslie E. Brown, the new 1st MAW commander, believed that the Seventh Air Force did not make efficient use of MAG-15 because of adherence to fixed flight schedules that kept the Marine sortie rate down.[H] As a result, on 28 April, General Brown proposed to General Metzger that MAG-15 augment the Navy's TF 77 combat air patrol requirements with four sorties a day.[15] While sortie rate had operational applications, it was also viewed by analysts as an important indication of readiness and effectiveness, especially at the JCS level. The rate was greatly influenced by other factors such as combat demands, weather, policies for scheduling, and location. General Brown also cautioned against mistaking sortie rate, bomb damage assessments, and bombing tonnage for effectiveness against the enemy, as the air strikes were in high threat areas where post-strike observation was impractical — obscured by smoke and not verified by

---

(G) This also served to avoid the appearance of "The Marines have landed" for political reasons in an election year and also demonstrated respect for Thai sensibilities.

(H) Sortie rate is the average number of combat missions flown per aircraft per day.

ground units. And finally, there was a dependence upon airborne forward air controllers who operated under different limitations than did ground-based tactical air control parties.[16]

While MAG-15 flew daily combat missions in MR 1 and MR 2, 1st MAW prepared plans in May to move the group to another location. A compelling consideration was the possible loss of MR 1 with the fall of Quang Tri City and the subsequent Communist drive on Hue.[17] As additional Air Force units arrived from the United States, Marine squadrons were logical candidates for withdrawal from Vietnam.[I] The situation in Vietnam and Southeast Asia, however, did not permit the Marine air units to return to their home stations; most units were redeployed within the region to continue the support of the South Vietnamese. The question faced by General Metzger and the 1st MAW commander, General Brown, was "where?"[J] When this was decided, the "how" took care of itself.

While this was underway, the situation in Quang Tri and Bien Hoa Provinces required General Metzger to move security forces to South Vietnam. On 25 May, the advance party of Company M, 9th Marinesarrived at Da Nang to protect MAG-15. By 4 June, 365 Marines of Companies M and L, 9th Marines were deployed as ground security forces. The infantry Marines did not have long to settle in, as MAG-15 (Forward) was scheduled to vacate Da Nang by 15 June for Thailand.[K][18]

Support to the Air Force, MAG-12 Operations

The North Vietnamese attack towards Saigon in April resulted in the fall of Loc Ninh and a "siege" of the provincial capital, An Loc. There was a single squadron of Air Force Cessna A-37 Dragonflies to support operations in MR 3, other air support coming from TF 77 aircraft carriers and from Thailand. The situation at An Loc required dedicated close air support aircraft and this requirement was met by the dependable A-4E Skyhawks of Marine Aircraft Group 12 (Forward). Soon after 1st MAW deployed fighters to Da Nang, General Metzger issued a warning order to General Brown to send squadrons to Bien Hoa Air Base north of Saigon.[19] Lieutenant Colonel Willis E. Wilson's "Avengers" of Marine Attack Squadron (VMA) 211 and Lieutenant Colonel Kevin M. Johnston's "Tomcats" of VMA-311 were sent "on a training mission" to forward bases in the Philippines in anticipation of going to Vietnam.[20] This began the second major deployment of 1st MAW aircraft on independent operations, providing support to embattled MR 3 and An Loc.

(I) From the June 1972 ceiling of 60,000 Americans in Vietnam, MACV allocated the Marines 1,383 billets, a number to be reached by 1 July.

(J) FMFPac's General Jones had been General Brown's battalion commander in World War II, when General Brown had been an infantry officer.

(K) Replacement personnel for Companies L and M were made from 3d Marine Division to MAG-15. Company I remained with MAG-12 at Bien Hoa until its departure from Vietnam in 1973.

General Brown issued movement orders on 16 May for 10 A-4s at Naval Air Station Cubi Point and 22 aircraft at Marine Corps Air Station, Iwakuni. Commitment orders were sent on 17 May. That same day Marine Skyhawks came up on TACAN[L] Channel 73 of "BNH" and began the approach to Bien Hoa's 10,000-foot runway, the first of 32 A-4s to arrive "in country."[M] Supporting elements of MAG-12 followed with Military Airlift Command (MAC) C-141 and C-130 flights delivering 870 Marines and material of H&MS-12 and MABS-12 Detachments. General Brown remembered the MAC airplanes arriving at Iwakuni literally "from all over the world. It was an absolutely superior performance."[21]

With a crisis at hand, the Marines of MAG-12 found themselves fully committed to the defense of Saigon.[22] Fortunately, Bien Hoa Air Base was a fully developed Vietnamese and U.S. Air Force base with support facilities, riveted parking aprons, and rocket resistant "Wonder-Arch" hangars.[N] Flight indoctrination by the USAF 8th Special Operations Squadron at Bien Hoa started that day with orientation flights over MR 3 in Air Force A-37s. Lieutenant Colonel Wilson noted the first death of a group pilot "on one of these orientation/strike missions."[23]

A gradual buildup of the group's sortie rate began on 19 May and reached 36 flights a day by the end of the month.[24] Like their fellow Marines in MAG-15, the aircrews of MAG-12 found themselves with a variety of singular missions and situations. Three NVA divisions were advancing upon the provincial capital of An Loc. Enemy forces included the *5th, 7th,* and *9th NVA Divisions, 33d NVA Infantry Regiment, 274th VC Regiment,* and the *74B NVA Regiment.*[25] The Communist use of conventional military forces resulted in a plethora of targets, including fixed positions, vulnerable road and bridge networks, and exposed logistical areas. There were tanks and armored personnel carriers, as well as the ubiquitous SA-7 and other antiaircraft weapons in locations and densities not experienced heretofore in Vietnam.

The 3d Regional Assistance Command under Major General James F. Hollingsworth, USA, at Long Binh, and the ARVN III Corps and 3d AirDivision at Bien Hoa, controlled operations. The MAG supported the 5th ARVN Division, 21st ARVN Division, 3d ARVN Ranger Group, and the 3d ARVN Armored Brigade. Air control was by the DASC at Bien Hoa, the TACC at Tan Son Nhut, and by the 21st Air Support Squadron and VNAF flying airborne FACs out of Tan Son Nhut. MAG-12's mission was part of a massive employment of tactical air power that included B-52, AC-130,

---

(L) Tactical Air Navigation (TACAN), ultra-high frequency, pulse-type, omni-directional range and distance measuring equipment used in air control.

(M) As with the MAG-15 move, MAG-12's sooner-than-expected appearance "in country" was noticed by JCS and others in the chain of command.

(N) The "Wonder Arch" hangars were constructed from pre-fabricated metal frames covered with sprayed-on concrete to provide overhead protection to aircraft and maintenance facilities.

A-37, A-1E, F-4, and helicopter gunships of the American and Vietnamese forces. This required "superhuman" efforts on the part of airborne air controllers to manage from their light observation aircraft, which, according to General Brown, they did "like real Pros."[(0)26]

American aircraft provided close and direct air support using bombs, rockets, and cannon. The highly maneuverable A-4, with speed and stability, was the ideal aircraft for accurate and responsive close air support. The ARVN defenders of An Loc and their American advisors praised the Marine air support which continued until other ARVN units reopened highway QL-13, labeled the "Road of Death" by the Communists.[27] Most operations were from 5 to 50 miles from Bien Hoa. MAG-12's Colonel Dean C. Macho recalled at times "... it was common to see, hear, and feel air strikes flown by MAG-12 A-4s as close as three to five miles from the field." This served as an incentive to the Marines who kept the aircraft flying.[28] Later, air operations expanded to cover MR 4 and Cambodia. Operations were even flown to MR 2 with the addition of a second external fuel tank and a reduced bomb load, or aerial refueling.

Because of the proximity of the fighting and the continued withdrawal of neighboring American units, Colonel Macho considered ground defense of the base to be his number one problem. The lack of ground forces and the constant threat of rocket attacks could not be adequately countered by his Marines.[29] At the request of 1st MAW, General Metzger ordered a rifle company from 3d Battalion, 9th Marines sent TAD (temporary additional duty) to Bien Hoa for 90 days. On 21 May, five officers, and 161 Marines of Company K, 9th Marines found themselves as part of MAG-12. Captain Nathaniel R. Hoskot, Jr., and his company began their stay by moving the company into prepared defensive positions, setting up crew-served weapons, and securing the group area. If needed, the South Vietnamese were to provide supporting-arms fire. By way of a welcome, on 23 May, the enemy struck MAG-12 with its first rocket attack.

MAG-12's sortie rate increased to 52 sorties a day in July.[30] Generals Abrams and Vogt, requested that VMA-211 and VMA-311 be retained in Vietnam despite continuing withdrawals of American forces.[31] The sortie and availability rate was the direct result of the support and maintenance efforts of MAG-12 ground crews. These Marines kept the planes in the air with a 12-hours-day, seven-days-a-week effort. Sergeant Warren F. Winn, an ordnance man with VMA-211, explained the accomplishment:

---

(0) For example, 1,077 fighter-bomber sorties had been allocated by MACV to An Loc and MR 3 alone from 11 through 14 May 1972.

> ... when we first arrived here and weren't in the groove of working
> together we had a hell of a time keeping up. As soon as we would load a
> plane they'd take it away and we'd start all over from scratch. Now
> working as a team, we are able to stay just one step ahead no matter what.[32]

Lieutenant General William K. Jones commented that "Performance of this excellence does not just happen, it results from superior leadership, a high degree of professional competence, team work and a lot of hard work."[33]

MAG-12's effort was not lost on the Communists, who subjected the Bien Hoa Air Base to continuing attacks beginning in August in an effort to disrupt flight operations.[34] The heaviest attack consisted of 101 rockets on 1 August that killed one Marine, wounded six others, and damaged the MAG-12 supply, headquarters, and operations areas.[35] The Vietnamese and Americans repaired the runway and flights, although delayed, continued. Since the rockets had come from the north, the pilots took off and worked over an area five miles north of the base that day. The attack reminded the group of the value of dispersion and individual security measures and resulted in a major effort to sandbag working and living spaces.[(P)]

The group logistics officer, Major Angelo M. Inglisa, wrote that it was surprising the attack was not more damaging: "The NVA/VC apparently tried to use the rockets as artillery and aimed for point targets," rather than employing the rockets "as area weapons as designed." He reflected a belief held within MAG-12 that civilian contract construction workers had surveyed the base for the Communists to locate targets prior to the attack.[36]

On 10 August, the initial elements of Company I, 9th Marines, arrived to assume the group security mission from Company K, which was returned to Okinawa. Captain Michael S. Kelly, the company commander, understood that this rotation of units would occur every few months, but events proved otherwise and his company stayed with MAG-12 until the end. Base defense was a "tripartite" affair with the Vietnamese Air Force Base Defense Force, the U.S. Air Force Security Police Squadron, and the Marine Security Element of MAG-12. Kelly wrote that, "I worked closely with Colonel Dean Macho and our Air Force Security Police counterparts to enhance base security."[37] "India 3/9" brought with them a section of mortars, trucks, and a detachment from the 3d Marine Division's Sensor Control and Management Platoon. According to Kelly, they "used various types of surveillance devices to enhance base security, specifically outside the ammunition dump." The mission was tedious, but necessary and these ground Marines "learned the tough tasks that the 'air-wing' Marines had."[38]

(P) Of the more than 800 rockets that hit Bien Hoa over the nine month period, 417 rockets hit in the MAG-12 area, killing two and wounding eight Marines; six A-4s were damaged.

The adjacent VNAF ordnance dump blew up on 10 September, wounding four Marines and damaging the MAG-12 supply building with the blast and debris.[39] Unable to determine the cause of this disaster, Colonel Macho, nevertheless, organized additional reaction forces of two 30-man "platoons" made up of maintenance and support personnel. These ad hoc units deployed at night in billeting and flight-line areas. Four A-4s were kept armed and fueled on 15-minute strip alert for support. With these precautions, the air war continued.

For Captain James P. "Waldo" Walsh of VMA-211, 26 September began as other days at Bien Hoa. The 26-year-old A-4 pilot from Hartford, Connecticut, had been flying combat missions with his squadron since arriving in Vietnam in June. His mission was to hit the heart of enemy-held territory near An Loc, the Quan Loi Airfield, an area known by MAG-12 pilots for the density of antiaircraft fire ranging from small arms to 37mm AAA. After preflight and take-off, Captain Walsh and his wingman met the airborne FAC near the operating area and were given a target.

After Walsh pulled out of his bomb run, his A-4E was hit by multiple rounds of gunfire. The Skyhawk shook uncontrollably and the controls went slack. When his instrument panel warning lights went red, Walsh instinctively pulled his ejection handle. According to a Marine report, the "stricken A-4 was emitting sheets of flame from the tailpipe and had pitched violently nose down as the pilot ejected." With a good parachute canopy overhead, he looked around at the rapidly approaching rubber plantation for signs of the NVA and a lay up position to take until help could arrive. The FAC lost sight of Captain Walsh's parachute as it disappeared through the tree tops. With no visual contact and only an intermittent "beeper" radio signal, the SAR helicopter recovery team had little to go on when it arrived. The lead helicopter was struck by ground fire and turned back from the area and with approaching darkness the SAR effort was postponed. Local thunderstorms even drove the airborne FAC away from Quon Loi that night.[40]

Captain Walsh hit the deck in the middle of a Communist campsite. Shrugging out of his parachute harness, he dodged through the rubber trees for about one hundred meters before being surrounded and trapped. In this standoff he had a single choice, surrender or die. Later he made a brief attempt to escape by diving underwater during a stream crossing. A Communist soldier waited for him to surface and took him prisoner. Captain Walsh was listed as missing in action by his squadron. Walsh, however, was neither missing nor dead, he was the last Marine to be captured by the North Vietnamese Communists.[(Q)][41]

Anticipated ground attacks at Bien Hoa failed to materialize, but on 22 October, the Communists fired 61 rockets onto the base. Colonel Macho considered the group's

---

(Q) Captain Walsh was released by the Communists in 1973. See Chapter 15.

effort at civic action to be a factor in limiting attacks on the base. Based on MAG-12's previous experience at Chu Lai, the group provided support to a local orphanage and children's hospital at Ke-Sat.[42]

Fall weather hindered the bombing effort and required using Air Force LORAN, TACAN, and other expedients, to put ordnance on target. Maintenance crews activated a then-dormant avionics component of the A-4E, first in VMA-211 and then VMA-311. A combination of training and maintenance with this system allowed continued support during periods of reduced visibility by enabling the aircraft to pull out of high-angle dives at 6,000 feet.[43]

Marine Aircraft Group 12 flew its 10,000th combat sortie on 9 December 1972, after having averaged 49 combat sorties a day over a seven-month period. By year's end, MAG-12 had completed combat operations, flying 12,574 combat sorties totaling 15,214 hours and dropping 18,903 tons of ordnance. Combat losses included three A-4s, three Marines killed, one missing, and 11 wounded.[44] Secretary of the Navy John W. Warner cited MAG-12's efforts during the battles to defend Hue, Kontum, and An Loc, when the group "provided close air support within 50 meters of friendly positions, contributing materially to the success of the allied effort in these campaigns."[45]

Task Force Delta

While MAG-15 and MAG-12 conducted operations from Da Nang and Bien Hoa, the 1st MAW completed efforts to relocate a portion of these units outside of South Vietnam. Initial relocation sites included Udorn, Ubon, and Utapao in Thailand. These bases were operating at maximum capacity with Air Force units, and the search also considered other locations. Fifteen miles northeast of the town of Khon Kaen, Thailand, was a 10,000-foot concrete runway built by the U.S. Air Force in 1967. Used as an emergency landing field and little else, it was situated centrally 340 miles west of Da Nang and 300 miles southwest of Hanoi. General Brown recalled:

> ... when we started gluing this thing together, there were just three or
> four guys who were in on it from the beginning. Brigadier General
> [Andrew W.] Andy O'Donnell, who was my assistant wing commander
> at the time, and a couple of other guys asking each other where the hell
> is Nam Phong? So we spread out the maps on the floor of my office and
> got down on our hands and knees and finally located the place.[(R) 46]

Maps and old intelligence reports indicated to General Brown that "there just wasn't anything there." There was no power, little water, fuel would have to come from the ports at Utapao and Sattahip by truck, and it was barely within flying range of MR 1

(R) Both Generals Brown and O'Donnell later commanded FMFPac.

for MAG-15's fighters. From General Brown's perspective "... All the place had really was a runway and nothing else except a lot of rain, a lot of heat, and a lot of logistical problems to be resolved."[47] The location did have a greater degree of physical security than Da Nang, was large enough to accommodate the entire MAG, and it was usable for operations if aircraft were refueled in the air or on the ground in MR 1.

On 11 May, Admiral Thomas H. Moorer and the JCS approved the plan to move MAG-15 to Thailand, specifying that the opening of Nam Phong would be on an "austere" basis — which was "a gross understatement," according to General Brown. On 14 May, a planning conference was held on Okinawa by General Metzger with 1st Marine Aircraft Wing, 3d Marine Division, and 3d Force Service Support Regiment to consider the task. The immediate result was to send a survey team headed by Brigadier General O'Donnell, the assistant wing commander, to Thailand to determine existing facilities and to coordinate with the U.S. Embassy, the Military Advisory Command, Thailand (MACThai), Seventh Air Force, and other supporting agencies.

General O'Donnell and a Marine and Navy staff arrived in Thailand on 18 May, went to Bangkok, and then on to Nam Phong. There they found a runway, taxiway, parking apron, six Butler buildings, and an 8,000-square foot hangar. As General Brown had expected, the main challenges to operations were logistical. Nam Phong was a U.S. Special Forces camp for the training of Laotian irregulars, who occupied the existing buildings and had constructed six other structures and training facilities. The 50 or so U.S. Army "Green Berets" and other advisors present found their pastoral surroundings altered by the arrival of the Marines. General O'Donnell concluded from his inspection that Nam Phong had potential for MAG-15 operations, but would require extensive development for the 60-to-90 day deployment envisioned by Admirals McCain and Moorer. While in Thailand, O'Donnell negotiated terms of occupancy as a "Royal Thai Air Base" and arranged support agreements with the U.S. Army Support Activity, Thailand, for a logistical base through the port of Sattahip. General O'Donnell then returned to Japan and briefed General Brown on what was needed to support MAG-15.

A special organization, designated Task Force Delta (TF Delta), was formed at Iwakuni, Japan, on 24 May 1972, and it remained in existence until well after the end of the American involvement in Vietnam. General O'Donnell commanded the task force with a mission of opening the base at Nam Phong and assuming control of MAG-15. His initial task was to make the airfield ready to support tactical flight operations. This was undertaken by U.S. Navy Mobile Construction Battalion 5, MABS-15, and H&MS-15. General O'Donnell also maintained liaison with Seventh Air Force, the Royal Thai Air Force, and the Military Advisory Command Thailand (MACThai).

A KC-130 tanker from Marine Aerial Refueler Transport Squadron (VMGR) 152 arrived at Nam Phong on 24 May with 39 Marines, beginning the buildup of forces to over 3,200 men. The establishment of a U.S. Air Force aerial port detachment triggered the airlift of the advance party of 377 Marines, 94 U.S. Navy "Seabees," 3 civilians, and 1,399 tons of material by MAC C-141s and C-5 transports.[S][48]

Construction began at once on 310 strong-back huts, 128 administrative and maintenance structures, a bomb dump, a 200,000 gallon Tactical Aviation Fuel Dispensing system, and storage for 360,000 gallons of bulk fuel.[T][49] Generals Brown and O'Donnell developed a deep respect for the "Seabees," the majority of whom arrived by ship and trucked inland to Nam Phong. Brown recalled "they worked hard and fast and never quit" on the base construction.[50]

The movement of MAG-15 aircraft began on 16 June when 11 F4Bs of VMFA-115 launched from Da Nang, completed air strikes enroute, and landed at Nam Phong. They began flying sorties from Nam Phong on 17 June.[51] By 20 June, VMFA-232 and Marine All-Weather Attack Squadron (VMA[AW]) 533 also arrived at Nam Phong. The A-6As "Hawks" of VMA(AW)-533 provided MAG-15 with an all-weather and night capability of 12 aircraft. Additional aircraft came from VMGR-152 Detachment Delta's four KC-130s for aerial refueling and a H&MS-36 Detachment of four CH-46s for search and rescue. By 30 June Task Force Delta consisted of 17 F-4s, 12 A-6s, 4 KC-130s, and 4 CH-46s.[U] In view of the JCS directed "austere" nature of this deployment, General Jones at FMFPac and General Brown at 1st MAW were personally involved with the "somewhat overwhelming" logistics support required, particularly for the A-6s.[52]

As it turned out, the A-6A proved its worth during this deployment with "full-systems" readiness. Lieutenant Colonel James C. Brown, the A-6 squadron commander, believed the deployment of MAG-15 reinforced the expeditionary capability of the U.S. Marines in an age of sophisticated aircraft and "especially sophisticated" ground support equipment with all its specific power and environment requirements. "The A-6 aircraft required a higher degree of ground support facilities than either the F-4 or A-4. These requirements were met at Nam Phong after a difficult start-up period." Lieutenant Brown credits this accomplishment to the innovation, perseverance, and hard work of individual Marines.[V][53]

(S) The combined movement of MAG-15, MCB-5, Logistics Support Group Delta, and supporting detachments to Nam Phong required 278 aircraft loads to move 6,259 tons of material and 2,064 passengers to make the field operational.

(T) The type and priority of construction are detailed in CNA MarActySEA, pp. 95-96.

(U) The TA-4 "Fast Fac" Detachment with MAG-15 returned to Iwakuni, Japan, and VMFA-212 returned to Hawaii instead of going to Thailand.

(V) Lieutenant Colonel Brown, VMA (AW)-533's commander, highlighted the joining of an attack squadron to be a fighter group as a classic example of Marine task organization. But, "there were some subtle lessons to be learned from integrating our attack orientation with a fighter oriented aircraft group." (Brown Comments)

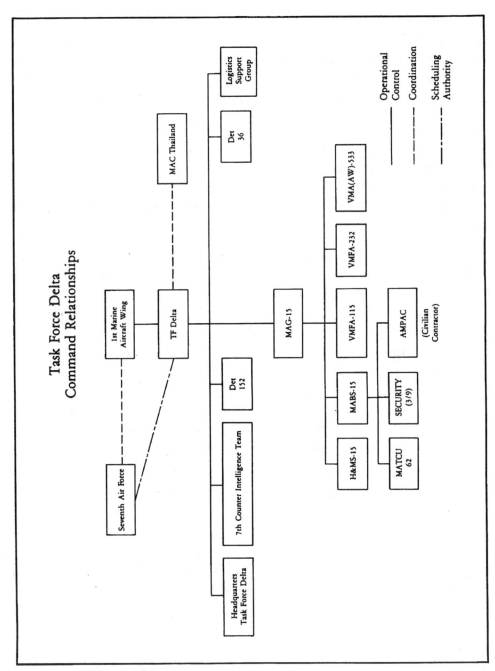

Task Force Delta
Command Relationships

Operational Control
Coordination
Scheduling Authority

1st Marine Aircraft Wing

TF Delta

MAC Thailand

Det 36

Logistics Support Group

Seventh Air Force

Headquarters Task Force Delta

7th Counter Intelligence Team

Det 152

MAG-15

H&MS-15

MABS-15

VMFA-115

VMFA-232

VMA(AW)-533

MATCU 62

SECURITY (3/9)

AMPAC (Civilian Contractor)

Adapted from Task Force Delta Material

The deployment and activation of TF Delta accomplished, the Commandant, General Robert E. Cushman, Jr., noted:

> .... such an achievement was made possible only through the team work of dedicated professionals and numerous personal sacrifices. This matter is of considerable pride to me and should be a source of great individual self-satisfaction.[54]

While the activation of Nam Phong stands as an accomplishment in its own right, ultimately its significance rests on the purpose for which it was constructed, the destruction of Communist forces. General Vogt tasked General O'Donnell with conducting air operations over North and South Vietnam. For General O'Donnell this meant finding out what the Air Force wanted, as well as ensuring that General Vogt understood the capabilities of MAG-15's pilots and planes. What resulted from this interaction with the Seventh Air Force was a variety of new tasks and missions for Marine aircrews. General O'Donnell personally flew F-4 combat missions which earned him great credibility with the pilots of the task force and when discussing operational matters with the Air Force.[W]

The distance from MR 1 required airborne refueling and landing at Da Nang. The average flight time increased from one to two hours and the ordnance load was reduced by 500 pounds to compensate for extra fuel. Support of operations from Nam Phong required three H&MS-15 detachments to "turn around" aircraft: Detachment Alpha at Da Nang to rearm and refuel, Detachment Bravo at Cubi Point for maintenance work, and Detachment Charlie at Iwakuni for administrative and logistical liaison with 1st MAW.[55] Detachment Alpha started at Da Nang on 3 July, increasing mission and sortie rate. On 8 July 1972, TFD aircraft intercepted two Communist MiG-19 Farmers over North Vietnam, the task force's first air-to-air encounter with the enemy in its new area of operations.[56]

Ground security considerations for the task force were different from those at Da Nang and Bien Hoa. Although Companies L and M, 9th Marines, moved into Thailand with MAG-15, Nam Phong's location removed the immediate threat of ground attack that had existed in South Vietnam. The infantry Marines were formed into the TF Delta security element and designated "Sub Unit 1" (SU1) of MABS-15.[57] The commanding officer was Major John M. Campanelli, an experienced infantry officer, assisted by Captain Philip F. Reynolds as executive officer and Captain Thomas D. Martin as operations officer.[58] The Sub Unit consisted of 11 officers and 363 Marines organized along the lines of a small infantry battalion — rifle companies with headquarters and service company support, including communications, 81mm mortars, motor transport, and medical sections. Its mission was to provide base

---

(W) An unspoken consideration was the clear risk of his becoming a prisoner if downed.

security and military police support to the task force. The Marines were armed with the full range of small arms, but were restricted to illumination rounds from their M79 grenade launchers and mortars. With no known external threat, Major Campanelli concentrated his efforts on interior guard and security of vital areas: the fuel and ordnance dumps, the flight line, and maintenance facilities. Guard towers, bunkers, barbed wire and chain-link security fences were built to control the perimeter and vital areas. The size of the base required more men for guards than SU1 could provide and it was augmented by MABS-15 and the flying squadrons. After the initial 90-day TAD period passed for the "Grunts," Headquarters Marine Corps assigned infantry replacements directly to 1st MAW. Major Campanelli hired 100 Thai auxiliary security guards from the Special Forces Camp to augment the Marines and, on 30 July, 12 guard dogs arrived.

The Rose Garden Grows

Task Force Delta air operations were of three distinct types: day fighter-cover, day ground-attack, and night ground-attack. These missions in turn were associated with specific geographic areas and targets. Most numerous were daytime flights supporting MACV and the South Vietnamese in MR 1, MR 2, and Route Package 1 during the combat to regain Quang Tri Province. These tasks were conducted with F-4s and A-6s using bombs, rockets, and cannon fire. Sorties normally consisted of two or three aircraft each. Daily the aircraft lined up on Nam Phong's single runway with engines screaming at 100 percent power as the pilots checked engine instruments. Each aircraft then took off in turn and quickly rendezvoused on its climb out to the target area. Many of the Marine flights hit a target, flew to Da Nang to refuel and rearm, and then flew another mission on the return to Nam Phong.

Fighter cover was in support of the ongoing strikes by Seventh Air Force against the North Vietnamese political and economic infrastructure. The strikes, which had begun on 8 May, were part of an extensive naval and air campaign to pressure the North Vietnamese into a negotiated settlement. The campaign included the mining of harbors, attacks against economic targets, the use of precision-guided munitions ("smart bombs"), and a massive increase in the size and duration of strikes with the aim of reducing the flow of supplies into North Vietnam and support to operations in South Vietnam. In contrast to the previous, graduated campaigns, commanders took all necessary steps to ensure target destruction.[X][59]

(X) The final analysis of air power in the Linebacker Campaign of 1972 is outside the scope of this study. The U.S. Air Force review of this section questioned whether the difference between Rolling Thunder and Linebacker was one of target destruction or a shift from attacking the economy to disrupting the storage and distribution of supplies. (Bernard C. Nalty, comment on draft ms, 3Jan90 [Vietnam Comment File])

Marine F-4s conducted combat air patrols to protect support aircraft from North Vietnamese reaction. This required them to fly a specified orbit point from which to cover tanker, command and control, electronic warfare, and rescue aircraft over Route Packages 4, 5, and 6. From orbit points they could track and engage North Vietnamese interceptors and air defense positions. The Marine KC-130s refueled the fighters going in and coming out. These missions witnessed Marine air integrated with the Air Force in air-to-air and deep-penetration flight profiles.[60]

The interdiction of roads and trails in the Barrel Roll and Steel Tiger areas of Laos were the missions assigned the VMA(AW)-533 crews with their night armed reconnaissance abilities. Lieutenant Colonel Brown wrote his squadron "... began interdicting convoys on Route Package 1 on 12 August and, like our entire effort, it was relentless. To the enemy, this incessant bludgeoning was crippling ...."[61] First Lieutenant Gary W. Dolgin described the aircraft and men engaged in these night flights in 1972:

> Aircraft 155707 ... has a long shadow cast behind her indicating a time late in the afternoon. She sits quietly, fueled, armed, and with power unit attached. In a few hours a crew of one pilot and one bombardier-navigator will walk out to her. The sun will have since set. The crew will do a pre-flight inspection, strap in, fire up, check out the entire aircraft system, and take off. An hour or so later they will be inside North Vietnam terrain following at 420 knots over mountains and down in valleys headed for a target regardless of weather.[62]

General O'Donnell passed command of Task Force Delta to Brigadier General Robert W. Taylor on 23 August. Three days later, VMFA-232 lost an aircraft to a MiG-21 Fishbed over Laos. Both crewmembers ejected — the intercept officer was recovered and the pilot was missing in action.[63] Colonel Aubrey W. "Tal" Talbert, Jr., commanding MAG-15, reported that to support the continued effort, the "... maintenance and supply effort to provide the full system aircraft needed in the hostile skies of North Vietnam has been substantial."[64] For maintenance crews, the beginning and end of all efforts was to get their pilots and planes in the air on time, "the primary objective to achieve a Marine aerial victory over enemy aircraft."[65] Life in Nam Phong or the "Rose Garden,"[Y] as it was now popularly known by its Marine occupants, revolved around the cycle of fragging, scheduling, briefing, arming, fueling, launch, and recovery activities that always appeared at odds with the normal routine of living. The routines of day, night, sleep, meals, and the calendar had relatively little meaning in the operational and maintenance cycles of air units at war.

(Y) A nickname Nam Phong acquired from a contemporary Marine recruiting slogan, "We Don't Promise You A Rose Garden," and a popular song by Lynn Anderson with similar lyrics. General Metzger observed a single scraggly rose bush planted in the middle of the camp, "with typical Marine humor." (Metzger Comments)

The need for adequate ground security was highlighted by terrorist attacks on Ubon and Udorn Air Bases in October. Concern for base security was at its peak at Nam Phong, recalled First Lieutenant George R. "Ross" Dunham of VMGR-152 Detachment Delta, when the sound of an explosion from the flight line brought cries of "Incoming, hit the bunkers!" from the billeting area. When the smoke had cleared, investigation determined that the accidental discharge of an air-to-ground rocket had occurred in the arming area.[66] The ground threats to the safety of TF Delta remained self-induced or those from the burgeoning local "black market" and economic enterprises outside the base. Major Kent C. Bateman, the VMA(AW)-533 executive officer, believed that this situation precluded a real sense of involvement by the enlisted Marines. As only the aircrews experienced combat, "there was little sense of urgency by the ground and support personnel."[67]

When Major Kenneth N. Zike took command of MABS-15's Sub Unit 1 on 26 November, it had expanded to include 200 Thai auxiliaries. Patrolling outside of the perimeter, out to 16 kilometers from the base, was now the responsibility of Thai military forces, because of the reluctance of the Thai Supreme Command to allow the U.S. Marines a ground combat role in Thailand. General Taylor and Royal Thai Air Force Special Colonel Supot, the base commander, signed a joint base defense plan at the year's end, alleviating the remaining security concerns. This plan tasked SU 1 with manning 27 bunkers and towers of the internal defensive position. The Thais manned the remaining 53 positions. Lighting and fencing continued to be installed and improved by the Marines. Two mobile reaction platoons were formed: one established near the combat operations center and the other at the bomb storage area. MABS-15 provided an additional civil disturbance platoon for riot duty.

With the arrival of the fall monsoon weather, conditions for visual delivery of ordnance declined. For the F-4s this meant level bombing using release points obtained from TACAN cuts, LORAN-equipped aircraft, and USAF Combat Skyspot control stations.[68] The A-6s continued to operate day and night over the roads and trails of Route Package 1.[69] By now, at the political level, Linebacker operations and successful South Vietnamese resistance brought the North Vietnamese to the negotiating table. Operations continued through the 23 October halt of bombing North Vietnam above the 20th Parallel. The Seventh Air Force noted in November that VMFA-115 and VMFA-232 had the highest sortie rate of any land-based F-4 units in Southeast Asia.[70] The offensive operations resumed with all-out air attacks against the North beginning on 18 December, and continued until combat flights in Vietnam ceased at year's end.[71]

Statistics can only indicate the magnitude of the effort by TF Delta and MAG-15. Figures only implied the human costs and achievements of the aircrews and men who kept them operating; the personnel of Task Force Delta contributed toward the South Vietnamese defense and the U.S. air offensive of 1972.[72] The North Vietnamese Army's transition to mobile warfare made it dependent on fuel, ammunition, and other supplies that were vulnerable to destruction from the air. In the resulting battle of attrition, airpower had a crushing effect on the enemy. Vice Admiral James B. Stockdale, USN, as a prisoner of war and an eyewitness to American airpower from the North Vietnamese capital in 1972, stated that, "If I learned nothing else during the eight years in wartime Hanoi, it was that Clausewitz is as right today as he was during the Napoleonic Wars; the name of the game in war is to break the enemy's will."[73] This was the stated purpose of airpower. The North Vietnamese relied, however, on Ho Chi Minh's rejoinder to the air effort: "Hanoi, Haiphong, and other cities and certain enterprises may be destroyed, but the Vietnamese people will not be intimidated! Nothing is more precious than independence and freedom!"[74]

CHAPTER ELEVEN ENDNOTES

Unless otherwise noted material in this chapter is derived from: FMFPac MarOpsSEA; CNA MarActySEA; Seventh Air Force Command Histories 1972 and 1973, hereafter SeventhAF ComdHist; 1st MAW AAR on TF Delta dtd 6Jan75, hereafter TFD AAR; MAG-12 and 15 ComdC, Apr-Dec72; and Assistant Secretary of Defense (Comptroller), U.S. Aircraft Losses in SEA, Hostile Action, dtd 17Oct73, hereafter OSAD(C) AirLoss. See also LtCol John J. Lane, Jr., *Command and Control and Communications Structures in Southeast Asia*, (Maxwell AFB, Air University, 1981); Gen William W. Momyer, *The Vietnamese Air Force*, 1951–1975, Monograph 4 (Washington, D.C., OAFH, 1975); BGen James R. McCarthy and LtCol George B. Allison, *Linebacker II: The View From the Rock*, Monograph 8 (Washington, D.C.: Office of Air Force History, 1979); Carl Berger, ed., *The United States Air Force in Southeast Asia*, (Washington, D.C.: Office of Air Force History, 1977); and USAF, *Air War-Vietnam*, (New York: Arno Press, 1978).

The Storm Breaks – Marine Air Responds

1   MCCC, Status of Forces, dtd 30Mar72. See also SeventhAF, The USAF Response to the Spring 1972 Offensive: Situation & Redeployment, Project CHECO report dtd 10Oct72, hereafter CHECO Redeployment.

2   Col Richard D. Revie, comments on draft ms, dtd 20Dec89 (Vietnam Comment File).

3   Metzger comments; MGen Leslie E. Brown, 1st Marine Aircraft Wing Achievements and Milestones, dtd 8Apr76, pp. 1-2, 7, hereafter Brown (Vietnam Comment File). LtCol Curtis G. Arnold, "1st Marine Air Wing Supports Operations in Vietnam," hereafter Arnold (ms, MCHC, Washington, D.C., 1976), p. 2; Col Albert R. Pytko, "An Epoch of Need," *Marine Corps Gazette*, May73, pp. 194–200.

Support to the Air Force, MAG-15 Operations

4   ComSeventhFlt msg to CG1stMAW dtd 6Apr72 (Vietnam Comment File).

5   FMFPac MarOpsSEA, p. 2-19 to 2-20, Brown, 1-2.

6   FRAC Intsum 125-72, dtd 3May72 (Vietnam Comment Files).

7   CNA MarActySEA, pp. 109-111; AFSpComCen msg to CinCPac dtd 5Sep72 (Vietnam Comment File).

8   MAG-15 ComdC, Jul72, p. 6.

9   MCCC, Climatology Study, dtd 18Nov70.

10   FMFPac MarOpsSEA, pp. 2-25, 3-20; CNA MarActySEA, pp. 17-18.

11   LtGen Leslie E. Brown, Comments on draft ms, dtd 11Feb90 (Vietnam Comment File).

12   CNA MarActySEA, p. 94.

13   LtCol Roger P. Fox, *Air Base Defense in the Republic of Vietnam, 1961–1973*, (Washington, D.C.: Office of Air Force History, 1979, p. 201, hereafter *Base Defense*. See also MACV/EACSJ2, "VC/NVA Rocket Artillery," 1967 (PersPapers, MCHC, Washington, D.C.).

14 Arnold, p. 5.

15 CNA MarActySEA, pp. 85-91; this covers the sortie rate buildup in detail.

16 1stMAW SitRpt dtd 20May72 (Vietnam Comment File).

17 TFD AAR, pp. 1-1 to 1-3.

18 3/9 ComdC, Jun72, p. 5; Dec72, pp. 3-4; and Jun73, p. 3.

Support to the Air Force, MAG-12 Operations
19 III MAF msg to 1stMAW dtd 12May72 (Vietnam Comment File).

20 Brown comments.

21 Ibid.

22 SeventhAF, "The Battle for An Loc, 5 April-26 June 1972," Project CHECO Report, dtd 31Jan73, hereafter CHECO AnLoc.

23 LtCol Willis E. Wilson, Jr., comments on the draft ms, dtd 29Nov89 (Vietnam Comment File).

24 Col Dean C. Macho intvw dtd Apr73 (OralHistColl, MCHC, Washington, D.C.); Brown, p. 5.

25 MAG12 ComdC, Dec72, p. 4.

26 Brown comments; CHECO AnLoc, pp. 53-54.

27 "Road 13 — Road of Death," *Vietnam* No. 172, 1972, pp. 6-7 (Besch comments).

28 MAG-12 ComdC, Nov72, p.5.

29 Macho intvw.

30 Brown, p. 5.

31 FMFPac MarOpsSEA, p. 3-18.

32 MAG-12 ComdC, Dec72, Tab A-12.

33 FMFPac MarOpsSEA, p. 3-19.

34 MAG-12 ComdC, Jan73, p. 7.

35 MAG12 ComdC, Dec72. p. 6; Jan73, p. 7.

36 Maj Angelo M. Inglisa, comments on the draft ms, dtd 29Nov89 (Vietnam Comment File).

37 LtCol Michael S. Kelly, comments on draft ms, dtd 2Apr90 (Vietnam Comment File).

38 Kelly comments.

39 MAG-12 ComdC, Dec72, p. 9.

40 MAG-12 ComdC, Sept72, pp. 4-5.

41 HQMC Report of Casualty No. 991-72.

42 Arnold, p. 10.

43 MAG-12 ComdC, Sept72, p. 4.

44 MAG-12 ComdC, Jan73, p. 8; OSAD(C) AirLoss, p. 4.

45 Marine Aircraft Group 12 Navy Unit Commendation citation (RefSec, MCHC, Washington, D.C.).

Task Force Delta
46 Arnold, p. 15.

47 Brown, p. 3; TFD AAR, p. 1-3.

48 CNA MarActySEA, p. 80

49 Task Force Delta Command Brief dtd 17Jun73, Tab A, Tab B, hereafter TFDBrief (Vietnam Comment File).

50 Brown comments.

51 TFD AAR, p. 1-7.

52 Brown comments.

53 LtCol James C. Brown, comments on the draft ms, dtd 3Jan90 (Vietnam Comment File).

54 FMFPac MarOpsSEA, p. 3-18.

55 CNA MarActySEA, p. 93.

56 FMFPac MarOpsSea, p. 3-18; TFDBrief, Operations.

57 MABS-15 ComdC, Jan73.

58 LtCol John M. Campanelli, comments on draft ms, dtd 5Jan90 (Vietnam Comment File).

The Rose Garden Grows
59 *Air War-Vietnam*, op. cit., pp. 203-204; Also see Karl J. Eschman, *Linebacker* (New York: Ivy Books, 1989); Mark Clodfelter, *The Limits of Airpower* (New York: The Free Press, 1989).

60 Brown comments.

61 1stLt Ronald S. Mullisen, 1stLt Gary W. Dolgin, and 1stLt Jerry D. Owen, eds., *Marine All-Weather Attack Squadron 533* (Marceline: Walsworth Publishing Company, 1972), p. 9.

62 Ibid., p. 55

63 FMFPac MarOpsSEA, p. 4-16.

64 MAG-15 ComdC, Aug72, p. 2.

65 Ibid.

66 Maj George R. Dunham intvw dtd 16Jun87 (Vietnam Comment File).

67 Col Kent C. Bateman, comments on draft ms, dtd 12Dec89 (Vietnam Comment File).

68 MAG-15 ComdC, Nov72, p. 3.

69 TFDBrief, Tab H, Operations.

70 FMFPac MarOpsSEA, p. 5-8.

71 TFD AAR, pp. 1-12 to 1-15.

72 Task Force Delta Navy Unit Commendation citation (RefSec, MCHC, Washington, D.C.).

73 VAdm James B. Stockdale, *A Vietnam Experience* (Stanford: Hoover Press, 1984), p. 145.

74 Democratic Republic of Vietnam, "The Late December 1972 Blitz on North Vietnam," special communique, dtd 3Dec72 (Hanoi, 1973), p. 56 (Vietnam Comment File).

CHAPTER TWELVE
ON YANKEE STATION

Support to the Navy, Task Force 77 • All-Weather Attack •
More Support to the Navy, VMCJ • Snakes at Sea • Fighters over the North

Support to the Navy, Task Force 77

While Marine air groups were supporting the U.S. Air Force, other air units were with the Seventh Fleet's Attack Carrier Strike Force (Task Force 77) of Vice Admiral Damon W. Cooper in the Tonkin Gulf. At the time of the 1972 Communist offensive, four carrier battle groups were in the Tonkin Gulf rather than the normal two. This increased to six by June and then to seven carrier groups by the end of the year.[A]

Vice Admiral William P. Mack, commanding Seventh Fleet, and Admiral Cooper, commanding Task Force 77, positioned carrier groups for air strikes from the Tonkin Gulf in response to the NVA attack. Other ships moved to support the increased tempo of carrier operations. Nine to 13 destroyers provided a screen to intercept North Vietnamese aircraft and torpedo boats. Destroyers and amphibious ships operated two northern search and rescue (SAR) stations, two positive identification and radar advisory zones (PIRAZ), a middle SAR station, and a southern SAR station, which was later renamed Picket Station Alpha to counter the threat of North Vietnamese missile boats.[1]

Admiral Cooper concentrated air attacks in Route Packages 1 and 2 with the resumption of naval gunfire and bombing in North Vietnam on 7 April 1972. These struck at troop and logistic targets in the Panhandle, Finger Lake, and Mu Gia Pass

---

(A) Carrier air wings (CVW) were task-organized mixes of aircraft and facilities on a self-contained floating airfield. Composition of CVW's during this period, as for example CVW-15 on the *Coral Sea* in 1972, included two squadrons of A-7 Corsairs, two squadrons of F-4 Phantoms, a Marine squadron of A-6s, and detachments of RF-8G Crusaders (photo), EKA-3Bs (tankers), E-1Bs (early warning), and SH-3G Sea Kings (rescue). Marine squadrons operated from three carriers in 1972; the USS *Coral Sea* (CVA 43), the *Saratoga* (CVA 60), and the *America* (CVA 66). Units that supported TF 77 included VMA(AW)-224, VMFA-333, HMA 369, and detachments from VMCJ-1, VMCJ-2, and H&MS-15.

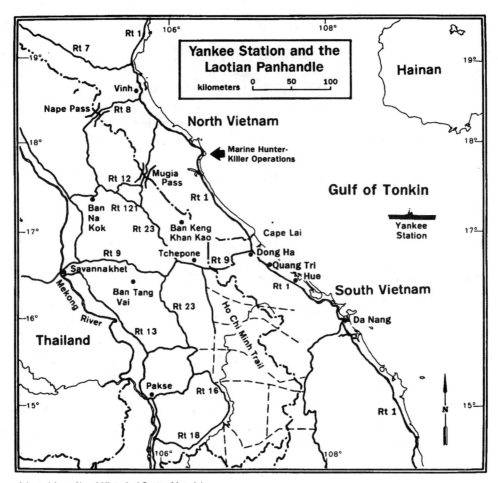

Adapted from Naval Historical Center Material

regions through low clouds and the fire of heavy antiaircraft defenses. One or more carrier groups remained dedicated to direct air support in South Vietnam, primarily in MR 1 during the critical days of April and May. The Marine squadrons flew the same missions as the Navy fighter and attack squadrons to maintain air superiority, interdict lines of communications, and attack economic targets in support of political goals. Major air attacks were flown against Vinh, Thanh Hoa, Haiphong, and Hanoi in 1972 by multiple aircraft employed in self-contained forces which were aimed at single target areas — the carrier-launched "Alpha Strikes."[B]

All-Weather Attack

The previous winter, the USS *Coral Sea* arrived on Yankee Station with VMA(AW)-224 on board as part of Carrier Air Wing (CVW)-15. The "Bengals" were from the 2d Marine Aircraft Wing, Marine Corps Air Station (MCAS), Cherry Point, North Carolina. Their arrival in the Western Pacific Ocean was part of a scheduled six-month cruise. Lieutenant Colonel Billy R. Standley's unit consisted of 44 officers, 290 enlisted men, with eight Grumman A-6A Intruder all-weather bombers, three A-6 Bs, and four KA-6D tankers. Initial operations were strikes against Ben Karai and Mu Gai Passes to interdict enemy convoys along the so-called Ho Chi Minh Trail in Laos. During the day the A-6s acted as pathfinders for other carrier flights, dropping impact and delayed-fuze bombs through cloud cover. At night the A-6s operated with the Air Force's "Commando Bolt" system using sensors and on-board moving target indicators to knock out trucks on the numerous feeder roads to the trail.[2] For the NVA soldiers, this continuous attack brought mixed emotions. One recalled:

> I could tell when we started to get close to the Vietnam border .... We could
> hear the rumble of bombings in the distance. Everyone stopped to listen to
> it — a dull continuous roar. A surge of fear went through everyone in the
> group I was traveling with. I was sick and half-starved and scared to death.
> But I was near home. It had taken six months to get here ....[3]

The *Coral Sea* and VMA(AW)-224 were at Subic Bay, Philippines, on 30 March when Admiral Mack hurriedly recalled them to the Gulf of Tonkin to help stem the NVA invasion force. Lieutenant Colonel Standley and his squadron found themselves engaged in air strikes ranging the entire length of North Vietnam for the next 50 days.[4] The squadron flew Commando Bolt missions at night and attack missions near the DMZ during the day. In one instance, providing close air support to a fire support base on 9 April in northern MR 1, Lieutenant Colonel Ralph E. Brubaker observed his "aircraft delivered their ordnance with deadly accuracy ...."[C] When the smoke from the A-6's bomb load cleared, the firebase commander radioed the flight that they had "saved his position."[5]

(B) An attack was launched in sequence beginning with reconnaissance, missile and antiaircraft artillery suppression, ordnance runs, and post-strike damage assessment aircraft.

(C) Lieutenant Colonel Brubaker later commanded the squadron in 1972.

In addition to these tasks, the Navy air group commander (CAG) assigned the squadron's A-6s to destroy SAM and radar sites with "Standard Arm" AGM-78 missiles guiding in on radar transmissions from the targets. These flights continued until a new phase of air operations began on 8 May. Unlike previous air operations, targeting was at the theater level rather than the "Commander-in-Chief" level.[D] Air Force B-52s and naval tactical aircraft were used simultaneously against the same targets.

The new operations called upon VMA(AW)-224 to play a role in mining North Vietnamese waterways and harbors. On the direct orders of President Nixon, Operation Pocket Money sealed Haiphong Harbor. Admiral Mack stated he was required by the President to drop the first mine "within seconds of nine o'clock because the President was going to announce the mining to the American public at that precise moment back in the United States."[6] That bright sun-lit morning, three Marine A-6As and six Navy A-7Es thundered up the defended approach to Haiphong at low level. The aircraft overflew local junks on the sparkling waterway and skirted its shoreline. Air and gunfire strikes silenced Communist missile and antiaircraft positions for aircrews who, according to Admiral Mack:

> ... had to know exactly where they were going and then drop mines in a
> very narrow channel regardless of fog, rain, or darkness. The drop had to
> be planned so that several aircraft could pick a point in the harbor area
> and drop their mines at 200 feet, microseconds apart, while going 300 to
> 400 knots.[7]

Captain William D. Carr, Jr., the bombardier-navigator in the lead Marine A-6A, established the critical attack azimuth for the Haiphong Harbor attack on 9 May. His aircraft dropped the first of 36 MK52-2 mines seconds after 0900 and completed the mission within the hour. For the main channel, 12 miles long and up to 250 feet wide, the U.S. forces used 75 mines in three minefields to block the waterway. Another 700 MK36 destructors were dropped in shallow water to deny passage to local shipping.[E]

After a three-day grace period before the mines armed, 26 merchant ships remained trapped in Haiphong Harbor. Air-dropped mines closed the ports of Hon Gai and Cam Pha north of Haiphong; the ports of Thanh Hoa, Vinh, Quang Khe, and Dong Hoi to the south. After using more than 8,000 mines in the coastal areas and another 3,000 in inland waterways, the Navy believed it had stopped the flow of material into North Vietnam from the sea. With 80 percent of needed supplies entering the country this way, and the rest by rail, air interdiction brought North Vietnam's economy and military to a standstill.

(D) Under the previous Rolling Thunder campaign, targets were selected for apparent political value within the considerations of "graduated response." At times, selection and approval of specific missions were from The White House (*Air War-Vietnam*, pp. 251–252).

(E) Special fuzing on a general-purpose MK82 500-pound aircraft bomb produced the destructor.

Relief on Yankee Station came in July with the arrival of the USS *America* (CV 66). By then VMFA(AW)-224 had flown 2,800 combat sorties with 4,500 hours of flight time and the loss of four aircraft and crews. With Operation Pocket Money, the Marine A-6s and crews played a crucial role in delivering "... one of the most significant blows to the enemy since the beginning of the Vietnamese conflict."[8]

More Support to the Navy, VMCJ

In the spring of 1972, with the increase in operations from the Tonkin Gulf, Lieutenant General Louis Metzger, the III MAF commanding general, tasked the 1st MAW commander, Major General Robert G. Owens, Jr., to provide electronic warfare support to Seventh Fleet and TF 77. This responded to a Seventh Fleet shortage of the specialized aircraft for this task and exercised the capabilities of 1st MAW's Grumman EA-6A Intruders. The Intruders of the VMCJ-1 "Golden Hawks" were well-enough equipped to allow American pilots to penetrate what was considered the third heaviest air defense system in the world.[F][9] Electronic warfare permitted the interception, recording, and jamming of communications and radar systems used in North Vietnamese air defense. As a "combat-multiplier," the "soft kills" of interception or jamming aided other attack and fighter aircraft to enter defended areas for "hard kills" with ordnance. On 3 April, General Owens ordered the immediate deployment of a six-plane detachment from VMCJ-1 to NAS Cubi Point.[6] Major John D. Carlton's detachment began missions in support of TF 77 on 7 April. Later in the month, on 20 April, four "Playboy" EA-6As of Detachment X, VMCJ-2 off the USS *Saratoga* (CVA 60) arrived as reinforcements.[10] The resulting composite detachment of 221 Marines included crews and KC-130s from VMGR-152 and personnel and support equipment from H&MS-15.[11]

Aircraft flew from Cubi Point to Da Nang Air Base for combat missions. Marines at Da Nang serviced the aircraft using fuel, revetments parking, and "ready room" space provided by the Navy's Fleet Air Reconnaissance Squadron (VQ) 1. Routinely, an early morning flight of four EA-6s and a KC-130 with additional flight crews departed the Philippines for Da Nang. Once there, pilots were briefed for morning sorties and the EA-6s were fueled and serviced. After briefings and inspections, the planes launched to support Navy and Air Force strikes over North Vietnam. Morning missions completed, they returned to Da Nang for fuel and replacement crews to fly in the afternoon. After completing these final missions, the aircraft landed at Da Nang for refueling and returned to Cubi Point with an accompanying KC-130.

Admiral Cooper commented in April 1972 on the effective electronic warfare support TF 77 received from the Marines and their EA-6A aircraft , declaring that on "the five

---

(F) After the Soviet Union and Israel.

(G) The detachment could still operate from carrier flight decks if required.

strikes they have supported, SAM guidance has been erratic and no aircraft have been hit."[12] This was critical support in conducting carrier-air operations into Route Packages 2 and 3. Major General Leslie E. Brown, while 1st MAW commander, concluded:

> ... ECM missions provided CTF 77 the primary EW support necessary to support intensive Alpha Strikes against North Vietnam without sustaining prohibitive aircraft losses.[13]

Operations continued at this pace through the October 1972 bombing halt, when the detachment's mission shifted to passive surveillance of North Vietnam to obtain an electronic order of battle. The 18 December 1972 resumption of bombings found the detachment engaged again in active support of Navy and Air Force attacks on Hanoi and Haiphong. The NVA commander for air defense of Hanoi, Tran Nhan, recalled that when the bombs fell in December "radar screens for the nine missile batteries around Hanoi remained blank."[14]

At the ceasefire, the VMCJ-2 detachment returned to 2d MAW in North Carolina, while the VMCJ-1 detachment remained at Cubi Point supporting the Seventh Fleet. The composite detachment flew 2,496 combat sorties and 5,356 hours, losing one aircraft.[(H)15] Vice Admiral James L. Holloway III, commanding Seventh Fleet when the detachment returned to III MAF control on 18 February 1973, told the departing Marine pilots that their "unique role in electronic warfare provided invaluable support to the U.S. air striking forces which were penetrating a most formidable and sophisticated anti-air warfare environment."[16]

Snakes at Sea

Another aircraft singular to the inventory of 1st MAW supported the Seventh Fleet, the newly arrived Bell AH-1J Seacobras of Marine Helicopter Attack Squadron (HMA) 369. Cobra gunships flew from amphibious ships to locate and destroy North Vietnamese sampans ferrying cargo from merchant ships to landing sites along the coast of North Vietnam and attempting to avoid the mines of Operation Pocket Money.

The squadron was still forming and had just received its AH-1Js when the Spring Offensive occurred. A detachment was sent to the 9th MAB, and on 11 June 1972, Admiral McCain called upon General Metzger to provide gunship support to TF 77. The origin of the Marine Hunter Killer ("MarHuk") operation arose from the desire of Admiral Holloway and Admiral Cooper to ensure that the blockade of North Vietnam's seaward approaches was complete and that not a "grain of rice" made it ashore through the use of small, expendable, boats that avoided the normal sea lanes. The use of fixed-wing carrier aircraft for this role diverted them from more critical

---

(H) Excluding KC-130 sorties of 1,440 hours and 568 combat flights.

interdiction missions. The solution rested in a more flexible low-performance aircraft, the helicopter gunship.[17] With the demise of Navy light attack helicopter squadrons, III MAF had the only immediate source of armed helicopters. General Metzger believed, however, the value of stopping a sampan and its cargo was not worth the possible loss of a gunship. He also objected to depriving General Miller and the 9th MAB of both amphibious transports and gunships during a critical period. One consequence was the use of U.S. Army Cobras for helicopter escort during the amphibious landings.[18]

Despite official reservations over the mission, General Brown warned the acting squadron commander, Captain Ronald G. Osborne, to be ready to go. As Major Dawson P. "Rusty" Hansen assumed command of the squadron on 15 June, it was loading on board ship to assume its role as the Marine Corps sea-based attack helicopter squadron.[19] At the time, 18 officers, 99 enlisted men, and seven helicopters squeezed into limited deck and hangar space on board the USS *Denver*. A troop transport, the ship lacked aircraft support and maintenance facilities. In fact, Admiral Holloway initially desired to use a helicopter carrier (LPH) for this mission, but none was available because of 9th MAB combat and ready operations. Major Hansen and his maintenance officer, Captain David L. Caldon, overcame problems related to supply, missile countermeasure modifications, avionics support, ordnance handling, and the acquisition of Zuni 5-inch rockets not normally used by helicopters.[20] Without doctrine or experience to go by, "innovation and imagination were the keys" for the self-styled "Marhuckers."[21]

Major Hansen and Captain David C. Corbett, the operations officer, developed a concept of employment and techniques to accomplish the mission assigned by Seventh Fleet. This had two parts: the surveillance of merchant ships at the Hon La Anchorage, and the destruction of sampans running cargo ashore from these ships.[(I)] As the merchant ships were from the People's Republic of China, they were not to be attacked or threatened by the Marines. Rules of engagement kept the Marines at least 500 yards away from the merchants and over the water at all times. Task Force 77 controlled daily sorties and coordinated air, gunfire, and rescue support. Over time, tactics evolved from a single morning and afternoon flight to random launches during the day. Finally, continuous night flights were conducted under illumination shells fired by accompanying destroyers. Because the AH-1J lacked radio cryptologic equipment, the use of radio silence was often mandatory to prevent and deceive North Vietnamese monitoring.[22] Flying without radio communications at night over the open sea was one measure of the squadron's skill.

The North Vietnamese positioned 23mm, 37mm, and 57mm antiaircraft guns for air defense around the three-sided Hon La anchorage. These weapons and a variety of

---

(I) Four merchant ships were anchored at Hon La. Another anchorage site was at Non Nieu.

small arms hit nine helicopters in 140 firing incidents.[23] Enemy fire from the anchorage and the beach increased threefold over the six-month period of operations, but "very early the enemy realized that if they fired on the AH-1Js they could expect Cobras, NGF, and/or fixed wing to engage them. This has made the enemy fire short unsustained bursts and thus reduced their volume and accuracy."[24] Major Hansen and his relief, Major David L. Ross, believed the Sea Cobra's small profile, maneuverability, and fire power prevented losses.

The AH-1Js fought back with 20mm guns and rockets and were also able to "call for" naval gunfire and tactical air. Two air observers were assigned the squadron as airborne controllers, Chief Warrant Officers James F. Doner, Jr., and James R. Owens. The two flying "gunners" soon had the squadron pilots trained in airborne spotting and the squadron consequently, could hit targets with more than just their on-board weapons, giving the North Vietnamese cause not to arouse the airborne Cobras. During one flight Chief Warrant Officer Doner's Sea Cobra was fired upon by a 12.7mm machine gun. The pilot turned his nose towards the gun position and let loose with a 5-inch Zuni rocket. This was Doner's first experience with the Zuni, and "the pilot didn't tell me he was about to fire it." The rocket enveloped the Cobra with smoke and sparks from its motor, rattling the aircraft, and had Doner yeling "We've been hit ..!"[25]

In August, the squadron moved to the USS *Cleveland* (LPD 7), and continued full-time combat operations. On 17 August, a concerted effort was made to ensure continued "permissive environment" for the gunships using carrier-based A-6s and Vought A-7 Corsairs and the fire support of seven naval gunfire ships, including the *Newport News*. After this, hostile ground fire slackened. Operating periods alternated with port visits through December, with a final move to the USS *Dubuque* (LPD 8).

When operations ended on 26 January 1973, HMA-369 had flown 981 combat sorties, destroying or damaging 123 sampans carrying an estimated 5,444 100-pound bags of rice. The merchant ships resorted to dumping cargo into the sea in waterproof containers in an effort to float cargo ashore.[26] A 1973 Center for Naval Analyses study concluded that the employment of HMA-369 released two destroyers and carrier aircraft otherwise required for this mission.[27] The Secretary of the Navy recognized that the squadron maintained a sustained pace of heavy combat operations during all types of weather, "responding gallantly to the almost overwhelming tasks of providing a three-fold role of attack, supply movement interdiction, and constant surveillance of the enemy."[28] Major Ross also provided a fitting summary of the period when he stated the squadron did more than just shoot-up sampans, "... most of all, the last six months of operations have given the AH-1J the opportunity to prove it deserves the designation of an attack helicopter ..."[29]

Fighters over the North

The USS *America* (CVA 66) arrived in the Tonkin Gulf in July 1972 with a Marine squadron on board, Marine Fighter Squadron (VMFA) 333. The 40 officers and 280 enlisted Marines of Lieutenant Colonel John K. Cochrane's squadron considered themselves "gunfighters," the special breed of aviators who flew fighters, even if their 12 McDonnell Douglas F-4J Phantoms had seen more Vietnam service in a close air support role. The "Shamrocks," a 2d Marine Aircraft Wing unit, were expecting to operate in the Mediterranean, when it was ordered by the Chief of Naval Operations to report to CinCPac and the Tonkin Gulf.[30] Operations in the skies over North Vietnam began on 14 July; half the missions were fighter patrols and the rest were ground attacks in Route Packages 3 and 4. In August, the air group commander ordered the squadron on night armed-reconnaissance missions, but no NVA aircraft were encountered. These tasks continued through the fall, with port visits to the Philippines and Hong Kong.[31]

In September, flight operations in Route Package 6b began. During this period two F-4s, call signs "Red One" and "Red Two," launched on a scheduled combat air patrol. Major Lee T. "Bear" Lasseter, the squadron operations officer and his radar intercept officer Captain John D. "Li'l John" Cummings flew aircraft "Red One," Captains Andrew S. "Scotty" Dudley, Jr., and James W. "Diamond Jim" Brady manned "Red Two." Lasseter and Cummings were an old team with nearly 5,000 hours of Phantom time between them as air combat instructors and from previous tours. Dudley and Brady were on their first flights into the heavily defended airspace of the far North. This was their second flight of the day to cover air attacks of targets on the coast north of Haiphong. Both F-4Js were armed with four Sparrow AIM-7E-2 and four Sidewinder AIM-9D missiles, a combination mandated by the different capabilities of the two missiles.[32] The tactical air commander and ground control intercept operator controlled the flight from the USS *England* (CG 22).

The previous day, 10 September, Lasseter and Cummings had been directed to intercept a North Vietnamese MiG aircraft, contact was made, but lost due to equipment failure. The 11th was different. Launched at 1700, after a delay in link-up because of radio silence, the flight proceeded to meet an airborne KA-6 tanker to top-off with fuel for the mission. "Red One" was filled and "Red Two" was refueling when the strike force they were assigned to protect began its attack. There was not enough time to complete refueling, but Lasseter felt that his wingman had enough fuel for the mission and ordered Dudley to follow him to their assigned combat air patrol station. Prior to reaching the orbit point, Chief Radarman Dutch Schultz on the

England gave Lasseter a flight vector to two MiGs 20,000 feet over Phuc Yen Airfield 10 miles northwest of Hanoi. With intermittent radar contact, the F-4s closed to seven miles of a pair of MiG-21 Fishbeds at 1,000 feet altitude. The aircraft sighted each other at about the same time, Lasseter commenting "we didn't surprise them." Dudley made the first call, "Tally-Ho! Tally-Ho! Twelve O'Clock. Keep going straight." The MiGs were flying one behind the other when Lasseter and Cummings locked on to the lead aircraft, "OK John, go boresight. Boresight now! Are we cleared to shoot?"[J] Lasseter launched two Sparrows which the silver-colored MiG dodged with an inside turn to gain altitude on "Red One." The second MiG reversed course and flew out of the engagement to the north.

During the next four and a half minutes Lasseter and the MIG engaged in subsonic maneuvers below 1,000 feet over the Phuc Yen runway. Cummings stated that "ground fire and SAM warnings were continuous." Lasseter executed a "high yo-yo" to gain altitude and a firing position on his opponent as Dudley pressed the MiG. Lasseter launched two Sparrows and two Sidewinders during the melee but the MiG stayed low and evaded the missiles with continued left turns. Four minutes into the fight, Dudley was dangerously low on fuel and had to disengage. Suddenly the MiG reversed his turn and gave Lasseter a clean shot at it: "Ha! We got him John! OK, splash one MiG-21!" Lasseter said later, the "MiG-21 exploded and disintegrated." Cummings added the Sidewinder "really did a job on that MiG. Everything aft of the cockpit was gone and what was left was in an almost-90-degree dive for the ground at about 500 feet."

"Red One" and "Red Two" joined, and started back to the *America* when, according to Lasseter, a third MiG "made a run on my wingman." Lasseter and Cummings fired their remaining Sidewinder, which got the MiG's "attention and sent him scooting towards home ...." By now Dudley was low on fuel as both aircraft slowed and climbed to 14,000 feet to reach the safety of the sea. They also shortened their exit route, flying straight over Haiphong. Electronic counter-measure gear continued to emit SAM and AAA warnings as the North Vietnamese attempted to hit them with a "tremendous amount of groundfire."

In the confusion that followed, "Red One" was damaged by a surface-launched missile. Unable to link up with a tanker and out of fuel, "Red Two" stayed with his leader. Crossing the beach, Lasseter's aircraft was burning and its engine flamed out, forcing him and Cummings to eject "feet wet" into the Tonkin Gulf. Dudley and Brady now out of fuel, complicated by possible battle damage, also ejected over the sea. The *England* launched Helicopter Combat Support Squadron (HC) 7 "Big Mother" SAR helicopter to pick up Lasseter and Cummings; Dudley and Brady were recovered by the USS *Biddle* (DLG 21).

(J) Because of the number of American aircraft over North Vietnam, visual identification and permission from a control agency was required before missiles could be used.

This was the only MiG kill of the war by a Marine Corps unit and an engagement with mixed results.[K] A second section of F-4s was diverted to the MiG fray, some 60 miles from assigned air cover positions on the coast, resulting in no fighter cover for the strike. Another consideration raised later by Captain Cummings was that "... the North Vietnamese used our aggressiveness and desire to bag a MiG to lure us into a trap consisting of AAA, SAMs, and MiGs."[33]

The air war for VMFA-333 continued through the end of the year, with the squadron flying armed reconnaissance missions during the bombing halt above the 20th Parallel in October 1972. By this time, the winter weather restricted the squadron to instrument-controlled bombing through cloud cover. The *America's* air commander ordered VMFA-333 to conduct attack missions with the resumption of bombing on 18 December 1972. In this month Major Lasseter took command of the squadron after Lieutenant Colonel Cochrane was shot down and injured, and he brought the squadron home at the end of its tour in March 1973.

As the Marine Corps is the landward extension of the U.S. Navy, Marine air is the landward continuation of naval airpower, demonstrated by the Marine units with the Seventh Fleet during the Spring Offensive. In 1972, these Marine electronic warfare, attack helicopter, attack, and fighter aircraft their share of Task Force 77's 65,285 sorties flown over North Vietnam and 35,730 sorties in South Vietnam that helped push the Communists further toward signing a ceasefire agreement.[34]

(K) Two other Marines had shot down enemy aircraft during the war, flying as exchange officers with the U.S. Air Force: Captain Doyle D. Baker on 17 December 1967 with the 13th Fighter Squadron and Captain Lawrence G. Richard on 11 August 1972 with the 585th Tactical Fighter Squadron.

CHAPTER TWELVE ENDNOTES

Unless otherwise noted, material in this chapter is derived from FMFPac MarOpsSEA, SeventhFlt ComdHist72, CNA MarActySEA. See also Clarke Van Fleet, "Year of Action-1972," *Naval Aviation News*, Feb73, pp. 6-25, hereafter Van Fleet; VAdm Malcolm W. Cagle, "Task Force 77 in Action Off Vietnam," *Naval Review 1972*, May72, pp. 66-109; and Edward J. Marolda and George W. Pryce III, *A Short History of the United States Navy and the Southeast Asian Conflict* (Washington, D.C.: Naval Historical Center, 1984).

Support to the Navy, Task Force 77
1 SeventhFlt ComdHist72, p. 4. Also Van Fleet, passim.

All-Weather Attack
2 VMA(AW)-224 ComdC, Jul72, p. 4.

3 Xuan Vu, quoted by David Chanoff and Doan Van Toi, ed., *Portrait of the Enemy* (New York: Random House, 1986), p. 184.

4 CWO2 Edward Scheiner, ed., *The Coral Scene*; (Picshel Yearbooks, Inc., 1972), p. 73.

5 VMA(AW)-224 ComdC, Jul72, p. 4.

6 Nixon, op. cit., pp. 583-587.

7 SeventhFlt ComdHist72, p. 10. Van Fleet, p. 17.

8 FMFPac MarOpsSEA, p. 3-22; Cmdr Ulrik Luckow, "Victory Over Ignorance and Fear: The U.S. Minelaying Attack on North Vietnam," *Naval War College Review*, Jan-Feb82, pp. 17-27. USS *Coral Sea* and Carrier Wing 15 Navy Unit Commendation citation (RefSec, MCHC, Washington, D.C.).

More Support to the Navy, VMCJ
9 CNA MarActySEA, pp. 74-75.

10 FMFPac MarOpsSEA, p. 2-21. ComNavAirLant msg to CVW-3 dtd 11Apr72.

11 MCCC, Chronology dtd 18May72, p. 5; Brown, pp. 9-10.

12 FMFPac MarOpsSEA, p. 2-21.

13 Brown, p. 9.

14 *Indochina Chronology*, Oct-Dec87, p. 19.

15 Brown, p. 10.

16 FMFPac, MarOpsSEA, p. 6-9.

Snakes at Sea
17 HMA-369 ComDC, Dec72; LtGen Louis Metzger intvw by FMFPac MarOpsSEA, Jan73, Tape 5060 (Oral HistColl, MCHC).

18 Metzger intvw.

19 CNA MarActySEA, P.17; Brown, pp.6-7. Also Mike Verier, "Marhuk," *Aviation News*, 18-31 Mar88, pp.1011-1017, and Kenneth P. Werrell, "MARHUK: Marine Helicopters Over Vietnam" (ms, Radford College, 29May87)

20 FMFPac MarOpsSEA, pp. 3-26 to 3-27; HMA-369 ComdC, Jun72, pp. 4-6

21 CTG79.8/HMA-369 AAR, 29Dec72, p. 2.

22 Brown, pp. 6-7; FMFPac, MarOpsSea, pp. 3-22 to 3-24.

23 Maj David L. Ross, Comments on draft ms, 9Jan90 (Vietnam Comment File); CTG79.8/HMA-369 AAR, p. 3.

24 CTG79.8/HMA-369 AAR, p. 5, Ross comments.

25 JO2 Julius L. Evans, "Gunner, One of a Few Good Men," *Naval Aviation News*, Jul-Aug82, p. 24.

26 FMFPac, MarOpsSEA

27 CNA MarActySEA, p. 116.

28 HMA-369 Navy Unit Commendation citation (RefSec, MCHC, Washington, D.C.)

29 HMA-369 ComdC, Dec72, p. 7.

Fighters over the North
30 VMFA-333 ComdC, Jun72, p. 4.

31 VMFA-333 ComdC, Dec72, pp. 3-5.

32 Col John D. Cummings, comments on draft ms, dtd 11Jan90 (Vietnam Comment File).

33 VMFA-333 ComdC, Dec72, pp. 3-4; Cummings comments. Also "Marine Mig Kill," transcript of ICS conversation (Vietnam Comment File); LtCol John Cummings ltr to Mr. Michael O'Connor dtd 25Jun84 (RefSec, MCHC, Washington, D.C.); Capt Joseph Boyle, ed., *WestPac* 72-73 cruise book (Norfolk, Tiffany Publishing Co., 1973), p. 77.

34 SeventhFlt ComdHist72, pp. 3-5, 8-10.

CHAPTER THIRTEEN
OTHER MARINE ACTIVITIES

Leadership, Morale, and Readiness • Beans, Bullets, and Av Gas: Logistics •
Thunder from the Sea, Fire from the Sky • War in the Ether

Leadership, Morale, and Readiness

At this time, commanders in FMFPac and III MAF had to address the intangible, as well as the physical, needs of their organizations: concerns related to the leadership, training, and morale of the Marines who made up the tactical units. The conduct of Marines who formed these units, in effect reflected the situation in contemporary American society. In June 1971, this condition was described by military historian and commentator Colonel Robert Debs Heinl, Jr., USMC (Retired), as "... the lowest state of military morale in the history of the country."[1]

From his experience as a division and corps-level commander, Lieutenant General Louis Metzger recalled, "personnel problems were a major challenge during this period."[2] One squadron executive officer and commander, Major Kent C. Bateman, concluded that "anti-war feelings of the period and the drug culture mindset presented a leadership dilemma that was imponderable."[3] Some officers and noncommissioned officers, faced with this situation, appeared to avoid the career risks of leading these Marines for less demanding assignments. A company-grade officer replied this was not quite accurate, "we were doing the best we could with the people and equipment on hand."[4]

Actually, many of these personnel problems stemmed from the fact that the Marine Corps, unable to call up Reserves, was forced by declining recruitment to take in substandard entrants. Once enlisted, certain of these disadvantaged young men found it difficult to meet military standards and were either unwilling or unable to accept military discipline. Marine historian Allan R. Millet observed that this was accepted by the Marine Corps at the time "as a calculated risk to keep up end strength."[5]

A later study by Headquarters Marine Corps provided the following statistics on Marine manpower at the start of the decade: In 1971, 21 percent of all recruits were discharged prior to completion of the short 78-day period of recruit training; 70 percent of enlisted Marines in this period, privates through sergeants, were 21 years of age or less, and 49 percent of this group acknowledged some illegal drug usage. Only five percent of the "first termers" eligible to re-enlist did so, indicative of service conditions at the time. This lack of quality manpower was also reflected in disciplinary problems which resulted in 587 general courts-martials and 6,655 special courts-martial. In 1971, desertions numbered 11,852 and unauthorized absences, 35,174, or at the rates of 56.1 and 166.6 per 1,000 respectively.[A] In 1973 alone, 10,045 Marines were discharged prior to completion of obligated service. Recruiting standards were lowered to the point that, by this same year, only 46 percent of incoming enlisted recruits held high school diplomas. Within the ranks of the lowest four enlisted grades of private through corporal, high school graduates composed 50 percent of ground combat units; 51 percent of support units; and 65 percent of aviation units. One division commander reported his troops' average general classification test (GCT) scores as 85, with 100 and above being required for training most technical skills.[B][6]

Serving overseas when their country appeared torn by antiwar dissension, Marines went to a bob-tailed division on Okinawa or an air wing spread over the Pacific from Hawaii to Japan. Officers and men served a 12-month tour, "unaccompanied" by families, alongside the more generous U.S. Army and Air Force family policies. Efforts to reconstitute the 3d Marine Division and the 1st Marine Aircraft Wing did not appear to be the highest priority to those on "the Rock," as Okinawa was known. Facilities and equipment showed the effects of the previous six years of war and the vagaries of the defense budget system that seemed to be unable to afford basic necessities on a cyclic basis. For some Marines the local culture seemed strange and unintelligible.

As Marine Corps units departed Vietnam in 1971, those men with less than nine months overseas were reassigned within III MAF to finish their overseas tours. They arrived with an outlook and disdain for garrison living that negated the experience they brought as "combat veterans." The resultant high turnover of personnel and the demands of additional duty and fleet augmentation programs adversely influenced combat effectiveness and unit cohesion. Racial conflict, alcohol and drug abuse, and criminal activity that placed demands on the small-unit leaders beyond their capacity were other manifestations of institutional stress.[7]

As commander of FMF Pacific, Lieutenant General William K. Jones conducted a survey that examined perceptions by Marines of duty assignments, the legal system,

---

(A) Rate per 1,000 equals number of incidents divided by average enlisted strength x 1,000. Length of unauthorized absences historically averaged 10 days.

(B) GCT scores are roughly similar to Intelligence Quotients (IQ); a GCT of 100 is believed to indicate average learning and reasoning ability.

racial conflict, drug use, and leadership. It reached a number of conclusions, among them the observation that:

> ... throughout all these areas of major concern are negative attitudes or indications which appear repeatedly. Principal among these was the distrust of the young Marines for the "establishment" — representing authority, one's superiors, the chain of command, the legal structure.[8]

Leadership was believed to be the weakest at the lowest level, the point at which conflicts appeared and where "... the apparent intolerance and insulation of the white SNCOs [represented] the focal point of the generation gap" and the communications breakdown.[9] This was not as much in routine official duties, but rather in the inability to establish personal trust and confidence during informal contacts with the young Marines. A factor in this was the loss of experienced staff noncommissioned officers who had been made temporary officers in the middle-1960s.[10]

The poll went on to conclude that drug use in the lower ranks was abetted by a "no-squeal" syndrome, race relations broke down in black perceptions of inequities, Article 15 nonjudicial punishment was used arbitrarily, and, in leadership relations, respect did not equate to trust between ranks. General Jones instituted a number of command programs to get at the essence of these social problems and took steps to get the Marine Corps to do the same, with limited results.[C] While General Leonard F. Chapman, Jr., then Commandant, approved the FMFPac programs, he "was reluctant to take action since he was soon to leave office and preferred to leave it to his successor," General Robert E. Cushman, Jr.[11]

The conflict of legitimate civil rights reforms and disruptive demands for "black power" were resolved as earlier steps taken by the Marine Corps to address this national social issue began to take effect. At Headquarters Marine Corps, the Equal Opportunity Branch and the CMC Advisory Committee for Minority Affairs continued efforts to remove inequities from the system. By late 1971, 1.2 percent of Marine officers and 12.1 percent of Marine enlisted personnel were African-Americans. Personnel distribution policies placed 17.97 percent of these Marines in combat arms and 16.18 percent in support and service occupational specialties. It was in FMF combat and support units that unrest was greatest. Racial incidents continued, but were now being recognized as not isolated but rather symptomatic of something more than poor discipline. In September 1971, the 3d Marine Division targeted disruptive behavior by blacks in the base mess halls by prohibiting "power salutes." This resulted in 34 Marines being charged with violations of the division order.

(C) Lest this situation appear unique to the 1971–1973 period, it should be noted that one of General Jones' contributions was an FMFPac newsletter, *The Marine Leader*, which included previous leadership challenges and solutions noted in his "Base Plate McGurk" series, first published in the *Marine Corps Gazette* in the late 1940's.

Further efforts were made to suppress provocative posters, banners, and clothing deemed to contain a racial content. The year ended with 116 racial incidents reported to Headquarters Marine Corps, which commented that the apparent increase in assaults and incidents of racial tension was a result of a "more responsive and sensitive" reporting system. By April 1972, racial incident reporting and "salt and pepper" personnel reports (a unit's strength broken down by "race" groupings) were further revised and standardized by Marine Corps order. The human relations program had begun within III MAF units. Inspection trips by the Commandant's Advisory Committee for Minority Affairs and the Department of Defense reported that the effort in the Western Pacific was overcoming both discrimination and the resultant black backlash.[12]

To counter overall divisive elements, small-unit leaders at all levels had to establish conditions that promoted what FMFPac called "job satisfaction." Nothing was too insignificant if it impacted adversely on this, particularly in barracks, the mess halls, and enlisted clubs. The commands emphasized unit identity, recognition of abilities and initiative, and an equitable promotion system. Leadership, as always, was a full-time demanding affair. It was a tough time, particularly in garrison for small-unit leaders: one second lieutenant recalled that the human relations program, while not a substitute for effective leadership, "was an attempt to allow Marines to better understand one another."[13] Another platoon leader, Second Lieutenant, Mark B. Pizzo, remarked that, officers and staff noncommissioned officers "were open to constant threats and reprisals."[14] As III MAF soldiered on, one result of the termination of the Vietnam War was the start of a self-conscious internal review of mission, force structure, manpower, and quality.[D][15]

Rear Admiral Wycliffe D. Toole, Jr., and Task Force 76 had to resolve "disturbing racial and disciplinary problems both ashore and afloat." Admiral Toole went on to state that he appreciated the "untiring efforts" of Major General Joseph C. Fegan, Jr., Brigadier General Edward J. Miller, and Brigadier General Paul G. Graham, to resolve these matters: "Without their constant personal attention...the situation could have easily escalated into disruptive physical violence."[16]

Despite units' internal turmoil, these same Marines and sailors responded automatically to the contingencies in 1972 with the speed and intensity of previous generations of U.S. Marines, particularly during the critical period of April and May. This desire to participate was reflected in shipboard activities and the intense

---

(D) This was completed when General Louis H. Wilson, Jr., as Commandant of the Marine Corps in 1975, wrote Senator Sam Nunn saying: "We have taken a hard look at ourselves. Self discipline requires that we take such account as a routine matter at all times; but, periodically, we must look deeper into institutional assumptions as well as operational realities. The Marine Corps has benefited from this extensive review." (HQMC manpower study, p. 3)

competition to be assigned to any duties contributing to combat efforts. As Marine Lance Corporal Donald L. Samuels of BLT 1/9 expressed it, unit pride gave "us a little something extra and makes us work harder."[17] Samuels' First Sergeant, Robert S. Ynacay, agreed that morale was highest afloat "when the Marines got to participate in U.S. Navy duties with the members of the crew."[18]

On troop transports, jungle-utility-clad Marines appeared on deck with shorn heads cleaning individual weapons "without being told to." Aviation crews pulled together as teams to meet the back-breaking demands of wartime sortie rates. Lieutenant Colonel Eddie R. Maag, the MAG-12 logistics officer, maintained that when a private-first-class aircraft mechanic "will spend his own buck on a flashlight, and hold it in his mouth to ready a $15 million Phantom for the next mission, you have to be impressed."[19] The knowledge that there was a war on and Marines had a part to play in it was a major factor that did much to restore their self-image as America's "first to fight."[20] It helped sustain them while "boring holes in the ocean" as a member of the so-called "Tonkin Gulf Yacht Club" and while experiencing the day-to-day sameness of forward-area living. As Thomas Hobbes stated in 1651, "War consisteth not in battle only, or the act of fighting; but in a tract of time, wherein the will to contend by battle is sufficiently known ...."[21]

Individual and unit quality as combat units, rather than social beings or groupings, was measured in areas such as readiness as well as in discipline and morale. Throughout this period, III MAF units conducted individual and unit training to ensure readiness for combat and contingency operations. Such training was more than the simple repetition of skills. It included physical and mental conditioning, instilling unit cohesion, sharing doctrine, ensuring material readiness, and providing leadership. Transition from peacetime to combat was not as difficult for most naval and aviation units, as their normal duties are demanding in themselves. Even they had something to learn from the experience of rapid deployment to combat with ensuing around-the-clock operations. Observed Lieutenant Colonel James C. Brown, commanding VMA(AW)-533, there were shortfalls "regarding readiness inspection procedures in garrison" that only became apparent in the field.[22] For the amphibious units oriented towards ground combat, landing exercises and additional preparations were conducted at the Zambales Training Area, Philippines. Once at sea, readiness was conducted at the small-unit level with what was called on-the-job training (OJT) for anything that could be accomplished within an individual ship's plan of the day. Most units took advantage of the opportunities made available during operations to accomplish needed improvements in readiness. This included rehearsals for landings, communications exercises, as well as general quarters drills.[23]

Maintaining combat readiness for 70 separate units, on 20 different ships, with more than 6,000 men for months at a time was especially difficult. Training of ground units on board ship is difficult under the best of conditions; the demand of combat readiness did not make it easier. The aviation units were already geared to a high tempo of operations that did not allow, for them at least, this benefit. The long periods afloat and ashore were tempered by the proximity of fighting in Vietnam. These operations reversed the normal relation of staff to line, with headquarters personnel being more actively involved in the conduct of the war and the riflemen and platoon leaders standing by. First Lieutenant Laurence W. Rush, an HMM-165 pilot, noted that they had to content themselves with monitoring the radios and listening to Air Force and Navy pilots flying "in country," "We listened to strafing and bombing runs, army chopper strikes, rescue ops and Arc Lights — that was B-52 high-altitude bombing strikes. We listened and thought that soon we were going to get our chance."[24]

Beans, Bullets, and AvGas: Logistics

Under the existing military assistance programs, direct replacement of "service unique" equipment was authorized to the South Vietnamese. To the U.S. Marine Corps, this meant the reconstitution of equipment and supplies lost in combat, as well as programs to upgrade the VNMC's potential. In addition to advisory personnel, additional material support was provided to the Vietnamese through the Marine Advisory Unit. To Colonel Dorsey, most significant was the emergency air shipment that brought 105mm howitzers, trucks, individual and crew served weapons, gas masks, and other "combat essential items to Da Nang Air Base less than six days after the initial combat loss report had been received in Washington, D.C."[25] The logistics advisor, Major Stanley G. Pratt, had direct telephone contact to Headquarters Marine Corps by way of the headquarters command center. Supported by the Assistant Commandant of the Marine Corps, General Earl E. Anderson, the Installation and Logistics Division, sent timely replacement of unit equipment lost in the spring battles. The close rapport between the Vietnamese Marines and the U.S. Marines paid dividends, as direct flights of replacement stocks were made into Da Nang before the start of the Lam Son counteroffensive.

General Metzger, as III MAF commander, was involved in a number of support activities cutting across the spectrum of deployed units on land, sea, and air. Units of the 3d Marine Division and 1st Marine Aircraft Wing units also required an extensive logistics effort. During 1972, this III MAF logistic "tail" stretched from ships in the Tonkin Gulf and depots in the jungles of Thailand back to the Philippines, Taiwan, Japan, and even to the United States. As the wing commander, Major General Leslie

E. Brown, felt his major achievement during the period was the coordination of the deployment of tactical and support units to combat in Southeast Asia at several far-flung sites.[26] The cost to the 1st MAW alone in terms of maintenance, ordnance, and fuel was significant. The 9th MAB commander, General Miller, later wrote that the 3d Marine Commander, Major General Joseph C. Fegan, had "turned his division 'inside-out' in terms of personnel and equipment" to support III MAF.[27]

There was a need was to maintain all manner of equipment at workshop (3d echelon) and depot (4th echelon) level at locations where facilities and support agreements did not exist. The continued readiness of the 9th MAB, MAG-12, and MAG-15 depended upon their organic maintenance program to provide maintenance for machines and Marines, not an easy task on a constantly moving amphibious transport or at a remote airfield. Material readiness depended on maintenance of equipment and on the availability of parts for repair, and replacement of items that could not be serviced on ship. Restricted space, facilities, diverse organizations, and constraints due to contingencies were also factors to overcome. General Miller's units with Task Force 76 lacked the extensive facilities in Vietnam that existed prior to 1972. Units at sea were dependent upon Admiral William P. Mack's Underway Replenishment Group for the supply of fuel, oil, lubricants, and food from supply ships. Moreover, combat essential parts or equipment took up to 14 days to arrive from Okinawa and the Philippines.

When battalions and squadrons arrived in the Vietnam theater in April, they were able to take advantage of the U.S. Army's departure from Vietnam to replace or obtain supplies and equipment informally from stocks being left that would otherwise have gone to the South Vietnamese. While common equipment could be "scrounged" from Navy, Army, and Air Force units, General Miller needed more reliable means to maintain forces afloat. On 16 April, General Metzger directed that high priority items be sent to Fleet Air Support Unit, Da Nang, for transfer by helicopter to units at sea. This effort was supported by daily VMGR-152 flights that arrived from Iwakuni, Japan, via Okinawa and the Philippines. The initial efforts to establish needed coordination in Da Nang ran afoul of the JCS-imposed personnel ceilings on General Creighton W. Abrams that prohibited Marine helicopters and personnel remaining ashore overnight. As a result, Fleet Air Support Unit (FASU), Da Nang was unable to establish a Marine liaison team to handle the increase of cargo. The Navy met this demand by bringing in sailors from the FASU at Cubi Point in the Philippines, and the Marines in turn sent their men to replace the sailors at Cubi Point.

III MAF Amphibious Assault Force Buildup in 1972

STRENGTH

	2 Apr	9 Apr	27 Apr	23 May	25 May	13 Jun	21 Jun	26 Jun	17 Jul
6000				6042					
				MAB					
				BLT					
5000				BLT					
				MAU	5005				
			4614	MAU	MAB		4902		
4000			MAB		BLT	4331	MAB		
			BLT		MAU	MAB	HMA		
			MAU		MAU	BLT	BLT		
			MAU			MAU	MAU	3639	
3000		3045					MAU	MAB	
		MAB						HMA	
		BLT						MAU	
2000		MAU						MAU	
									1924
									MAB
1000	1424								HMA
	MAU								MAU

Adapted from FMFPac MarOpsSEA and CNA MarActySEA Material

This system reduced the delivery time for critical items to three and four days and mail, a high-priority morale item, averaged a four-day delivery time from the United States.[28] Personnel movement to and from the brigade paralleled these supply lines. Outgoing Marines on emergency leave, transfer, liaison, or advance parties traveled from ship via Marine helicopters to Hue or Da Nang and connected with flights to Okinawa or the Philippines from Da Nang. Incoming personnel arrived at Da Nang by air or ship and were picked up at FASU by helicopter for transport to their units. Replacements who had left the United States for service in Okinawa were often in a state of shock when they were sent on to Vietnam at a time when there were reportedly no Marines left "in country." "Prado's Bunker" and "The Red Dog Inn," the most convenient transient quarters and bar, became familiar landmarks to FASU "customers" as they flowed along the supply and replacement routes serving the seabased 9th MAB for almost 12 months.

Air transport was vital to the employment of MAG-12 and MAG-15 during the Spring Offensive. Advance parties flew to the operating area in Marine KC-130s as soon as warning orders were received to coordinate for the reception and support of the incoming squadrons to Vietnam. Concurrently, flying squadrons deployed directly to Vietnam or through NAS Cubi Point, Philippines. Squadron support personnel and material flew to forward locations in air transport obtained from a variety of sources, including the Military Airlift Command (MAC) and Pacific Air Transport Management Agency (PATMA), while remaining supplies followed on military and civilian sealift.

VMGR-152 tankers and crews assigned to the detachment at NAS Cubi Point met initial air refueling requirements. The Hercules tanker version could carry 32,140 pounds of fuel and could refuel two aircraft at the same time. The cargo version could carry up to 92 passengers or 26,913 pounds of cargo. Both VMGR aircraft provided direct support to fighter and attack squadrons moving into Da Nang, Bien Hoa, and Nam Phong. VMFA-212 employed the services of six tankers and a cargo aircraft in its move from Kaneohe Bay, Hawaii, to Da Nang during its Pacific transit from Hawaii. Eventually another four tankers were stationed in Thailand with TF Delta. A factor in the heavy demands placed on the tankers was the incompatibility of Navy and Air Force refueling systems, although the Air Force tankers could reconfigure with advance notice. The magnitude of tanker support is indicated by statistics from the four-plane VMGR-152 Detachment Delta at Nam Phong. In the year it was deployed, it flew 4,721 hours, refueled 3,239 aircraft, and transferred 4,434,280 gallons of JP-4 fuel.[29]

III MAF Aviation Force Buildup in 1972
(Excluding units with Seventh Fleet)

STRENGTH

Date	6 Apr	10 Apr	16 May	31 May	13 Jun	18 Jun	21 Jun	24 Jun	1 Jul
									3633
					3578	3578		3477	MAG
3000					MAG	MAG	3113	MAG	MAG
					MAG	MAG	MAG	MAG	TFD
					TFD	TFD	MAG	TFD	
2000							TFD		
				2141					
			1639	MAG					
			MAG	MAG					
1000		1008	MAG	TFD					
		MAG							
	700	MAG							
	MAG								

Y-axis: 6000, 5000, 4000, 3000, 2000, 1000

Adapted from FMFPac MarOpsSEA and CNA MarActySEA Material

The KC-130 served to fly Marine logistic (MarLog) runs as well as for refueling. These same VMGR planes constituted an intratheater airlift between MAC and commercial air support to the forward locations. Starting in April, a daily MarLog flight ran from Iwakuni, to Okinawa, Cubi Point, and Da Nang, where helicopters ferried material to the 9th MAB. These flights were expanded to include Bien Hoa and Nam Phong as landing sites.[30] The demand upon the available planes and crews from Futema required additional reinforcement. VMGR-352 aircraft deployed in April, bringing the total of KC-130s to 15 in the Western Pacific, of which eight were configured for tanker operations.

General Metzger was also concerned about his ability to support sustained operations at the new locations, combined with increasing demands for logistic support made upon General Abrams and General Vogt.[31] The support structures in Vietnam developed by the Marines in the 1960s were no longer in place, including accurate information about existing facilities and services. Deployments to Da Nang and Bien Hoa resulted in support from Seventh Air Force of common items such as ordnance and fuel. Uncommon support, including rework facilities, came from the FASU at Cubi Point and through the use of the ubiquitous MarLog for high-priority items. On 27 April 1972, General Brown established Detachment Bravo, H&MS-15 at Cubi Point to conduct scheduled inspections, engine buildups, and provide intermediate maintenance activity (AIMD) support for deployed squadrons. Remote from Vietnam, it was a secure location to work on aircraft shuttled in and out of the combat zone.[32]

The deployments of MAG-12 and MAG-15 presented substantially different problems: MAG-12 moved into existing facilities with direct support from Seventh Air Force and MACV; the MAG-15 movement to Nam Phong was to an empty airstrip. For MAG-15, base development was the initial priority. Support at Nam Phong was predicated on the Air Force's definition of "bare base" operations that required "...no physical facilities other than a usable runway, taxiway, parking area, and source of water."[33] General Jones at FMFPac authorized several actions to free material for the construction of facilities after receiving a report dated 10 May from Brigadier General Andrew W. O'Donnell and the Officer in Charge of Construction, Thailand. The FMFPac commander directed General Metzger to ship to Nam Phong AM-2 matting from MCAS Futema, "Butler" buildings from Camp Butler, Quonset huts from the 3d Marine Division, and contingency construction material held by 3d Force Service Regiment.

To build the base required the efforts of Mobile Construction Battalion 5, the Marine Wing Support Group, and contract civilian construction companies to install fuel storage, navigational aids, parking ramps, ordnance storage, cargo handling facilities, and the road network. The MAG was able to fly limited sorties after fuel became available and air controllers were in the field's towers. Renovation of existing buildings, development of a water system, and construction of warehouses and security positions were followed by laying concrete for a helicopter pad and constructing housing, mess hall, and seven concrete "Wonder Arch" aircraft shelters. Support of TF Delta was dependent upon airlift to bring in 7,400 tons of cargo and 3,000 men with MAC C-141s. Seven weeks later the USS *Tuscaloosa* (LST 1187), USS *Mobile*, and the MSC *American Ranger* delivered another 628 tons of cargo, mostly vehicles, through Sattahip. Despite General Jones' personal interest in building up Nam Phong, it still took from 24 May until 17 June for the first combat flights to be flown from the base.

General O'Donnell also had to consider the availability of repair parts from the logistics support group, the lack of storage facilities, and the less-than-effective response from the Naval Supply Center at Cubi Bay and the 3d FSR at Okinawa to supply requests. Repair parts for electronic and ordnance items were not stocked at levels adequate to meet increased failure rates from combat usage. All of this was complicated by the different locations of MAG-15 and the extended distances involved with the supply "pipeline." In June 1972, when MK46 and MK47 decoy flares were expended at a rate that was greater than the receipt of replacement stocks from the United States, General Jones expedited their resupply.[34] Also by 17 June, the PATMA airlift was only half completed, with a supply backlog at NAS Cubi Point. A solution had to be found before shortages affected the tempo of operations. On 4 July, Lieutenant Colonel Raneley A. Brown's KC-130s began an emergency shuttle of critical cargo from Cubi Point to Nam Phong, to build up stocks of fuel and ordnance. Without a 15-to-30 day amount of supplies on hand, General O'Donnell believed TF Delta would be dependent upon a constant flow of daily shipments from the Air Force at Udorn, 77 road kilometers to the north.[35]

Other difficulties arose when supplies of matting, generators, and lighting became short. Shared group and wing ground support equipment (GSE) was in short supply because the number and dispersion of detachments exceeded authorized allowances of equipment. A solution to this was the consolidation of maintenance Marines and equipment at common locations to support a number of detachments. Further problems cited for sustained operations at Nam Phong were with TACAN and liquid oxygen equipment failures. This situation was compounded by clouds of insects that jammed filters and heavy rains that virtually turned the area into a swamp.[36]

Thunder from the Sea, Fire from the Sky

During 1972, Marine advisors believed their value to the South Vietnamese was directly related to their ability to request and control supporting arms — aircraft, artillery, and naval gunfire. They were only a "troop without a rifle" if they could not. In fire support coordination, the efforts of Marine Advisory Unit and ANGLICO personnel merged, with advisors becoming supporting arms coordinators and ANGLICO members becoming involved with tactical advice. Colonel Donald L. Price remembered that every move or stop he made with his VNMC battalion caused him to go down his supporting arms checklist from mortars, artillery, naval gunfire, and air to medevac agencies and procedures; all as taught in Marine Corps service schools and observed closely by the Vietnamese Marines who saw it work when needed.[37]

The South Vietnamese relied on supporting arms because the number of enemy forces and defenses made tactical surprise difficult to achieve, particularly after the battlefield had become immovable along fixed lines. The success of the assault landings conducted by the 9th MAB and the Vietnamese Marines depended, in part, on the availability, control, and coordination of firepower from Vietnamese and American forces.[E] This effort was hindered earlier in the year by a lack of controlling agencies and later on by the volume and complexity of fire coordination efforts required to use this support effectively.[38] Therefore the majority of the American Marines sent to Vietnam during 1972 had fire-support and communications backgrounds.

Previous VNMC work in fire-support coordination was based upon battalion- and brigade-level experience where the commander had direct-support artillery. The VNMC unit commanders, some of whom had been trained in U.S. Marine schools, observed their advisor's effort at the unit level in plotting fire support down to the battalion-level mortars and were aware of the vital need to integrate the various weapons systems. Their orientation was not conducive to control and coordination by the division, which lacked the requisite personnel and communications equipment.[39]

During the 1972 period, American supporting units often required complete and detailed planning earlier than could reasonably be expected from the South Vietnamese in I Corps.[F] The Vietnamese Marine Division, with its attached American advisors and ANGLICO personnel, met these requirements in most cases. In this process General Lan and his staff selected specific objectives, while General Miller

---

(E) For the period from June through December 1972, the Vietnamese Marine Division was supported by the expenditure of 1,457,142 105mm artillery rounds; 161,058 155mm artillery rounds, 289,963 naval gunfire rounds, 4,959 tactical air sorties; and 698 Arc Light sorties. (Marine Advisory Unit Historical Summary, 1972)

(F) The combat operations in northern MR1 were land operations supported from the sea rather than purely amphibious operations.

and his staff determined landing zones and beaches. Fire-support plans then developed for two to three hours of preparatory fire from air, naval gunfire, and the VNMC Division and ARVN corps artillery; B-52 bombing of the landing zone or beaches; and tactical air strikes just prior to landing the assault forces (see chart with this chapter).[40]

General Lan's staff used overlays and target lists to plan helicopter approach and retirement lanes, landing zones, friendly positions, and required fires. ANGLICO, in conjunction with USAF and VNMC planners, produced joint schedules of fire that were based upon Arc Light support availability. Delivery of fires was made according to time schedules with fluctuations in tactical air availability being covered by artillery and naval fires. Plans remained flexible until the B-52 support was confirmed, usually by 1600 the day prior to the operation. The Seventh Air Force also needed air requests the day prior to execution, which conflicted with the Eighth Air Force confirmation schedule. This situation was alleviated when the Eighth Air Force confirmation time was changed to 1400 to coincide with the Seventh Air Force. The MR 1 Direct Air Support Center received its copies of plans from the USAF liaison officer of the VNMC Division, and also briefed the supporting tactical air support squadron for assignments, planned targets, on station aircraft, post-landing support, and air controller requirements. Artillery requirements were assigned to supporting units by the VNMC Division Artillery representative with VNMC brigade input in the form of requests via the artillery chain of command.

The VNMC Naval Gunfire Liaison Officer, or his I Corps counterpart, delivered completed plans to the Naval Gunfire Support Group (Task Group 70.8.9). The Naval Gunfire Support Group staff assigned targets, missions, and fire-support stations. Overall naval gunfire support in early 1972 was hampered by the decline in "gun" ships from 292 vessels in Fiscal Year 1965 to 128 in Fiscal Year 1973. When the Spring Offensive began, there was a shortage of ships to meet the demand for fire support.[G] Arrival of the USS *Newport News* (CA 148) arrival with 8" guns provided an increase in capabilities, if not in numbers, from the available destroyers and their 5"54 and 5"38 guns.[41] Demands for support multiplied as targets south of the DMZ increased and were further expanded as restrictions against targets in North Vietnam were removed.

Generals Metzger and Miller believed that any amphibious action ashore by American Marines required six to eight destroyers and a cruiser for support. Such operations also needed local air superiority provided by an estimated two aircraft carriers and two

---

(G) Lieutenant Colonel D'Wayne Gray of Sub Unit One and advisors with forward VNMC battalions credit two destroyers, the USS *Buchanan* (DDG 14) and the USS *Anderson* (DD 786) with blunting the NVA ground attack across the DMZ during the first days of the offensive, a time when poor weather restricted tactical air support. Captain John W. Ripley, stated that, at Dong Ha, naval gunfire was responsive to fire-requests in every case "... and was the only supporting arm which could respond with a volume of fire approaching that of the enemy's." (Ripley intvw)

VNMC Division Supporting Arms Schedule
for 11 July 1972 Assault

Naval Gunfire*

2400 — 0600	2,400 rounds harassment and interdiction fires
0600 — 0800	1,500 rounds preparation fires
0800 — L-Hour	On-call direct-support fires
	(Two direct-support ships for VNMC Brigade 147 on D-1, three direct-support ships as of 0800 D-Day)

Artillery

2400 — 0600	Harassment and interdiction fires
0600 — 0800	Preparation fires
0800 — L-Hour	On-call direct-support fires

Tactical Air

0800 — 1140	Ten flights of tactical air
	(Six sorties of U.S. aircraft with M84 bombs, two sorties of VNAF aircraft with CBU55s — between third and fourth B-52 Arc Lights)
	One airborne U.S. forward air controller on station until 1900**

On-Call Tactical Air

1200 — 1230	One sortie with bombs and napalm
1230 — 1300	One sortie with bombs and napalm
1300 — 1900	Two sorties per hour

Air Cavalry

Command and control helicopter
Two light observation helicopters
Eight helicopter gunships
Two search and rescue helicopters

*An alternate naval gunfire plan was developed for 0800 — 1140 should weather preclude the use of tactical air during this period.

**A naval gunfire spotter was airborne with the FAC aircraft. The FAC was available to control airstrikes if naval gunfire targets were not available; however, priority was given to naval gunfire missions in the objective area.

Adapted from the Song Than 9-72 Folder, Marine Advisory Unit File

Da Nang-based fighter squadrons. On 19 April 1972, General Miller noted that the Navy, engaged in Operation Linebacker, could not provide the necessary forces to support amphibious landings in North Vietnam. FRAC's Major General Frederick J. Kroesen, Jr., voiced his opposition to amphibious operations north of the DMZ, that would result in reduced naval gunfire support to MR 1 at a crucial time. The demands for support for both Seventh Fleet operations and MACV operations were in constant conflict, influencing 9th MAB relations with VNMC and FRAC. A related constraint on naval gunfire was the availability of aerial spotting. Adequate numbers of USAF aircraft to meet ANGLICO needs, as well as aircraft capable of surviving aloft in northern MR 1 and North Vietnam, were not available. As a result, naval gunfire was limited to either direct or unobserved fires of decreased effectiveness.

ANGLICO's Lieutenant Colonel George E. Jones believed that the problem of quality and quantity of naval gunfire support resolved itself by mid-year when targets of opportunity declined along the coast and support to the ARVN Airborne Division increased in the drive towards Quang Tri City. The need for qualified fire support personnel and communications equipment for the South Vietnamese was recognized, but never organized prior to the ceasefire and withdrawal of American assets.[42]

A subjective comment on the battlefield effect of concentrated firepower was provided by a North Vietnamese Army veteran of the 1972 Quang Tri City fighting who recalled a B-52 Arc Light. As the battlefield became very quiet and he knew something was going to happen:

> I just looked up into the sky and saw how beautiful the day was, the sun was shining. And then we saw the bombs, round big black discs ... the noise of the bombs and you couldn't see anything at all because of the smoke and the dust and we couldn't hear anything at all.[43]

War in the Ether

No less a part of effective firepower was the targeting efforts by Captain Clarence W. Phillips with 12 men of Detachment "N," 1st Radio Battalion. This support reached the VNMC Division through Captain Frank M. Izenout, Jr., the Marine advisor with the main division command post at Hue.

Detachment "N" had originally deployed with the 9th MAB for the exercise in Korea. Integrated with the Task Force 76 Joint Intelligence Center and operating from the supplemental radio spaces of the USS *Blue Ridge* using input from the service cryptologic agencies in Southeast Asia, the detachment provided signal-intelligence information. On 18 April, signal-intelligence tasking authority was passed to General

Miller, commanding 9th MAB, and the next day the detachment was augmented by another officer and 11 enlisted operators from the 1st Radio Battalion in Hawaii.

Operating from the *Blue Ridge* posed reception problems because of the distance from shore. From 24 April 1972, two or three direct support elements were in operation from naval gunfire ships at any one time, with control remaining at the headquarters element on the *Blue Ridge*. An additional 10 operators expanded the detachment, with further resources available as needed from the Marine Support Battalion.[H]

In July, Captain Phillips and his men moved to the USS *Paul Revere* (LPA 248) with the 9th MAB staff when the USS *Blue Ridge* returned to the United States. The detachment analysts relocated to the Naval Communications Station, San Miguel, Philippines, until 21 January 1973, when Detachment "N" was deactivated. It provided timely and continuous support throughout the III MAF response to the North Vietnamese invasion.[44]

(H) The Marine Support Battalion was a component of the Naval Security Group and consisted of companies that were assigned with Naval Security Group Activities worldwide.

CHAPTER THIRTEEN ENDNOTES

Unless otherwise noted, material in this section is derived from MGen Leslie E. Brown, "1st Marine Aircraft Wing Achievements and Milestones," dtd 8Apr76; MGen Joseph C. Fegan, Jr., intvw dtd 8Jan73, Tape 5062 (OralHistColl, MCHC, Washington, D.C.); FMFPac, "Analysis of Human Affairs Poll," dtd Jul72, hereafter FMFPac Human Affairs; and HQMC, "Report on Marine Corps Manpower Quality and Force Structure," dtd 31Dec75, hereafter HQMC Manpower study. See also Henry I. Shaw, Jr., and Ralph W. Donnelly, *Blacks in the Marine Corps* (Washington, D.C.: Hist&MusDiv, 1975), hereafter Shaw and Donnelly; The BDM Corporation, *A Study of the Strategic Lessons Learned in Vietnam*, 8 vols (McLean, Va.: 1980), Vol. 6, "The Soldier."

Leadership, Morale, and Readiness

1 Col Robert D. Heinl, Jr., "The Collapse of the Armed Forces," *Armed Forces Journal*, 7Jun71, p. 31.

2 Metzger comments.

3 Bateman comments.

4 Dr. V. Keith Fleming, Jr., comments on draft ms, dtd 15Dec89 (Vietnam Comment File).

5 Dr. Allan R. Millet, comments on draft ms, dtd 21Dec89 (Vietnam Comment File).

6 HQMC Manpower study, pp. 4, 13-14; "Deserters and Absentees" CMC Reference Notebook 1973, Tab II-H-6; "Courts-Martial During Second Half of Calendar Year 1973," CMC Reference Notebook 1974, Tab II-H-3.

7 Fegan intvw; See also Heinl, op. cit., pp. 30-37 and Dr Thomas C. Bond, "Fragging: A Study," Army, Apr77, pp. 45-47.

8 FMFPac Human Affairs, p. iv.

9 Ibid.

10 Bernard C. Nalty and LtCol Ralph F. Moody, *A Brief History of U.S. Marine Corps Officer Procurement 1775–1969* (Washington, D.C.: Hist&MusDiv, 1970), pp. 20-25.

11 Jones comments.

12 HQMC(AP12), "USMC Statistical Report on Military Personnel Strength and Turnover by Race," dtd 30 Sept 71, Tables I, II, and III (RefSec, MCHC, Washington, D.C.); HQMC(AO1K), Summary of Significant Racial Incidents at Marine Corps Installations, Aug68-Nov71 (RefSec, MCHC, Washington, D.C.); "Summary of Significant Racial Incidents at Marine Corps Installations," CMC Reference Notebook 1974, Tab II-H-9; Shaw and Donnelly, pp. 69-83; Brown comments; Fegan intvw.

13 Fogleman comments.

14 LtCol Mark B. Pizzo, Comments on draft ms, dtd 13Apr90 (Vietnam Comment File).

15 HQMC Manpower study, p. 3.

16 RAdm Wycliffe D. Toole, Jr., Comments on draft ms, dtd 29Nov89 (Vietnam Comment File).

17 "D Company Has Formula For Morale," *Okinawa Marine*, 14Jul72 (Vietnam Comment File).

18 Ynacay comments.

19 LtCol Eddie R. Maag, comments on draft ms, dtd 28Dec89 (Vietnam Comment File).

20 LtCol Gary D. Solis, *Marines and Military Law in Vietnam: Trial by Fire* (Washington, D.C.: Hist&MusDiv, 1989), pp. 231-244; Cosmas and Murray, op. cit., pp. 344-369.

21 Thomas Hobbes, *Leviathan*, I, (Chicago: Encyclopedia Brittanica, Inc.), 1952, p. 85.

22 Brown comments.

23 CNA MarActySEA, pp. 57-58.

24 Rush, op. cit., p. 71.

Beans, Bullets, and AvGas: Logistics
Unless otherwise noted, material in this section is derived from FMFPac MarOpsSEA and CNA MarActySEA.

25 Col Stanley G. Pratt comment, CSC symposium; SMA HistSum 1972, pp. 4-5.

26 Brown, pp. 10-11.

27 Miller comment.

28 FMFPac MarOpsSEA, pp. 2-29 to 2-30; CNA MarActySEA, pp. 16, 57-58.

29 TFD Brief, Tab H, Operations.

30 CNA MarActySEA, p. 78.

31 FMFPac MarOpsSEA, pp. 2-29 to 2-31.

32 CNA MarActySEA, p. 93.

33 USAF Tactical Air Command Project 3782, "Bare Base Mobility;" CNA MarActySEA, pp. 14, 95-101.

34 FMFPac MarOpsSEA, p. 3-27.

35 CNA MarActySEA, pp. 99-101.

36 CNA MarActySEA, pp. 93-94.

Thunder from the Sea, Fire from the Sky

Unless otherwise noted, material in this section is from Operations Analysis Group, "Defense of Hue and Quang Tri City, The 1972 NVA Invasion of MR-1," ONR study CNS 1035 dtd May74, hereafter CNA Defense of Hue; and CHECO Invasion 72.

37 Price comments.

38 Gray memo; CNA Defense of Hue, pp. 1-2.

39 Artillery advisor memo to ASMA, dtd 21Mar72, SMA memo to CGFRAC dtd 23Jan73, MarAdvU Turnover Folder (MarAdvU File).

40 CNA MarActySEA, pp. 62ff.

41 Gray comments; Ripley intvw; CNA MarActySEA, p. 14.

42 Jones Comments; SMA memo dtd 26Dec72, MarAdvU Turnover Folder (MarAdvU File).

43 Nguyen Ngoc Hoang, television intvw by Morley Safer, dtd 19Mar89, CBS "60 Minutes" (Vietnam Comment File).

War in the Ether

Unless otherwise noted, material in this chapter is derived from 1stRadBn ComdC, Mar72-Jan73; LtCol John K. Hyatt, Jr., comments on draft ms, dtd 10Aug88 (Vietnam Comment File).

44 CNA MarOpsSea, PP. 58-61.

PART V

REPRISE AND ASSESSMENT

CHAPTER FOURTEEN
CEASEFIRE AND CONSOLIDATION

The Final Act • Operation Countdown, 'On the Land' •
Operation Countdown, ' and Sea' • Operation Countdown, 'and Air'

The Final Act

General Frederick C. Weyand, the last MACV commander, insisted to General Metzger that he had to have the Marines off the coast of South Vietnam to ensure the security of the remaining American personnel in the country, support that could only be provided by Metzger's III MAF. At a minimum, this was with two Marine Amphibious Units (MAUs) at sea and the planes of Marine Aircraft Groups 12 and 15. General Metzger later asserted that this period of the Vietnam War "repeatedly demonstrated the many functions that only amphibious forces can perform."[1]

Determined resistance of the South Vietnamese and the direct support by the Americans, including the air campaign against North Vietnam, halted and then reversed the Communist "Nguyen-Hue" Spring Invasion. President Nixon had used intensive diplomatic and military pressure to bring about a settlement of the war as the South Vietnamese regained lost territory and the aerial bombing and mining of North Vietnam took effect. By 11 October 1972, the mining and bombing efforts had closed ports through which North Vietnam had obtained 85 percent of its foreign trade: "seaborne imports into North Vietnam have been cut from over 250,000 tons a month to almost none."[2] By then, U.S. authorities believed the North Vietnamese wanted to reach an agreement. As a result, on 23 October 1972, U.S. Armed Forces stopped air and naval gunfire bombardment north of the 20th Parallel. But numerous false starts and recriminations by both parties and their allies occurred as the proposed ceasefire approached.

President Nixon authorized Operation Linebacker II on 18 December 1972 when the North Vietnamese failed to act in good faith on the previous ceasefire proposals, opening the way to the Christmas bombing of Hanoi and the virtual destruction of critical targets in North Vietnam. Referring to the "late December 1972 US Blitz on

North Vietnam," the Communists stated that the Nixon Administration had mobilized almost all its strategic bombers in Southeast Asia and the Pacific, and tactical aircraft in South Vietnam, Thailand, and with the Seventh Fleet "to conduct a strategic bombing operation against North Viet Nam the savageness of which is unprecedented in the whole history of the US war of aggression in this country."[3] The intensity of operations was unmatched by any of the previous eight years of strikes against North Vietnam. Linebacker II's blows against military and economic targets brought the North Vietnamese back to the negotiating table.

The "Agreement on Ending the War and Restoring Peace in Vietnam" was signed as the result of negotiations by Dr. Henry Kissinger and Le Duc Tho at the Paris Conference on Vietnam. The ceasefire was a part of an accord that met both American and North Vietnamese demands that had evolved during the course of the conflict. It was a unilateral accord with the less-than-wholehearted concurrence of the Republic of South Vietnam and the Communist "Provisional Revolutionary Government." It called for cessation of all military operations in North and South Vietnam to go into effect at 2400 Greenwich Mean Time, 27 January 1973. All forces would remain in place, with disengagement supervised by a Two Party Joint Military Commission; only replacement of existing equipment and supplies was authorized.[4] Within 60 days all Americans would withdraw, all prisoners of war would be returned, and all U.S. mines would be cleared from North Vietnamese waterways. Seventh Fleet and III MAF operations in both North and South Vietnam ceased on 28 January 1973 with the signing of these accords. For the Americans, including the U.S. Marines, this agreement brought an end of combat and support operations.[(A)] The ceasefire campaign was over.[5]

For the Vietnamese of both sides, the struggle continued, fought hard from the morning of the ceasefire and for a month or two thereafter. The Communists throughout South Vietnam had put out the red and blue flags of the National Liberation Front in a land-grab effort just prior to the ceasefire, expecting the South Vietnamese to be hampered by the terms and timing of the agreement. The South Vietnamese countered with military attacks during and after the ceasefire, which were successful in defending territory they already held.

While the major American equipment and resupply effort ended with the ceasefire, the NVA infiltration effort continued. This included numbers of armored vehicles and artillery moved into base areas in South Vietnam. Although the ARVN and NVA had equal numbers of armored vehicles inside South Vietnam, the North Vietnamese had twice as many with trained crews. Similar buildups were detected in artillery and antiaircraft weapons that countered any South Vietnamese air superiority.[6]

(A) Operations continued in Laos until 21 February 1973 and in Cambodia until 15 August 1973.

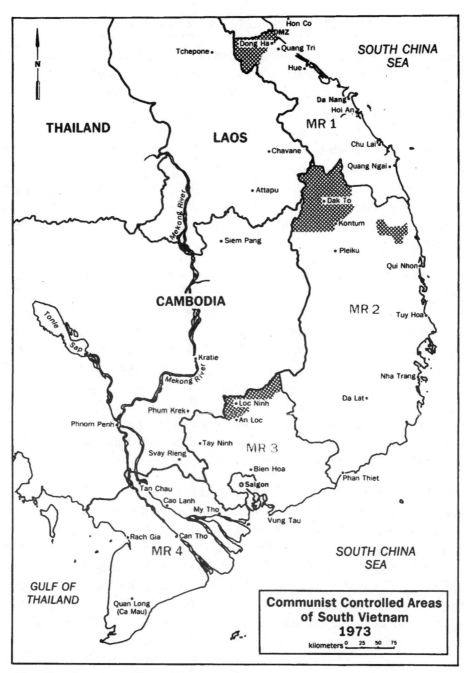

Adapted from Government of Vietnam Material

Operation Countdown, 'On the Land'

Operation Countdown, the final withdrawal of Free World forces from Vietnam, began immediately after the agreement was signed and the withdrawal of Marine Corps units followed on schedule.[B] First to leave was Sub Unit One, 1st ANGLICO. From 1 April through 10 September 1972, this specialized unit bore the brunt of the increased demands for air and naval gunfire support throughout the whole of Vietnam.[C]7 Lieutenant General Louis H. Wilson, Jr., the FMF Pacific commander, observed that Sub Unit One's departure made it the last Fleet Marine Force unit to leave Vietnam and that the aggressive spirit displayed by ANGLICO airborne and ground spotters, combined with the firepower of Seventh Fleet naval gunfire ships, "was given considerable credit for stemming the tide of the NVA invasion in MR 1 during March/April 1972."[8]

Lieutenant Colonel George E. Jones, Sub Unit One's last commander in Vietnam, recorded that on the morning of 28 January 1973 his Marines and sailors throughout Vietnam's four military regions ceased active operations in support of the South Vietnamese. Like other redeploying units, there was an incremental transfer of personnel and equipment phased by "X-days."[D] Jones stated simply on 17 February 1973 that Sub Unit One, 1st ANGLICO, "ceased to have an operational mission and all efforts were directed towards the deactivation of the unit."[9] With a majority of personnel and equipment gone, the remaining members boarded flights for duty stations elsewhere in the Marine Corps. This marked the end of eight continuous years of combat support to the South Vietnamese Armed Forces and their allies.[10] Sub Unit One, 1st ANGLICO, transferred to FMFPac and deactivated as a unit on 14 March 1973.

The Marine Advisory Unit was also deactivated by the ceasefire. It had been in the process of withdrawing battalion advisors and shifting the emphasis of support to logistics, training, and staff functions as part of the overall reduction of American forces at the beginning of 1972. The NVA invasion reversed this as the unit was totally committed to the fight. The advisor structure had been reinforced by additional ANGLICO, U.S. Army, U.S. Air Force, and U.S. Navy personnel as it deployed to MR 1 in April 1972. According to the Senior Marine Advisor, they all "encountered exceptionally intense and continuous enemy artillery attacks-by-fire, ground attacks, and the introduction of large numbers of enemy armored units."[11] To compensate for casualties, disease, and exhaustion among the Marines, nine additional temporary-duty advisors were assigned.[E] The first of their number

---

(B) As of 31 January 1973, there were 21,821 American servicemen in South Vietnam. (MACV ComdHist 1973, p. 476)

(C) Sub Unit One lost three killed and three missing and suffered fourteen wounded in action.

(D) X-Day being the ceasefire date of 28 January 1973.

(E) Fourteen advisors were wounded in action during 1972.

arrived in July and a second group in October 1972. At the peak of the Spring Offensive, the advisory unit reached a strength of 66, including U.S. Navy medical personnel.

Anticipating the withdrawal of American forces at the end of 1972 and possible restrictions on support, the Departments of Defense and State sought to accelerate the delivery of equipment approved for Vietnamization programs. Project Enhance Plus began on 14 October 1972 and was completed with the delivery of 39 armored personnel carriers from the U.S. Army, 7 Air Force aircraft, and 31 amphibian tractors from the Marines. These high-priority items, except for the amphibian tractors, were delivered by air, interrupted only by the tentative ceasefire with North Vietnam.[12]

The U.S. Marines provided the Vietnamese Marines 1 LVTR-5, 2 LVTC-5s, and 28 LVTP-5s, all amphibian tractors in recovery, command, or personnel carrier configurations. These tractors were taken from III MAF inventories to hasten delivery and loaded on U.S. Navy amphibious ships at Okinawa beginning 8 November 1972. Delivery was completed by 27 November 1972, when all the vehicles were unloaded at the VNMC compound near Saigon. American Marines from the 1st Amphibian Tractor Battalion and the 3d Force Service Regiment accompanied these tracked vehicles to provide needed instruction in their use and maintenance. Follow-on training was arranged by Major Oliver M. Whipple, Jr., advisor to Captain Doan Thien Niem's fledgling Amphibian Tractor Company, including rehearsals at sea with the 9th MAB and Seventh Fleet amphibious groups.[13]

General Wilson at FMFPac and the senior advisor, Colonel Dorsey, believed the arrival of these amphibian tractors provided the VNMC Division with an assault capability previously lacking, a capability that allowed operations to be conducted north of the DMZ. In reality, the VNMC was saddled with additional maintenance and supply problems and amphibious capability was never established because the Vietnamese Navy did not assign ships for amphibious operations or training.[F][14] Secretary of Defense Melvin R. Laird allowed the Marine Corps to fund $714 million in Fiscal Year 1974 to provide replacement LVT-7 series amphibian tractors. As the new model LVTP-7s became available, they were to be exchanged on a one-for-one basis for the LVTP-5s. This decision was approved by the Joint Chiefs of Staff in November 1972, but was then canceled by Secretary Laird in January 1973, putting an effective end to the program.

Colonel Dorsey and his staff had approached the ceasefire "in accordance with MACV directives" and planned as if for any other military evolution. They conceived three

---

(F) In June 1974, VNMC Logistic Support Branch head, LtCol George E. "Jody" Strickland justified the continued existence of the LVT program to the Defense Attache Office because of cross-country mobility and armored-infantry attack value rather than the amphibious assault value. (LtCol George E. Strickland, Comments on draft ms, dtd 4Jan90)

phases, keyed on "X-Day:" standdown (prior to X-Day), withdrawal (X to X + 45), and rollup (X + 45 to X + 60). Specific tasks had to be accomplished during each phase along the lines of standard military staff responsibilities: personnel; intelligence; operations; and logistics. The unit-level advisory effort continued through 16 February 1973, when the last two Marine advisors departed from the brigade and battalion levels. The American authorities in South Vietnam at the time reported that the "active USMC field advisory effort is terminated."

Living side-by-side with their counterparts, U.S. Marine advisors had provided sound tactical advice and enhanced Vietnamese Marine Corps combat effectiveness. The advisory unit "contributed immeasurably towards the development of the Vietnamese Marine Corps into a thoroughly professional fighting organization."[15] The last Senior Marine Advisor wrote in his final historical report about the division's finest hour, when two brigades of Vietnamese Marines were ordered to hold the invading Communist army at the My Chanh River, "and hold they did. The My Chanh Line was subjected to tremendous pressure and although it bent at times, it never broke. This was due to responsive supporting arms fire plans, excellent small-unit leadership, and the courage and tenacity of individual Vietnamese Marines."

In addition to standown affairs, Colonel Dorsey had to request spare parts for the LVT-5s which had not been included in the previous support agreements because of the planned acquisition of the LVT-7s. In March 1973, General Wilson and Admiral Bernard A. Clarey replied that spare parts were not available through the Marine Corps, but suggested the Republic of China as a source on a "government to government" basis. By that time, the advisory group believed the Vietnamese Marine Division was "almost totally self-sufficient in tactical operations and had made giant strides in self-sufficiency in all other areas."[16] The Americans described General Lan as a tough, professional Marine who demanded high standards of discipline and obedience. The Vietnamese Marines were seen as a "sharp, effective fighting unit" with ability and experience in independent, combined, and joint operations.

Colonel Dorsey reported on 27 March 1973, with the exception of minor alterations to withdrawal plans "the phase down of the Marine Advisory Unit was accomplished in a professional manner without appreciable problems. Until the end, the Marine Advisory Unit maintained a readiness to return to combat operations in support of the Vietnamese Marine Corps."[17]

The Marine Advisory Unit closed down on 29 March 1973 after serving with the Vietnamese Marine Corps for 18 years. That same day, Commander, Naval Forces Vietnam and the Naval Advisory Group ended an era of commitment to the

Vietnamese Navy and Marine Corps. All remaining tasks were turned over to the VNMC Logistics Support Branch, Navy Division, of the Defense Attache Office (DAO).[18] The improvement of amphibious capability and equipment maintenance were felt to be the two areas where "major DAO assistance is required."[19] These problems were passed to Lieutenant Colonel Walter D. Fillmore to resolve as head of the recently created Vietnamese Marine Corps Logistic Support Branch of the Defense Attache's Office in Saigon.[20]

Headed by a U.S. Marine lieutenant colonel, the VNMC Logistic Support Branch consisted of five U.S. Department of Defense civilians and 27 Vietnamese civilians. Functions of the Naval Advisory Group, Vietnam, were continued for maintenance and supply under existing support agreements through the Office of the Chief, Navy Division. This organization was a component of Army Major General John E. Murray's Defense Attache Office, which superseded MACV in March 1973. General Murray had previously served as the CinCPac J-4 and had been Admiral McCain's representative to MACV during the Spring Offensive. Instead of traditional attache duties, Murray's terms of reference in this assignment were for "cleaning up the battle fields" with the assistance of the Defense Logistics Agency.[21]

Lieutenant Colonel Fillmore, monitored, managed, and coordinated supply and maintenance requirements for U.S. Marine-peculiar and U.S. Army-common equipment transferred to the Vietnamese Marines. In his initial report, Fillmore indicated the difference between his logistics branch and the former Marine Advisory Unit. Because of the physical separation of the VNMC Logistics Support Branch in Saigon from the Vietnamese Marine Division in Quang Tri Province and with the limited number of personnel within the branch, "it is extremely difficult for the branch to accurately report on VNMC operational matters."[22]

Operation Countdown, 'and Sea'

Brigadier General Paul G. Graham's tour as 9th Marine Amphibious Brigade commander began on 16 November 1972. It was characterized by the preparation of contingency plans and liaison with MACV to support final troop withdrawals and the recovery of American prisoners. The 31st MAU and 33d MAU rotated in providing an amphibious force off the coast of MR 1. During this period, HMM-164 recovered the crew of a downed Air Force B-52 bomber from the Tonkin Gulf. The Marines provided troop training to the VNMC in December 1972 and January 1973. Colonel Charles T. Williamson, the 33d MAU commander, recalled that he worked closely with the advisory unit in late January 1973, and that this involved launching and maneuvering the LVT-5 tractors in the water: "I had been watching the tractors being driven by the Vietnamese until around noon and was just leaving the bridge of the flagship, USS *Cleveland* (LPD 7), when the Commodore called me back and handed me a 'flash' message," a ceasefire had been signed and the Amphibious Ready Group would return to Okinawa to prepare for Operation End Sweep. After going ashore to the 1st Regional Advisory Command (FRAC) headquarters in Da Nang to coordinate the abrupt discontinuation of the joint training, Colonel Williamson returned to the *Cleveland* at dusk, "As we lifted off, I looked down at Da Nang, which I had first seen in the Spring of 1965 .... I never had such an empty feeling."[23]

After the ceasefire, the 9th MAB Headquarters returned to Okinawa and operational control of afloat Marine amphibious units was turned over to III MAF. General Graham reported existing operational schedules as well as the task organization and missions of the 9th MAB and its subordinate units quickly changed: "No longer did the contingency evacuation or security responsibilities have priority. Instead emphasis was placed on using MAB and amphibious assets to support Operation Homecoming Afloat and Operation End Sweep."[24] On 31 January 1973, Seventh Fleet directed the commanders of the 9th MAB and TF 76 to work out the details for organizing a surface ready group to support contingency operations in support of FRAC and the American Embassy in Saigon.[25]

The military situation in MR 1, according to the 9th MAB liaison officer with FRAC, Major Howard L. Richey, indicated that NVA and ARVN activity would not pose an immediate threat to Americans in the region. On 2 February 1973, Major Richey observed a state of "cautious optimism" prevailing towards the ceasefire in MR 1 and that Da Nang "is in full observance of Tet."[26] Of a more prophetic note was the 5 February situation report that observed that South Vietnamese commanders "at all levels in MR 1 expressed deep concern over withdrawal of U.S. advisors at this time. Equally concerned over failure of ICCS (International Commission of Control and Supervision) to appear on scene to ensure compliance with cease fire, and failure of NVA to respect terms of Paris agreement."[27]

The 9th MAB stood down from operations and deactivated on 9 February 1973, becoming the 9th MAB nucleus staff and III MAF forward command post on the flagship of Task Force 76, the USS *Paul Revere* (LPA 248).[28] The 31st MAU remained on ships as the available ready force. Colonel Ray A. Stephens wrote that his unit was directed through a series of evolutions to assist in prisoner recovery and mine clearing at the same time. Then III MAF "cancelled this assignment and alerted the MAU to reconfigure for evacuation operations in South Vietnam."[29] This was altered drastically when Seventh Fleet assigned ARG Alpha and Bravo amphibious ships to support the Mine Counter Measures Force, Task Force 78. Control of HMM-165 and HMH-164 also went to TF 78 as it gathered forces. Fleet Marine Force, Pacific cryptically recorded that "until mine sweeping operations were completed, III MAF forces would be forced to operate without its full complement of helicopters."[30] Seventh Fleet and III MAF reconstituted the amphibious ready force by organizing a surface assault configured ready group of five ships from Amphibious Squadron One: an LKA, LSD, and three LSTs.[G][31] Headquarters, 31st MAU remained on the USS *Cleveland* and Batallion Landing Team 3/4 was BLT Alpha. Through March 1973, the amphibious ready group and BLT Alpha remained afloat off Da Nang on a 12-hour recall to MR 1. By April 1973, the 33d MAU on Okinawa was deactivated and the Western Pacific afloat forces returned to the posture of the previous year, the 31st MAU with Amphibious Ready Group Alpha and BLT Bravo with ARG Bravo.[32]

Operation Countdown, 'and Air'

The year 1972 had witnessed Marines flying 15,412 sorties over South Vietnam[H] and 539 sorties over North Vietnam, mostly in Route Package 1.[33] The New Year began on a discordant note with an air strike on Da Nang on 8 January 1973, causing damage and casualties to units on the ground. A flight of Marine and Navy aircraft, under U.S. Air Force control, bombed the western corner of the airbase because of an F-4 "Loran Bird" cockpit error.[34] Despite this, operations continued throughout the region.

Marine Aircraft Group 12 flight operations continued in South Vietnam and in Cambodia during January 1973. Colonel Dean Macho claimed credit for 864 enemy casualties and 293 buildings and 956 bunkers destroyed or damaged during this final period. MAG-12's 2,123 tons of ordnance destroyed 8 tanks, 12 artillery positions, 28 trucks, and 20 sampans, with numerous fires and secondary explosions being reported by the aircrews.[35] During the group's eighth month in combat, longer and heavier work loads were experienced to meet combat and withdrawal requirements. Air strikes in Cambodia were three times more frequent than previous months with the "Cambodian Reds" moving south through Kiampong Thom and Ankor Wat towards Phnom Penh. In January, according to Colonel Macho, air strikes within 200 yards of friendly positions "were not uncommon." The threat from antiaircraft gunfire and missiles remained high over the target areas. Weather was clear, even if inaccurate weather reports from Tan Son Nhut and Bien Hoa caused the MAG-12 duty officer to "back door" estimates of the ceiling and visibility used for crew briefs.[36] On 15 January 1973, Vietnamese Air Force controllers (FACs) took over control of all air strikes. Initial difficulties with language and procedures were overcome. By the end of the month Marine aviators were speaking pidgin Vietnamese as well as the FACs spoke

---

(G) These were the USS *Tulare* (LKA 112), *Monticello* (LSD 35), *San Bernardino* (LST 1189), *Racine* (LST 1191), and *Fresno* (LST 1182).

(H) 19 percent of the tactical air effort.

pidgin English: "problems were few, courtesy was high, and the Vietnamese fliers were a pleasure to work with."[37]

A single volley of 122mm rockets hit the group area at 0227 on 26 January 1973. The Marine killed during the rocket attack, Private First Class Mark J. Miller, was the last Marine killed in action prior to the ceasefire. This was the same day as the final combat flights, with MAG-12 becoming the last American fixed-wing aviation unit to depart Vietnam.[38] With the cessation of combat operations throughout Vietnam on 27 January 1973, the group made preparations to return to Iwakuni, Japan. Colonel Macho felt the move was "smooth and orderly with no major problems." This was through the efforts of First Lieutenant Edward J. Jobin, the MAG-12 embarkation officer, and the MAG-12 (Rear) Logistic Coordination Center under Chief Warrant Officer Larry G. Cravens at Iwakuni.[39] MAG-12 (Forward) aircraft departed Bien Hoa on 29 January 1973. The retrograde began within 24 hours of the ceasefire, requiring the support of 70 transport "lifts" flying around the clock to move 600 Marines and 2,791,000 pounds of cargo over the next five days.[40] The MAG's 28 A-4s arrived at Iwakuni, Japan, on 1 February 1973 at 1430 and the remaining men and equipment followed on 3 February.

For Task Force Delta, 1972 ended with the Bob Hope Christmas Show making an appearance at Nam Phong. Mr. Hope's arrival marked the seventh month of what had been perceived by some as a "90-day" deployment. Colonel Aubrey W. Talbert, Jr., of MAG-15 recalled that the end of 1972 was characterized by continued planning for the several possible contingencies which might result from a cessation of hostilities in South Vietnam and "two major changes in the geographical areas into which combat sorties were flown."[41] Air operations in South Vietnam concentrated on direct support to Republic of Vietnam units in MR 1 until 26 January 1973, after which they were directed to missions in Laos and Cambodia. That same day a rocket attack at Da Nang damaged two MAG-15 Phantoms on the ground being rearmed.

By the end of January 1973, 380 tons of excess material were shipped to Japan. Preparations to leave Nam Phong began with the ceasefire agreement, but the uncertainty of the ceasefire and continued flights over Laos necessitated continued effort to remain an effective force. Operations were flown against North Vietnamese targets in Laos until 21 February 1973 when a ceasefire agreement was reached for this area. One Air Force "Raven" air controller working the Black Lion Operation near Pakse, Laos, wrote VMA-115 to tell them "when you guys say that close air support is your business, you don't kid around .... I know it, the ground pounders know it, and the NVA know it."[42] While prepared to "retrograde," TF Delta was kept at Nam Phong by the Joint Chiefs of Staff to support any contingencies, particularly the enforcement of the ceasefire agreement, the recovery of American prisoners, and the mine-clearing operations in North Vietnam. The emphasis on combat again changed to training and waiting.

To cite the chronology of significant events at the Marine Corps Command Center for 29 March 1973, "Operation Countdown completed," marking the end of the Marines involvement in America's long war in Southeast Asia. This was the day after the last-known Marine prisoner of war was released and as Marine participation in "post-war" operations continued. In accordance with the ceasefire accords, the U.S. had left a residual force of less than 200 American servicemen in South Vietnam. There remained three U.S. Marines "in country" with the Defense Attache Office and the 143-man State Department security guard.[I] The Vietnamese Communists stated of the period that for "the first time in 115 years, not a single foreign soldier was garrisoned on Vietnamese land."[43]

(I) The three DAO Marines were Col William B. Fleming with the Plans and Liaison Branch, LtCol Walter D. Fillmore with the VNMC Logistics Branch, and Maj Richard F. Johnson with the Operations and Training Branch.

CHAPTER FOURTEEN ENDNOTES

Unless otherwise noted, material in this chapter is derived from CinCPac ComdHist73; MACV ComdHist73; FMFPac MarOpsSEA; SeventhFlt ComdHist73; MarAdvU Files; and the Defense Attache Office Saigon, "History of the Defense Attache" (Federal Records Center, Suitland, Md), hereafter DAOHist.

The Final Act

1 Metzger intvw and comments.

2 Van Fleet, *Aviation*, p. 17.

3 DRVN, op. cit., Foreign Ministry statement, dtd 29Dec72, p. 19.

4 Office of the White House Secretary, "Agreement on Ending the War and Restoring Peace in Vietnam," dtd 24Jan73, Articles 1 through 23 and amended protocols, hereafter Peace Accords (Vietnam Comment File).

5 SeventhFlt ComdHist73, "Planning Decisions and Conclusions," p. 2.

6 Besch comments.

Operation Countdown, 'On the Land'

7 Sub Unit One, 1st ANGLICO Navy Unit Commendation citation (RefSec, MCHC, Washington, D.C.).

8 FMFPac MarOpsSEA, p.6-5.

9 Sub Unit One ComdC, Feb73, p.3.

10 CMC msg to FMFPac dtd 9Feb73; MACV msg to FMFPac, dtd 4Mar73 (Jone's comments).

11 MarAdvU HistSum72, pp.2-3; MarAdvU Phase Down Log, dtd 28Jan73-16Feb73; Daily OpSum Folder, Feb73 (MarAdvU File).

12 Office of the Assistant Secretary of Defense (Installations and Logistics), Memo for the President, dtd 17Nov72 (Vietnam Comment File).

13 MarAdvU HistSum 72, p. 4; Ordnance/Maintenance Folder, CWO3 Bobby E. Dusek memo, 16Feb73; MarAdvU Turnover Folder, Narrative Evaluation of VNMC 2dQtrFY73, pp. 4-5 (MarAdv File).

14 DAOHist 2CYQ73, pp. 78-83; FMFPac MarOpsSEA, p. 5-16.

15 Marine Advisory Unit Navy Unit Commendation citation (RefSec, MCHC, Washington, D.C.).

16 FMFPac MarOpsSEA, p. 6-19.

17 SMA After Action Report to ComdrNavForV, dtd 27Mar88, hereafter SMA AAR, pp. 4-5 (MarAdvU File).

18 SMA msg to ComNavForV, dtd 13Mar73 (MarAdvU File); DAOHist, 1CYQ73, pp. 8-14; FMFPac MarOpsSEA, pp. 6-14 to 6-19.

19 DAOHist, 1CYQ73, p.80.

20 DAOHist, 1CYQ73, p. 21.

21 MajGen John E. Murray, comments on draft ms, dtd 3Feb90 (Vietnam Comment File).

22 DAOHist, 1CYQ73, p. 1.

Operation Countdown, 'and Sea'

23 Williamson comments.

24 9thMAB ComdC, Jan73, p. 1.

25 ComSeventhFlt msg to 9thMAB dtd 31Jan73 (Vietnam Comment File).

26 9thMAB ComdC, Feb73, p.3-1.

27 Ibid.

28 FMFPac MarOpsSEA, pp. 6-1 to 6-5; 9thMAB ComdC, Jan73, pp.1-4.

29 Col Ray A. Stephens, Comments on draft ms, dtd 12Dec89 (Vietnam Comment File).

30 FMFPac MarOpsSEA, p. 6-14.

31 FMFPac MarOpsSEA, p. 5-15.

32 FMFPac MarOpsSEA, p. 6-20.

Operation Countdown, 'and Air'

33 Kenneth P. Werrell, "U.S. Marine Corps Aviation and North Vietnam," ms, 1989, p. 18 (Vietnam Comment File).

34 *New York Times*, "U.S. Planes Bomb Da Nang by Mistake, Wounding 10," 8Jan73, pp. 1, 6.

35 FMFPac MarOpsSEA, pp.6-6 to 6-7; MAG-12 ComdC, Jun73, pp.6-7.

36 MAG-12, ComdC, Jun73, p.6.

37 Ibid.

38 FMFPac MarOpsSEA pp. 6-6 to 6-8; MAG-12 ComdC, Jab73, pp. 7

39 MAG-12 ComdC, Jan73, pp. 6-9.

40 MAG-12 ComdC, Jan73, pp. 4, 8-9; Jun73, p.8.

41 MAG-15 ComdC, Jun73, p. 5.

42 TFD AAR, p. 1-15.

43 Nguyen Khac Vien, ed., *Indochina: The 1972–73 Turning Point* (Hanoi: Xunhasaba, 1974), p. 22.

CHAPTER FIFTEEN
IN ENEMY HANDS

Combatants or Hostages? • Egress Recap and Other Contingencies • Operation Homecoming • Welcome Home Marine • Code of Conduct • MIAs: The Joint Casualty Resolution Center

Combatants or Hostages?

By 1972, the return of missing and captured Americans in Southeast Asia had become a national objective for the United States. For the U.S. Marine Corps, this meant finding some 136 missing Marines thought possibly to be in Communist captivity.[1] During 1972 alone, 23 Marines were lost in action from III MAF and only four of these returned as prisoners the next year.[A] Other Americans, including Marines, had been saved from capture or loss by search and rescue efforts; 232 individual recoveries were made during 1972, including the American advisors from the Quang Tri Citadel in May.[B]

The Communists claimed they treated "enemy soldiers who have surrendered" with humanity. But a captured Marine's probability of living or dying depended upon a number of circumstances, including his captor's perception of the chances for evasion or escape and the immediate tactical situation. When captured, prisoners heard something like "you are now captured. We do not kill you. Just follow our command! We will have your arms tied up and take you to a safe place. Stand up and follow us right now!"[2] From then, their ordeal was essentially an individual experience.[C]

Headquarters Marine Corps monitored the status of Marines in captivity and tracked them as individuals in both the Intelligence and Manpower Divisions. As near as can be determined, 48 of all the Americans captured in Southeast Asia were U.S.

(A) Missing Marines included nine in North Vietnam, seven in South Vietnam, and three in Laos. Most were aircrews.

(B) The chance of successful rescue depended upon where an individual was "lost." Only seven Americans were recovered from North Vietnam out of 149 American fixed-wing aircraft lost there in 1972 A total of 239 American and South Vietnamese fixed-wing aircraft were lost in combat in Southeast Asia during 1972.

(C) This chapter is intended to document the return of some of these men in 1973. Any complete narrative about their ordeal will have to be based on the debriefs conducted upon their return and take into account the diverse circumstances of captivity, release, and rank. These debriefs, along with the majority of material on prisoners, remain classified by executive order for privacy and security. (OASD[ISA] ltr dtd 3Jan87)

Marines. Of these: 9 died in captivity, 10 escaped, 2 were released prior to 1973, 26 returned during Operation Homecoming, and 1 — Private First Class Robert R. Garwood — returned in 1979.[D][3]

Individual conduct could not be evaluated while these men were prisoners, as the only information about them was dependent upon press reports and statements by visiting delegations in North Vietnam. Published stories or broadcasts by prisoners did not indicate the circumstances under which these statements were made. Prisoners were allowed to write a monthly letter, but most were never sent, except through "anti-war" groups favorable to the North Vietnamese.[E][4]

Over time, it became evident to the United States Government that the North Vietnamese were not abiding by the Geneva Convention and that all prisoners were not living up to the U.S. Armed Forces Code of Conduct. The Code of Conduct was written and published after the Korean War to provide principles to follow while in captivity. It is neither law nor regulation. It reads:

> I am an American fighting man. I serve in the forces which guard my country and our way of life. I am prepared to give my life in their defense.
>
> I will never surrender of my own free will. If in command, I will never surrender my men while they still have the means to resist.
>
> If I am captured, I will continue to resist by all means available. I will make every effort to escape and aid others to escape. I will accept neither parole nor special favors from the enemy.
>
> If I am a prisoner of war, I will keep faith with my fellow prisoners. I will give no information or take part in any action which might be harmful to my comrades. If I am senior, I will take command. If not, I will obey the lawful orders of those appointed over me and will back them up in every way.
>
> When questioned, should I become a prisoner of war, I am bound to give only name, rank, service number, and date of birth. I will evade answering further questions to the utmost of my ability. I will make no oral or written statements disloyal to my country and its allies or harmful to their cause.
>
> I will never forget that I am an American Fighting Man, responsible for my actions, and dedicated to the principles which made my country free. I will trust in my God and in the United States of America.

(D) The first Marine prisoner was taken on 31 December 1964 and the last was captured on 26 September 1972.

(E) Prisoners did not receive mail until the late 1960s, and by the war's end only 13 relatives of Marine prisoners had received outgoing letters, nine from North Vietnam and four from South Vietnam.

The Communists refused to furnish complete listings of names or numbers of detained prisoners, refused inspection of prison camps by the International Red Cross, neither announced the locations nor otherwise marked prison camps, publicly paraded American prisoners for propaganda purpose, allowed few prisoners to correspond with their next of kin, and tortured or otherwise coerced prisoners to make public confessions of criminal activity and anti-American statements. The Department of Defense concluded that "their captors could obtain a statement from any POW from whom they wanted one [and] all POWs made statements in one form or another."[5]

Before 1971, there had been three separate groups of Marine prisoners in Southeast Asia.[F] In North Vietnam were 11 Marines, all aviators and officers, their average age 30 years at time of capture. Some spent up to eight years in captivity, with 5.2 the mean. Two groups were captured in South Vietnam. These Marines were younger, mostly enlisted, and subject to a higher death rate in captivity.[6] They were confined in temporary camps in South Vietnam, Cambodia, and Laos for up to two and a half years. Most were moved to camps in North Vietnam by 1971.

The "Southern Group" in MR 1 suffered the highest death toll of all as the result of harsh living conditions, rather than maltreatment during indoctrination and interrogation. The Communists originally kept about two dozen allied prisoners in a variety of jungle locations in the "Tam Ky Complex" of South Vietnam. These prisoners were confined in bamboo "tiger cage" enclosures or were shackled to their "beds." Of 10 Marines in this group: one was killed trying to escape, one was released, one remained with the Communists, and five died of various causes related to malnutrition.[G] Corporal Jose J. Anzaldua, Jr., of H&S Company 2/5, observed that the minute anyone of this group quit "he was as good as dead. There was no retrieving a man once he despaired."[H][7] Only 12 of these allied prisoners reached North Vietnam in 1971, where they were known as "The Dirty Dozen" by the other Americans already held in the North.

According to First Lieutenant Bruce R. Archer of HMM-165, the prisoners were forced to maintain a six-day week consisting of identical morning and evening schedules. A bell woke them up at the break of dawn, when "we were then required to fold up our gear neatly. The prisoners were taken out of their cells one at a time

---

(F) Locations where Marines were held and the nicknames given them by prisoners, were as follows (those with an asterisk were used during 1972–1973): Cambodia and border area; Tam Ky Complex (Camps I, II, III), SVN; Hoa Lo (Hanoi Hilton-Camp Unity), NVN*; Cu Loc (Zoo), NVN*; Xom Ap Lo (Briar Patch), NVN; Thermal Power Plant (Dirty Bird), NVN; Son Tay (Camp Hope), NVN; Citadel (Plantation), NVN*; Dan Hoi (Camp Faith), NVN; Bang Liet (Skid Row), NVN; Luong Lang (Dog Patch), NVN*; Noi Coc (Rock Pile), NVN*; Duong Ke (Farnsworth), NVN; Ba Cao (Bao Cao), NVN.

(G) The Marine who stayed behind was PFC Robert R. Garwood.

(H) Ranks used in text are as of time of capture.

to dump their toilet buckets, brush their teeth, and were then locked up again." Meals were a big event of the day, if lacking in quality and quantity.

At times, food consisted of two daily meals, one largely of rice and squash soup, the other of pork fat. Archer continued, "in the South we were eating chicken, some kind of vegetable soup and rice. In North Vietnam, after we settled into our camp site, they started feeding us bread. We were getting a bowl of soup and a hard roll twice a day, with plenty of water."[8] Captain Paul J. Montague, also from HMM-165 and captured with Archer, commented that the situation was actually worse. In the early years, "meat of any sort was only given to us in minute pieces, if any at all."[9] Another prisoner wrote that in South Vietnam he was fed "manioc, bamboo, and salt water and so was the camp commander."[10] The diet was so lacking in basic vitamins and protein that survival was a wonder. Corporal Anzaldua remembered that the "only protein we had consisted of an occasional rat, lizard, or snake we could catch with our hands."[11] Common to all prisoners at release was a weight loss of 45 to 60 pounds.

An overall death rate of 15% occurred, with those surviving being healthier than expected when examined upon release.[12] Medical care by the North Vietnamese was limited. Marines suffered from malnutrition, malaria, dysentery, beri-beri, open sores, rashes, typhoid, dental problems, ejection injuries, and psychological stress.[13] All suffered from nutritional deficiencies, torture, filthy living conditions, and solitary confinement.

The American raid on the empty prison camp at Son Tay marked the start of major changes in how the North Vietnamese treated their prisoners. The raid demonstrated that the Americans could enter North Vietnam at will and were determined to get their countrymen back. As a result of this and other considerations, the Communist improved conditions, diet, and treatment for the better. Most of the dispersed and isolated prisoners were eventually confined at the Hoa Lo Prison (Hanoi Hilton) complex. Men were brought together who had not seen another American in years; they now lived 30 to 50 men confined to a room.

When Captains Orson G. Swindle III of Marine Wing Headquarters Group and Lawrence V. Friese of Marine Aircraft Group (MAG) 12 arrived following a suffocating ride in a refrigerator truck, they found scrawled on a cell door "Marine Corps Barracks Hanoi."

With their concentration in one place, the prisoners were able to organize and resist to a greater degree. The prisoners needed to psychologically exhibit group solidarity and to interact with each other to overcome guilt feelings caused by their inevitable

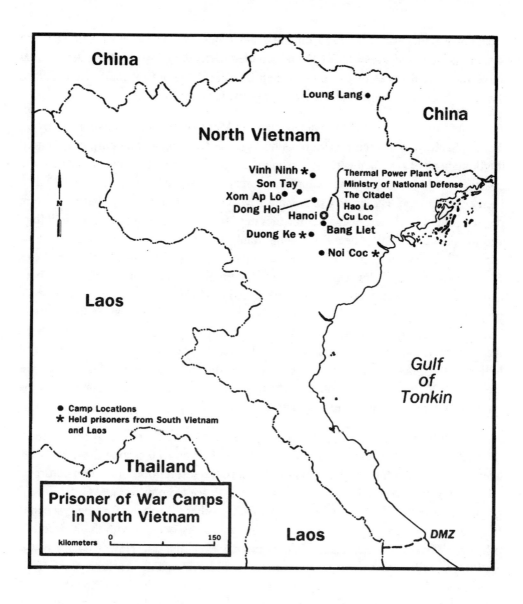

China

North Vietnam

China

Loung Lang ●

Vinh Ninh ✱ ●
Son Tay ●
Xom Ap Lo ●
Dong Hoi
Hanoi ⊙
Thermal Power Plant
Ministry of National Defense
The Citadel
Hao Lo
Cu Loc
Bang Liet
Duong Ke ✱ ●
● Noi Coc ✱

N

Laos

Gulf
of
Tonkin

● Camp Locations
✱ Held prisoners from South Vietnam
and Laos

Thailand

**Prisoner of War Camps
in North Vietnam**

kilometers   0 ———————— 150

Laos

DMZ

breakdown under torture. Based on the main points of the Code of Conduct, the system that evolved stressed: (1) Do not condemn, deny, or say anything detrimental about the United States or its allies or their cause; (2) Do not give aid or comfort to the enemy; and (3) Do not accept special favors, including parole.[14]

The object was to continue the war against the Vietnamese Communists by denying them the ability to use the prisoners as hostages or for propaganda purposes. Within the limitations of confinement, the prisoners had evolved over the years from helpless hostages at the mercy of their captors to organized combatants in a war of wills. Lieutenant Colonel Harlan P. Chapman, of MAG-13, noted that this was of a "joint service nature" and there was a senior ranking officer "for each room, each building, and for the camp. Date of rank was important but it did not matter what branch of service."[15] For example, Major John H. Dunn, of MAG-11, established these policies while senior officer at Son Tay under the acronym of Blades: "Bitch constantly about necessities, luxuries bitch about occasionally, absurdities debunk, discourage propaganda, everyone participates, select what is to be bitched about individually."[16] Techniques used to resist included the discouragement of visits by family members, the refusal to view live entertainment, the resistance to Vietnamese sponsored holidays, the celebration of American holidays, the stopping of recreation that was viewed by Vietnamese-sponsored delegations, and the refusal to comment during interrogation on any subject except personal needs.[I][17]

As Linebacker air attacks on the North increased in May 1972, the NVA moved more than 200 prisoners to Luong Lang near the Chinese border. At the same time, the North Vietnamese used groups of prisoners to denounce the resumption of air bombardment with statements and broadcasts, this included the "Peace Committee" or "Outer Seven" group of prisoners.[J] They were called this by other prisoners for their separate treatment by, and cooperation with, the Communists. Associated with them were two officers, VMFA-323's Lieutenant Colonel Edison W. Miller and Navy Captain Walter E. Wilber.[18] Miller later wrote, "I most certainly did, during the last three years of my confinement, express my views on the Vietnam War. It has not changed. The prosecution of the Vietnam War has to be one of the major mistakes of our country ...."[19]

Renewed air action also resulted in new prisoners arriving. On 11 June 1972, Captain William K. Angus of VMA(AW)-224 was captured when his A-6 was struck by

---

(I) Prisoner resistance was all that could be accomplished under the circumstances, but was isolated and individual in nature until late in the war. LtCol Swindle recalled that the standards of conduct for Marines in the North were set by Chapman, Dunn, and Frederick. (Swindle comments) VAdm James B. Stockdale, the senior naval service officer held in captivity, takes exception to the concept of a "4th Allied POW Wing," which he regarded as a publicity device after the fact. (Stockdale comments).

(J) These were SP4 Michael P. Branch, USA; SSgt Robert P. Chenoweth, USA; SSgt James A. Daly, Jr., USA; Pvt Frederick L. Elbert, Jr., USMC; Sgt Able L. Kavanaugh, USMC; SSgt King D. Rayford, Jr., USA; SSgt Alfonso R. Riate, USMC; and SSgt John A. Young, USA.

ground fire during a bombing run. North Vietnamese subjected him to brutal interrogation, with the same results as with earlier prisoners: despair and guilt for going beyond the "big four"[K] under torture.[20] But to the men who had remained in the north for so long, it seemed these newcomers brought attitudes that threatened those held by earlier prisoners.[L] Major Leo Thorsness, USAF, felt these men had been on college campuses in the 1960s when he had been taken prisoner and they "were not hard-core resisters." They asked him, "Why in the world should we be tortured to say things that everybody in the states is already saying?"[21]

This last year of captivity for the prisoners also saw tragic hardships. During July 1972, the Luong Lang camp suffered a typhoid epidemic due to the crowded and unsanitary conditions. One of those who died was Chief Warrant Officer John W. Frederick, Jr., of MAG-11, who had survived seven years of confinement.

That same month, a group of prisoners met with actress Jane Fonda and later in August with former U.S. Attorney General Ramsey Clark, meetings that were staged for newsmen.[M] One prisoner who met with them at that time explained, "I had no idea who she was, but every young officer in the camp (The Zoo) I was in at the time, viewed her as a sex symbol and wanted to see her."[22] This, and other incidents, brought accusations of American prisoners of cooperating with the Communists, accusations a court of law never resolved.[23]

One Marine prisoner concluded after his release that not everyone resisted to the best of his abilities. Jose J. Anzaldua felt that some prisoners put together peace statements for the enemy in exchange for better treatment or a few paltry privileges, a little more food or a few cigarettes. "I tried to think of them simply as 'weak sisters' but ultimately I hated them — and I hate them still. Beyond a certain point no man's fear or suffering was greater than anothers. We all had the same choices."[24]

(K) Name, rank, serial number, and date of birth being the only four questions a prisoner was required to answer for his captors.

(L) VAdm Stockdale commented that the years of "heavy" torure were prior to 31 March 1968. After that, he felt that it was continued by the North Vietnamese against those with whom they still had grudges. A greater threat was from the early-release offers. By 1 December 1971, "all torture was a thing of the past." (Stockdale comments)

(M) On 13 July 1972, a group of 16 American prisoners made statements denouncing the war. Jane Fonda also made broadcasts on Radio Hanoi that were heard by American forces at the time, including Marine units. This led an unknown Marine with VMFA-333 to quip: "Guess the end-of-the-cruise date and win a date with Jane." On 9 August 1972, Clark broadcast over Radio Hanoi that there "is no excuse for bombing North Vietnam," but appealed for the release of prisoners of war. At the time, he was a member of the Stockholm-based International Commission of Inquiry on war crimes in Indochina. (Vietnam Comment File)

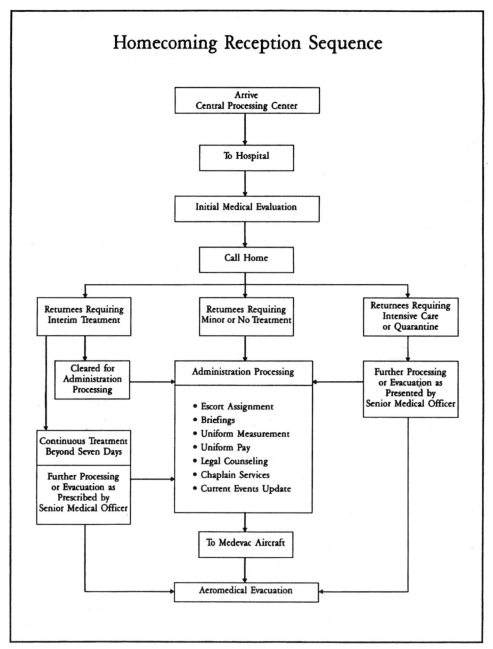

Homecoming Reception Sequence

Adapted from Department of Defense Material

Egress Recap and Other Contingencies

Active prisoner recovery operations, including contingencies for prisoners in North Vietnam continued through the end of the war and beyond. The Deputy Director for Operations of the Joint Chiefs of Staff began a special operations project that envisioned the recovery of American prisoners from Hanoi. Lieutenant General Hugh J. Elwood, the Deputy Chief of Staff for Plans and Programs at HQMC, assigned Colonel William J. Davis as the Marine Corps action officer and representative. Project planners proposed operations using U.S. Army and U.S. Marine forces to rescue prisoners from the enemy capital. These concepts remained in the planning stage because of the success of military operations in South Vietnam and negotiations in Paris.[25]

In 1972, Major William B. Clark was the Headquarters Marine Corps action officer concerned with monitoring status of captured Marines when a special Department of Defense prisoner task force formed. In August 1972, he attended the DOD/CinCPac planning conference on recovery contingencies. He reported back to the Assistant Chief of Staff, G-1, that a great deal of meaningful and productive action had taken place since the previous World Wide Conference on Prisoners of War. In his opinion, there were "processing sites ready and waiting with every conceivable problem examined," medical, personnel, and personal files were on station and up to date, next of kin telephone procedures were established, security precautions taken, public affairs press guidance promulgated, and casualty transportation to the United States laid on.[26]

The task force on the prisoners of war and missing in action was headed by Dr. Roger E. Shields from the office of the Assistant Secretary of Defense for International Security Affairs. During Operation Homecoming he dealt directly with CinCPac and the Services. These efforts were coordinated under a Pacific Command plan known Egress Recap, later renamed Operation Homecoming.[27] This called for a three-phase operation and delegated responsibility among the Services. Phase one and phase two were controlled by the Homecoming Operations Center at Pacific Command's headquarters in Hawaii. Phase one was the recovery of the prisoners by Thirteenth Air Force from the Communists. Phase two was their processing at an intermediate facility, the Joint Homecoming Reception Center (JHRC) at Clark Air Force Base, Philippines. Phase three was the return of these Americans to the United States, as the responsibility of the individual services.[28] In addition, the U.S. delegation to the Four Party Joint Military Commission established by the ceasefire agreement had a two-man POW liaison division provided by MACV.[29]

More than 2,880 American government and military personnel were involved with the first two phases of Homecoming, which directly involved 62 Marines. The III MAF

Marines worked within the organizational framework of the Joint Homecoming Reception Center at Clark Air Force Base, Philippines, to include the command post, base hospital, Joint Debriefing and Casualty Reporting Center, Joint Reception and Support Center, Joint Information Bureau, and the Quick Reaction Team/Reception Support Team. Military Airlift Command and the Pacific Air Force provided aircraft support. General William G. Moore described the command post as "the hub of all activity" for the command element, the Service deputy site commanders and State Department team chief, and representatives of key support agencies.[30]

Marine Corps participation in Operation Homecoming ranged from the prisoners themselves to Marine action officers in Washington, D.C. Major General Michael P. Ryan, then Commanding General, III MAF, assigned Colonel John W. Clayborne as his representative with the Joint Homecoming Reception Center at Clark. There he was a service deputy JHRC commander under General Moore. Colonel Clayborne headed the Marine contingent of 32 officers and 28 enlisted men who comprised the Marine Processing Team at Clark and the escort team on board the Military Airlift Command aircraft. The III MAF team began operations on 13 December 1972 when Major John J. Burton reported to Clark as the III MAF liaison officer, assisted by Staff Sergeant Thomas W. Bohnenkamp, an administrative chief, and Master Sergeant Fred A. Norvell, the Camp Butler uniform custodian. Planning and briefings continued with the Air Force, as well as with Brigadier General Paul G. Graham's 9th MAB and 31st MAU for Homecoming Afloat if it were necessary to transport the returnees by sea rather than by air.[31]

On 26 December 1972, the prisoners at The Citadel moved to Hoa Lo Prison. Indication of a prisoner exchange came to the Americans in North Vietnam when lists of prisoners by the date of capture were arranged to establish the order in which prisoners were released. In January 1973, the "Dirty Dozen" prisoners of the MR 1 group were also moved to Hoa Lo and joined the other Hanoi prisoners for release. For Corporal Anzaldua the word of the pending relief came in formation with the other prisoners in the main yard of the prison. The camp commander, speaking through an interpreter, told them "You will be released in 30 days." There was no visible response from the assembled prisoners: "No one believed him, for all we knew it was a trick." Stated Anzaldua, "We dared not hope. We were beyond hope."[32]

When the ceasefire agreement was imminent, the JCS Chairman, Admiral Thomas H. Moorer, notified the Pacific Command that during "the next 60 days the most important single event will be the return of our prisoners of war."[33] The recovery and accountability of Americans held by the Communists in Southeast Asia had become a national objective and a specific goal of negotiation with the North Vietnamese. At this point, the prisoners were the only leverage the Communists could exert, and President Nixon personally followed the daily progress of the prisoner release and final troop withdrawals.[34]

The prisoner release was dependent on the removal of U.S. naval mines from North Vietnamese waterways, the withdrawal of remaining U.S. forces from South Vietnam, and the exchange of some 5,000 South Vietnamese and 26,508 Communist prisoners.[35] Under the terms of the Vietnam Agreement, the internationally supervised ceasefire went into effect throughout South and North Vietnam at 0800 Saigon time, 28 January 1973. Within 60 days all American prisoners and remaining military forces would leave Vietnam, and there were 23,335 Americans, 35,396 Koreans, and 113 other allies to withdraw.[36] It also began the long-awaited recovery of American prisoners from Hanoi. Homecoming was no longer a plan, it was operational.

Operation Homecoming

In order to support round-the-clock processing of these men in the transition from Communist to American control, a facility was established and manned by the Services to provide medical, financial, psychological, and humanitarian support. On 28 January 1973, these reception stations were manned with the announcement of the names of the Americans to be released. Included were the names of 26 Marine returnees, and eight others who had died in captivity. When the JHRC was activated, it was believed that the prisoners would be released in roughly equal groups at 15-day intervals.

Families were notified, records audited, current promotions, awards, and uniforms were on hand to be issued upon arrival at Clark Air Force Base. Representatives from the various Services were assigned to each pickup aircraft; however, they were not escorts for specific returnees. Marine escorts were assigned to each Marine returnee to accompany him to the JHRC and then to the United States.[37] The processing at the JHRC was designed to allow a smooth transition of the returnees back into the Marine Corps. Information was provided to bring the Marines up on the events of the last few years, and to allow them to make contact with their families.

As February 1973 began, prisoners in Hanoi began the transfer to their final holding facility, known as "Showplace" because the Vietnamese made efforts to improve the condition and appearances of prisoners prior to release. Operation Homecoming had started for them at last. One of the prisoner leadership's last instructions was the "Go Home Guidance." These provided specifics on "dress, press, debrief, violators." The prisoners used military formations to display pride and dignity. Any emotionalism or arrogance was kept in check. Priority for release were the sick or wounded, enlisted, civilians, and officers in order of capture. But, this was ultimately controlled by the Communists. An experience that began for a diverse group of individuals ended as a unifying event.[38]

On 12 February 1973, the first phase began with the release of 116 prisoners at Gia Lam Airfield in North Vietnam and 19 prisoners in South Vietnam who left from Saigon. These first groups included three Marines from the north and Captain James P. Walsh from the south. Other prisoners were released from the same locations and from the British Crown Colony of Hong Kong. In accordance with the provisions of the Agreement and Protocol, transactions were observed by teams from the Four Party Joint Military Commission and the International Commission of Control and Supervision.

As the first prisoners were transferred from their Vietnamese bus, their way to the aircraft was blocked by newsmen. However, Air Force plane crews pushed the newsmen aside and escorted the men to the waiting C-141. Colonel James R. Dennet, USAF, who headed the 18-man reception support team, reported, "One of the POWs told me that this was the high point of the whole operation."[39] Dennet was impressed with the discipline displayed as the former prisoners got off the bus at Hanoi, "The senior man took charge and marched them to the turnover point. Some were limping, but there was full control." The releases that followed were based upon agreements reached in Paris and on the spot in North Vietnam. Delays in negotiations at exchange sites made subsequent releases irregular. In all, 20 MAC flights by C-141s and C-9s were used to bring the men to the Philippines. When the last flights arrived, 591 Americans and nine foreign nationals had been repatriated.[N]

After arriving in the Philippines, the former prisoners began the next phase of Homecoming. Processing began with an initial medical examination. The returned Marines were then debriefed. The purpose of this was to determine the status of the remaining prisoners and to elicit information on missing persons who may have been encountered in captivity.[40] Captain William C. Howey led the five-man debrief team and recalled the actual debriefs began on 13 February 1973 with Lieutenant Colonel John H. Dunn and Lieutenant Colonel Harlan P. Chapman.[O] Lieutenant Colonel Edison W. Miller "was not debriefed by direction of FMFPac."[41] Returnees then met their escorts, received personal information briefings on their home situations, met with a chaplain (if desired), and called their families. Changes to initial hospital assignments were made at this time. After that, a post exchange call was made for necessities and measurement for uniforms in which to return home.[42]

(N) Marines were released on the flights on 12 February 1973 and on 5, 14, 16, 27, and 28 March.

(O) LtCol Howey commented that it took an estimated 45 manhours to process the Dunn and Chapman debriefs to collate, cross-check, and verify names mentioned. Other prisoners were specifically designated to serve as "name memory banks" for the prisoners.

The men were in a euphoric state that lasted through their stay at Clark. The returning Americans "were greeted by large crowds of well-wishers at the flight line and along the ambulance bus routes to the hospital."[43] These crowds of dependents and service personnel from Clark were the returning prisoner's first indication that their experience was appreciated by their fellow citizens. The returning Marines adjusted promptly to eating a normal American diet. To Colonel Clayborne, surprisingly, "though subjected to the most primitive living conditions and cruelties, together with long years of imprisonment, (they) did not appear psychologically or mentally affected in most cases."[44] They were especially interested in the details of their capture and information about their units following their capture. Colonel Clayborne credited a strong prisoner unity with maintaining a sense of military discipline and providing the men a sense of purpose. Standing out in his recollections, was the rapport between the Marine returnees and their escorts.[45]

Colonel Dennet had initial concerns for demonstrations against the North Vietnamese by the returning prisoners. On 16 March 1973, Dennet was prepared for possible demonstrations against the United States from a group of 32 prisoners in Hanoi, including seven Marines, three of whom were subsequently charged with misconduct after their return.[46] His concern for this particular release was due primarily to the personalities among the returnees themselves, some "individuals in this group had been identified as having anti-war and most particularly anti-U.S. military sentiments." Captain Howey had received derogatory information about some of these returnees during his debriefing sessions and passed this information on to Colonel Clayborne, who informed Fleet Marine Force Pacific and Headquarters Marine Corps.[47]

The returnees were cleared for "medical evacuation" to the United States as soon as they were ready to go, an average of 68 hours of processing time. Thirty-six MAC C-141 flights were made to take all the men back to Hawaii. The first Marine to arrive was Lieutenant Colonel Harlan P. Chapman, to be welcomed by the Commanding General of FMF Pacific, General Louis H. Wilson, Jr. Chapman was the Marine held the longest by the enemy, from his capture on 5 November 1965. General Wilson shook his hand and said, "Welcome back to the Marine Corps," Chapman replied, "Thank you General, but I never left."[48] Others followed and this "process" continued until the arrival of Captain William K. Angus on 28 March 1973, the last Marine prisoner out of North Vietnam. As Captain Angus boarded the aircraft that returned him to the United States he took the "salute of a formation of Marines who were enroute to Nam Phong."[49]

The third phase of Operation Homecoming began after notification of a Marine's return was sent to his family. The returnee was then assigned to one of seven United

States naval hospitals.[P] The returning Marines were given more intensive medical care and counseling. They were then debriefed further and given time to spend with families and friends to catch up on lost years. This was controlled by Headquarters Marine Corps, with a program called Operation Homecoming Marine. Headquarters formed a group under Brigadier General Edward A. Parnell for the Manpower Division. As in the preoperation planning, these action officers at Headquarters supervised this with the assistance of the respective hospitals and with local Marine representatives.[Q] [50] They also had to assist the survivors of those Marines who were not coming home.

Welcome Home Marine

Chief Warrant Officer William E. Thomas, Jr., arrived at NAS Miramar, California, at 1815 on 30 March 1973. The 36-year-old native of Pennsylvania was serving as an air observer with Sub Unit One, 1st ANGLICO, when shot down near the demilitarized zone in 1972. At the time, he had been "controlling naval gunfire on enemy positions along Route 555" from an Air Force OV-10. He was escorted to the United States by Major John H. Messick to Camp Pendleton, California. Previously Warrant Officer Thomas had met his wife and two children in Hawaii during a brief stopover at Hickam. Thomas recalled, "I arrived with Sgt Anzaldua, we (Joe and I) arrived late due to aircraft problems." A Marine Corps sedan and reception party drove them to Camp Pendleton naval hospital where they were greeted by the base commander, Major General Herman Poggemeyer, Jr.; Major General John N. McLaughlin, Commanding General, 4th Marine Division, himself a former POW from the Korean War; and the naval hospital commander. Assigned to the Operation Homecoming Ward 22A, Warrant Officer Thomas was once again reunited with his family.

In the days that followed, Chief Warrant Officer Joseph A. Canonico and Sergeant William C. Westerlund of the 1st Counterintelligence Team conducted detailed debriefings, in conjunction with medical and dental treatment. Decorations and awards were initiated or completed during this period, as well as administrative matters relating to pay and legal assistance. Family visits and liberty were authorized consistent with medical, administrative, and debriefing schedules. On 16 April 1973, Chief Warrant Officer Thomas conducted a press conference and began a 90-day convalescent leave.[51]

(P) These were U.S. Naval Hospitals in Oakland, California; Camp Pendleton, California; Great Lakes, Illinois; St. Albans, New York; Bethesda, Maryland; Camp Lejeune, North Carolina; and Philadelphia, Pennsylvania. USNHs in San Diego, California and Jacksonville, Florida, also participated.

(Q) Units involved were Marine Corps Base (MCB) Camp Pendleton, California; Marine Barracks, Great Lakes, Illinois; Marine Barracks, Brooklyn, New York; Marine Barracks, Jacksonville, Florida; Marine Barracks, Treasure Island, California; and MCB Camp Lejeune, North Carolina.

With variations in detail this same sequence was followed by the 25 other Marines who had returned during Homecoming. An important element of this program was the public relations exploitation of the returned Marines that allowed them to have press conferences, make public speaking engagements, and hold interviews designed to capitalize on the massive public response to their return. The Marines were welcomed home at the national level by General Robert E. Cushman, Jr., and by President Nixon with a White House reception.[52]

Shortly after the prisoners were returned, General Cushman received a letter from Mr. Douglas K. Ramsey that would focus his personal attention on a Marine Corps officer, a prisoner who had been dead for six years in Vietnam. Ramsey, a civilian language officer, had been held a prisoner by the Communists from 1966 until his release during Operation Homecoming in 1973. His letter told the story of Captain Donald G. Cook, USMC.[53] Captain Cook went to Vietnam as an observer from Communications Company, Headquarters Battalion, 3d Marine Division. He was assigned to the 4th Battalion of the Vietnamese Marines. On 31 December 1964 he was wounded and captured during fighting near Binh Gia, Phuoc Thy Province, in III Corps.[54] Captain Cook was held prisoner by the Viet Cong until his death. The 33-year-old native of New York and father of four set an example of courage and conduct in the face of the enemy.

Held in various camps in South Vietnam near the Cambodian border, Cook reportedly assumed a rigid adherence to the Code of Conduct that won him the respect of his fellow prisoners and his Communist captors. Observed a fellow prisoner, after a 14-day forced march to a new camp, Captain Cook's determination and fortitude "was commended by the VC camp commander ... like a physicist being praised by Einstein."[55] Although seriously ill, Cook refused to allow other prisoners to carry him or his pack. He set the example for others by assuming leadership, nursing the sick, sharing his rations, organizing the prisoners, attempting to escape, and resisting the Vietnamese at every turn. The strain of this effort eventually cost him his life. Fellow prisoners believed "that Cook could have negotiated his own early release, had he been willing to pay the price of a signed statement or tape" against the United States' policy in Vietnam. Captain Cook's 1967 death from malaria was announced to other prisoners as his having "gone to a camp rather far from here." The North Vietnamese finally notified the American government of Captain Donald G. Cook's death in 1973 during Operation Homecoming.[R]

The return of Marine prisoners also brought disciplinary action for some. Rear Admiral James B. Stockdale, the senior naval officer in captivity, was met the day after his arrival at Clark Air Force Base by CinCPac's Rear Admiral Earl P. Yates. A telephone call made in Stockdale's name to the Chief of Naval Personnel in

---

(R) He was declared legally dead by the Department of Defense on 26 February 1980. On 16 May 1980 Colonel Donald G. Cook's widow received his Medal of Honor from Secretary of the Navy Edward Hidalgo.

Washington, D.C., concerning Navy Captain Walter E. Wilber and Lieutenant Colonel Edison W. Miller, demanded that they be removed for their own safety as there "are released ex-prisoners who don't want to be in the same hospital with them."[56]

The telephone call appeared to have been motivated by Miller and Wilber being on the first flights out of Hanoi, which Stockdale felt "may not have been either Miller's idea, or the North Vietnamese's." Colonel Clayborne's opinion was that Wilber and Miller's place on the initial plane was because of the North Vietnamese control and manipulation of the process. Reasons proposed for this were for the Communists to "get some favorable media exposure" or as "a gesture of contempt" to continue to exploit division among the returnees.[57] In regards to his release date, though one of the more seriously injured returnees, Miller himself said he had declined early repatriation, but was told with the others by the North Vietnamese that "we would all leave the country when told to."[58] At this point, CinCPac and Washington's concern was to move Miller and Wilber out as soon as possible. Stockdale observed that there "are a lot of loose ends here ...."[59]

In June 1973, Admiral Stockdale, brought charges against these same two officers, in accordance with the Secretary of Defense policy that charges against returnees would have to be brought by other former prisoners. They were charged with conspiracy to solicit mutiny, solicitation of mutiny, mutiny, violation of orders, communications with the enemy, and urging others to cooperate with the enemy.[60] Stockdale recalled these charges had been drafted by the Judge Advocate General of the Navy based in part on some 50 depositions collected by the Naval Investigative Service from returnees.[61] Miller stated that "my critics have preferred as much anonymity and distance as possible" and that Admiral Stockdale "has never spoken with me or met me."[62]

Air Force Lieutenant Colonel Theodore Guy brought charges of misconduct against eight enlisted men under him as the senior ranking officer at The Citadel. Three Marines and five soldiers were accused. The Marines were Staff Sergeant Alfonso R. Riate, Sergeant Able L. Kavanaugh, and Private Frederick L. Elbert, Jr. All were accused of making propaganda statements, cooperating with the enemy, disobedience of orders, attempting to persuade others to disobey orders, and wrongfully communicating with the enemy about other prisoners.(S) [63] Sergeant Kavanaugh committed suicide soon after the charges were published.

A divergence of opinion existed between the prisoners, the Pentagon, the Services, and White House on how this situation should have been handled. Secretary of the Navy John Warner ordered the Navy Judge Advocate General conduct an investigation

---

(S) The legal and command background on these charges is covered extensively in LtCol Gary D. Solis, *Marines and Military Law: Trial by Fire* (Washington, D.C.: History and Museums Division, U.S. Marine Corps, 1989), pp. 218-221.

and Warner himself interviewed some 19 former prisoners and reached two separate determinations. On 3 July 1973, Warner dismissed the charges against the enlisted Marines: on 27 September, he dismissed those against the officers. All of them received secretarial letters of censure.[T] In October 1973, Secretary Warner dropped additional charges against the enlisted Marines following additional investigation and consideration of the legal and policy issues involved. Secretary Warner directed that no further action be taken relating to accusations of misconduct while a prisoner. When the Secretary of the Navy announced his decision he concluded that the convening of a pretrial investigation under Article 32 of the Uniform Code of Military Justice was warranted by the evidence, but felt that "further proceedings, with their attendant publicity, would subject many former prisoners of war and their families ... to additional serious disruption and hardship disproportionate to any national interest which could conceivably be served."[64] In a similar decision, the Secretary of the Army also dismissed the charges against the soldiers involved.

A short time later, the Department of Defense convened a committee to review the Code of Conduct and it considered the handling of the investigations into misconduct. It concluded that "the investigations were minimal, and the rationale supporting dismissal was very weak."[65] While recognizing the "emotional climate" that was disinclined to prosecute any returnees and the Defense Department policy that there would be no prosecution based solely on propaganda statements, the committee was struck by the depth of bitterness expressed by the returnees interviewed. The consensus of returnees was that those who violated the Uniform Code of Military Justice had not been required to account for their actions: "they were put to no test of justice; and their apparent immunity would serve to undermine command authority in any future [prisoner-of-war] organizations."[66]

The Pacific Command's Homecoming organization continued through 2 October 1973 when the Assistant Secretary of Defense for International Security Affairs believed that there would be no other releases. By 1 December 1973, the last vestiges of Homecoming had faded away.[67] Admiral Noel A. M. Gayler's CinCPac command history quoted a *Time* magazine observation that the "exercise was worthy of a major offensive .... The U.S. military's planning for the operation had been meticulous and even loving, in an official way."[68]

(T) LtCol Miller's censure stated in part, he "placed personal comfort and welfare above that of ... fellow prisoners of war." (BGen Walter J. Donovan memo to CMC dtd 29May85. [Vietnam Comment File])

Code of Conduct

The wartime experience of the Marine prisoners was examined from debriefs conducted as part of Operation Homecoming Marine. Areas examined included general treatment, interrogation, indoctrination, prisoner organization, prisoner communications, and effectiveness of training received prior to capture. An acronym "*Sere*," stood for *s*urvival, *e*vasion, *r*esistance, and *e*scape. These four words summarized the ordeal of the Marines at the hands of the Communists in Southeast Asia.[69] Regardless of background and training, all Marines had been indoctrinated in the Code of Conduct. This code was drafted after the Korean War, when there was a need perceived to delineate acceptable behavior in captivity. The degree of success or failure in this endeavor varied with each individual and his relative circumstances. Conduct in the enemy camp was influenced by two sets of standards, those of international law and those of the American military. While survival was a goal in itself, the quality of that survival was measured against the criteria of resistance to the North Vietnamese. This goal had been set by the Code of Conduct and the service senior ranking officers in the Vietnamese camps.[70]

The Marine Corps had used the Code of Conduct for training and instruction intended to promote in Marines the positive attitude that they could oppose and defeat any enemy of their country, even if they were captured. In recruit training, individual combat training, and during predeployment training, Marines received instruction in the Geneva Convention, the Code of Conduct, and survival, evasion, resistance, and escape techniques. The emphasis on the Code of Conduct and the Geneva Convention before and during the war in Vietnam had been oriented towards "big four only" statements — name, rank, serial number, and date of birth. This left nothing to fall back upon when a Marine was not treated as a prisoner of war by the Communists, but as a "war criminal." The Code of Conduct did provide a sound philosophy, but previous training in it did not allow flexibility. Returning prisoners considered this preparation inadequate for what they experienced. "What does one do when unable to stick to the big four?" was the most discussed question during Homecoming debriefings.[71] As one Marine stated, "I was mentally unprepared for internment. I had guilt feelings of a traitorous nature because of my conduct."[72]

As could be expected, the application of the code varied with individuals and military service. The standards of the Code of Conduct were those that Marines carried with them into captivity in Vietnam. The experience they brought out, generally reaffirmed the importance of the Code, with minor variation in wording.[73] Captain Montague wrote that it was a "beautiful code," but that the way it was taught aided the enemy.

When there is time, as in Vietnam, "all can [be] and were broken by our enemy." It is the subsequent guilt that is exploited, until "we realized we had done our best, and had gone to the extreme" and were then able to pick up the pieces and continue the fight.[74]

MIAs: The Joint Casualty Resolution Center

The Paris Accords in 1973 called for signatories to report the location of missing persons as well as prisoners. The North Vietnamese for their part claimed an estimated one million missing to be reconciled. More than a statistic, each missing U.S. Marine was a loss to loved ones, a loss to his unit, and an unresolved individual tragedy that did not diminish with the passing of time and the fading of memory. The missing became an issue for the same reasons that the prisoners became hostages during the war. The domestic pressure of families on elected representatives caused the government to mobilize its efforts to resolve the status of these men, which included 290 Marines in two categories at the end of the war: those considered missing and possibly captured (believed to be 136 Marines in 1973) and those considered killed with their bodies not being recovered. After Operation Homecoming did not provide further insight into the status of the remaining missing, Secretary of the Navy Warner directed that "no action be taken to change the status of Vietnam MIA's" without his personal knowledge.[75] This policy continued until procedures were agreed upon that allowed a judicious determination of a "final" status in each case. Since the 1973 ceasefire, the Department of Defense has maintained that the status review process and the accounting for missing are two separate and distinct issues.[76]

When the MACV Special Operations Group-Joint Personnel Recovery Center (JPRC) was deactivated, its prisoner recovery functions were turned over to the Joint Casualty Resolution Center (JCRC).[U] U.S. Army Brigadier General Robert C. Kingston's Thailand-based organization's mission was to resolve the status of 2,441 Americans missing in action in Southeast Asia.[77] The task force interviewed refugees, conducted searches of identified crash sites, and participated in the "technical" talks with the North Vietnamese. In conjunction with the JCRC, the U.S. Army Central Identification Laboratory provided support with the recovery and identification of remains. The Joint Casualty Resolution Center continued to resolve the status of missing Marines after the completion of Homecoming.

One Marine who did not return during Homecoming was Private First Class Robert R. Garwood. Garwood's initial loss had been treated as capture by the Communists, even after reports that he had chosen to remain with them after being offered release in 1967. The Marine Corps believed him to be collaborating with the enemy at the time of Operation Homecoming in 1973. Reports by prisoners who had been held with

---

(U) First located in Saigon, the JCRC moved to Thailand in February 1973. In May 1976, JCRC moved to NAS Barbers Point, Hawaii.

him confirmed these suspicions. Intelligence gathered by DIA (Defense Intelligence Agency) as late as 1975 indicated he operated with Communist forces in Eastern Quang Nam and Quang Ngai provinces. It was reported that Garwood "spoke Vietnamese fluently, had become a Communist Party member and had recently been promoted to the rank of major."[78] With his return to the United States in 1979, it was alleged during his subsequent trial, that he acted as an interpreter, interrogator, informer, and indoctrinator of his fellow prisoners. At one point he was said to have served as armed guard and to have struck several prisoners for the death of the camp commander's cat. Other prisoners testified that he also provided help to his fellow Americans and that his behavior was the result of manipulation by the Communists.[V][79]

Since the fall of South Vietnam in 1975, and up to 1990, the Defense Intelligence Agency has processed 4,564 reports pertaining to Americans in Southeast Asia: information on grave sites, crash sites, dog tags, live sightings, hearsay, and even prison camp locations. Of 672 Americans indicated in these accounts: 78 percent had already returned alive, remains were located for 15 percent, and 7 percent were unaccounted for. As a matter of national policy, should "any report prove true, we will take appropriate action to ensure the return of those involved." Of the "live" sightings of Americans in Southeast Asia by 1986, 97 were "under continuing investigation in an attempt to confirm the information." Over half of these sightings were considered not related to prisoner of war situations.[80]

(V) Garwood's trial is covered in detail in LtCol Gary D. Solis' *Marines and Military Law in Vietnam: Trial by Fire* (Washington, D.C.: History and Museums Division, U.S. Marine Corps, 1989).

CHAPTER FIFTEEN ENDNOTES

Unless otherwise noted, this chapter is based on HQMC(INTC), "Experience of POWs," study dtd 1973, hereafter POW study; 11thCIT, "Camp Location Study," dtd 22Sept71, hereafter Camp study; Fourth Allied Prisoner of War Wing Debrief dtd 16Apr73, hereafter POW debrief; and HQMC(M), "US Marine Prisoners of War and Missing in Action Summary" dtd 17Oct72, hereafter POW summary. Additional material resides in the Judge Advocate Division files for specific prisoners and subjects, hereafter JAR Files. Operation Homecoming material is derived from JCS Hist73; CinCPac ComdHist73; Thirteenth Air Force Joint Homecoming Reception Center AAR dtd 6Jun73, hereafter Thirteenth AF AAR; III MAF Operation Homecoming AAR dtd 5Apr73, hereafter IIIMAF AAR, and Marine Corps Operation Homecoming AAR dtd 25Jul73, hereafter HQMC AAR. See also DOD, "Operation Homecoming," *Commanders Digest*, Mar73; and Berger, op. cit., pp. 321-339. See also the various hearings by the Subcommittee on National Security Policy and Scientific Developments of the House Committee on Foreign Affairs, 1971 through 1973.

Combatants or Hostages?

1   POW summary, p. 1.

2   Communist "pointy-talkee" card captured in 1969 in MR 1 from an NVA medic, Maj Edward J. Wages, Comments on draft ms, dtd 20Nov90 (Vietnam Comment File).

3   Defense Intelligence Agency, "Citizens and Dependents, Captured, Missing, Detained or Voluntarily Remained in SEA," dtd 10Nov79 (RefSec, MCHC, Washington, D.C.); and POW summary.

4   "Information Concerning PW Mail," Tab III-H-7, CMC Reference Notebooks 1971-72.

5   RAdm Horace B. Robertson, Jr., memo to SecNav, dtd 16Jul73 (JAR File); "PW Treatment in North and South Vietnam;" "PW Statistics and Marines Who May be Assisting the Enemy," Tab III-H-7, CMC Reference Notebooks 1971-72; HQMC(INTC) memo, dtd 14Mar79, "Comment and Report of American Collaborators and Deserters in South Vietnam," hereafter INTC comments. Also Bernard B. Fall, "Communist POW Treatment in Indochina," (Norfolk: Composite Interrogation Translation Team, FMFLant), dtd Jan61; and LCdr John M. McGrath, *Prisoner of War* (Annapolis, Naval Institute Press, 1975), for conditions in captivity.

6   POW study, pp. H-19 to H-19f.

7   Maj Jose J. Anzaldua intvw by MCAS New River Public Affairs Office, *Marines*, Sep85, pp. 6-9.

8   Maj Bruce R. Archer intvw by MCDEC Public Affairs Office, dtd 12Mar87 (Vietnam Comment File).

9   Maj Paul J. Montague, Comments on draft ms, dtd 16Nov89 (Vietnam Comment File).

10 Douglas K. Ramsey ltr to Gen Robert E. Cushman, Jr., dtd 3Apr73, hereafter Ramsey ltr, p. 3, in Capt Donald G. Cook biographic file (RefSec, MCHC, Washington, D.C.).

11 Anzaldua intvw.

12 POW study, pp. H22 to H24; Also, Frank Bormann, "U.S. Prisoners of War in Southeast Asia," *Congressional Record*, 22Sep70, p. H9019.

13 LCdr William Berg, "Injuries and Illnesses of Vietnam War POWs: Marine POWs," *Military Medicine*, Sep77, pp. 678–80.

14 POW study, Tab-Wing Policies.

15 LtCol Harlan P. Chapman, Comments on draft ms, dtd 18Jan90 (Vietnam Comment File).

16 POW study, Tab-SRO Policy Son Tay.

17 LtCol Orson G. Swindle, Comments on draft ms, dtd 15Nov89; POW debrief, passim; VAdm James B. Stockdale, comments on draft ms, dtd 28Jan89 (Vietnam Comment File).

18 "I heard the tapes he made ...." Chapman comments.

19 Col Edison W. Miller, Comments on draft ms, dtd 21Jan90 (Vietnam Comment File).

20 POW study, p. S14.

21 Hank Whitmore, "Fear Can Be Your Best Friend," *Parade Magazine*, 19Apr85, p. 5.

22 Miller comments.

23 RAdm Horace B. Robertson, Jr. memo to SecNav, dtd 16Jul73 (JAR File); LtCol Edson W. Miller biographical file and POW subject files; (RefSec, MCHC, Washington, D.C.).

24 Anzaldua intvw, p. 8.

Egress Recap and Other Contingencies

25 MGen Leroy J. Manor ltr to Deputy Chief of Staff, Plans and Policies, HQMC, dtd 12Oct72 (Vietnam Comment File). See also Benjamin F. Schemmer, *The Raid* (New York: Harper & Row, Publishers, 1976), pp. 261–263.

26 HQMC AAR, p. 2.

27 CinCPacInst 3461.1C, dtd 3Aug72 and 13thAF OPlan Egress Recap, dtd 1 Dec 72.

28 ThirteenthAF AAR, pp. 1-25 for background and conduct, pp. 26-45 for conclusions.

29 The White House, "Fact Sheet: International Commission of Control and Supervision," dtd 24Jan73 (Vietnam Comment File).

30 ThirteenthAF AAR, p. 7.

31 Col John W. Clayborne, comments on draft ms, dtd 29Dec89 (Vietnam Comment File).

32 Anzaldua intvw.

33 JCS msg to CinCPac, dtd 25Jan73 (Vietnam Comment File).

34 JCS Hist73, pp. 714, 721.

35 Peace Accords, Article 8, p. 3.

36 JCS Hist73, p. 723.

Operation Homecoming
37 Clayborne comments.

38 POW study, Tab-Go Home Guidance.

39 ThirteenthAF AAR, pp. 15-21, 15-25.

40 LtCol William C. Howey, Comments on draft ms, dtd 17Nov89 (Vietnam Comment File).

41 Howey comments.

42 Clayborne comments.

43 ThirteenthAF AAR, p. 13.

44 IIIMAF AAR, p. 29.

45 Clayborne comments.

46 ThirteenthAF AAR, p. 15-45.

47 Howey comments.

48 Chapman comments.

49 IIIMAF AAR, p. 25.

50 CMC ltr to Casualty Assistance Call Officers, dtd 6Dec 72.

Welcome Home Marine
51 Capt William E. Thomas, Jr., Comments on draft ms, dtd 20Dec89; MCB Camp Pendleton, "Historical Documentation of Phase III Prisoner of War Repatriation Activities," dtd 5Jun73, in HQMC AAR (Vietnam Comment File).

52 Operation Homecoming (Public Affairs), dtd 20 Apr 1973, in HQMC AAR.

53 Capt Donald G. Cook biographical file (RefSec, MCHC, Washington, D.C.).

54 Ramsey ltr, p.3.

55 Ramsey ltr, p. 2.

56 Stockdale comments.

57 Clayborne comments.

58 Miller comments.

59 Stockdale comments.

60 RAdm Merlin H. Staring memo to SecNav, dtd 16Jul73; Col James P. King memo to ACMC, dtd 1Aug79 (JAR File).

61 Stockdale comments.

62 Miller comments.

63 RAdm Horace B. Robertson, Jr. memo to SecNav, dtd 22Jun73; Col John R. DeBarr memo to CMC, dtd 5Jul73 and 2Aug73 (JAR File).

64 BGen Walter J. Donovan, memo to CMC, dtd 29May85 (JAR File); HQMC(PA), "Fact Sheet: Operation Homecoming; Disciplinary Action Against Returnees" (Vietnam Comment File).

65 *Report Defense Review Committee for the Code of Conduct* (Washington D.C.: Department of Defense, 1976), pp.15-17, hereafter the Code of Conduct Review (Vietnam Comment File).

66 Code of Conduct review, p. 16

67 CinCPac ComdHist73, pp. 599-603.

68 *Time*, 19Feb73, p. 13, in CinCPac ComdHist73, p. 600.

Code of Conduct

69 For Vietnam era SERE doctrine see DA, FM21-76 *Survival, Evasion, Resistance, and Escape*, dtd Mar69; FM21-77 A *Joint World Wide Evasion and Escape Manual*; and DAPAM30-101 *Communist Interrogation, Indoctrination, and Exploitation of Prisoners* of War, dtd May56.

70 "Code of Conduct," Tab III-F-1-0, CMC Reference Notebooks 1971–72.

71 Ibid., pp. H-22 to H-29.

72 POW study, Tab-Code of Conduct.

73 Code of Conduct review, p. 17. Also Maj Terrence P. Murray, "Code of Conduct—A Sound Doctrine," *Marine Corps Gazette*, Dec83, pp. 56-62; and Maj Edward F. Wells, "Operation Homecoming" (ms, MCHC, Washington, D.C., 1985)

74 Montague comments.

MIAs: The Joint Casualty Resolution Center

75 SecNav memo to CMC/CNO, dtd 6Jul73 (JAR File).

76 OASD(ISA) memo to SecDef, dtd 4May77 (JAR File).

77 LtCol Richard H. Esau, Jr., "Da Nang After the Armistice," *Marine Corps Gazette*, Jul74, pp. 49-50.

78 INTC comments, p. 36.

79 Garwood Folder (JAR File); "Return of PFC Robert Russell Garwood, USMC, from Vietnam," AAR, dtd 20Apr79; MCB Camp Lejeune, "Public Affairs and the GCM of PFC Robert R. Garwood, USMC," AAR, dtd 5Mar81; and PFC Robert R. Garwood biographical file (RefSec, MCHC, Washington, D.C.).

80 SecDef msg to CMC, dtd 30Jun82, SecDef msg to SecNav, dtd 25Mar83; SecDef msg to CMC, dtd 11Jul85; and OASD(ISA), "Status Reviews and Accounting for Servicemen Missing in Southeast Asia," dtd 4May77. See also OASD(PA), "Americans Unaccounted for in Indochina," dtd 2Jan89; "Joint Casualty Resolution Center," dtd 2Jan86; "U.S. Army Central Identification Laboratory," dtd 2Jan86; "Remains Identified as American," dtd 2Jan86; "Technical Talks," dtd 24Feb86; "Principal Sources of POW/MIA Information," dtd 24Feb86; and "Official U.S. Government Live Sighting Position," dtd 24Feb86 (Vietnam Comment File).

CHAPTER SIXTEEN
CONTINUITY AND CHANGE

Operation End Sweep • Task Force Delta, The Tigers Depart • To What End?

Operation End Sweep

The final withdrawal of III MAF units from Vietnam as part of the Paris Accords was contingent upon the release of allied prisoners held by the Communists and the clearing of the American mines from the harbors of North Vietnam. When these waterways were mined in May 1972, the possibility of the U.S. having to clear them had been recognized. These mines were a significant factor in negotiations, as the North Vietnamese possessed only rudimentary mineclearing capabilities and apparently their Soviet and Chinese allies were not prepared to test theirs.

This was the mission of Seventh Fleet's Mine Countermeasure Force (Task Force 78) under Rear Admiral Brian McCauley, a Naval Academy graduate with a degree in physics from Harvard and a surface warfare career in destroyers. Earlier reductions in size had left the Seventh Fleet with few minesweeping assets. Surface units resided mainly in the reserve, rather than in the active, force structure. As a result, the majority of any minesweeping had to be accomplished by helicopter units and the Navy possessed a single 13-aircraft squadron. Planning for the clearing of mines, codenamed Formation Sentry, began in November 1972 when JCS ordered the Charleston, South Carolina-based Mine Countermeasure Command (MCMC) and Helicopter Mine Countermeasure Squadron (HC) 12 to Cubi Point, Philippines.[A][1]

Task Force 78 was formed at Subic Bay on 24 November around the Mine Countermeasure Command staff, including the Navy helicopter squadron HM-12, and

---

(A) Formation Sentry I, the original mineclearing plan, was drafted by Commander Paul L. Gruendl, USN, and other members of the mine countermeasure staff on temporary duty with CinCPac in 1972. It called for fewer assets to cover the same area in sequence over a longer period of time. The later Formation Sentry II planned for simultaneous sweep with more assets involved. (Gruendl Comments)

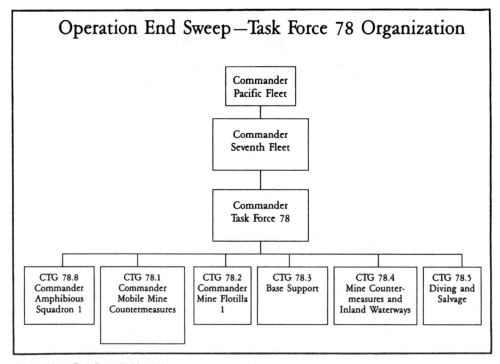

Operation End Sweep—Task Force 78 Organization

Adapted from Task Force 78 Material

the Guam-based Mine Flotilla 1, augmented by other West Coast units. Marine Corps representatives on the force staff were Lieutenant Colonel James C. Robinson, Lieutenant Colonel Charles B. Redman, and, later, Lieutenant Colonel Victor M. Lee. Admiral McCauley's initial concept envisioned a single airborne mine countermeasure (AMCM) unit of eight aircraft supported by an LPH and LPD to clear five ports. As planning progressed, the complexity of the task and the desire to complete the clearing as soon as possible made it evident that the command did not possess the necessary forces to accomplish the mission. Admiral McCauley wrote, "Operation End Sweep had the highest priority in the Pacific Fleet. It commenced with the ceasefire and, as a result, people, ships, and aircraft, which in a wartime scenario would have been otherwise occupied, were made available."[2] Major General Leslie E. Brown, the 1st Marine Aircraft Wing (MAW) commander, recalled that the decision was made at the "highest levels to employ USMC helicopters." The JCS and CinCPac staff directed Lieutenant General Louis H. Wilson, Jr., the FMFPac commanding general, to support the Navy with Marine CH-53s, which were basically the same as the HM-12 aircraft. Commander Paul L. Gruendl, Chief of Staff of the Mine Countermeasure Force, recalled the CH-53 had been adapted by the Secretary of the Navy with this mission in mind and that the hard-point fittings for towing equipment were already in place and "the aircraft was not modified."[3] All of this caused concern to Lieutenant General Louis Metzger at III MAF regarding roles, missions, and, more important, the loss of 9th MAB amphibious lift and aircraft.[4] General Metzger realized the implications of losing both helicopter squadrons and five amphibious ships because of the mineclearing commitment, units upon which many demands had been made in the previous six months. Brigadier General Paul G. Graham of 9th MAB removed his Marine units from the appointed ships and changed their organization to provide ship-based support for MACV, without helicopter assets. If required, the amphibious assault ships (LPHs) from Task Force 78 would be made available to 9th MAB for amphibious operations.

Operation End Sweep sent workhorse Marine helicopter squadrons where they least expected to fly, North Vietnam. End Sweep was also a new mission: airborne mineclearing. To support the task force, FMFPac assigned Major John Van Nortwick III's Hawaii-based Marine Heavy Helicopter Squadron (HMH) 463 to 1st MAW. General Brown, the wing commander, assigned Lieutenant Colonel Charles H. Egger's composite Marine Medium Helicopter Squadron (HMM) 165 to this mission as well, reinforced with the CH-53 Sea Stallions of HMH-462 and additional CH-46 Sea Knights from HMM-164. Command elements were organized around the existing headquarters of HMH-463 and HMM-165, with aircraft and crews coming from all the assigned Marine squadrons. The four supporting squadrons were at various locations throughout the Western Pacific prior to Task Force 78 activation: HMM-165 with three CH-53s, two UH-1s, and five CH-46s on the USS *New Orleans* (LPH 11) and HMH-463 with nine CH-53s, six CH-46s, and two UH-1s on the USS *Inchon* (LPH 12) and three CH-53s on the USS *Cleveland*. Nine HMH-462 CH-53s at Cubi Point, Philippines, and at Futema, Okinawa, and all 12 of HMM-164's aircraft at Futema could provide additional support if necessary."[5]

By 7 December 1972, the assigned forces had been identified 10 ocean minesweepers, 9 amphibious ships, 6 fleet tugs, 3 salvage ships, 6 destroyers, 45 helicopters, and more than 5,000 men serving with TF 78.[6] Carrier- and land-based air support was available to protect the task force and additional support was provided by logistic and picket ships.[7] Four surface mine-countermeasure (SMCM) units were configured around the ocean-going minesweepers (MSOs). The four airborne mine-countermeasure (AMCM) units arranged to clear extensive areas of seven ports and 15 inland waterways. According to the final concept, Marine CH-53s were to be used in minesweeping operations, CH-46s for logistics and search and rescue support, and UH-1s for command and control. Some missions were not covered by existing tactical procedures, as in how to conduct search-and-rescue operations in a minefield? Aircraft and aircrew familiarization began at Naval Air Station, Cubi Point, early in December 1972. The month witnessed intensified unit training at Subic Bay to qualify the Marine units in the technique of sweeping mines from the air.

Following the final ceasefire agreement, on 24 January 1973, the Joint Chiefs of Staff named the operation End Sweep and directed it to start on 1 February 1973.[8] General Metzger passed control of designated Marine units to Admiral McCauley on 1 February. Control of Task Force 76's Amphibious Squadron 1 (ARGs Alpha and Bravo) went to Task Force 78 at the same time. According to HMM-165's Lieutenant Colonel Egger, the Vietnamese ceasefire became a reality when his unit's stay in Singapore was cut short and the unit was rushed back to Subic Bay for "a new and important assignment."[9] At Subic Bay, further intensive training brought the Marine aircrews up to the skill level of their Navy counterparts. Major Van Nortwick reported that in the short period, 50 pilots and 50 crewmen were given at least three training flights towing countermeasure devices. When the force departed Subic for North Vietnam, HMM-165 was on the USS *New Orleans* and HMH-463 was on board the USS *Inchon*. The Marine helicopters and crews were now integrated into five Navy-led AMCM units.[B] [10]

The task force's mission required the clearing of ports and coastal locations of more than 11,000 MK52-2 mines and MK36 destructors that had been used during the course of the mining campaign. These devices were equipped with magnetic and acoustic fuses that detonated when a target was close enough to activate the mine. Most were located in restricted water as shallow as three feet and the devices had been set to detonate or deactivate after a given period of time.

At an initial meeting on 5 February 1973, at the Duyen Hai Hotel in Haiphong, Admiral McCauley negotiated with North Vietnamese Colonel Hoan Nuu Thai to establish procedures and the sequence of areas to be cleared. This set the pattern for subsequent negotiations which were often more political than technical. North Vietnamese demands were accompanied by thinly veiled threats that United States and Democratic Republic of Vietnam relations would not improve unless the Americans met all requirements, including the completion of mine clearing by 28 March. If not, the North Vietnamese intimated that the release of American prisoners would not go smoothly.[11]

(B) Flagship/Command Unit (*New Orleans* with 10 USMC CH-46s, 2 USMC UH-1s, 7 USN CH-53s, 1 USN CH-46); AMCM Unit Alpha (*Cleveland* with 3 USN CH-53s); AMCM Unit Bravo (*Ogden* with 3 USN CH-53s); AMCM Unit Charlie (*Inchon* with 9 USMC CH-53s, 10 USMC CH-46s, 2 USMC UH-1s, 1 USN CH-46); AMCM Unit Delta (*Dubuque* with 3 USMC CH-53s).

On 23 February 1973, AMCM Units Alpha and Bravo arrived at an anchorage off of Haiphong. The next day, Marines flew the command negotiating team to the Cat Bi Airfield for consultations with the North Vietnamese. Logistic runs to this airfield continued throughout the period, while additional flights transported men and equipment to install three Raydist[(C)] sites around Haiphong Harbor. Admiral Noel A. M. Gayler, CinCPac, suspended operations soon after they began and ordered Task Force 78 from the anchorage on 28 February, when the release of American prisoners was delayed, demonstrating that continued clearing was dependent upon prisoner release. The task force moved to a holding area at sea where the units practiced flight and sweep procedures until 4 March. On 7 March 1973, Marine CH-53s began sweeping the Haiphong Channel with MK105 towed sleds.[(D)] Five days later, HMH-463 made its first sweeps of the Lach Huyen River.[12] On 17 March, Airborne Mine Counter Measure Unit Charlie and Inchon began sweeping the Hon Gai approaches.

In their daily routines, the helicopter crews swept a specific area. They used navigational aids located both on shore and on board minesweepers to ensure accurate location. The sweep flights themselves were time-consuming, repetitive passes over an assigned stretch of waterway at less than a 100 feet above the surface. One pilot from HMH-463 described a typical minesweep sortie which began with the towing of the magnetic pipe from the LPD to the minefield under radar control, approximately a 30-minute process:

> At this time radar coverage from the LPD was lost and the actual two-hour
> sweep was conducted by pilot judgment utilizing previously prepared
> charts. A 30-minute return to the LPD followed. If operational planning
> was correct and no mechanical difficulties were encountered, an incoming
> relief helicopter passed the outgoing one at the minefield boundary.[13]

This was an exhaustive effort that required concentration and was flown in the knowledge of a possible pass too near the blast of a detonated mine. Other difficulties were North Vietnamese constraints on navigational airspace and sea lanes and poor flying weather. Major Joseph L. James, the HMM-165 executive officer, stated that "for 63 days, ship and squadron personnel, while performing their new mission, encountered low ceilings, fog, and instrument flight conditions."[14] The helicopters delivered supplies and equipment to North Vietnamese engineers at various inland waterway clearing sites. Flight routes into North Vietnam required strict compliance to stated arrival and departure times.[15]

(C) A precise navigation system installed on the AMCM helicopters which used shore-based signal antennas. For political reasons it was only used in the Haiphong channel.

(D) The MK105 sled on one of the five mine countermeasure devices used. It was an influence minesweeping system using a float and foils to trail electrode trails. The other common device towed by Marines was the Magnetic Orange Pipe (MOP) using acoustic and magnetic systems.

Sweeps continued despite operational casualties, breakdowns in communication with the North Vietnamese, and others delays, until each area was ready for a surface test run by the MSS-2, a decommissioned LST (the former USS *Washtenaw County*). When the deactivation date of the mines was reached, flights became less demanding as check- or demonstration-only sweeps were made, rather than protracted clearance sweeps. The CH-53's suspended flight operations for a time in late March and early April 1973 after two of the helicopters crashed during towing operations. By 13 April 1973, clearing operations in the main Haiphong shipping channel were finished.

Four days later, Vice Admiral James L. Holloway III, Seventh Fleet commander, ordered Admiral McCauley to withdraw the task force, without notice to the North Vietnamese, because of continued delays in the release of prisoners. The units of the task force made port visits to Hong Kong and Subic Bay and conducted needed maintenance and training. Marine Captain Raul A. Sifuentes, commanding AMCM Unit Delta, "crossdecked" his unit to the USS *Vancouver* (LPD-2) while at Subic Bay and on 20 April 1973, HMM-165 moved from the *Inchon* to the USS *Tripoli*. Finally, in response to a joint American and North Vietnamese communique signed in Paris, Task Force 78 sailed for North Vietnam to resume clearing operations, which began again on 18 June. It had been agreed in Paris that sweeping would resume within five days and that it would be completed within 35 days. On 20 June 1973, after MSS-2 made four transits of the Haiphong channel to prove the safety of the area, Admiral McCauley notified the North Vietnamese that the "United States has concluded mine clearance operations in the Nan Trieu [Haiphong] Main Channel."[16]

The clearance of Haiphong allowed the minesweeping units to concentrate now on the other harbors and coastal areas. The Marines of AMCM Unit Charlie were assigned the channel to Hon Gai and AMCM Unit Delta to the Cam Pha channel. The North Vietnamese continued inland sweeping using American equipment and training. By 26 June 1973, these tasks were completed and the mines had either been detonated or were inert. Operations shifted further south to the Vinh area where, on 28 June, AMCMs Charlie and Delta started to sweep and check the seaward entrance to the Giang Song River. On 2 July, AMCM Unit Delta proceeded to the Cua Sot coastal area to check-sweep, supported by the USS *Ogden* (LPD 5), *Impervious* (MSO 779), and the *Moctobi* (ATF 105). There, one of HMH-463's helicopters made a forced water landing, Navy ships recovered both the crew and the wreckage.

Admiral McCauley declared the Vinh, Hon La, Cua Sot, and Quang Hung areas clear on 4 July 1973. Ship-based HMM-165 and HMH-463 departed North Vietnam for Subic Bay, evading Typhoon Anita enroute. Logistic support of the inland waterways operations by the Democratic Republic of Vietnam personnel continued through mid-

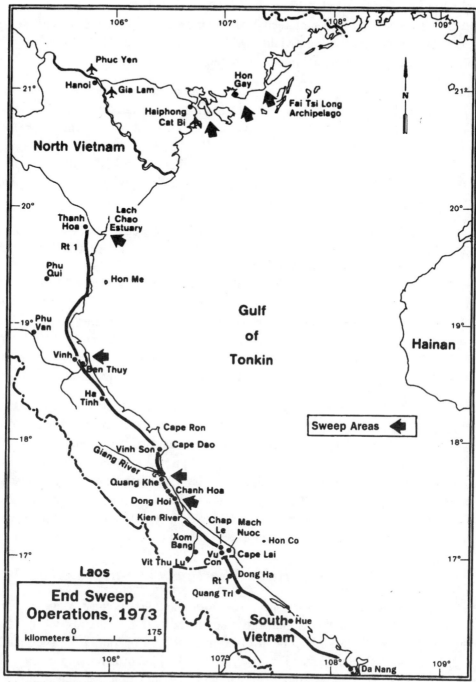

Adapted from Task Force 78 Material

July when End Sweep ended. Admiral McCauley informed the North Vietnamese the End Sweep forces would depart their waters on 18 July. A final U.S. and North Vietnamese disagreement prevented the sweeping of the ports of Than Hoa and Dong Hoi, as well as small minefields in coastal waters.[17]

Admiral McCauley shifted his flag on shore at Subic Bay and Task Force 78 was disestablished. Detached on 24 July 1973, the Marines returned to III MAF after seven demanding months with Task Force 78 that had placed a toll on men and machines, even with the credible maintenance effort. HMH-463 flew a total of 2,147 hours, including 745 hours of the task force's 2,000 hours under tow with AMCM operations, while HMM-165 flew 3,444 sorties, for 1,690 hours.[18] In flying these hours, the squadrons of the AMCM group swept 27,000 miles of water.[19]

Squadrons had learned new procedures in conducting mine countermeasures, search and rescue, water survival, aircraft modifications, and evaluations. As HMH-463's Major Van Nortwick said, they "once again proved that Marine Corps Aviation can operate in any environment, at any time, with skill and professionalism.[20] The Marines anticipated a return to the home stations, Hawaii for HMH-463 and Okinawa for HMM-165, to conduct needed maintenance and refitting not possible on ship. The continuing war in Southeast Asia found HMM-165 retained on the *Tripoli* to support the 31st MAU tasked with Operation Eagle Pull, the evacuation of American personnel from Cambodia. As one crisis was over another was beginning.[21]

Admiral McCauley cautioned in his after-action report, that it "would be a mistake to attempt to devise general, long-standing mine warfare conclusions from the specific operational and political arena in which End Sweep was conducted." End Sweep was a unique solution to a unique problem and did not present a challenge of nearly the magnitude that can be expected in the future.[22] General Metzger, III MAF, and General Wilson, FMFPac, realized that the Navy's shortage of mine countermeasure ships and helicopters meant that Marine Corps assets had to be diverted from an amphibious to a fleet role to perform End Sweep, even if they did not relish it.

Task Force Delta, The Tigers Depart

As Operations Homecoming and End Sweep were completed, some Marines were still at war. Task Force Delta combat sorties continued in Cambodia, just when "... it appeared that MAG-15 would not be involved in combat air operations."[23] The March 1973 dry season saw the Khmer Rouge trying to take Phnom Penh, and closing all major highways into the Cambodian capital. The situation for the Lon Nol government was critical with the interdiction of the Mekong River, the major supply artery from South Vietnam. The defense of the capital and the reopening of the river required direct American air support to the Cambodian Army. Marine Aircraft Group (MAG) 15 continued operations in April, flying missions assigned by Seventh Air Force for daytime bombing and strafing controlled by airborne controllers. This involved the F-4s of Marine Fighter Attack (VMFA) 115 and 232, flying 12 to 20 sorties a day. "Moderate to heavy" antiaircraft fire by the Communists was received from 23mm, 37mm, and SA7 weapons in positions set up along major communications routes. Previously, the Khmer Rouge had used small arms and 12.7mm machine guns.[24] Beginning 11 May 1973, the Marine All Weather Attach Squadron (VMA[AW]) 533 conducted strikes using its airborne moving target indicator and ground radar beacons to carry out armed road reconnaissance at a rate of five sorties a night. The distances flown to the targets required inflight refueling by the Marine Aerial Refueling Squadron 152 Detachment Delta before and after the target areas were hit.[25] By June, the beginning of the annual monsoon, the ground crisis had passed with the help of MAG-15. By not authorizing continued funding, Congress brought an end to this support that summer. By then, Task Force Delta had flown 10,215 combat sorties involving a total of 30,998 flight hours and 24,584 tons of ordnance. Three A-6s and two F-4s were lost in combat.[26]

The "on again, off again" nature of Task Force Delta's deployment, its isolation, and the proximity of Thai civilians and available "recreational" drugs, increased the importance of law enforcement as the duration of the stay in Thailand extended beyond the ceasefire. As the unifying effect of combat was removed, the social tensions that had been suppressed manifested themselves in unrest, drink- and drug-related incidents, and violations of military law.[27] A serious incident of racial unrest occurred in July 1973 with a series of confrontations among black and white Marines that escalated into a mess-hall riot and resultant bitterness.[28] In the subsequent investigations and court cases, it developed that the mixture of air and ground Marines was a factor in this turmoil, compounded by the short-term rotational nature of personnel assignments.[E] Major John T. "Jack" Dyer, Jr., a combat artist from Headquarters Marine Corps, assigned to Nam Phong that summer, recorded the scene in words and pictures in 1973:

> .... The Rose Garden experience will soon be history, remembered most
> vividly by those who were there. With the passage of time the unpleasant
> heat, dust, mud, long hours of hard work, nightmarish combat flights,
> tepid showers when available, four-holers and Montezuma's revenge will
> slowly fade from memory. Until the next time. "The Marines don't
> promise you a Rose Garden, just one good deal after another."[29]

(E) While the leadership problems were similar in division and wing, the leadership styles used to solve them were different. Innovative programs were tried by 1st MAW in Japan to achieve these ends: human relations instruction, counseling centers for addicts and alcoholics, a hotline telephone service, a "coffee house," and cultural center. These programs were not in place at Nam Phong.

This was the situation faced by Colonel Darrel E. Bjorklund who assumed command of MAG-15 from Colonel Talbert on 26 July 1973. Increased concerns for internal security brought increased emphasis on SU 1 defense forces, which now included a "K-9" dog section, a criminal investigation detachment, customs inspectors, and a military police platoon. Their functions included manning roadblocks, running patrols, and maintaining a temporary detention facility. Marine commanders also employed more positive solutions in providing adequate recreation, education, and personal-services support to meet the wing commander's goals of "racial harmony and the elimination of drug/alcohol abuse."[30] Some of the more innovative "human relations" methods conflicted with the more traditional ones. These were grounded in obedience to orders as opposed to sensitive treatment of social minorities. As in other Marine Corps units, the answer to leadership problems was found in pride and purpose. Whether innovative programs or traditional leadership values resolved the social issues found in American society remains a matter of conjecture.[31]

All the while, planning continued and was completed to withdraw the Marines and to return Nam Phong to the Thai government. Task Force Delta's Operation Plan (Op Plan) 1-73 (Operation Sunset) was used as the basis for the 10 August 1973 program directive from the Military Assistance Command, Thailand (MACThai), that standardized the anticipated base closure. Brigadier General Manning T. Jannell replaced General Taylor as commanding general on 14 August 1973. Jannell arrived from Headquarters Marine Corps in Washington, D.C., where he had been the Assistant Quartermaster General. The withdrawal of the Marines seemed imminent, but no date was set. After 15 August, efforts were made to ready Task Force Delta for departure while maintaining a high level of operational readiness.[32] Marine Corps units by their expeditionary nature are prepared to deploy with standing embarkation plans and special containers and packing material for all items of equipment. Inspections by the MAG-15 embarkation officer, Major Frederick J. Schober, uncovered a major problem in the disintegration of "embarkation boxes" from exposure to the elements in the tropical conditions of the Rose Garden.

General Jannell was directed to carry out OpPlan 1-73 on 27 August 1973 when the Joint Chiefs of Staff had approved the shut down of Nam Phong with a target date of 30 August. Task Force Delta's command chronology recorded, "received execute order for retrograde. Today is designated as 'R' day."[33] After U.S. notification of the Thai and Japanese Governments of the move, General Jannell proceeded to relocate all tactical aircraft, 4.5 million pounds of cargo, and 2,147 men. This had to be carried out so as to ensure the least disruption of combat readiness of the units involved.[F] The movement itself consisted of the fly-away of tactical aircraft, air transport for people,

---

(F) Brigadier General Victor A. Armstrong, the deputy chief of staff of FMFPac, observed that the total wear and tear on aircraft and equipment was significant, and that the "Marine Corps lived with some of these problems for several years." (Armstrong Comments)

and sealift for equipment. The airlift required 106 MAC C-141s and C-5s; in addition, VMGR-152 and the Pacific Air Traffic Management Agency used their C-130s throughout the 11-day movement. At 0600, 30 August 1973, the A-6s of VMA(AW)-533 launched down the runway at Nam Phong for the last time. They were followed on the next day by VMFA-115 and on 1 September by VMFA-232. Because of the previous planning and anticipation of the move, the final withdrawal from Thailand took on its own momentum. Some delay occurred to obtain commercial trucks to move the sea echelon 400 miles to Sattahip. Once at the port of embarkation, the officer-in-charge of the movement unit found that expected U.S. Navy amphibious ships were not available and that the Military Sealift Command's SS *Green Forest* and *Puerto Rico* would provide the lift for some seven million pounds of cargo, which was mainly the vehicles of the task force.[34]

General Jannell completed the turnover of facilities and remaining equipment to a representative of the Thai Supreme Command. After calls on the U.S. Embassy and MACThai, General Jannell supervised the final color detail at Royal Thai Air Force Base Nam Phong at 0800, 21 September 1973, as the "American flag was lowered ... signifying the departure of the final increment of the 2,100 U.S. Marines stationed at the facility in support of Cambodia air operations."[(G) 35] Present were the Thai Minister of Defense and the Commanding General of the 1st Marine Aircraft Wing. "Approximately 50 members of the press flew in from Bangkok to observe the final departure," recalled Jannell, who met them, along with MAG-15's Colonel Bjorklund.[36] The story of the "Rose Garden" was closed with this last official act.[37] By now most Marines were gone; on 23 September both commercial ships were on their way to Japan and on 2 November 1973, the task force was dissolved.

To What End?

The Vietnam scholar, Douglas Pike, observed that the North Vietnamese, under Soviet tutelage and with Chinese logistics support, mounted a conventional combined-arms invasion of South Vietnam after a decade of revolutionary war. Their efforts had progressed from dependence on manpower to a battle of technology fought on sea, air, and land. For the Communists this was a continuation of the process of military, political, and diplomatic efforts to achieve their goal of domination of the Indochina region. This aggression was met by the South Vietnamese with American support, primarily logistics and firepower.[38]

The Marines who came to symbolize the Marine commitment to Vietnam during the 1972 Spring Offensive were the advisors, the *Covans,* who with the Marines and

---

(G) On 24 September 1973, the Marine Corps Historical Division noted that "we should accept this time and date as being the official end of the U.S. Marine Corps participation in the Southeast Asian War." (HQMC[HD], Director of Marine Corps History memo dtd 24Sept73)

sailors of ANGLICO's Sub Unit One, served with the Vietnamese through the initial defeat and subsequent victories. Coming from diverse backgrounds and experience, their common characteristic was earlier successful combat tours. According to participant Lieutenant Colonel Andrew D. DeBona, they "were well trained and wanted to be there."[39]

The 9th Marine Amphibious Brigade, Marine Aircraft Group 12, and Marine Aircraft Group 15 were destined to serve in anonymity, their efforts not considered newsworthy at the time.[40] As a matter for the historical records, when the Vietnamese Marine Division moved from Saigon to defend Hue in April 1972, aggressive support by III MAF forces contributed to its success in defeating Communists there and at Quang Tri City. The contributions made by Marine Aircraft Group 12 to the defense of An Loc in Military Region 3 were also noteworthy.[41]

The Marine Corps response reflected the changing security requirements of the decade, as much as continuing the previous era of fighting in Vietnam. When considered in the context of maritime strategy, the variety of demands placed upon III MAF Marines in 1972 and 1973 can be viewed as post-war deployments that set a pattern for the next decade of contingencies in the Far East and elsewhere. These underscored the need for flexibility, versatility, and presence. As each crisis occurred, the first United States tactical units to respond were the forces deployed afloat, specifically the amphibious ready groups with embarked Marines.[42] The other major employment, the independent and expeditionary operation of Marine air forces, was demonstrated by MAG-12 and MAG-15 as landward extensions of naval aviation.

Previous contingency operations in Lebanon, the Dominican Republic, and by the Special Landing Force in Vietnam had shown the way. But, in 1972, there was no doctrine for the conduct of a "noncombatant evacuation" other than the seize, occupy, defend, and withdraw missions enunciated in FMFM 8-1, *Special Operations*.[(H)] What emerged from the 9th MAB experience was a more refined concept of the noncombatant evacuation and the use of "seabasing," rather than costly deployment ashore. Continued revisions took place in the Mediterranean contingencies of 1973, and were put to the test during the final evacuations of Phnom Phenh and Saigon in 1975.

The Marine Corps response to the North Vietnamese invasion brought together a number of diverse efforts and enterprises. For III MAF, the story of this period was of a campaign that saw the assembly and employment of amphibious and air forces to achieve political goals. General Metzger, the Marine commander who carried out this response stated that "... we were ready. We met every challenge," challenges that saw

---

(H) The edition of 13 May 1968 was then current. This was the reference used to prepare operations orders and plans for raids, demonstrations, and withdrawals. Concepts for evacuations have been published since, as non-combatant evacuation operations (NEO).

operations ranging from combat to contingency over a vast geographic area.[43] At what cost were the U.S. Marine Corps' efforts to be measured for this period? From mid-1971 until 29 January 1973, 21 Marines were killed, 82 wounded, 19 reported missing, and 4 captured. Twenty-four Marine aircraft were lost in combat during this same interval.[44] These casualties are added to the total of 13,005 Marines killed and 88,635 wounded over the course of the war from 1961 through 1973.[I] This fighting had the smallest Marine casualty rate of the war and in these limited terms "Vietnamization" was successful. But while the Marines endured, the Communists persisted. U.S. Army Colonel Harry G. Summers, Jr., commented to an NVA colonel in Hanoi in April 1975 that "you never defeated us on the battlefield." After a moment the North Vietnamese colonel replied, "That may be so, but it is also irrelevant."[45] The record of this period then, must reflect both direct and indirect costs to the Corps of the war that would not end.

(I) The Vietnam Memorial lists 14,809 total dead, including those missing and presumed dead. American casualities for this period of the war were established at 198 billed and 561 overall.

CHAPTER SIXTEEN ENDNOTES

Unless otherwise noted, material in this chapter is derived from CincPac ComdHist73; MACV ComdHist73; FMFPac MarOpsSEA; SeventhFlt ComdHist73; MAU Files; and the Defense Attache Office, History of the Defense Attache (National Records Center, Suitland, Md.), hereafter DAOHist. See also Brig F. B. Serong, "The 1972 Easter Offensive," Southeast Asian Perspectives, Summer 74; Sir Robert Thompson, Peace is Not at Hand (New York: David McKay Company, Inc., 1974); and Nguyen Khac Vien, ed., Indochina: The 1972–73 Turning Point (Hanoi: Xunhasaba, 1974).

Operation End Sweep

Unless otherwise noted, material in this section is derived from FMFPac MarOpsSEA; SeventhFlt ComdHist73; "Operation Endsweep" is derived from Office of Naval Research, "Operation Endsweep," ONR study CRC 277, dtd Feb75 (CNA, Washington, D.C.), hereafter CNA Endsweep; and HMM-165, HMM-164, HMH-463 ComdChron, Feb-Aug73. See also RAdm Brian McCauley, "Operation End Sweep, *Naval Institute Proceedings*, Mar74, pp. 19-25, hereafter McCauley Endsweep; and LtCol John Van Nortwick, "Endsweep," *Marine Corps Gazette*, May74, pp. 29-36, hereafter Van Nortwick.

1 FMFPac MarOpsSEA, pp. 5-14 to 5-17; Capt Paul L. Gruendl, comments on draft ms, dtd 10Dec89 (Vietnam Comment File).

2 McCauley, Endsweep, p. 23.

3 Gruendl comments.

4 HMM-165, Special Operation Report (Endsweep), dtd 21Aug73, passim, hereafter HMM-165 SOR.

5 FMFPac MarOpsSEA, p. 6-12.

6 CNA Endsweep, pp. C1 to C3.

7 CNA Endsweep, pp. B-1 to B-3.

8 JCS Historical Division, Comments on draft ms, dtd 5Dec89 (Vietnam Comment File).

9 HMM-165 ComdC, Feb73, p. 21.

10 Brown, pp. 8-9.

11 CNA Endsweep, p. 5-7.

12 HMM-165 ComdC, Feb73, p. 22.

13 Van Nortwick, pp. 31-32.

14 HMM-165 ComdC, Feb73, p. 22.

15 Gruendl comments.

16 CNA Endsweep, p. E-9.

17 JCS comments.

18 HMH-463 ComdC, Jun73, p. 7; HMM-165 SOR, p. 14.

19 Van Nortwick, p. 33 (which does not reflect command chronology totals).

20 HMH-463 ComdC, Jun73, p. 7. See Van Nortwick and HMM-165 SOR for detailed lessons learned.

21 SeventhFlt OpOrd 9-73, dtd 26Jul73. SeventhFlt ComdHist73, Encl (2), p. 1.

22 McCauley, Endsweep, p. 23

Task Force Delta, The Tigers Depart
Unless otherwise noted, material in this section is derived from the TFD AAR, TFD Brief, and MAG-15 ComdC, Jan-Sept73.

23 FMFPac MarOpsSEA, pp. 6-6 to 6-8; MAG-15 ComdC, Jun73, p. 10.

24 MAG-15 ComdC, Jun73, Encl (1), p. 4.

25 TFD ComdC Sept73, p. II-1

26 TFD AAR, pp. 1-28 to 1-30; Maj George R. Dunham, "The Khmer Flex Their Muscle" (ms, MCHC, Washington, D.C.) pp. 28-33.

27 TFD Brief, Tab E; TFD AAR, pp. 3-1 to 3-5.

28 TFD AAR, pp. 6-1 to 6-14.

29 Maj John T. Dyer, "Impressions of a 'Rose Garden,'" *Fortitudine*, Fall 1973, pp. 4-6.

30 Brown, pp. 10-11, 13; SecDef ltr to MajGen Brown dtd 7Sept72; Brown comments.

31 FMFPac, Human Affairs, passim; HQMC, Manpower study, pp. 2-4.

32 TFD ComdC, Sept73, p. II-1.

33 TFD ComdC, Sept73, p. III-2.

34 BGen Manning T. Jannell, Comments on draft ms, dtd 29Oct89 (Vietnam Comment File).

35 CGMACThai msg to SecDef, dtd 21Sept73 (Vietnam Comment File).

36 Jannell comments.

37 TFD AAR, pp. 1-15 to 1-21.

To What End?
Unless otherwise noted, material in this section is derived from LtCol Gerald H. Turley, "Time of Change in Modern Warfare," *Marine Corps Gazette*, Dec74, pp. 16-20; BGen Edwin H. Simmons, "The Marines: Now and in the Future," *Naval Review 1975*, pp. 102-117; MajGen Bernard E. Trainor, "New Thoughts on War," *Marine Corps Gazette*, Dec80, pp. 49-51; and Allan R. Millett, "The U.S. Marine Corps, Adaptation in the Post-Vietnam Era," *Armed Forces and Society*, Spring 83, pp. 363-392.

38 Douglas Pike, *PAVN: People's Army of Vietnam* (Novato, Calif: Presidio Press, 1986), pp. 48-49, 103, 229; also ColGen Van Tien Dung, "Some Problems Concerning the Art of Military Campaigns of the Vietnamese People's War," *People's Army Magazine*, Dec73, pp. 61-65 (Vietnam Comment File).

39 LtCol Andrew D. DeBona, CSC symposium.

40 Peter Braestrup, CSC symposium.

41 FMFPac MarOpsSEA, p. 6-14; SMA msg to CTF76&79, dtd 30Jun72 (Vietnam Comment File).

42 HQMC, "Contingency Operations involving U.S. Marine Forces in Evacuation or Rescue Missions, 1956–1975," study, dtd 21Apr81 (Ref Sec, MCHC, Washington, D.C.).

43 Metzger intvw.

44 MCCC Chron, 12 Jul 73, Tab 41-10; OASD(C) AirLoss, Tables 351 and 352; Tab II-H-1, CMC Reference Notebook 1975, Tab II-H-1, "USMC Casualties in SEASIA."

45 Col Harry G. Summers, Jr., *On Strategy* (Carlisle Barracks, Pa.: U.S. Army War College, 1981) p. 1.

APPENDICES

APPENDIX A
COMMAND AND STAFF LIST
MARINE ADVISORY UNITS

Marine Advisory Unit
(MarAdvU)
1Jul7–31Mar73

SMA Col Francis W. Tief	1Jul71–10Jul71
Col Joshua W. Dorsey, III	11Jul71–31Mar73

VNMC Advisor Assignments
1Mar72–30Sep72

Capt James B. Archer	Infantry *
Capt Russell F. Bailes, Jr.	Unit Hq, Engineer
Maj James D. Beans	Infantry
Maj Walter E. Boomer	Infantry
Maj Gerald W. Boston	Infantry*
Capt James A. Brabham, Jr.	Engineer
CWO3 Shella R. Bray, Jr.	Engineer
CWO3 Ferris D. Brown	Engineer
Maj Jack R. Campbell, Jr.	Infantry*
Capt Reid O. Carlock	Infantry*
Maj Paul L. Carlson	Infantry*
Capt Philip C. Cisneros	Infantry*
Capt William A. Clark III	Infantry
SSgt Richard E. Clemens	Unit Hq
Maj Robert C. Cockell	Infantry
Capt Clelland D. Collins, Jr.	Infantry
Maj Patrick G. Collins	Infantry*
Capt Allen M. Coward	Motor Transport
Sgt Bobbie G. Crowl	Unit Hq
HMC Ronald C. Fitzgerald, USN	Medical
Maj Andrew D. Debona	Infantry
Capt Gary D. Dockendorff	G-1

CWO3 Bobby E. Dusek	Communications
Maj Jon T. Easley	G-4, Training
Capt Clark D. Embrey	Infantry
Capt Robert S. Evasick	Artillery
Sgt Gary M. Fauteck	Unit Hq
LtCol Walter D. Fillmore	Assistant SMA
HMC Ronald C. Fitzgerald, USN	Medical
CWO2 George M. Francis	Unit Hq
GySgt David F. Fureigh	Unit Hq
Maj Thomas E. Gnibus	Artillery
Maj Charles J. Goode, Jr.	Training, Infantry, Unit Hq
Capt Samuel T. Gray	Supply
GySgt Ronald C. Guilliams	Motor Transport
Capt Ronald C. Harrington	Infantry
Capt David D. Harris	Infantry
Maj William R. Hart	Artillery
Capt Stephen M. Hartnett	Infantry
SSgt Jerry W. Harvey	Unit Hq
SSgt Richard L. Helm	Communications
Maj Porter K. Henderson	Infantry*
CWO3 James E. Hill	Ordnance
Capt Richard W. Hodory	Infantry
Capt Terry L. Howard	Supply
Maj Emmett S. Huff, Jr.	Infantry
Capt Frank M. Izenour, Jr.	G-3, G-2
Capt Harry Jensen, Jr.	Infantry*
Capt James E. Johnson	Infantry
Lt(jg) Wesley J. Johnson, USN	Medical
Maj Clyde J. Johnston	Artillery

Maj Duncan H. Jones	Artillery	Sgt Calvin L. Pitchford	Unit Hq
Capt Walter F. Jones	Infantry	LtCol James A. Poland	G-3
Maj Jim R. Joy	Infantry, G-3	CWO1 William T. Pope	Ordnance
Maj Gordon W. Keiser	Infantry	Maj Stanley G. Pratt	G-4
Maj Robert D. Kelley	Infantry, OIC Rear	Maj Donald L. Price	Infantry
Maj William M. Keys	Infantry	SSgt Paul A. Prusak	Unit Hq
Capt Charles W. King	Infantry, Unit Hq	Capt David S. Randall, Jr.	Artillery
Capt Earl A. Kruger	Infantry	Capt Charles L. Redding	Infantry*
Capt John J. Lacy	G-1, PsyOps, Training	Capt Robert K. Redlin	Infantry
Sgt Robert R. Langdon	Unit Hq	Capt Ronald R. Rice	Infantry
Capt Alastair J. Livingston	Infantry, Training	Capt John W. Ripley	Infantry
Capt Lawerence H Livingston	Infantry, Training	Capt Joe D. Robinson	Infantry
GySgt John C. Lowery	Unit Hq	Capt Wayne E. Rollings	Infantry*
Capt Charles A. Lyle	Infantry	Maj Geoffrey H. Root	G-4
Sgt Daniel L. Mason	Unit Hq	Maj Richard B. Rothwell	Infantry
GySgt Robert L. McElyea	Unit Hq	Capt James W. Seal	Infantry
GySgt Roscoe A. McGuire	Unit Hq	Capt Merlyn A. Sexton	Infantry
Maj Robert C. McInteer	Amphibious Support	Maj Robert F. Sheridan	Training, Infantry
Maj Paul A. McLaughlin	Artillery	Maj Robert D. Shoptaw	G-4
Capt Eric W. Mezger	Infantry*	Capt Ray L. Smith	Infantry
Sgt Charles J. Miller	Unit Hq	Capt William J. Spangler	Infantry*
Capt William H. Miller	Motor Transport	GySgt Bernard J. Sturzl	Unit Hq
Capt Charles J. Miller	Infantry	Maj William T. Sweeney	Infantry
Capt Charles P. Minor III	Infantry*	LtCol William G. Swigert	Assistant SMA
Capt Peter S. Morosoff	Infantry	GySgt Joseph Sykora, Jr.	Unit Hq
GySgt James A. Morris	Unit Hq	Capt John W. Theisen	G-2
Capt John D. Murray	Infantry	Maj James M. Tulley	Unit Hq
Capt Allen D. Nettleingham	Infantry	LtCol Gerald H. Turley	Assistant SMA, G-3
Capt Phillip C. Norton	Infantry	Maj William R. Warren	Infantry, Unit Hq
Maj Joseph J. O'Brien	Infantry	Capt Marshall R. Wells	Infantry, G-3
Capt Jerome X. O'Donovan, Jr.	Infantry	Maj Oliver M. Whipple, Jr.	Amphibious Support, Infantry
LCdr R.S. Oldham, USN	Medical		
Capt Thomas F. O'Toole, Jr.	G-2	Capt Jonathan W. Wilbor	Infantry*
Capt Robert A. Packard, Jr.	Infantry	Capt William D. Wischmeyer	Infantry
Maj Donald C. Pease	Infantry*	Sgt William D. Wisecarver	Unit Hq
Capt Harry W. Peterson III	Infantry*	Maj Regan R. Wright	Infantry
Capt George Philip III	Artillery	Capt Thomas Zalewski	Communications
Maj John Pipta	Unit Hq	Capt Jon L. Zellers	Infantry

*Indicates temporary assignment

APPENDIX B
COMMAND AND STAFF LIST
MARINE GROUND UNITS

Sub Unit One
1st Air Naval Gunfire Liaison Company
(SU1 1stANGLICO)
1Jul71–14Mar73*

CO LtCol Eugene E. Shoults	¹Jul71-24Jul71
LtCol D'Wayne Gray	25Jul71-16Jul72
LtCol George E. Jones	17Jul72-14Mar73
XO Maj Edward J. Dyer, Jr.	25Feb72-3Jun72
Maj Glen Golden	4Jun72-31Jul72
Maj John S. Vogt	11Aug72-28Jan73
Maj William A. Hall	29Jan73-14Mar73
SgtMaj 1stSgt Elvis W. Lane	1Jul71-7Dec71
1stSgt Ernest Benjamin	8Dec71-31Oct72
1stSgt Kenneth R. Buehl	1Nov72-14Mar73
S-1 1stLt Richard E. Scott	1Jul71-23Jan73
1stLt John H. Cole, Jr.	24Jan73-14Mar73
S-3 LCdr Richard M. Kreassing,USN	1Jul71-16Nov71
Lt(jg) David P. Throop, USN	17Nov71-7Dec71
Capt Ronald W. Marsteller	8Dec71-10Apr72
Lt(jg) David P. Throop, USN	11Apr72-8May72
Lt Robert I. Still, USN	9May72-31Oct72
1stLt William E. Corcoran	1Nov72-14Mar73
S-4 CWO3 Joseph R. Morrissette	1Jul71-10Nov71
CWO4 Roy K. Harris	11Nov71-25Oct72
1stLt Frank Rivas, Jr.	26Oct72-14Mar73

*Deactiviated with return to FMFPac on 14Mar73.

Hq, 31st Marine Amphibious Unit
(31st MAU/CTG 79.4)
1Jan72–31Mar73

CO Col Walter C. Kelly	1Jan72-31May72

Col Donald E. Newton	1Jun72-28Nov7
Col Thomas J. Stevens	29Nov72-31Mar73
XO LtCol Glen T. Beauchamp	1Jan72-31Mar72
LtCol Thomas E. Bradley	1Apr72-24Nov72
LtCol Gerit L. Fenenga	25Nov72-31Mar73
S-1 CWO2 Donald J. Mossey	1Jan72-21Feb72
Maj Jules C. Rivera, Jr.	22Feb72-6Mar72
CWO2 James N. Deitrich	7Mar72-16Jan73
1stLt Leonard L. Touney	17Jan73-9Feb73
2dLt Billy R. Newman	10Feb73-31Mar73
S-2 Maj Grady V. Gardner	1Jan72-20Jan72
Maj William L. Shearer	21Jan72-23Sep72
Maj William P. Eshelman	24Sept72-31Mar73
S-3 Maj James H. Yarnell	1Jan72-4Jan72
Maj Julian P. Stienon	4Mar72-31Mar72
Maj John W. O'Donnell	1Apr72-7Jul72
Maj Joseph W. Gibbs III	8Jul72-15Mar73
Maj Robert J. Graham	16Mar73-31Mar73
S-4 Maj Berlis F. Ennis	1Jan72-28Jan72
Maj Harold E. Itchkawich	29Jan72-10Nov72
Maj Bobbie K. Brodie	11Nov72-31Mar73

Hq, 9th Marine Amphibious Brigade
(9thMAB/CTG 79.1)
3Apr72–9Feb73*

CG BGen Edward J. Miller	3Apr72-15Nov72
BGen Paul G. Graham	16Nov72-9Feb73
C/S Col Sumner A. Vale	3Apr72-27Jul72
Col Kenneth G. Fiegnener	28Jul72-9Feb73
G-1 LtCol William C. Bradley	3Apr72-14Jun72

Capt Herbert F. Posey	15Jun72-2Aug72
Maj David D. Johns	3Aug72-9Feb73
G-2 Maj James A. Miller	3Apr72-12Jun72
Maj William I. Ferrier	13Jun72-11Aug72
Maj Fred L. Edwards, Jr.	12Aug72-9Feb73
G-3 LtCol James L. Shanahan	3Apr72-20Oct72
LtCol James L. Day	21Oct72-9Feb73
G-4 LtCol Frank S. Cannon	3Apr72-11Aug72
LtCol Richard L. Etter	1Jul72-2Jan73
LtCol Jimmie R. Phillips	3Jan73-9Feb73
G-5 LtCol George B. Crist	3Apr72-11Aug72 **

*Deactivated with return to III MAF on 9Feb73.

**Command Chronologies incomplete.

Hq, 33d Marine Amphibious Unit
(33d MAU/CTG 79.5)
18Apr72–26Apr73*

CO Col Robert J. Perrich	1May72-4Aug72
Col Charles T. Williamson	5Aug72-26Apr73
XO LtCol Julius M. Lewis, Jr.	1May72-1Sep72
LtCol Bobby T. Ladd	2Sep72-26Apr73
S-1 Maj Dougal A. Cameron III	1May72-31May72
CWO2 James R. Milner	12Jun72-31Dec72
CWO3 John M. Larson	1Jan73-26Apr73
S-2 Maj John F. Delaney	17Apr72-16Aug72
Maj Henry W. Austin	12Jun72-16Aug72
Capt Jerrold T. Irons	11Sep72-26Apr73
S-3 Maj William H. Leonard	13Apr72-5May72
Maj Dougal A. Cameron III	6May72-7Jun72
Maj Raymond M. Kostesky	12Jun72-4Aug72
Maj Jerry D. Peterson	5Aug72-14Jan73
Maj David J. McGraw	15Jan73-26Jan73
S-4 Maj David J. Ryan	13Apr72-5May72
Maj Leonard K. Slusher	12Jun72-12Nov72
Capt Emile W. Hoffman	13Nov72-26Jan73

*Deactivated 26Apr73.

1st Battalion, 4th Marines
1Jan72–31Dec72

CO LtCol Clyde D. Dean	1Jan72-16Aug72
LtCol Floyd A. Karker, Jr.	17Aug72-31Dec72
XO Maj Robert E. Hamilton	1Jan72-9Aug72

Maj Herbert L. Seay	10Aug72-31Dec72
H&S Capt Robert E. Happy	1Jan72-31Dec72
A Co Capt Joseph E. Freed	1Jan72-12Jul72
1stLt Charles C. Emmons	13Jul72-31Dec72
B Co Capt Robert W. Carswell	1Jan72-28Aug72
C Co Capt Donald R. Huskey	1Jan72-9Jun72
1stLt Donald L. Martin	10Jun72-12Jul72
1stLt John H. Young	13Jul72-31Dec72
D Co Capt John S. Leffen, Jr.	1Jan72-1Jul72
1stLt James G. Zumwalt II	2Jul72-31Dec72

2d Battalion, 4th Marines
1Jan72–31Dec72

CO LtCol John Phillips	1Jan72-23Jun72
LtCol Robert W. Kirby	24Jun72-31Dec72
XO Maj John W. Hemingway	1Jan72-21Jul72
Maj Henry W. Tutterow, Jr.	22Jul72-27Dec72
Maj Robert R. Babbin	28Dec72-31Dec72
H&S Capt Robert T. Willis	1Jan72-29Mar72
1stLt Robert W. Clark	30Mar72-24Nov72
1stLt Everitt P. Clark, Jr.	25Nov72-31Dec72
E Co Capt Carlton W. Fulford, Jr.	1Jan72-7Apr72
Capt Robert G. Nunnally	8Apr72-13Apr72
1stLt Robert P. McAleer	14Apr72-22Apr72
Capt Fred R. Crowley	23Apr72-19Dec72
Capt William J. Johnston III	20Dec72-31Dec72
F Co Capt Guy A. Pete, Jr.	1Jan72-31Jan72
Capt William R. J. Masciangelo	1Feb72-13Apr72
1stLt Allan H. Vargas	14Apr72-19Dec72
Capt Larry S. Schmidt	20Dec72-31Dec72
G Co Capt George S. Ford	1Jan72-3Apr72
Capt Carlos D. Espinoza	4Apr72-13Apr72
1stLt Peter R. Dorn	14Apr72-22Apr72
Capt Laurens J. Jansen	23Apr72-31Dec72
H Co Capt Bruce E. Griesmer	1Jan72-30May72
Capt George J. Eschenfelder	1May72-31Dec72

3d Battalion, 4th Marines
1Jan72–31Dec72

CO LtCol William R. Von Harten	1Jan72-30Jun72
LtCol Bruce A. Truesdale	14Oct72-31Dec72

H&S Capt John S. Lowery, Jr.	1Jan72-22Feb72
1stLt Dennis J. Hellman	23Feb72-8Mar72
Capt Walter E. Deese	9Mar72-12May72
1stLt Thomas E. Mitchell, Jr.	13May72-14Jun72
Capt Thomas A. Hobbs	15Jun72-31Dec72
I Co Capt Samuel M. Garland	1Jul72-31Dec72
K Co Capt Jack M. Moore	1Jan72-24Apr72
1stLt Paul R. Ottinger	25Apr72-14Jun72
Capt Eugene G. Meiners	15Jun72-31Dec72
L Co Capt Harry C. Dolan	1Jan72-12May72
1stLt Perry S. Shimanoff	13May72-14Jun72
Capt Richard T. Kohl	15Jun72-31Dec72
M Co Capt Walter E. Deese	1Jan72-8Mar72
Capt Dennis B. Fryrear	9Mar72-14Jun72
Capt Thomas E. Mitchell, Jr.	15Jun72-31Dec72

1st Battalion, 9th Marines
1Jan72–31Dec72

CO LtCol Phillip B. Friedrichs	1Jan72-2Jul72
LtCol Robert A. Monfort	3Jul72-31Dec72
XO Maj Joseph P. Hoar	1Jan72-18Jun72
Maj Phillip A. Forbes	19Jun72-24Aug72
Maj Bayliss L. Spivey, Jr.	25Aug72-31Dec72
H&S Capt Robert J. Arboleda	1Jan72-14Apr72
1stLt Robert W. Geary	15Apr72-19Sep72
Capt Howard W. Langdon, Jr.	20Sep72-31Dec72
A Co 1stLt Charles Demello	1Jan72-13Apr72
1stLt John C. Dowell	14Apr72-31Dec72
B Co 1stLt Charles D. Melson	1Jan72-13Feb72
Capt Lynn J. Kimball	14Feb72-24Jun72
1stLt Robert G. Sikorski	25Jun72-31Dec72
C Co Capt John D. Haaland	1Jan72-1Sep72
1stLt Paul R. Gerdes	2Sep72-9Sep72
Capt Robert E. Logan, Jr.	10Sep72-31Dec72
D Co Capt Dennis R. Kendig	1Jan72-1Sep72
1stLt Peter J. Cammarano	2Sep72-14Sep72
Capt Donald R. Dunagan	15Sep72-31Dec72

2d Battalion, 9th Marines
1Jan72–31Dec72

| CO LtCol John C. Gonzales | 1Jan72-22Mar72 |

LtCol Jerome P. Trehy	25Mar72-27Jul72
LtCol Ray A. Stephens	28Jul72-31Dec72
XO Maj Richard A. Johnson	1Jan72-8Mar72
Maj Edward H. Boyd	9Mar72-17Dec72
Maj Richard W. Marsden	18Dec72-31Dec72
H&S Capt Richard D. Camp, Jr.	1Jan72-10Apr72
Capt Albert P. Johns	11Apr72-17Oct72
Capt John M. Holladay	18Oct72-19Nov72
Capt Paul L. Snead	20Nov72-19Dec72
1stLt Donald Thomley	20Dec72-31Dec72
E Co 1stLt Kevin G. Crouthamel	1Jan72-13Apr72
Capt Robert G. Nunnally	14Apr72-19Nov72
Capt John M. Holladay	20Nov72-31Dec72
F Co 1stLt Robert A. Thomas	1Jan72-6Mar72
1stLt Andrew N. Pratt	7Mar72-13Apr72
Capt William R. J. Masiangelo	14Apr72-30Jun72
1stLt Andrew N. Pratt	1Jul72-17Oct72
Capt Albert P. Johns	18Oct72-31Dec72
G Co 1stLt Askold T. Haywas	1Jan72-28Mar72
Capt Peter N. Vidito	29Mar72-17Oct72
1stLt Gary M. Alden	18Oct72-31Dec72
H Co Capt Coy T. Best, Jr.	1Jan72-5Feb72
1stLt Thomas J. Short	6Feb72-1Mar72
1stLt Leo W. Billings	2Mar72-12Apr72
Capt Carlos D. Espinoza	13Apr72-31Dec72

3d Battalion, 9th Marines
1Jan72–31Dec72

CO LtCol George B. Crist	1Jan72-16Jan72
LtCol Ronald A. Clark	17Jan72-10Oct72
LtCol Richard J. Alger	11Oct72-31Dec72
XO Maj Richard C. Ossenfort	1Jan72-15Jul72
Maj Daniel E. Mullally, Jr.	28Jul72-9Nov72
Maj Samuel E. Black	10Nov72-31Dec72
H&S Capt Thomas D. Martin	1Jan72-13Mar72
1stLt David E. Vlasak	14Mar72-18Apr72
1stLt George W. Ball	19Apr72-5May72
Capt Robert E. Tschan	6May72-31Dec72
Co I Capt Richard A. Crowe	1Jan72-20Apr72
1stLt John G. Nemec, Jr.	21Apr72-3May72

1stLt Frederick C. Williams	4May72-19May72
Capt Michael S. Kelly	20May72-24Aug72*
Co K Capt Richard J. Muller	1Jan72-21Feb72
1stLt Carl J. Loguidice	22Feb72-5Apr72
Capt Nathaniel R. Hoskot, Jr.	6Apr72-20May72**
Co L Capt Gary W. McDowell	1Jan72-1Mar72
1stLt Jeffrey M. Parkinson	2Mar72-4May72

1stLt Roger F. Harris	5May72-25May72
Capt Philip F. Reynolds	26May72-3Jun72***
Co M Capt Klaus D. Schreiber	1Jan72-3Jan72
1stLt Raymond M. Kruse	4Jan72-22Feb72
1stLt Gregg C. Kubu	23Feb72-17Apr72
1stLt David E. Vlasak	18Apr72-24May72
Capt Thomas D. Martin	25May72-2Jun72****

*To MAG-12, 25Aug72.

**To MAG-12, 21May72.

***To MAG-15, 4Jun72.

****To MAG-15, 3Jun72.

APPENDIX C
COMMAND AND STAFF LIST
MARINE AIR UNITS

Hq, Task Force Delta
24May72–21Sep73*

CG BGen Andrew W. O'Donnell	10Jun72-22Aug72
BGen Robert W. Taylor	23Aug72-13Aug73
BGen Manning T. Jannell	14Aug73-2Nov73
C/S Col Richard E. Hawes, Jr.	24May72-30Sept72
LtCol Guy R. Campo	1Oct72-28Aug73
LtCol Louis W. Schwindt	29Aug73-2Nov73
G-1 Capt Mathew Pallo, Jr.	10Jun72-15May73
CWO2 Dennis Egan	16May73-2Nov73
G-2 Maj James M. Barnhart	10Jun72-12Sept72
G-3 LtCol Mervyn J. Burns	10Jun72-10Nov72
Maj Paul M. Cole	11Nov72-3Feb73
Maj Arthur P. Loring, Jr.	4Feb73-1Jun73
LtCol Robert Plant	2Jun73-28Aug73
LtCol Norman A. Smith	29Aug73-2Nov73
G-4 LtCol Vincil W. Hazelbaker	10Jun72-28May73
LtCol Robert C. Tashjian	29May73-21Sept73
G-5 Capt Theodore D. Owens	19Aug72-12Sept72
3/9 Security Element	
Maj John M. Campanelli	20Jun72-25Nov72
Maj Kenneth N. Zike	26Nov72-21Sept73

*Deactivated with return to III MAF on 2Nov73.

Hq, Marine Air Group 12
(Forward) (MAG-12)
17May72–1Feb73*

CO Col Dean C. Macho	17May72-1Feb73
XO LtCol John M. Rapp	17May72-9Sep72
LtCol Eddie R. Maag	10Sep72-29Jan73
LtCol Harold L. Jackson, Jr.	30Jan73-1Feb73
S-1 Maj Theodore R. McElroy	17May72-27Jul72
CO LtCol Kent A. McFerren	1Apr72-23Jun72
Capt Marvin F. Pixton III	28Jul72-31Jul72
Maj John T. Cline	1Aug72-19Dec72
Maj John H. Ditto	20Dec72-1Feb73
S-2 CWO2 Arnoldo T. Serrata	17May72-31Dec72
S-3 Maj Richard T. Poore	17May72-31Jul72
Maj Kenneth D. Holland	1Aug72-29Jan73
Maj Jack L. Omer	30Jan73-1Feb73
S-4 Maj Angelo M. Inglisa	17May72-11Sep72
Maj Robert C. Blackington	12Sept72-29Jan73
Maj James B. Harrison, Jr.	30Jan73-1Feb73
3/9 Security Element	
Capt Nathaniel R. Hoskot, Jr.	21May72-24Aug72
Capt Michael S. Kelly	25Aug72-2Feb73

*Date returned to 1st MAW.

Hq, Marine Air Group 15
(Forward) (MAG-15)
1Apr72–21Sep73

CO Col Keith O'Keefe	1Apr72-8Aug72
Col Aubrey W. Talbert, Jr.	9Aug72-24Jul73
Col Darrel E. Bjorklund	25Jul73-21Sep73
XO LtCol Don A. Mickle	1Apr72-5May72
LtCol Rodney O. Lawrence	6May72-7Sep72
LtCol Don J. Slee	8Sep72-8May73
LtCol Arvid W. Realsen	9May73-21Sep73
S-1 Maj Daniel C. Escalara	1Apr72-20Feb72
LtCol John T. Tyler	21Feb72-20Jul72

Maj Martin W. Meredith	21Jul72-20Apr73
Capt Bruce E. Welch	21Apr73-21Sep73
S-2 Capt Donald L. Schussele	1Apr72-15Apr72
Capt Bruce M. Wincentsen	16Apr72-31Jul72
CWO2 Thomas R. Burnham	1Aug72-12Dec72
CWO3 Richard D. Webb	23Jun73-21Sep73
S-3 Maj Joseph B. Wuertz	1Apr72-5Jun72
LtCol Ernest J. Andersen	6Jun72-5May73
Maj Arthur P. Loring, Jr.	6May73-26May73
LtCol Robert Plant	27May73-21Sep73
S-4 Maj Jack P. Smith	1Apr72-2Jul72
Maj William F. Tremper	3Jul72-31Aug72
Maj William J. Cooper	1Sep72-24Apr73
Maj Jay N. Bibler	25Apr73-21Sep73
3/9 Security Element	
Capt Philip F. Reynolds	25May72-19June72

*Date returned to 1st MAW.

Marine Fighter Attack Squadron 115E (VMFA-115) 1Apr72-21Sep73

CO LtCol Kent A. McFerren	1Apr72-23Jun72
Maj Gerald Dejong	24Jun72-14Jul72
LtCol Henry C. Ivy, Jr.	15Jul72-2Jul72
LtCol Charles V. Smillie, Jr.	3Jul73-21Sep73
XO Maj Thomas K. Duffy	1Apr72-27Apr72
Maj Gerald Dejong	19May72-23Jun72
Maj Jay N. Bibler	18Sep72-25Apr73
Maj William J. Cooper	26Apr73-1Aug73
Maj Philip R. Kruse	2Aug73-21Sep73

Marine Aerial Refueler Transport Squadron 152 (VMGR-152), Detachment Delta 8 June 72-21 Sep73

OIC Maj Francis T. O'Conner	8Jun72-6Aug72
Maj Anton E. Therriault	7Aug72-5Oct72
Capt Andrew D. Larson	6Oct72-12Dec72
Capt David D. Hundley	13Dec72-31Jan73
Capt Larry W. Allen	1Feb73-1Aug73
Capt Harry F. Clemence, Jr.	2Aug73-21Sept73

Marine Medium Helicopter Squadron 164 (HMM-164) 1Jan72-31Dec72

CO LtCol Edward C. Hertberg	1Jan72-11Jan72
Maj David J. Moore	12Jan72-27Jan72
LtCol Edward C. Hertberg	28Jan72-31Jul72
LtCol Donald E. Schneider	1Aug72-31Dec72
XO Maj David J. Moore	1Jan72-11Jan72
Maj Achille J. Verbeck, Jr.	12Jan72-27Jan72
Maj David J. Moore	28Jan72-17Jul72
Maj Harrison A. Makeever	18Aug72-31Dec72

Marine Medium Helicopter Squadron 165 (HMM-165) 1Jan72-31Jul73*

CO LtCol Paul L. Moreau	1Jan72-15Jun72
LtCol Charles H. F. Egger	16Jun72-1May73
LtCol Arthur B. Colbert	2May73-31Jul73
XO Maj Donnie M. Griffay	1Jan72-15May72
Maj Thomas A. B. Goldsborough	16May72-30Jun72
Maj Davis Sayes	1Jul72-10Oct72
Maj Robert P. Rogers	11Oct72-31Jul73

*OpCon TF 78, 1Feb73 until 24Jul73.

Marine Attack Squadron 211 (VMA-211) 17May72-1Feb73

CO LtCol Willis E. Wilson, Jr.	17May72-23May72
LtCol Delbert G. Ranney	24May72-1Feb73
XO Maj Richard A. Bishop	17May72-13Apr72
Maj Donald M. Ferris	14Apr72-6May72
Maj Lonnie S. Underhill	7May72-8Jul72
Maj William H. Horner	9Jul72-1Feb73

Marine Fighter Attack Squadron 212 (VMFA-212) 1Apr72-30Jun72*

CO LtCol Richard D. Revie	1Apr72-30Jun72
XO Maj James B. Leonard, Jr.	1Apr72-30Jun72

*Unit departed RVN for Hawaii, 24Jun72.

Marine All-Weather Attack Squadron 224 (VMA[AW]-224)
1Jan72–31Jul72*

CO LtCol Billey R. Standley	1Jan72-1Jul72
LtCol Ralph E. Brubaker	2Jul72-31Jul72
XO LtCol Ralph E. Brubkaer	1Jan72-29May72
Maj Robert L. Gondek	30May72-31Jul72

Deployed for operations in Southeast Asia on the USS Coral Sea, 8Dec71 until 11Jul72.

Marine Fighter Attack Squadron 232 (VMFA-232)
1Apr72-21Sep73

CO LtCol Joe L. Gregorcyk	1Apr72-9May72
LtCol Eddie R. Maag	10May72-8Sep72
LtCol Rodney O. Lawrence	9Sept72-19Apr73
Maj James M. Mead	20Apr73-21Sept73
XO Maj Daniel C. Escalera	1Apr72-31May72
Maj Jacob K. Albright, Jr.	1Jun72-10Sep72
Maj William T. McFall	11Sep72-16Jun73
Maj Dave G. Drewelow	17Jun73-21Sep73

Marine Attack Squadron 311E (VMA-311)
17May72-1Feb73

CO LtCol Kevin M. Johnston	17May72-7Sep72
LtCol John J. Caldas, Jr.	8Sep72-1Feb73
XO Maj Thomas L. Elser	17May72-31Dec72
Maj John T. Cline	1Jan73-1Feb73

Marine Fighter Attack Squadron 333 (VMFA-333)
1Jul72-4Mar73*

CO LtCol John K. Cochran	1Jul72-23Dec72
Maj Lee T. Lasseter	24Dec72-4Mar73

XO Maj Lee T. Lasseter	1Jul72-23Dec72
Maj Thomas Lyman	24Dec72-4Mar73

Deployed for operations in Southeast Asia on the USS America, 1Jul72 until 4Mar73.

Marine Attack Helicopter Squadron 369 (HMA-369)
16Jun72-26Jan73*

CO Maj Dawson P. Hansen	16Jun72-23Oct72
Maj David L. Ross	24Oct72-26Jan73
XO Capt Ronald G. Osborne	16Jun72-17Jun72
Maj James H. Marshall	18Jun72-23Oct72
Maj Dawson P. Hansen	24Oct72-26Jan73

OpCon TF 77, 22Jun72 until 26Jan73.

Marine Heavy Helicopter Squadron 463 (HMH-463)
1Jan73-31Jul73*

CO Maj John Van Nortwick III	1Jan73-4Jun73
Maj William J. Smith	5Jun73-31Jul73
XO Maj William J. Smith	1Jan73-4Jun73
Maj Bruce L. Shapiro	5Jun73-31Jul73

OpCon to TF 78, 1Feb73 until 24Jul73.

Marine All Weather Attack Squadron 533 (VMA[AW]-533)
20Jun72-21Sep73

CO LtCol James C. Brown	20Jun72-19Apr73
Maj Kent C. Bateman	20Apr73-24Jun73
Maj Ronald E. Merrihew	25Jun73-21Sep73
XO Maj John A. Martin	20Jun72-31Jul72
Maj Kent C. Bateman	1Aug72-19Apr73
Maj Ronald E. Merrihew	29Apr73-24Jun73
Capt Ronald M. D'Amura	25Jun73-30Jun73
Maj Thomas W. Krimminger	31Aug73-21Sep73

APPENDIX D
OPERATION HOMECOMING

Marine prisoners-of-war recovered prior to Operation Homecoming*

Cpl Santos J. Agosto	captured	12May67	released	23Jan68
Sgt James Dodson	captured	6May66	escaped	5Jun66
LCpl Walter Eckes	captured	10May66	escaped	20Jun66
LCpl Walter D. Hamilton	captured	18Oct65	escaped	29Oct65
Sgt Frank C. Iodice	captured	30May68	escaped	1Jun68
LCpl Steven D. Nelson	captured	7Jan68	escaped	21Jan68
Pvt Joseph S. North, Jr.	captured	10Oct65	escaped	19Oct65
Sgt Albert J. Potter	captured	30May68	escaped	1Jun68
Maj Richard F. Risner	captured	20Sep68	escaped	22Sep68
Pvt Michael R. Roha	captured	7Jan68	escaped	21Jan68
Sgt Jon M. Sweeney	captured	19Feb69	released	17Sep70
Cpl William P. Tallaferro	captured	6Feb68	escaped	13Feb68

* Ranks at time of capture

Marines missing-in-action during operations in 1972*

CWO2 Bruce E. Boltze	lost	6Oct72	over water
Capt Donald C. Breuer	lost	20Nov72	Laos
Capt Ralph J. Chipman	lost	27Dec72	North Vietnam
1stLt John M. Christensen	lost	13Apr72	over water
Capt John W. Consolvo, Jr.	lost	7May72	South Vietnam
1stLt Sam G. Cordova	lost	26Aug72	Laos
Cpl Kenneth L. Crody	lost	11Jul72	South Vietnam
1stLt Ronald W. Forrester	lost	27Dec72	North Vietnam
SSgt Jerry W. Hendrix	lost	11Jul72	South Vietnam
1stLt Scott D. Ketchie	lost	9Apr72	Laos
Capt David L. Leet	lost	13Apr72	over water

1stLt Joseph W. McDonald	lost	3May72	North Vietnam
Capt John R. Peacock II	lost	12Oct72	North Vietnam
1stLt Larry F. Potts	lost	7Apr72	South Vietnam
1stLt William M. Price	lost	12Oct72	North Vietnam
1stLt Dwight G. Rickman	lost	25Dec72	South Vietnam
Capt Leonard Robertson	lost	7Jul72	South Vietnam
Capt David B. Williams	lost	3May72	North Vietnam
Cpl James F. Worth	lost	1Apr72	South Vietnam

*Ranks at time of loss.

Marine returnees during Operation Homecoming*

Capt William K. Angus	captured	11Jun72	released	28Mar73
Sgt Jose J. Anzaldua	captured	23Jan70	released	27Mar73
Capt Bruce R. Archer	captured	28Mar68	released	16Mar73
Capt Paul G. Brown	captured	25Jul68	released	14Mar73
Sgt Leonard R. Budd, Jr.	captured	21Aug67	released	5Mar73
Sgt Richard G. Burgess	captured	25Sep66	released	5Mar73
LtCol Harlan P. Chapman	captured	5Nov65	released	12Feb73
SSgt Frank E. Cius, Jr.	captured	3Jun66	released	5Mar73
SSgt John A. Deering	captured	3Feb68	released	5Mar73
Capt James V. Dibernardo	captured	3Feb68	released	5Mar73
LtCol John H. Dunn	captured	7Dec65	released	12Feb73
Pvt Fred L. Elbert, Jr.	captured	16Aug68	released	16Mar73
Capt Lawrence V. Friese	captured	24Feb68	released	14Mar73
Sgt Robert R. Helle	captured	24Apr68	released	16Mar73
Sgt Abel L. Kavanaugh	captured	24Apr68	released	16Mar73
1stLt Alan J. Kroboth	captured	7Jul72	released	27Mar73
LtCol Jerry W. Marvel	captured	24Feb68	released	14Mar73
LtCol Edison W. Miller	captured	13Oct68	released	12Feb73
Maj Paul J. Montague	captured	26Mar68	released	16Mar73
SSgt Alfonso R. Riate	captured	26Apr67	released	16Mar73
Sgt Ronald L. Ridgeway	captured	25Feb68	released	16Mar73
Maj Orson G. Swindle III	captured	11Nov66	released	4Mar73
Sgt Dennis A. Tellier	captured	19Jun69	released	27Mar73
CWO3 William E. Thomas, Jr.	captured	19May72	released	27Mar73
Capt James P. Walsh	captured	26Sep72	released	12Feb73
Capt James H. Warner	captured	13Oct67	released	14Mar73

*Ranks at time of release.

Marines recovered after Operation Homecoming

PFC Robert R. Garwood   captured   28Sep65   returned   21Mar79

III MAF Operation Homecoming Marine Processing Team
8Jan73–2Oct73

Deputy Commander	Col John W. Clayborne
Team Chief	Maj John J. Paganelli
Asst Team Chief	Maj Richard L. Brown
Admin Team	Capt Gerald S. Duncan
	Capt Robert E. Spiker
	SSgt Richard V. Anderson
	Sgt Thomas W. Bohnenkamp
	Sgt Frank R. Lawson
	Sgt Orville J. Pierce
Chaplain	Capt S. R. Hardman, USN
	Cdr J. G. Newton, USN
Medical Team	Capt M. A. Vasquez, USN
	Cdr P. O. O'Halloran, USN
	HM1 T. J. Taylor, USN
Public Affairs	2dLt Thomas E. Kingry
Legal	LtCol Joseph A. Mallery, Jr.
	Maj Neal T. Rountree
	CWO2 Lawrence T. Mullin
Debrief Team	Capt William C. Howey
	CWO3 Vaughan E. Delk
	CWO3 Claude R. Cordell, Jr.
	GySgt Cleslie H. Evans
	GySgt Lloyd H. Link
Uniform Team	MSgt Fred A. Norvell
	SSgt William C. Dahlquist
	SSgt Ronald E. Clemons
Escort Team Chief	LtCol Melvin H. Sautter
FMFPac POW Action Officer	Maj Thomas Y. Barton, Jr.

HQMC POW Action Officers

Policy, G-1	Maj William B. Clark
Casualty, G-1	Capt James A. Johnson
Intelligence, G-2	Capt Thomas H. Marino
Public Affairs	Capt James A. Amendolia
Judge Advocate	Maj David M. Brahms

APPENDIX E
VIETNAMESE MARINE CORPS (VNMC)
JANUARY 1972–JANUARY 1973

CMC	LtGen Le Nguyen Khang
	BGen Bui The Lan
AsstCMC	Col Bui The Lan
	Col Nguyen Thanh Tri
C/S	Col Le Dinh Que
	Maj Nguyen Van Hay
IG Inspector	Col Ton That Soan
AdjGen	Maj Nguyen Van Dien
Asst	Capt Nguyen Van Hanh
Social Welfare	Capt Tran Thi Huy Le, WACF
DC/S Ops and Log	LtCol Nguyen The Luong
(C/S Forward)	Col Pham Van Chung
G-1	Capt Tran Van Nuoi
Asst	Capt Nguyen Van Hanh
G-2	Maj Le Van Hien
Asst	Capt Tran Kim Hoang
G-3	LtCol Do Ky
Asst	Maj Tran Van Hien
G-3 TOC	LtCol Nguyen Huu Cat
G-3 Ops	Maj Le Van Cuu
G-3 Plans	Maj Phan Cong Ton
G-3 Trng	Capt Le Hoang Nghi
G-4	Maj Nguyen Van Nhieu
G-4 Tran	Maj Ngo Nhat Thang

G-4 Plans	2dLt Nguyen Van Le
DC/S Polwar	LtCol Bui Van Pham
Psywar	Capt Le Dinh Bao
Psyops Trng	Capt Huynh Van Phu
DivArty/FSC	LtCol Nguyen Van Truoc
Asst	Maj Vo Dang Phuong
DivCEO	LtCol Hoang Ngoc Bao
Asst	Maj Nguyen Nhu Chu

Headquarters Battalion

CO	LtCol Vo Kinh
	LtCol Pham Nha
XO	Maj Dang Van Hoc

Communications Battalion

CO	LtCol Hoang Ngoc Bao
XO	Maj Nguyen Van Dong

Medical Battalion

CO	Maj Nguyen Van The
XO	Maj Tran Manh Tuong
	Maj Nguyen Manh Tuong

Amphibious Support Battalion

CO	Maj Phan Van Sat
XO	Maj Vuong Van Tai

Engineer Battalion

CO	Maj Do Van Ty
XO	Capt Cao Van Tam
	Maj Dang Van Tuyen

Long Range Reconnaissance Company 147

CO	1stLt Phan Van Than

Long Range Reconnaissance Company 258

CO	Capt Duong Van Buu

Long Range Reconnaissance Company 369

CO	Capt Tran Van Chi

Brigade 147

CO	Col Nguyen Nang Bao
XO	LtCol Phan Van Thang
	LtCol Nguyen Xuan Phuc

Brigade 258

CO	Col Ngo Van Dinh
XO	LtCol Do Dinh Vuong
	LtCol Do Huu Tung

Brigade 369

CO	Col Pham Van Chung
	LtCol Nguyen The Luong
XO	LtCol Pham Nha
	LtCol Doan Thuc

1st Infantry Battalion

CO	Maj Nguyen Dang Tong
	Maj Nguyen Dang Hoa
XO	Maj Doan Duc Nghi
	Maj Nguyen Cao Nghiem

2d Infantry Battalion

CO	LtCol Nguyen Xuan Phuc
	Maj Tran Van Hop
XO	Maj Tran Van Ho
	Maj Le Quang Lien

3d Infantry Battalion

CO	Maj Le Ba Binh
	Maj Nguyen Van Canh
XO	Capt Duong Van Hung

4th Infantry Battalion

CO	Maj Tran Xuan Quang
	LtCol Nguyen Dang Tong
XO	Maj Nguyen Dang Hoa
	Maj Pham Kim Tien

5th Infantry Battalion

CO	LtCol Ho Quang Lich
XO	Maj Tran Ba
	Capt Ngo Thanh Huu

6th Infantry Battalion

CO	Maj Do Huu Tung
	Maj Tran Van Hien
XO	Maj Nguyen Van Canh
	Maj Nguyen Van Su

7th Infantry Battalion

CO	Maj Vo Tri Hue
	Maj Nguyen Van Kim
XO	Capt Nguyen Van Kim
	Capt Ton That Tran

8th Infantry Battalion

CO	Maj Nguyen Van Phan
XO	Capt Le Van Huyen
	Maj Nguyen Phuc Dinh

9th Infantry Battalion

CO	LtCol Nguyen Kim De
XO	Maj Pham Cang

1st Artillery Battalion

CO	LtCol Doan Trong Cao
XO	Maj Nguyen Huu Lac

2d Artillery Battalion

CO	LtCol Dang Ba Dat
XO	Maj Truong Cong Thong

3d Artillery Battalion

CO	LtCol Tran Thien Hieu
XO	Capt Ha Tien Chuong

Song Than Base

CO	Maj Tran Ngoc Toan
	LtCol Le Ba Binh

Training Center

CO	LtCol Nguyen Duc An
XO	Capt Le Van Do
	Capt Tran Xuan Bang

APPENDIX F
GLOSSARY OF TERMS AND ABBREVIATIONS

A

A-1 – Douglas Skyraider, a single-engine, propeller-driven, attack aircraft.

A-4 – McDonnell Douglas Skyhawk, a single-seat jet, attack aircraft in service on board carriers of the U.S. Navy and with land-based Marine attack squadrons.

A-6 – Grumman Intruder, a twin-jet, twin-seat attack aircraft specifically designed to deliver weapons on targets completely obscured by weather or darkness.

A-7 – Vought Corsair, a single-seat, jet attack aircraft.

A-37 – Cessna Dragonfly, a twin-jet, dual-seat, light attack aircraft.

AAA – Antiaircraft Artillery.

ABCCC – Airborne Battlefield Command and Control Center, a U.S. Air Force aircraft equipped with communications, data link, and display equipment; it may be employed as an airborne command post or a communications and intelligence relay facility.

AC-47 – Douglas Spooky, a twin-engine, propeller-driven gunship armed with four 7.62mm mini-guns and illumination.

AC-119 – Fairchild Shadow and Stinger, a twin-engine, propeller-driven gunship armed with four 7.62mm mini-guns and illumination.

AC-130 – Lockheed Spectre, a four-engine, turboprop gunship armed with 20mm and 40mm guns, illumination, and infrared capability.

ACBLT – Air Contingency Battalion Landing Team, also Air BLT.

ACCS – Airborne Command and Control Squadron.

ACT – U.S. Air Cavalry Troop.

ACTIV – Army Concept Team in Vietnam.

ADC – Assistant Division Commander.

AdminO – Administrative Officer.

Adv – Advanced.

AH-1J – Bell Sea Cobra, twin-engine, single rotor helicopter specifically designed for helicopter escort and gunship support with 20mm cannon, rockets, and flares.

AID – Agency for International Development.

AIK – Assistance In Kind.

Air America – U.S. Government-sponsored proprietary air transport company.

AK-47 – Kalashnikov-designed, gas-operated, air-cooled, magazine-fed, 7.62mm automatic rifle, with an effective range of 400 meters. Standard rifle of the North Vietnamese Army.

ALC – Area Logistical Command.

A&L CO – Administrative and Direct Support Logistics Company.

Alladin – Air Force FAC operating at night using starlight scope and flares to control night air strikes.

AlMar – All Marines, a Commandant of the Marine Corps bulletin directed to all Marine Corps personnel.

ALO – Air Liaison Officer, a naval aviator/flight officer attached to a ground unit who is the primary advisor to the ground commander on air operation matters.

AMTI – Airborne Moving Target Indicator on the A-6 aircraft.

ANGLICO – Air and Naval Gunfire Liaison Company, a unit composed of Marine and Navy personnel specially qualified for control of naval gunfire and close air support. ANGLICO personnel normally provided this service while attached to U.S. and allied units.

AO – Air Observer, brief for naval aviation observer (tactical), an individual whose primary mission is to observe from light aircraft in order to adjust supporting arms fire and to obtain information.

AO – Area of Operations.

AOA – Amphibious Objective Area, a defined geographical area within which is located the area or areas to be captured by an amphibious task force.

AOE – Fast Combat Support Ship.

Apache – Call sign of "A" Troop, 7/1 Air Cavalry Squadron (ACS).

APC – Armored Personnel Carrier.

APD – Airborne Personnel Detector.

Arc Light – Codename for B-52 bombing missions in South Vietnam.

ARG – Amphibious Ready Group.

ARRS – Aerospace Rescue and Recovery Squadron.

Arty – Artillery.

ARVN – Army of the Republic of Vietnam (South Vietnam).

ASP – Ammunition Supply Point.

ASPB – Assault Support Patrol Boat.

ASRT – Air Support Radar Team, a subordinate operational component of a tactical air control system which provides ground controlled precision flight path guidance and weapons release for attack aircraft.

ATC – Armored Troop Carrier, nicknamed "Tango boat."

ATCO – Air Transportation Coordination Officer.

ATSB – Advanced Tactical Support Base.

Autumn Mist – A helicopter defoliation mission utilizing one UH-1 spray aircraft which may or may not be accompanied by a light fire team.

A/W – Automatic Weapons.

B-3 – North Vietnamese military command established in the Central Highlands of South Vietnam to control military operations in Kontum, Dar Lac, and Pleiku Provinces.

B-5 – North Vietnamese military command established along the Demilitarized Zone.

B-40 – Communist rocket-propelled grenade launcher.

B-52 – Boeing Stratofortress, U.S. Air Force eight-engine jet, swept-wing heavy bomber.

BA – Base Area.

Barrel Roll – Codename for air interdiction operations in Laos.

BCC – Boarder Control Center.

BDC – Base Defense Commander.

BGen – Brigadier General.

BLT – Battalion Landing Team.

Bn – Battalion.

Brig – Brigade.

Bronco – OV-10 – North American Rockwell Bronco, twin-engine, turboprop, counter insurgency aircraft.

Bushmaster – An operation conducted by a company-sized unit inserted into an area, to establish a clandestine base of operations and to interdict enemy infiltration routes using coordinated platoon-sized night ambushes.

C

C-5 – Lockheed Galaxy, four-engine jet transport aircraft.

C-7 – De Havilland Caribou, twin-engine, propeller-driven transport aircraft.

C-117 – Douglas Skytrain, a twin-engine, propeller-driven transport aircraft. The C-117 was an improved version of the C-47, the military version of the DC-3.

C-123 – Fairchild Provider, twin-engine, propeller-driven transport aircraft.

C-130 – Lockheed Hercules, a four-engine, turboprop transport aircraft.

C-141 – Lockheed Starlifter, a four-engine, jet transport aircraft.

Capt – Captain.

CARE – Co-operation for American Relief Everywhere.

CAS – Close Air Support.

CBU – Cluster Bomb Unit.

CCB – Command and Communications Boat.

CCC – Combined Campaign Plan.

Cdr – Commander.

CEC – Construction Engineer Corps.

CG – Commanding General.

CH-46 – Boeing Vertol Sea Knight, a twin-engine, tandem-rotor transport helicopter designed to carry a four-man crew and 17 combat-loaded troops.

CH-47 – Boeing Vertol Chinook, a twin-engine, tandem-rotor transport helicopter designed to carry a four-man crew and 33 combat-loaded troops.

CH-53 – Sikorsky Sea Stallion, a twin-engine, single-rotor, heavy transport helicopter with an average payload of 12,800 pounds. Carries a crew of three and 38 combat-loaded troops.

ChiCom – Chinese Communist.

Chieu Hoi – "Open Arms" program which welcomes returnees to the side of the Government of South Vietnam.

CIA – Central Intelligence Agency.

CICV – Combined Intelligence Center Vietnam.

CID – Criminal Investigative Division.

CIDG – Civilian Irregular Defense Groups, mercenaries of Vietnamese, Laotian, and Cambodian descent who fight primarily around their own villages.

CinCPac – Commander in Chief, Pacific.

CinCPacFlt – Commander in Chief, Pacific Fleet.

CIT – Counter-Intelligence Team.

Class I, II, III et al. – Categories of military supplies, e.g., Class I, rations; Class II, petroleum-oil-lubricants; Class V, ammunition.

Claymore – M18A1 U.S. directional antipersonnel mine.

CMC – Commandant of the Marine Corps.

CMD – Capital Military District.

CMH – Center of Military History, Department of the Army.

CNO – Chief of Naval Operations.

CO – Commanding Officer.

COC – Combat Operations Center.

Col – Colonel.

Combat Skyspot – High altitude, radar directed, level-flight bombing employing various types of aircraft.

ComdC – Command Chronology.

ComdHist – Command History.

Comm – Communications.

ComUSMACThai – Commander, U.S. Military Activities Command, Thailand.

ComUSMACV – Commander, U.S. Military Assistance Command, Vietnam.

ComNavForPac – Commander, Naval Forces, Pacific.

ComNavForV – Commander, Naval Forces, Vietnam.

CORDS – Civil Operations Revolutionary Development Support.

COSVN – Central Office of South Vietnam, the nominal Communist military and political headquarters in South Vietnam.

CP – Command Post.

CPX – Command Post Exercise.

CRC – Control and Reporting Center, an element of the U.S. Air Force tactical air control system, subordinate to the Tactical Air Control Center, which conducts radar and warning operations.

CRS – Catholic Relief Service.

CRDC – Central Revolutionary Development Council.

CRIMP – Consolidated Republic of Vietnam Improvement and Modernization Plan.

CRIP – Civilian Reconnaissance Intelligence Platoon.

CS – Riot agent, also know as "tear gas."

CSC – Communications Service Company.

CTZ – Corps Tactical Zone.

CV – Multipurpose aircraft carrier.

CVA – Attack aircraft carrier.

CZ – Coastal Zone.

DAO – Defense Attache Office.

DASC – Direct Air Support Center, a subordinate operational component of an air-control system designed for control of close air support and other direct air-support operations.

DC-8 – McDonnell Douglas Jet Trader, a four-engine, jet cargo and passenger transport aircraft.

D-Day – Day scheduled for the beginning of an operation.

DD – Destroyer.

DDG – Guided Missile Destroyer.

DE – Escort Destroyer.

DIA – Defense Intelligence Agency.

Div – Division.

DMZ – Demilitarized Zone separating North and South Vietnam.

DOD – Department of Defense.

DRV – Democratic Republic of Vietnam (North Vietnam).

DSA – District Senior Advisor.

DTA – Division Tactical Area.

Dtd – Dated.

DTZ – Division Tactical Zone.

Duffel Bag – Acoustical sensors used for surveillance.

Duster – Nickname for the U.S. M42 tracked vehicle which mounts dual 40mm automatic weapons.

Dust Off – Medical evacuation by helicopter.

E

EA-6 – Grumman Prowler, the electronic warfare version of the A-6A Intruder.

Eagle Flight – Air-cavalry-type operation using gunships and light helicopters to initiate contact, followed by helo insertions into contact areas.

Eagle Float – Troops embarked on river assault craft (RAC) who are inserted into a battle area on command.

EB-66 – Douglas Destroyer, twin-engine, jet, electronic warfare version of the B-66.

EC-130 – Lockheed, a four-engine, turbo-prop, electronic warfare and communications version of the C-130 Hercules.

ECM – Electronic Countermeasures, a major subdivision of electronic warfare involving actions against enemy electronic equipment or to exploit the use of electromagnetic radiations from such equipment.

ECCM – Electronic Counter Countermeasures, the procedures and equipment used to protect communications and electronic equipment from interference or exploitation by an enemy.

Elint – Electronic Intelligence, the intelligence information gained by monitoring radiations from enemy electronic equipment.

Engr – Engineer.

ENIFF – Enemy Initiated Fire Fight.

EOD – Explosive Ordnance Disposal.

ETA, ETD – Estimated Time of Arrival and Estimated Time of Departure.

F

F-4 – McDonnell Phantom II, a twin-engine, two-seat, long-range, all-weather jet interceptor and attack bomber.

F-5 – Northrop Freedom Fighter, a twin-engine, single-seat, jet fighter aircraft.

FAC – Forward Air Controller.

FAC(A) – Forward Air Controller (Airborne).

FANK – *Force Armee Nationale Khmer*, the Cambodian Army.

FDC – Fire Direction Center.

Firefly – A light fire team (LFT) with a flare or a light ship employed in a night airfield defense.

FMFPac – Fleet Marine Force, Pacific.

FO – Forward Observer.

Freedom Deal – Codename for air operations in Cambodia.

FRC – Federal Records Center.

Front 4 – Communist military headquarters responsible for Quang Nam Province.

FSB – Fire Support Base.

FSCC – Fire Support Coordination Center, a single location involved in the coordination of all forms of fire support.

FSR – Force Service Regiment.

Fwd – Forward.

FWMAF – Free World Military Assistance Forces.

FWMF – Free World Military Force.

FY – Fiscal Year, for example "FY-724."

G

G-1, -2 et al. – Military staff positions on a general staff, e.g., G-1 would refer to the staff member responsible for personnel; G-2, intelligence; G-3, operations; G-4, logistics; and G-5, civil affairs.

Gen – General.

Grenade Launcher – U.S. M79 or M203 single-shot, breech-loaded, shoulder weapon which fires 40mm projectiles and weighs approximately 6.5 pounds when loaded; it has a sustained rate of aimed fire of five to seven rounds per minute and an effective range of 375 meters.

Gun, 175mm – U.S. M107 self-propelled gun which weighs 62,000 pounds and fires a 147-pound projectile to a maximum range of 32,800 meters. Maximum rate of fire is one round every two minutes.

GVN – Government of Vietnam (South Vietnam).

H&I – Harassing and Interdiction fires.

H&MS – Headquarters and Maintenance Squadron.

H&S Co – Headquarters and Service Company.

HC(A) – Helicopter Commander (Airborne).

HDC – Helicopter Direction Center.

HE – High Explosive.

HEALT – Helicopter Employment And Landing Table.

HH-3 – Sikorsky Sea King, a single-rotor helicopter used for combat search and rescue.

HH-53 – Sikorsky Sea Stallion, twin-engine, single-rotor helicopter used for search and rescue in combat configurations.

H-Hour – Specific time an operation begins.

HLZ – Helicopter Landing Zone.

HMH – Marine Heavy Helicopter Squadron.

HMM – Marine Medium Helicopter Squadron, also the basis of the composite squadrons with deployed forces.

Hoi Chanh – A Chieu Hoi rallier.

Hook – CH-47 helicopters from an assault supply company (ASHC).

Howitzer, 8-inch – U.S. M55 self-propelled, heavy-artillery piece with a maximum range of 16,900 meters and a rate of fire of one round every two minutes.

Howitzer, 105mm – U.S. M101A1 towed, general purpose light artillery piece with a maximum range of 11,000 meters and maximum rate of fire of four rounds per minute.

Howitzer, 155mm – U.S.M114A towed and M109 self-propelled medium artillery with a maximum range of 15,080 meters and a maximum rate of fire of three rounds per minute. The newer and heavier self-propelled M109 was largely road-bound, while the lighter, towed M114A could be moved either by truck or by helicopter.

HST – Helicopter Support Team.

Huey – Bell Iroquois UH-1 series of helicopters.

HQMC – Headquarters Marine Corps.

I

ICCS – International Commission of Control and Supervision, established by the Paris Peace Accords of 1973 to supervise the implementation of the accords. Composed of members from Canada, Hungary, Poland, Indonesia, and Iran.

I MAF – I Marine Amphibious Force.

Intel – Intelligence.

Intvw – Interview.

IOD – Integrated Observation Device.

ITT – Interrogator/Translator Team.

J

J-1, -2 et al. – Designation for members of a joint staff which includes members of several services. J-1 refers to the staff member responsible for personnel; J-2, intelligence; J-3, operations; J-4, logistics; and J-5, civil affairs.

JCRC – Joint Casualty Resolution Center.

JCS – Joint Chiefs of Staff (U.S.).

JGS – Joint General Staff (South Vietnamese).

JMC – Joint Military Commission. The Four Party JMC representing the United States, South Vietnam, North Vietnam, and the Provisional Revolutionary Government established by the 1973 Paris Peace Accords. See also the Two Party JMC of RVN and the PRG.

JUSPAO – Joint U.S. Public Affairs Office.

K

K Bar – A platoon of gunships, one command and control ship, and at least five troop-carrying helicopters available for use by South Vietnamese provincial governments.

KC-130 – Lockheed, in-flight refueling tanker configuration of the C-130 Hercules.

Khmer Rouge – Cambodian Communists.

KIA – Killed in Action.

Kit Carson Scouts – Former Viet Cong who came over to the South Vietnamese side and served with allied units.

Knife – Call sign for USAF CH-53 helicopters.

L

LAAW – U.S. M72 light antitank assault weapon, also know as light antitank weapon (LAW).

LCC – Amphibious Command Ship.

LCM – Landing Craft, Mechanized, designed to land tanks, trucks, and trailers directly onto the beach. Also known as a "Mike boat."

LCPL – Landing Craft, Personnel, Large.

LCU – Landing Craft, Utility.

LCVP – Landing Craft, Vehicle, Personnel, a small craft with a bow ramp used to transport assault troops and light vehicles to the beach. Also known as a "Papa boat."

LGB – Laser Guided Bomb, popularly known as "smart bombs."

L-Hour – The specific time helicopters land in a helicopter landing zone (USMC); launch hour, when an aircraft leaves the ground (USAF).

Linebacker – Codename for the air and surface interdiction operations against North Vietnam in 1972.

LKA – Amphibious Cargo Ship.

LOC – Lines of Communication.

LOH – OH-6 Light Observation Helicopter.

LOI – Letter of Instruction.

LORAN – Long Range Navigation, a system of radio stations at known positions used for air and sea guidance.

LPD – Amphibious Transport Dock, a ship designed to transport and land troops, equipment, and supplies by means of embarked landing craft, amphibious vehicles, and helicopters. It had both a submersible well deck and a helicopter landing deck.

LPH – Amphibious Assault Ship, a ship designed or modified to transport and land troops, equipment, and supplies by means of embarked helicopters.

LRRP – Long Range Reconnaissance Patrol.

LSA – Logistic Support Area.

LSD – Landing Ship Dock, a landing ship designed to combat load, transport, and launch amphibious crafts or vehicles together with crews and embarked personnel, and to provide limited docking and repair services to small ships and crafts. It lacks the helicopter landing deck of the LPD.

LST – Tank Landing Ship, a landing ship designed to transport heavy vehicles and to land them on a beach.

LSU – Logistics Support Unit.

Lt – Lieutenant.

LtCol – Lieutenant Colonel.

LTDS – Laser Target Designation System.

LtGen – Lieutenant General.

Ltr – Letter.

LUFT – Light fire team (two helicopter gunships).

LVTC – Landing Vehicle, Tracked, Command, an amphibian vehicle fitted with radios for use as a command and control facility.

LVTE – Landing Vehicle, Tracked, Engineer, a lightly armored amphibian vehicle designed for minefield and obstacle clearance.

LVTP – Landing Vehicle, Tracked, Personnel, an amphibian vehicle used to land or transport personnel.

LZ – Landing Zone.

MAB – Marine Amphibious Brigade.

MABLEx – MAB Landing Exercise.

MABS – Marine Air Base Squadron.

MAC – Military Airlift Command.

Machine Gun, .50 Caliber – U.S. M2 belt-fed, recoil-operated, air-cooled automatic weapon, which weighs approximately 80 pounds without mount or ammunition; it has a sustained rate of fire of 100 rounds per minute and an effective range of 1,450 meters.

Machine Gun, 7.62mm – U.S. M60 belt-fed, gas-operated, air-cooled, automatic weapon, which weighs approximately 20 pounds without mount or ammunition; it has a sustained rate of fire of 100 rounds per minute and an effective range of 1,000 meters.

MACS – Marine Air Control Squadron, provides and operates ground facilities for the detection and interception of hostile aircraft and for the navigational direction of friendly aircraft in the conduct of support operations.

MACV – Military Assistance Command, Vietnam.

MAF – Marine Amphibious Force, current "MEF" (Marine Expeditionary Force).

MAG – Marine Aircraft Group.

Main Force – Refers to organized Viet Cong battalions and regiments opposed to local guerrilla groups.

Maj – Major.

MajGen – Major General.

MAP – Military Assistance Program.

MarDiv – Marine Division.

Marines – Designates an infantry regiment, e.g., 3d Marines.

MASF – Military Assistance Service Funded.

MASS – Marine Air Support Squadron, provides and operates facilities for the control of support aircraft operating in direct support of ground forces.

MAU – Marine Amphibious Unit, not to be confused with the Marine Advisory Unit of the Naval Advisory Group which administered the advisory effort to the South Vietnamese Marine Corps.

MarAdvU – Marine Advisory Unit.

MAW – Marine Aircraft Wing.

MCAF – Marine Corps Air Facility.

MCAS – Marine Corps Air Station.

MCCC – Marine Corps Command Center.

MCO – Marine Corps Order.

MCOAG – Marine Corps Operations Analysis Group of the Center for Naval Analyses (CNA).

MCSA – Marine Corps Supply Agency.

MedCAP – Medical Civic Action Program.

MedEvac – Medical Evacuation.

MEDTC – Military Equipment Delivery Team, Cambodia.

MIA – Missing in Action.

MiG – Mikoyan-Gurevich-designed Soviet aircraft.

MilCAP – Military Civic Action Program.

Mini-dust – Two or more helicopter spray ships accompanied by one or more light fire teams and employed in enemy base areas.

Mini-Package – A platoon of gunships, one command and control ship, and at least five troop-carrying helicopters available for the use of South Vietnamese provincial governments.

MO – Mount-Out, loaded and ready classes of supplies for contingency use by amphibious forces.

MOA – Mount Out Augmentation.

ModLoc – Modified Location, radius around a specified point from which naval ships may transit while waiting employment.

Monitor – Heavily armored LCM-6 with 40mm cannon, 105mm howitzer or flame gun.

Mortar, 4.2 inch – U.S. M30 rifled, muzzle-loaded, drop-fired weapon consisting of tube, base-plate and standard; weapon weighs 330 pounds and has maximum range of 4,020 meters. Rate of fire is 20 rounds per minute. Also known as the "Four-Deuce."

Mortar, 60mm – U.S. M19 smooth-bore, muzzle-loaded weapon, which weighs 45.2 pounds when assembled. It has a maximum rate of fire of 30 rounds per minute and a sustained rate of fire of 18 rounds per minute; the effective range is 2,000 meters.

Mortar, 81mm – U.S. M29 smooth-bore, muzzle-loaded weapon, which weighs approximately 115 pounds when assembled; it has a sustained rate of fire of two rounds per minute and an effective range of 2,300–3,650 meters, depending upon ammunition used.

Mortar, 82mm – Communist smooth-bore, single-shot, high angle of fire weapon which weighs approximately 123 pounds; it has a maximum rate of fire of 25 rounds per minute and a maximum range of 3,040 meters.

Mortar, 120mm – Communist smooth bore, drop- or trigger-fired weapon which weighs approximately 600 pounds; it has a maximum rate of fire of 15 rounds per minute and a maximum range of 5,700 meters.

MR – Military Region; South Vietnamese army corps tactical zones were redesignated military regions in 1970, e.g. I Corps Tactical Zone (ICTZ) became Military Region 1 (MR 1).

MRB – Mobile Riverine Base.

MRF – Mobile Riverine Force.

MR-5 – Communist political and military sector in South Vietnam, including all of MR1 Corps. NVA units in *MR-5* did not report to COSVN.

Ms – Manuscript.

MSB – Mine Sweeper Boat.

MSC – Military Sealift Command.

MSD – Mine Sweeper Drone.

MSG – Marine Security Guard.

Msg – Message.

N

NAG – Naval Advisory Group.

Nail – Call sign for USAF OV-10 aircraft.

NAS – Naval Air Station.

NATOPS – Naval Air Training and Operating Procedures Standardization.

NavLE – Naval Liaison Element.

NCC – Naval Component Commander.

NCO – Noncommissioned Officer.

NEO – Noncombatant Evacuation Operation.

NGLO – Naval Gunfire Liaison Officer.

NGS – Naval Gunfire Support.

NILO – Naval Intelligence Liaison Officer.

NKP – U.S. Air Force designation for Nakhon Phanom Air Base, Thailand.

NLF – National Liberation Front, the political arm of the Communist-led insurgency against the South Vietnamese Government.

NMCB – Naval Mobile Construction Battalion, whose members are known as "SeaBees."

NMCC – National Military Command Center.

NOD – Night Observation Device.

NPFF – National Police Field Force.

NSA – Naval Support Activity.

NSD – Naval Supply Depot.

Nui – Vietnamese word for hill or mountain.

Nung – Southeast Asian tribesman, of a ethnic group of probably Chinese origin.

NVA – North Vietnamese Army, the Peoples Army of Vietnam (PAVN); often used colloquially to refer to a single North Vietnamese soldier.

O

O-1 – Cessna Bird Dog, single-engine, propeller-driven observation aircraft.

O-2 – Cessna Skymaster, dual-engine, propeller-driven observation aircraft.

OH-6 – Hughes Cayuse, single-rotor light helicopter used for armed reconnaissance and observation. Also known as a "Loach."

OH-58 – Bell Kiowa, single-rotor light helicopter used for armed reconnaissance and observation.

OIC – Officer-In-Charge.

OpCon – Operational Control, the authority granted to a commander to direct forces assigned for specific missions or tasks which are usually limited by function, time, or location.

OpO – Operation Order, a directive issued by a commander to subordinate commanders for the execution of an operation.

OP – Observation Post.

OPlan – Operation Plan, a plan for a single or series of connected operations to be carried out simultaneously or in succession; it is the form of directive employed by higher authority to permit subordinate commanders to prepare supporting plans and orders.

OpSum – Operational Summary.

OV-10 – North American Rockwell Bronco, twin-engine turboprop, observation and light-attack aircraft.

P-3 – Lockheed Orion, four-engine, turboprop naval patrol aircraft.

Paddy Control – Air Force Tactical Radar Control Center for the Mekong River Delta, located at Binh Thuy Air Base.

PAT – People's Action Team or Political Action Team.

PATMA – Pacific Air Traffic Management Agency.

Pave Nail – Call sign for USAF OV-10 with laser-designator to control precision-guided munitions.

PAVN – Peoples Army of Vietnam (North Vietnam). This acronym was dropped by the Americans in favor of NVA.

PBR – Patrol Boat River.

PCF – Patrol Craft Fast, known as a "Swift boat."

Pegasus – CH-47 helicopters employed on a standby basis to drop bulk riot agent.

PF – Popular Force, Vietnamese militia who were usually employed in the defense of their own communities.

PG – Patrol Gunboat.

PGM – Precision-guided munitions, so-called "Smart Bombs."

PIIC – Photo Imagery Interpretation Center.

Platoon of Gunships – Two light fire teams (four helicopter gunships).

POL – Petroleum, Oil, and Lubricants.

PolWar – Political Warfare.

POW – Prisoner of War.

PRC25 – Standard, very high frequency radio used by Marine ground units in Vietnam for voice communication over distances up to 25 miles.

PRU – Provincial Reconnaissance Unit.

PSA – Provincial Sector Advisor.

PRG – People's Revolutionary Government (Viet Cong).

ProvMAG – Provisional Marine Aircraft Group.

PSA – Province Senior Advisor.

PsyOps – Psychological Operations.

Q

QL – Vietnamese acronym for national highway.

R

RaBFAC – Radar Beacon for Forward Air Control.

RAD – River Assault Division.

RAG – River Assault Group.

R&R – Rest and Relaxation.

RAID – River Assault and Interdiction Division (North Vietnam).

RAS – River Assault Squadron.

Recoilless Rifle, 106mm – U.S. M40 single-shot, recoilless, breech-loaded weapon which weighs 438 pounds when assembled and mounted for firing; it has a sustained rate of fire of six rounds per minute and an effective range of 1,365 meters.

Regt – Regiment.

RF – Regional Force, Vietnamese militia who were employed in a specific region.

RF-4 – Photographic-reconnaissance model of the F4B Phantom.

RF-8A – Vought reconnaissance version of the F-8 Crusader.

Rifle, M14 – U.S. gas-operated, magazine-fed, air-cooled, semi-automatic, 7.62mm shoulder weapon, which weighs 12 pounds with a full 20-round magazine; it has a sustained rate of fire of 30 rounds per minute and an effective range of 500 yards.

Rifle, M16 – U.S. gas-operated, magazine-fed, air-cooled, automatic, 5.56mm shoulder weapon, which weighs 3.1 pounds with a 20-round magazine; it has a sustained rate of fire of 12–15 rounds per minute and an effective range of 460 meters.

RLT – Regimental Landing Team.

ROK – Republic of Korea.

Rolling Thunder – Codename for initial U.S. air operations over North Vietnam.

ROE – Rules of Engagement.

Route Package – Numbered air control areas for the American bombing campaign in North Vietnam.

RPG – Rocket Propelled Grenade.

RR – Rural Reconstruction.

RSSZ – Rung Sat Special Zone.

RVN – Republic of Vietnam (South Vietnam).

RVNAF – Republic of Vietnam Armed Forces.

RZ – Reconnaissance Zone.

S

S-1, 2 et al. – Refers to staff positions on regimental and battalion levels. S-1 would refer to the staff member responsible for personnel; S-2, intelligence; S-3, operations; S-4, logistics; and S-5, civil affairs.

SAC – Strategic Air Command.

SACC – Supporting Arms Control Center.

SAM – Surface to Air Missile.

SAR – Search and Rescue.

SATS – Short Airfield for Tactical Support, an expeditionary airfield used by Marine Corps aviation that included a portable runway surface, aircraft launching and recovery devices, and other essential components.

SCAMP – Sensor Control and Management Platoon.

Sea-Lords – Codename for Southeast Asia naval campaign.

Seal – Sea, Air, Land, special six- to eight-man naval intelligence gathering detachment.

SEATO – Southeast Asia Treaty Organization.

Seawolves – Naval helicopter gunships operating as light or heavy fire teams.

SecDef – Secretary of Defense.

SecState – Secretary of State.

SeventhAF – Seventh Air Force, the major U.S. Air Force command in Southeast Asia.

SeventhFlt – The U.S. Navy fleet assigned to the Western Pacific.

Shadow – C-119 aircraft with four 7.62mm mini-guns and illumination.

SID – Seismic Intrusion Device, sensor used to monitor movement through ground vibrations.

SitRep – Situation Report.

SKS – Simonov-designed, gas-operated, 7.62mm semiautomatic rifle.

Slick – UH-1B helicopter.

SMA – Senior Marine Advisor.

SOG – Special Operations Group, MACV's joint unconventional warfare task force.

Song – Vietnamese for river.

SOP – Standing Operating Procedure, set of instructions laying out standardized procedures.

Sortie – An operational flight by one aircraft.

SOS – Special Operations Squadron.

SOW – Special Operations Wing.

Spectre – C-130 aircraft with 20mm and 40mm mini-guns, illumination, and infrared television for night observation support of troops.

SPG – Special Planning Group.

Spooky – C-47 aircraft with four 7.62mm mini-guns and flare illumination capability for night support of troops in contact.

SptRept – Spot Report.

SRF – Ship Repair Facility.

SSB – Swimmer Support Boat, also known as a "Skimmer."

Stinger – C-119K aircraft with 20mm mini-guns and illumination use for night observation in support of troops.

SVN – South Vietnam.

Swing Ship – UH-1D helicopter assigned to different sectors for administrative use.

T

T-39 – North American Rockwell Sabreliner, twin-engine, jet used as trainer and passenger aircraft.

TA-4 – McDonnell Douglas Skyhawk, dual-seat version of the A-4 used as trainer and FAC/TAC platform.

TAC(A) – Tactical Air Coordinator (Airborne), a designated aviator who controls and coordinates air support from an aircraft.

TACC – Tactical Air Control Center, the principal air operations installation for controlling all aircraft and air-warning functions of tactical air operations.

TACLOG – Tactical Logistics cell.

TACP – Tactical Air Control Party, a subordinate operational component of a tactical air control system designed to provide air liaison to land forces and for the control of aircraft.

TADC – Tactical Air Direction Center, an air operations installation under the Tactical Air Control Center, which directs aircraft and aircraft warning functions of the tactical air center.

TAFDS – Tactical Airfield Fuel Dispensing System, the expeditionary storage and dispensing system for aviation fuel at tactical airfields. It uses 10,000-gallon fabric tanks to store the fuel.

Tank, M48 – U.S. 50.7-ton tank with a crew of four; primary armament is a turret-mounted 90mm gun with one .30-caliber and one .50-caliber machine gun; has maximum road speed of 32 miles per hour and an average range of 195 miles.

TAOC – Tactical Air Operations Center, a subordinate component of the air command and control system which controls all air traffic and air defense operations.

TAOI – Tactical Area of Interest.

TAOR – Tactical Area of Responsibility, a defined area of land for which responsibility is specifically assigned to a commander for control of assigned forces and coordination of support.

TASS – Tactical Air Support Squadron.

TCN – Third Country National.

TE – Table of Equipment.

TE – Task Element.

TF – Task Force.

TG – Task Group.

Tiger Hound – Codename for air operations in Laos.

TO – Table of Organization.

TOW – U.S. M220 Tube-launched, Optically-tracked, Wire-guided antitank missile system.

TQLC – Thuy Quan Luc Chien (Vietnamese Marine Corps).

Trail Dust – Air Force C-123 dispensing defoliant or crop destruction chemical.

TSN – Tan Son Nhut, U.S. Air Force designation for South Vietnamese air base.

TU – Task Unit.

U-21 – Beechcraft King Air, twin-engine, turboprop utility and passenger aircraft.

UCMJ – Uniform Code of Military Justice.

UH-1 – Bell Iroquois, single-rotor, light helicopter noted for its maneuverability and firepower; carries a crew of three; it can be armed with air-to-ground rocket packs and fuselage-mounted, electrically fired machine guns. Also known as a "Huey."

USA – United States Army.

USAAG – U.S. Army Advisory Group.

USAF – United States Air Force.

USAID – U.S. Agency for International Development.

USARV – U.S. Army, Vietnam.

USASuppCom – U.S. Army Support Command.

USIA – U.S. Information Agency.

USIS – U.S. Information Service.

USMC – United States Marine Corps.

USN – United States Navy.

USSAG/SeventhAF – United States Support Activities Group/Seventh Air Force.

V

VC – Viet Cong.

Viet Cong – Term used to refer to the Communist guerrillas in South Vietnam adhering to the NLF and PRG; a contraction of the Vietnamese phrase meaning "Vietnamese Communists."

VCC – Viet Cong Captured.

VCI – Viet Cong Infrastructure.

VIS – Vietnamese Information Service (South Vietnam).

VMA – Marine Attack Squadron.

VMF(AW) – Marine Fighter Squadron (All-Weather).

VMFA – Marine Fighter Attack Squadron.

VMCJ – Marine Composite Reconnaissance Squadron.

VMGR – Marine Refueler Transport Squadron.

VMO – Marine Observation Squadron.

VN – Vietnam or Vietnamese.

VNAF – Vietnamese Air Force.

VNMC – Vietnamese Marine Corps.

VNMC LSB – Vietnamese Marine Corps Logistics Support Branch of the Navy Division, U.S. Defense Attache Office, Saigon.

VNN – Vietnamese Navy.

VT – Variable timed electronic fuze for an artillery shell which causes airburst over the target area.

W

WestPac – Western Pacific.

WIA – Wounded in Action.

Wild Weasel – Codename for special techniques and aircraft used to suppress radar systems.

WFRC – Washington Federal Records Center.

X

XO – Executive Officer.

Z

Zippo – Flame thrower equipped ATC or monitor.

APPENDIX G
CHRONOLOGY OF SIGNIFICANT EVENTS
JULY 1971–SEPTEMBER 1973

1971

1 July	Start of the Consolidation I Campaign.
9 July	American forces are no longer obligated to defend the region south of the Demilitarized Zone (DMZ) at the 17th parallel. The U.S. military had moved into this area in 1966 to reinforce the 1954 Geneva Convention agreement, prohibiting ground or artillery attacks from this buffer zone.
9–11 July	National Security Advisor Dr. Henry A. Kissinger visits China.
12 July	American troop strength in South Vietnam is at 236,000, decreasing at a rate of about 14,000 a month.
19 July	Redeployment of all major Marine Corps units from South Vietnam is completed.
18 August	Australia and New Zealand announce the withdrawal of their combat forces from Southeast Asia.
25 August	The Army's 173d Airborne Brigade withdraws from South Vietnam.
27 August	The Army's 1st Brigade, 5th Infantry Division (Mechanized) withdraws from Vietnam. It had operated along the western area of the DMZ since January 1971.
8 October	Operation Jefferson Glenn concludes, the last significant operation that included U.S. ground forces.
12 November	President Richard M. Nixon announces that American military forces are now taking a purely defensive stance, leaving the offensive role entirely up to the South Vietnamese.
29 November	An aid agreement with the Soviets is signed by the North Vietnamese in Moscow.
1 December	Start of the Consolidation II Campaign.
26 December	President Nixon allows the resumption of the bombing of North Vietnam as peace talks stall.
31 December	The strength of the American forces in South Vietnam is down to 156,800. As of this date, 45,626 American military had been killed in action.

1972

1 January	General Leonard F. Chapman, Jr., Commandant of the Marine Corps, is succeeded by General Robert E. Cushman, Jr.
12 January	Long Cheng, Laos, captured by Communist forces using artillery and armor.
25 January	New allied peace plan is announced by President Nixon and President Nguyen Van Thieu.
21 February	President Nixon arrives for talks in China. This results in changes in U.S. Pacific strategy.

10 March	Lon Nol was declared President of Cambodia. The U.S. 101st Airborne Division (Airmobile) withdraws from South Vietnam, the last Army division to leave.
23 March	The Paris peace talks are suspended at the behest of the American delegation, to be resumed when the North Vietnamese will engage in deliberations on specific topics.
30 March	The Communist Nguyen-Hue Offensive commences with major attacks across the DMZ. The Vietnam Ceasefire Campaign begins.
1 April	Marine landing forces and amphibious ready groups of the Seventh Fleet arrive off Military Region 1.
3 April	Marine reconnaissance squadron detachment arrives at Cubi Point, Philippines to support renewed air operations.
5 April	The North Vietnamese Army (NVA) attacks Loc Ninh in Military Region 3.
6 April	Marine Aircraft Group 15 arrives at Da Nang. Lieutenant General John D. Lavelle, USAF, is recalled from command of the Seventh Air Force for exceeding rules of engagement policies.
7 April	Loc Ninh captured and An Loc encircled by the NVA. The bombing of North Vietnam is resumed as Freedom Train and Linebacker Operations. The French Government is petitioned by the North Vietnamese in Paris to try to halt American bombing.
8 April	The 9th Marine Amphibious Brigade arrives in the Tonkin Gulf.
15 April	The bombing of Hanoi and Haiphong is resumed for the first time since 1968. Bombing restrictions are lifted for most other targets.
15–20 April	A wave of protests occurs in the United States as a result of the increase in fighting in Southeast Asia.
23 April	The NVA captures Dak To in Military Region 2.
27 April	Major NVA attacks occur against Quang Tri City in Military Region 1. The Paris peace talks are resumed.
28 April–2 May	NVA attacks on outlying defenses of Hue City in Military Region 1.
1 May	The NVA captures Quang Tri City.
3 May	NVA/NLF capture Bong Son in Military Region 2.
4 May	The Paris talks are again suspended indefinitely by the American and South Vietnamese delegations after the 149th session.
8 May	Haiphong and other North Vietnamese harbors are mined by the U.S. Navy. President Nixon offers to withdraw all U.S. forces within four months of a ceasefire agreement.
14 May–25 May	Major NVA attacks on Kontum in Military Region 2.
16 May	Marine Aircraft Group 12 arrives at Bien Hoa.
19 May	Soviet and Chinese delegations arrive in Hanoi to discuss support measures.
22 May	President Nixon visits Moscow.
17 June	Washington, D.C., office of Democratic National Committee is burglarized.
21 June	American troop strength in South Vietnam down to 60,000. First Marine combat sorties flown from Nam Phong, Thailand.
18 June	An Loc is relieved by South Vietnamese forces.
19 June	South Vietnamese counteroffensive begins in Military Region 2.
26 June	The 3d Brigade, 1st Cavalry Division (Airmobile) withdraws from Vietnam.
28 June	South Vietnamese counteroffensive begins in Military Region 1.

29 June	The 196th Infantry Brigade withdraws from Vietnam, the final Army ground combat unit to leave. General Fredrick C. Weyand, USA, becomes Commander of the U.S. Military Assistance Command Vietnam, succeeding General Creighton W. Abrams, USA.
13 July	The Paris peace talks are resumed.
22 July–15 August	The 9th Marine Amphibious Brigade conducts flood relief operations in the Philippines.
18–19 August	The NVA attacks Que Son and captures Fire Support Base Ross in Military Region 1.
1 September	Admiral Noel A. M. Gayler, USA, becomes Commander in Chief of the Pacific Command, replacing Admiral John S. McCain, Jr., USN.
16 September	Quang Tri City is recaptured by South Vietnamese forces.
26–27 September	More private talks are held between Dr. Kissinger and the North Vietnamese representatives in Paris.
8 October	A breakthrough in peace talks is announced by Dr. Kissinger.
19–20 October	Dr. Kissinger and President Thieu hold discussions in Saigon.
24 October	Operation Linebacker I ends as bombing north of the 20th parallel is curtailed as a peace gesture.
7 November	In U.S. presidential elections, President Nixon defeats Senator George S. McGovern.
11 November	Direct U.S. Army participation in the war concludes with relinquishment of the logistical base at Long Binh to the South Vietnamese.
20–21 November	More private talks are held between Dr. Kissinger and Le Duc Tho to design a final peace agreement.
13 December	Talks between Dr. Kissinger and Le Duc Tho reach a standstill.
14 December	President Nixon warns he will resume bombing if negotiations are not resumed.
18–29 December	Operation Linebacker II is launched against Hanoi and Haiphong, the "Christmas Bombing."
31 December	American troop strength in South Vietnam is at 24,200.

1973

8–12 January	Henry Kissinger and Le Duc Tho proceed with their private talks.
15 January	With progress with peace talks, President Nixon declares an end to all U.S. offensive operations against North Vietnam.
25 January	Joint Homecoming Reception Center activated at Clark Air Force Base, Philippines.
27 January	The Americans and North Vietnamese sign the Paris Peace Accords. The conclusion of the military draft is announced by the Department of Defense.
28 January	The Ceasefire Campaign ends as the final withdrawal of allied forces from South Vietnam begins.
30 January	Melvin R. Laird is succeeded by Elliot L. Richardson as the Secretary of Defense.
21 February	A ceasefire is reached in Laos.
25 February	Task Force Delta commences combat sorties in Cambodia.
31 January	Operation End Sweep mineclearing begins.
14 March	Sub Unit One, 1st ANGLICO, the last Marine unit to leave Vietnam, is transferred to Fleet Marine Force, Pacific.
29 March	The Headquarters of the U.S. Military Assistance Command Vietnam is closed. Marine advisory effort ends. The release of prisoners of war by the Communists and the departure of all American forces from South Vietnam is completed.
4 April	Joint Homecoming Reception Center reverts to a standby status.

22 May	Dr. Kissinger and Le Duc Tho conclude their discussions on Vietnam truce agreement.
13 June	A new treaty is signed by the Americans, South Vietnamese, National Liberation Front, and the North Vietnamese in an attempt to strengthen the ceasefire.
24 June	Ellsworth Bunker is replaced by Graham A. Martin as U.S. Ambassador to South Vietnam.
2 July	Elliot Richardson is replaced by James R. Schlesinger as Secretary of Defense.
14 August	Congress declares the cessation of all U.S.-funded military action in Southeast Asia. Marine combat operations from Nam Phong end.
21 September	Marines depart Nam Phong.
22 September	William P. Rogers is replaced by Dr. Kissinger as Secretary of State. Dr. Kissinger continues his post as National Security Advisor.

APPENDIX H
MEDAL OF HONOR AND NAVY CROSS CITATIONS
1971–1973

The President of the United States in the name of The Congress takes pride in presenting the MEDAL OF HONOR posthumously to

COLONEL DONALD G. COOK
UNITED STATES MARINE CORPS

for service as set forth in the following

CITATION

For conspicuous gallantry and intrepidity at the risk of his life above and beyond the call of duty while interned as a Prisoner of War by the Viet Cong in the Republic of Vietnam during the period 31 December 1964 to 8 December 1967. Despite the fact that by so doing he knew he would bring about harsher treatment for himself, Colonel (then Captain) Cook established himself as the senior prisoner, even though in actuality he was not. Repeatedly assuming more than his share of the manual labor in order that the other Prisoners of War could improve the state of their health, Colonel Cook willingly and unselfishly put the interests of his comrades before that of his own well-being and, eventually, his life. Giving more needy men his medicine and drug allowance while constantly nursing them, he risked infection from contagious diseases while in a rapidly deteriorating state of health. This unselfish and exemplary conduct, coupled with his refusal to stray even the slightest from the Code of Conduct, earned him the deepest respect from not only his fellow prisoners, but his captors as well. Rather than negotiate for his own release or better treatment, he steadfastly frustrated attempts by the Viet Cong to break his indomitable spirit, and passed this same resolve on to the men with whose well-being he so closely associated himself. Knowing his refusals would prevent his release prior to the end of the war, and also knowing his chances for prolonged survival would be small in the event of continued refusal, he chose nevertheless to adhere to a Code of Conduct far above that which could be expected. His personal valor and exceptional spirit of loyalty in the face of almost certain death reflected the highest credit upon Colonel Cook, the Marine Corps, and the United States Naval Service.

The President of the United States takes pride in presenting the NAVY CROSS to

CAPTAIN LARWRENCE H. LIVINGSTON
UNITED STATES MARINE CORPS

for service as set forth in the following

CITATION

For extraordinary heroism on 11 July 1972 while serving as Senior Advisor to the 1st Vietnamese Marine Corps Infantry Battalion during a heliborne assault into enemy-held territory northeast of Quang Tri City, Republic of Vietnam. When the battalion encountered unexpectedly heavy enemy fire while disembarking into the landing zone, and sustained numerous casualties, Captain Livingston moved throughout the hasty positions taken by the scattered and hesitant element and formed the Marines into an assault force. Despite the continuing heavy concentration of hostile fire, he began the assault on the initial objective — a treeline approximately 50 yards distant. Although blown from his feet by explosions and periodically delayed to reform and redirect his casualty-riddled force, he forged ahead, leading the Vietnamese Marines into the enemy-infested trench lines of the objective and a subsequent hand-to-hand battle. Upon seizure of the initial portion of the trenchline, Captain Livingston shed his combat equipment, emerged from the trenchline, and exposed himself to a hail of enemy fire to reach his wounded naval gunfire spotter to a position of relative safety. Captain Livingston's repeated acts of heroism in the face of heavy fire reflected great credit upon him and the Marine Corps and were in keeping with the highest traditions of the United States Naval Service.

The President of the United States takes pleasure in presenting the NAVY CROSS to

CAPTAIN JOHN W. RIPLEY
UNITED STATES MARINE CORPS

for service as set forth in the following

CITATION

For extraordinary heroism on 2 April 1972 while serving as the Senior Marine Advisor to the 3d Vietnamese Marine Corps Infantry Battalion in the Republic of Vietnam. Upon receipt of a report that a rapidly moving, mechanized, North Vietnamese army force, estimated at a reinforced divisional strength, was attacking south along Route 1, the 3d Vietnamese Marine Infantry Battalion was positioned to defend a key village in the surrounding area. It became imperative that a vital river bridge be destroyed if the overall security of the northern provinces of Military Region 1 was to be maintained. Advancing to the bridge to personally supervise this most dangerous but vitally important assignment, Captain Ripley located a large amount of explosives which had been prepositioned there earlier, access to which was blocked by a chain-link fence. In order to reposition the approximately 500 pounds of explosive, Captain Ripley was obligated to reach up and hand-walk along the beams while his body dangled beneath the bridge. On five separate occasions, in the face of constant enemy fire, he moved to points along the bridge and with the aid of another advisor who pushed the explosives to him, securely emplaced them. He detonated the charges and destroyed the bridge, thereby stopping enemy assault. By his heroic actions and extraordinary courage, Captain Ripley undoubtedly was instrumental in saving an untold number of lives. His inspiring efforts reflected great credit upon himself, the Marine Corps, and the United States Naval Service.

The President of the United States takes pleasure in presenting the NAVY CROSS to

CAPTAIN RAY L. SMITH
UNITED STATES MARINE CORPS

for service as set forth in the following

CITATION

For extraordinary heroism during the period 30 March to 1 April 1972 while serving as advisor to a Vietnamese command group numbering approximately 250 Vietnamese Marines located on a small hilltop outpost in the Republic of Vietnam. With the command group repulsing several savage enemy assaults, and subjected to a continuing hail of fire from an attacking force estimated to be of two-battalion strength, Captain Smith repeatedly exposed himself to the heavy fire while directing friendly air support. When adverse weather conditions precluded further close air support, he attempted to lead the group, now reduced to only 28 Vietnamese Marines, to the safety of friendly lines. An enemy soldier opened fire upon the Marines at the precise moment that they had balked when encountering an outer defense ring of barbed wire. Captain Smith returned accurate fire, disposing of the attacker, and then threw himself backwards on top of the booby-trap-infested wire barrier. Swiftly, the remaining Marines moved over the crushed wire, stepping on Captain Smith's prostrate body, until all had passed safely through the barrier. Although suffering severe cuts and bruises, Captain Smith succeeded in leading the Marines to the safety of friendly lines. His great personal valor and unrelenting devotion to duty reflected the highest credit upon himself, the Marine Corps, and the United States Naval Service.

APPENDIX I
FMF PACIFIC COMMAND RELATIONSHIPS, 1971

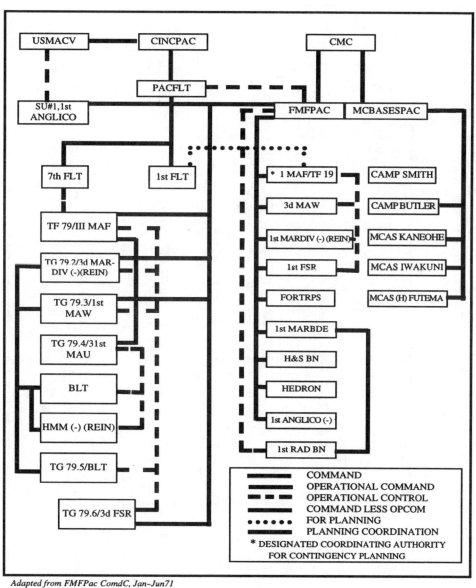

Adapted from FMFPac ComdC, Jan–Jun71

APPENDIX J
USMACV COMMAND RELATIONSHIPS, 1971

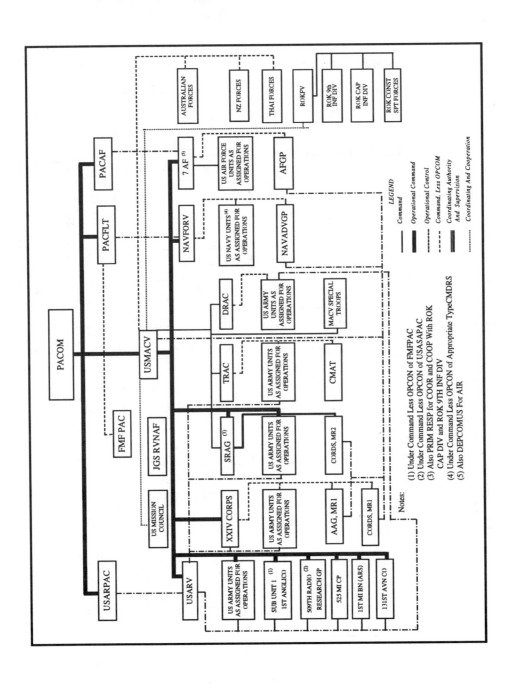

APPENDIX K
VIETNAMESE MARINE DIVISION, 1972

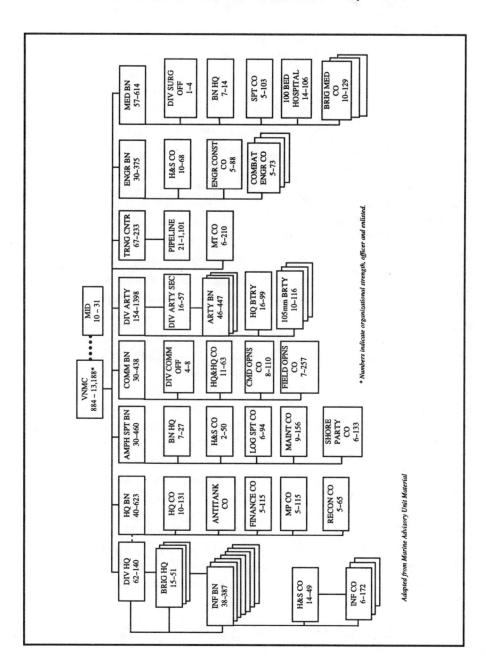

* Numbers indicate organizational strength, officer and enlisted.

Adapted from Marine Advisory Unit Material

APPENDIX L
LIST OF REVIEWERS

Marines

Gen Louis H. Wilson, Jr., USMC (Ret)
LtGen Leslie E. Brown, USMC (Ret)
LtGen Clyde D. Dean, USMC (Ret)
LtGen Joseph C. Fegan, Jr., USMC (Ret)
LtGen D'Wayne Gray, USMC (Ret)
LtGen William K. Jones, USMC (Ret)
LtGen Louis Metzger, USMC (Ret)
LtGen Edward J. Miller, USMC (Ret)
LtGen Andrew W. O'Donnell, USMC (Ret)
LtGen Donn J. Robertson, USMC (Ret)

MajGen Victor A. Armstrong, USMC (Ret)
MajGen Walter E. Boomer, USMC
MajGen William P. Eshelman, USMC
MajGen Donald R. Gardner, USMC
MajGen Kenneth J. Houghton, USMC (Ret)

BGen Darrel E. Bjorklund, USMC (Ret)
BGen Walter D. Fillmore, USMC (Ret)
BGen Paul G. Graham, USMC (Ret)
BGen Manning T. Jannell, USMC (Ret)
BGen Jim R. Joy, HQMC (Ret)

Col Kent C. Bateman, USMC (Ret)
Col John W. Clayborne, USMC (Ret)
Col Patrick G. Collins, USMC (Ret)
Col John D. Cummings, USMC
Col Kenneth G. Fiegener, USMC (Ret)

Col Herbert G. Fischer, USMC (Ret)
Col Charles H. Gallina, USMC
Col Charles J. Goode, Jr., USMC (Ret)
Col Richard E. Hawes, Jr., USMC (Ret)
Col Leo J. Kelly, USMC (Ret)
Col Robert W. Kirby, USMC (Ret)
Col Raymond M. Kostesky, USMC (Ret)
Col Jerry W. Marvel, USMC (Ret)
Col Edison W. Miller, USMC (Ret)
Col Robert J. Perrich, USMC (Ret)
Col Donald L. Price, USMC
Col John M. Rapp, USMC (Ret)
Col Richard D. Revie, USMC (Ret)
Col John W. Ripley, USMC
Col Donald E. Schneider, USMC (Ret)
Col James L. Shanahan, USMC (Ret)
Col Robert D. Shoptaw, USMC (Ret)
Col Charles V. V. Smillie, Jr., USMC (Ret)
Col William J. Smith, USMC (Ret)
Col Ray A. Stephens, USMC (Ret)
Col Thomas J. Stevens, USMC (Ret)
Col Aubrey W. Talbert, USMC (Ret)
Col Gerald H. Turley, USMCR (Ret)
Col Sumner A. Vale, USMC (Ret)
Col Charles T. Williamson, USMC (Ret)

LtCol Andrew E. Anderson, USMC (Ret)
LtCol Roger W. Badeker, USMC (Ret)

LtCol James C. Brown, USMC (Ret)
LtCol Mervyn J. Burns, USMC (Ret)
LtCol John M. Campanelli, USMC (Ret)
LtCol Harlan P. Chapman, USMC (Ret)
LtCol Andrew D. DeBona, USMC (Ret)
LtCol George S. Ford, USMC (Ret)
LtCol Thomas E. Gnibus, USMC (Ret)
LtCol Glen Golden, USMC (Ret)
LtCol James C. Hardee, USMC
LtCol William C. Howey, USMC (Ret)
LtCol Emmett S. Huff, USMC (Ret)
LtCol John K. Hyatt, Jr., USC (Ret)
LtCol George E. Jones, USMC (Ret)
LtCol Michael S. Kelly, USMC (Ret)
LtCol Eddie R. Maag, USMC (Ret)
LtCol Harrison A. Makeever, USMC (Ret)
LtCol David J. Moore, USMC (Ret)
LtCol Ronald S. Neubauer, USMC (Ret)
LtCol Nguyen Van Phan, VNMC (Ret)
LtCol George Philip, III, USMC (Ret)
LtCol Mark B. Pizzo, USMC
LtCol Michael L. Powell, USMC
LtCol David L. Ross, USMC (Ret)
LtCol Robert F. Sheridan, USMC (Ret)
LtCol James D. Simpson, USMC (Ret)
LtCol George E. Strickland, USMC (Ret)
LtCol Orson G. Swindle, III, USMC (Ret)
LtCol William R. Von Harten, USMC (Ret)
LtCol Marshall R. Wells, USMC
LtCol William E. Wilson, Jr., USMC (Ret)

Maj Stephen G. Biddulph, USMC
Maj Donald C. Brodie, USMC (Ret)
Maj Robert L. Gondek, USMC (Ret)
Maj Thomas W. Hoysa, USMC
Maj Angelo M. Inglisa, USMC (Ret)
Maj Dennis R. Kendig, USMCR (Ret)
Maj Paul J. Montague, USMC (Ret)
Maj John T. Paparone, USMC
Maj Anthony P. Shepard, USMC
Maj Edward J. Wages, USMC (Ret)

Capt Edwin W. Besch, USMC (Ret)
Capt Alan J. Kroboth, USMC (Ret)

Capt William E. Thomas, Jr., USMC (Ret)

SgtMaj Ernest Benjamin, USMC (Ret)
SgtMaj Robert S. Ynacay, USMC (Ret)
MGySgt Harry G. Lock, USMC (Ret)

Army

Gen Frederick J. Kroesen, USA (Ret)
LtGen Howard H. Cooksey, USA (Ret)
MajGen John E. Murray, USA (Ret)
LtCol William C. Camper, USA (Ret)
1stSgt Jimmy D. Evans, USA (Ret)

Navy

VAdm Walter D. Gaddis, USN (Ret)
VAdm William P. Mack, USN (Ret)
VAdm James B. Stockdale, USN (Ret)
RAdm Wycliffe D. Toole, Jr., USN (Ret)
Capt Paul L. Gruendl, USN (Ret)
LCdr Francis C. Brown, USN

Air Force

LtCol Darrel Whitcomb, USAFR

Others

Mr. Dale Andrade
LtCol William B. Barker, KSNG
Mr. Garnett M. Bell
Mr. Peter Braestrup
Mr. Robert J. Destatte
Mr. Howard C. H. Feng
Dr. V. Keith Fleming, Jr.
Mr. Stephen C. Fogleman
Dr. Nguyen M. Hung
Dr. Allan R. Millett
Mr. Douglas Pike
Mr. David K. Schmidt

Director of Naval History
Joint Chiefs of Staff Historical Division
Office of Air Force History
Office of the Chief of Military History
Office of the Secretary of Defense Historical Staff

APPENDIX M
DISTRIBUTION OF PERSONNEL
FLEET MARINE FORCE, PACIFIC

Unit	Unit Commander	Location	Strength USMC	Strength USN	Major Equipment
FMF			91,351	3,503	
MIDPAC			6,602	204	
FMFPAC	LTGEN W. K. Jones	Hawaii	55,621	2,212	
HQFMPAC			777	31	
H&SBN	COL R McClennan	CP Smith	729	24	
DET 2, 21ST Dental Co.	CAPT M. R. Hamilton (USN)			7	
HQ SQDN	LTCOL C. E.Dorffeld	Kaneohe	48		5/T-28B, 1/US-2B
1ST ANGLICO (-)	MAJ H. S. Morgan, Jr.	SDiego	104	4	
SU 1, 1ST ANGLICO (MACV)	LTCOL D. Gray	Saigon	102	8	
1ST RADIO BN	LTCOL J. K. Hyatt, Jr.	Kaneohe	450	8	
1ST MARINE BRIGADE	BGEN V. A. Armstrong	Kaneohe	5,169	153	
HQCO	CAPT H. J. Trautwein, Jr.		265	18	
1ST ITT	WO R. R. Scott		4		
11TH CIT (FMFPAC)	1STLT H. Jensen		13		
21ST Dental Co (-)	CAPT J. F. Hardin (USN)			33	
3D Marines (-) (REIN)	COL J. P. Connolly II	Kaneohe			
HQCO (-)	CAPT M. B. Brown		156	4	
1STBN	LTCOL L. H. Gaboury		703	40	6/106MM RR, 6/81 MORT
2DBN	MAJ R. J. Modrzejewski		432	16	8/81 MORT
CO A, 3D ENGR BN	1STLT R. A. Cheever		126		
CO A (REIN), 3D MT BN	CAPT M. G. Roth		58		
CO A (REIN), 3D SP BN	CAPT J. L. Spikerman		41		
CO A, 3D RECON BN (REIN)	CAPT C. A. Rodatz		38		
CO A, (REIN), 3D MED BN	HM1 R. F. Gray			32	
1STBN, 12TH MAR	LTCOL B. J. Coogan	Kaneohe	396	10	18/105 HOW TD
CO D, 3D AMTRAC BN	MAJ W. W. Bahnmaier		160		3/LVTP-5 COMD, 43/LVTP-5, 1/LVTR
COMM SPT CO, 7TH COMM BN	MAJ A. B. Ray		160		
PROV SERV BN	LTCOL J. W. Brown		486		1/LVTR
MAG-24	COL R. E. Carey	Kaneohe	2,133	43	
H&MS-24	MAJ F. M. Logan		403		1/C-117D, 3/TA-4F
MABS-24	LTCOL L. Gasparine, Jr.		305	36	
MATCU-70 (MAG-24)	CWO O. F. Gour, Jr.		45		
VMFA-122 (1ST MAW)	LTCOL L. Furstenberg	Iwakuni	252	3	7/F-4B
VMFA-212 (MAG-15 (FWD))	LTCOL R. D. Revie	Danang	294	4	11/F-4J
VMFA-235	LTCOL G. H. Leach	Kaneohe	222		12/F-4J
MACS-2	LTCOL D. T. Benn		193		
HMM-262	MAJ C. W. Lively		151		4/CH-46D, 17/CH-46F
HMM-463	LTCOL W. R. Ledbetter		173		13/CH-53D
DET, VMO-6	CAPT R. R. Critser		48		3/OV-10A

Unit	Unit Commander	Location	Strength USMC	Strength USN	Major Equipment
DET, HML-367	CAPT C. T. Crews		47		7/UH-1E
WESTPAC			23,748	1,033	
FMFPAC					
III MAF	LTGEN L. Metzger	CP Courtney	23,748	1,033	
H&S CO	MAJ T. P. Dickson		114		
9TH CIT	CAPT F. W. Schultz		11		
3D MARDIV (-) REIN (III) MAF	MAJGEN J. C. Fegan, Jr	CP Courtney	13,830	879	
HQBN	LTCOL S. Wawrzyniak		1,326	39	
3D ITT	WO T. F. Singley	CP Hansen			
7TH ITT	CWO S. M. Osenkoski				
11TH ITT	CAPT G. H. Johnson, Jr.				
15TH ITT	WO E. J. Croghan				
17TH ITT	WO A. F. Kent				
SCAMP	1STLT J. W. Kahler	CP Courtney	26		
3D CIT	CAPT D. D. James	CP Hansen	14		
1ST SSCT	CAPT G. L. Nason	CP Courtney	6		
3D DENTAL CO	CAPT P. J. Sydow (USN)		3	59	
4TH MARINES	COL R. J. Perrich	CP Hansen			
HQCO	CAPT P. H. Gesell		234	6	
1STBN (31ST MAU)	LTCOL C. D. Dean	Afloat WESTPA	1,037	38	8/106MM RR, 8/81 MORT
2DBN	LTCOL J. Phillips	CP Hansen	1,022	36	8/106MM RR, 4/81 MORT
3DBN (33D MAU)	LTCOL W. R VonHarten	Afloat WESTPA	1,059	44	7/106MM RR, 6/81 MORT
9TH MARINES	COL V. T. Blaz	CP Schwab			
HQCO	CAPT E. B. Burrow		286	9	
1STBN	LTCOL P. B. Friedrichs		1,258	65	7/106MM RR, 7/81 MORT
2DBN	LTCOL J. O. Trehy	Afloat WESTPA	937	49	8/106MM RR, 8/81 MORT
3DBN	LTCOL R. A. Clark	CP Schwab	983	39	8/106MM RR, 8/81 MORT
12TH MARINES	LTCOL W. A. Lawrence	FUJI			
HQ BTRY (-)	CAPT J. G. Collins		220	17	
2DBN	LTCOL E. D. Litzenberger		396	5	12/105MM HOW TD
3DBN	LTCOL M. D. Julian		388	8	12/105MM HOW TD
4THBN (-) (REIN)	LTCOL S. M. Gipson, Jr		551	9	18/155MM HOW TD
3D PLAT, 1ST 8" HOW BTRY SP					2/8" HOW SP
3D SERV BN (-)	COL E. B. Hart	CP Hansen	669	17	
3D TANK BN (-)	LTCOL G. B. Chaney		533	8	43/M48 TANK, 3/M51 VTR
9th MT BN (-)	LTCOL A. J. Eagan		230	5	
3D MED BN (-)	CMDR H. J. Boudreau (USN)		124	92	
1ST HOSPITAL CO	LT H. D. Cash (USN)		21	12	
3D MT BN (-)	LTCOL C. F. Hammel	CP Schwab	184	4	
10 RECON BN (-)	MAJ G. H. Douse	QNNA	294	16	
3D ENGR BN (-) (REIN)	LTCOL R. F. Goins	CP Hansen	532	5	
CO D (REIN), 7TH ENGR BN	CAPT H. L. Campbell		136	1	

Unit	Unit Commander	Location	Strength		Major Equipment
			USMC	USN	
1ST PLAT, 1ST BRIDGE CO	1STLT C. B. Maunders		33		
7TH COMM BN (-)	LTCOL R. C. Lafser		476	6	
3D SP BN (-)	LTCOL G. H. Ripley		273	8	
1ST AMTRAC BN (-)	LTCOL P. J. Saxton	CP Schwab	579	8	7/LVTP-5 COMD, 80 LVTP-5, 2/LVTR
1ST MAW (III MAF)	MAJGEN L. E. Brown	Iwakuni	7,214	119	
JAPAN (1ST MAW ELEMENTS)			4,867	98	
MMHS-1	LTCOL R. E. Hawes, Jr.	Iwakuni	645	13	
7TH CIT (1ST MAW)	CAPT S. L. Moyer		12		
11TH FORCE DENTAL CO	CMDR J. J. Lyons (USN)		4	35	
3D SSCT	CAPT C. J. Holloway		6		
MACG-18	COL E. M. Jones	Iwakuni			
H&HS-18	LTCOL L. B. Myers		151	7	
MASS-2 (-)	LTCOL J. H. Thompson		151	2	
MWCS-18	LTCOL R. V. Walker, Jr.		289		
MAG-12	COL D. C. Macho	Iwakuni			
DET A, MAG-12		Bien Hoa			
H&MS-12	LTCOL K. D. Curry, Jr.		528		2/TA-4F
MABS-12	LTCOL L. Dewolf		368	13	
MATCU-60 (MAG-12)	CAPT A. E. Peters	Iwakuni	59		
VMA-211	LTCOL W. E. Wilson	Bien Hoa	158		17/A-4E
DET A, VMA-211					
VMA-311	LTCOL K. M. Johnston		190		16/A-4E
Det A, VMA-311					
VMA(AW)-533	MAJ D. E. Cathcart	Iwakuni	231		9/A-6A
DET A, VMA(AW)-533					
OTHER					
SU 2, HS&M-36	MAJ J. J. Tharp	Atsugi	39		4/CH-46D
MAG-15	COL K. O'Keefe	Iwakuni			
H&MS-15	MAJ J. E. Herlocker		285		4/TA-4F
MABS-15	MAJ R. L. Beckwith		193	18	
MATCU-62 (MAG-15)	CAPT D. L. Hendrix		54		
VMFA-115	LTCOL K. A. McFerren	DaNang	241		14/F-4B
VMFA-232	LTCOL J. L. Gregorcyk		257		15/F-4J
VMCJ-1	MAJ J. D. Carlton	Iwakuni	303	1	5/EA-6A, 9/RF-4B
MWSG-17	COL M. G. McCool	Iwakuni			
H&MS-17	LTCOL D. C. Morgan		505	9	7/C-117D
WERS-17(-)	LTCOL A. L. Frucci		199		
OKINAWA (1ST MAW Elements)			2,347	21	
MAG-36	COL A. F. Garrotto	Futema			
H&MS-36 (-)	LTCOL E. J. Murphy		542		
MABS-36	MAJ F. J. Quadrini		390	14	

Unit	Unit Commander	Location	Strength USMC	Strength USN	Major Equipment
MATCU-66 (MAG-36)	CAPT T. A. Varrell		73		
HMM-164 (31ST MAU)	LTCOL E. C. Hertberg	Afloat WETPA	304	3	2/AH-1J, 14/CH-46D, 4/CH-53D, 2/UH-1E
HMM-165 (33D MAU)	LTCOL P. L. Moreau		290	3	14/CH-46D, 6/CH-53D, 4/UH-1E
HMM-462 (-)	LTCOL O. G. McDonald	Futema	169		15/CH-53D
VMO-6	LTCOL D. E. Dilley		140		16/OV-10A
VMGR-152 (1ST MAW)	LTCOL R. A. Brown		273	1	6/KC-130F
HML-367 (-)	MAJ W. T. Hewes		105		9/UH-1E
HMA-369	CAPT R. Osborne		61		2/AH-1J
OTHER					
DET, MASS-2		Futema			
SU1, WERS-17	WO L. A. Walker		31		
SU1, H&MS-12	CAPT R. D. Pitts	NAHA	42		
MACS-4	MAJ G. L. Collins	Futema	262	2	
3D FSR	COL R. E. Roeder, Jr.	CP Foster	2,579	35	
H&SBN	LTCOL J. B. Harris, Sr.		699	15	
SUPPLY BN	LTCOL J. W. Friberg		975	20	
NOP, 3D FSR (3D FSR)	CAPT T. R. Geries		48		
MAINT BN	LTCOL H. I. Frey		857		2/LVTE-1, 1/106MM RR, 1/81 MORT
EASTPAC			25,271	975	
FMFPAC					
1 MAF	MAJGEN R. T. Dwyer, Jr.	Campen	54		
1ST MARDIV(-) (REIN)	MAJGEN R. T. Dwyor, Jr.	Campen	11,332	716	
HQBN (REIN)	COL H. G. Robinson		1,709	72	
1ST CIT	CAPT B. B. Voronin		16		
5TH ITT	CWO R. G. Prefontaine				
9TH ITT	CWO R. L. Runkle	Campen			
19TH ITT	MSGT R. W. Anderton				
21ST ITT	2DLT M. M. Lincoln				
23D ITT	CWO F. W. Schaffer				
25TH ITT	1STLT G. D. Jennings				
2D SSCT	CWO E. L. Haney		6		
SCAMP	CWO A. L. Selleck, Jr.		47		
COMM SPT CO, 9TH COMM BN	CAPT J. M. Hartnett		87		
1ST CIVIL AFFAIRS GRP (CADRE)	1STLT R. S. Lind		15		
1ST MARINES	COL E. J. Bronars	Campen			
HQCO	CAPT V. L. Schultz		114	39	
1STBN	LTCOL C. A. Barstow		192	1	8/106MM RR, 8/81 MORT
2DBN	LTCOL A. Lukeman		170		8/106MM RR, 8/81 MORT
3DBN	LTCOL M. Hunter		221		8/106MM RR, 8/81 MORT
3DBN, 3D MARINES	LTCOL J. D. Noble	Campen	127	4	7/106MM RR, 8/81 MORT
5TH MARINES	COL R. N. Burhans	Campen			

Unit	Unit Commander	Location	Strength USMC	Strength USN	Major Equipment
HQCO	CAPT R. T. Peterson		147	60	
1STBN	LTCOL P. J. Ryan		238		8/106MM RR, 8/81 MORT
2DBN	MAJ J. A. Linnemann		179		2/106MM RR, 8/81 MORT
3DBN	MAJ J. D. Mattingly		165		8/106MM RR, 8/81 MORT
7TH MARINES	COL F. J. Hunt	Campen			
HQCO	CAPT E. P. Aldous		229	13	
1STBN	LTCOL R. W. Badeker		832	34	8/106MM RR, 8/81 MORT
2DBN	MAJ J. I. Hopkins		851	40	7/106MM RR, 8/81 MORT
3DBN	LTCOL T. R. Henderson		859	47	8/106MM RR, 8/81 MORT
11TH MARINES	COL W. R. Grubaugh	Campen			
HQ BTRY	CAPT S. C. Winegardner		197	34	
1STBN	MAJ C. D. Bailey		145		18/105 HOW TD
2DBN	MAJ E. F. Whipple, Jr.		154		18/105 HOW TD
3DBN	LTCOL R. J. Henley		587	4	18/105 HOW TD
1ST RECON BN	MAJ. C. R. Dunning	Campen	200	12	
1ST FORCE RECON CO	CAPT D. L. Cook		74	3	
1ST ENGR BN	MAJ C. N. Wall		430	9	
1ST TANK BN (REIN)	LTCOL H. G. Edebohls		646	18	5/M51 VTR, 16/103 TANK, 34/M48 TANK
CO D, 3D TANK BN (CADRE)					
1ST MT BN (REIN)	MAJ R. W. Smith		218	7	
CO B (REIN), 9TH MT BN	1STLT J. M. Barr		108		
1ST MED BN	LCDR C. A. Roper (USN)		89	157	
1ST SP BN	MAJ F. L. Edwards, Jr.		313	28	
1ST DENTAL CO	CAPT. J. F. King (USN)		4	60	
1ST SERV BN (REIN)	COL G. K. Reid		753	41	
1ST SEARCHLIGHT BTRY (CADRE)					
7TH SEP BULK FUEL CO (CADRE)					
3D AMTRAC BN (-)	LTCOL J. L. Saul		715	16	8/LVTP-5 COMD, 68/LVTP-5, 4/LVTR
7TH ENGR BN (-) (REIN)	LTCOL L. E. Ramsey		408	17	
1ST BRIDGE CO (-)	1STLT P. R. Fields		89		
FORCE TROOPS FMFPAC	BGEN P. G. Graham	29 Palms	1,547	54	
HQCO	MAJ R. J. Lucas		175	7	
PROV MAINT CO, 1ST FSR	LTCOL N. B. Wynn		145		
NOP, 1ST FSR	1STLT W. W. Steele		50		
9TH COMM BN (-)	LTCOL R. J. Lee		279	7	
13TH CIT (FORTRPS FMFPAC)	CWO W. J. Knipper		12		
DET 1, 21ST DENTAL CO	CMDR C. M. Johnson (USN)		1	12	
CO A (REIN) 7TH ENGR BN	CAPT H. L. Dietz		120		
3D HOSPITAL CO	LT C. E. Montgomery (USN)		18	14	
1ST FAG	LTCOL R. O. Gillick	29 Palms			
HQ BTRY, 1ST FAG	CAPT J.J. Folan		104	10	
1ST 8" HOW BTRY SP (-)	1STLT B. J. Roberts		138		1/M51 VTR, 4/8" HOW SP

Unit	Unit Commander	Location	Strength USMC	USN	Major Equipment
1ST 175MM GUN BTRY SP	CAPT C. I. Stanfield		65		1/M51 VTR, 6/175 GUN SP
3D 175MM GUN BTRY SP	CAPT G. C Windheim		74		6/175 GUN SP
4THBN, 11TH MAR (1ST FAG)	LTCOL D. W. Sanford		366	4	18/155 HOW SP
3D MAW	BGEN F. C. Lang	El Toro	10,342	171	
NWHS-3 (-)	LTCOL H. E Sexton		674	16	
SU 1, MWHS-3	MAJ P. J. Vogel		37		
6TH CIT	CAPT H. C. Cofty		16		
4TH SSCT	CWO D. J. Brown		7		
13TH FORCE DENTAL CO	CAPT F. P. Beall (USN)		1	29	
MAG-11	COL N. M. Trapnell	El Toro			
H&MS-11	LTCOL L. N. Levin		432		
MABS-11	LTCOL N. E. Douglas		187	21	
VMFA-314 (CADRE)	MAJ R. H. Brown		172		9/F4-B
VMFA-323	MAJ T. G. Leach		202		14/F-4B
VMFA-531	LTCOL J. T. Zych		235		12/F-4B
MAG-13	COL J. W. Parchen	El Toro			
H&MS-13	MAJ J. L. Shelton		637		1/A-4E, 8/TA-4F
MABS-13	MAJ J. Dermody		322	22	
MATCU-67 (MAG-13)	1STLT E. R. Spears		57		
VMCJ-3	LTCOL M. W. Dinnage		338		8/RF-4B, 5/EA-6A
VMA-214	LTCOL J. J. McCarthy		193		13/A-4F
VMA-223	LTCOL A. Oseguera		183		11/A-4F, 5/A-4E
VMA(AW)-225 (CADRE)	MAJ R. C. Tinsley		6		
VMA(AW)-242	LTCOL M. S. Newbill		252		10/A-6A
MAG-16 (-)	COL J. L. Sadowski	Santa Ana			
HS&M-16	LTCOL R. J. Eitel		443		4/AH-1G,2/UH-1E,5/OV-10A, 2/CH-53A, 3/CH-46F
MABS-16	MAJ B. G. Wilkison		379	13	
MATCU-74 (MAG 16 (-))	CAPT T. Gotta		40		
HMM-161	LTCOL G. W. Hintz		156		15/CH-46F
HMM-163	LTCOL J. H. Walker		174		21/CH-46F
HMM-361	MAJ R. F. Captor		188		16/CH-53A
HMM-363	MAJ V. M. Lee		201		17/CH53A
MHTG-30	COL R. D. Bianchi	Santa Ana			
H&MS-30	MAJ A. F. Ribbeck		251	1	5/CH-46F, 1/CH-53A
HMHT-301	MAJ F. A. Lock		129		9/CH-53A
HMMT-302	LTCOL R. G. Ritchie		163		13/CH-46F
MWSG-37	COL B. F. Frankovic	El Toro			
H&MS-37 (-)	LTCOL L. K. Warn		520	20	6/C-117D
SU 1, H&MS-37	MAJ L. C. Wallace, Jr.		55		
WERS-37	LTCOL M. Pallai		200		
VMGR-352 (3D MAW)	LTCOL G. L. Carlson		291		7/KC-130F

Unit	Unit Commander	Location	Strength		Major Equipment
			USMC	USN	
MACG-38	COL J. R. Omara	El Toro			
H&MHS-38	MAJ D. E. T. Wilson		150	19	
1ST REDEYE PLAT	1STLT W. E. Beals		26		
3D REDEYE PLAT	1STLT B. L. Kelly	AFLOAT WESTPAC	42		
MWCS-38	MAJ W. T Chwatek	El Toro	209		
MASS-3	MAJ V. J. Fulladosa		127		
DET, MAG-16		Campen			
SU 1, H&MS-16	MAJ F. Owlett		210	9	
SU1, MABS-16	CAPT M. R. Massie		100		
MATCU-75 (DET, MAG 16)	CAPT P. D. Haynes		38		
MACS-7 (REIN) (MACG-38)	MAJ P. J. Florio		191	1	
HMA-169	MAJ P. F. Cameron		149		8/AH-1G
HML-267	MAJ G. A. Olsen		195		24/UH-1E
VMO-2	MAJ D. A Caylor		185		14/OV-10A
MCRTG-10	COL R. B. Sinclair	Yuma			
H&MS-10	MAJ C. K. Conley		290	8	
VMFAT-101	LTCOL T. R. Moore		278	1	19/F-4B
VMAT-102	LTCOL R. D. Reid		192	2	20/A-4E
VMT-103	MAJ H. L. Searle		182	2	8/TA-4F, 13/TA-4J
MATCU-65 (MCCRTG-10)	1STLT A. W. Ustaveson		48		
2D LAAM BN (MACG-38)	LTCOL R. D. Foster	Yuma	546	7	
SU 1, H&S BTRY, 2D LAAM	CAPT M. Posthuma		60		
1ST FSR	COL H. C. Reed	Campen	1,996	34	
H&SBN	LTCOL J. W. Marks		629	18	
SUPPLY BN	LTCOL D. Muffi		683	16	
MAINT BN	LTCOL R. D. White		684		2/M51 VTR, 3/LVTR

APPENDIX N
IN THEIR OWN IMAGE

Author's Note:

The text in this appendix was funded in part by a research grant from the Marine Corps Historical Foundation and presented as a paper at the Royal Military College of Canada at Kingston for the Society of Military History, 20–24 May 1993.

During the North Vietnamese 1972 "Spring Offensive," the South Vietnamese 3d Division was defeated in a series of engagements that climaxed on May 1, 1972 with the loss of Quang Tri. The aftermath of defeat was muddled by acrimonious dispute between the Americans over the conduct of the defense of Quang Tri — which saw the U.S. Army advisors withdraw while the U.S. Marine advisors remained.[A]

This appendix will examine the claims of both the Army of the Republic of Vietnam (ARVN) and the U.S. Military Advisory Command Vietnam (MACV). Their claims state that the Vietnamese Marines were a main factor in this defeat for two reasons: 1) Marine commanders paid more attention to their service leader than their tactical commander; 2) This was caused by Vietnamese and American Marine pressure to fight as a division for the first time.[1]

Riverine Commandos to Marine Division

After 1954, a scattering of riverine commandos were designated as the "Marine Infantry" of the Vietnamese Navy, known as the Vietnamese Marine Corps (VNMC).[B] Present was a small advisory team of American Marines. The Americans had a background based on established naval amphibious forces, division-level employment, and a legislated structure. It was from this that the concept of a Vietnamese Marine Division arose, reflecting the doctrine and organization the Americans were familiar with. This was fostered by Vietnamese attendance at Marine Corps schools and the material support of the advisory effort.[2] Despite resistance from the Vietnamese and American command structure, from 1968, the goal of a full

---

(A) The tone of this is illustrated in the views of the Marine's most vocal participant, Col Gerald H. Turley. The debate his book began was not helped by attempts to discredit the story by repeating earlier unsubstantiated charges of Marine misconduct.

(B) It became part of the South Vietnamese armed forces general reserve and, in 1965, separated from the Vietnamese Navy, to answer only to the Joint General Staff of the Republic of Vietnam Armed Forces.

division of Marines was a priority for Lieutenant General Le Nguyen Khang, the VNMC commandant, and his advisors.[C]

In 1971, with the departure of American combat units from Military Region 1, Marine brigades were deployed in the I Corps area under the command of the Army division along the demilitarized zone of Quang Tri Province. Experience in Laos under Lieutenant General Hoang Xuan Lam, who commanded I Corps, had earned him the name "Bloody Hands" for his expenditure of Marine lives.[3] Khang and his advisors felt that General Lam failed to support the Marines in Laos. The extent to which politics overrode tactical decisions was "difficult to gauge" when Marine requests to withdraw had been met with Lam's "now the Marines will have to fight."[4]

Another concern from Lam Son 719 was that the Americans provided the critical control of maneuver and fire support which should have come from the Vietnamese. The senior American commander in Vietnam, General Creighton W. Abrams, concluded in July 1971 that the Vietnamese suffered from weak leadership and the inability to control American firepower. Public comments otherwise, he did not expect the American advisor "to play a major role in the improvement of South Vietnamese military forces."[5] In the fall of 1971, the 3d Division, the Ben Hai Division, was formed and assigned to the demilitarized zone. The Marines came under the command of Brigadier General Vu Van Giai, the division commander, for tactical matters, but remained firmly under Marine Corps control for material and political support.[D]

According to Major General Frederick J. Kroesen, the senior American in Military Region 1, General Giai was not satisfied with Marine "responsiveness to his orders," but the brigades were combat tested, fully reliable, and respected. Significantly, they were well supplied, equipped, and maintained at effective strength by Marine logistic and replacement channels.[6] General Kroesen observed that their ability to rotate forces proved vital in maintaining combat effectiveness.

Background to Defeat

This arrangement was tested on 30 March 1972 when the NVA launched attacks coinciding with the American exit. The Communist invasion, in brief, was part of an effort that struck toward Hue in Military Region 1, toward Kontum and Pleiku in Military Region 2, and at An Loc and Saigon in Military Region 3. They relied on bad

(C) There was speculation that the expenditure of Marine lives was to weaken Khang-Ky faction after the losses the Airborne incurred during Lam Son 719 weakened the Lam-Thieu faction. This same kind of argument was put forward about the Marine's action at Quang Tri City in 1972 as a scheme by Khang and Ky to discredit Lam and Thieu.

(D) The relationships of separate military organizations were based on the degree of support provided: general, direct, or attached. In theory, an attached unit is supposed to be the same as an organic unit; oftentimes in practice this is not the case.

weather and combined arms to defeat the South Vietnamese, who were believed to lack effective American support. The magnitude of the initial attack was such that six divisions entered South Vietnam on three fronts.[7] The American First Regional Assistance Command in Military Region 1 estimated three divisions, five separate infantry regiments, two independent battalions, seven sapper battalions, three or more artillery regiments, and two armored regiments — all of whom were used in the attacks in Quang Tri Province.[8]

On 3 April, the Vietnamese Joint General Staff sent the entire Marine Division to Military Region 1, where General Khang was directed to place his brigades under the operational control of I Corps.[9] The 3d Division suffered the surrender of its 56th Regiment and artillery group and suffered harrowing withdrawals by the 57th Regiment and Marine Brigade 147. Marine Brigade 258 and the 1st Armor Brigade barely held at Dong Ha as the division regrouped south of the Cua Viet River during the first week of April. While the 3d Division held Dong Ha, the emphasis of the battle shifted to the western approaches of the Ai Tu Combat Base and Quang Tri City, the province capital. Attempts by I Corp Commander General Lam to conduct a counteroffensive failed to get off the ground and the demands on his command and control system multiplied with reinforcements (up to 36 battalions). Kroesen pointed out that at no time was the 3d Division's communications or logistics resources expanded and links were maintained with outside commands to ensure needed support. Colonel Donald J. Metcalf, the senior advisor to General Giai and commander of the MACV Advisory Team 155, felt that this arrangement did not carry "the allegiance and loyalty" necessary for the conduct of combat operations.[10]

Despite apparent difficulties, Lam refused to use the Marines and Rangers — the two division-level headquarters placed at his command by the Joint General Staff. The chairman of the Joint General Staff, General Cao Van Vian, recalled they were "never utilized or given a mission." General Kroesen wrote that Lam dismissed suggestions to provide a multi-division structure to fight the battle north of the Hai Van Pass as "unnecessary and impractical." Lam's focus on a premature counteroffensive prevented him and his staff from even considering the problems of defending Quang Tri City or Hue.[11]

The effects of Lam Son 719 were felt, with Lam and Khang refusing to deal directly with each other, according to the Marine operations (G-3) advisor, Lieutenant Colonel Gerald H. Turley. General Kroesen and Colonel Joshua W. Dorsey III, the Marine advisor to General Khang, served as the only means of contact between the two Vietnamese generals. A sign of the lack of effective authority within I Corps, to Kroesen, was the participation of the Marine Division and Ranger Command in issuing guidance, responding to complaints and questions, and providing "unsought advice and counsel concerning their forces to anyone who would listen." According to Turley, Khang and his staff monitored "every move" and he waited impatiently "to assume control of his three infantry brigades."[12] General Lam compounded this by going directly to 3d Division units, particularly the 1st Armored Brigade, whose advisor, Lieutenant Colonel Louis C. Wagner, complained of orders from the Corps commander, his deputy, and operations officer.[13] General Kroesen concluded that all this undercut the authority of General Giai by planting the "seeds of distrust and disobedience" that would culminate at the end of the month "in near mutiny."[14]

General Giai's headquarters was at Quang Tri City in the "Citadel," along with Colonel Metcalf's Advisory Team 155. By the end of April 1972, the 3d Division was organized around five mixed task forces: the 1st Armored Brigade (with the 57th Regiment) held the area from Highway 1 to five kilometers to the west, bounded by the Cam Lo River on the north and the Ai Tu Combat Base, which conducted operations to the west.[15] The 2d Regiment defended the western area south of Ai Tu to the Thach Han River. The 1st Ranger Group was located below the Thach Han River and Marine Brigade 369 was farther south near Hai Lang.[16] General Kroesen saw a pattern of action established within the 3d Division's area and by this time "no orders, threats, or exhortations" were able to force subordinates to move or stay if they disagreed. They were willing to let air power win the fight for them and General Lam and Giai were losing control on the battlefield to this "general state of inertia."[17]

Actions at Quang Tri City

On 27 April, the North Vietnamese renewed their general offensive throughout the "Quang Tri Front." The 308th NVA Division attacked Dong Ha and, on the afternoon of 28 April, "liberated" it. The 304th NVA Division attacked the Ai Tu Combat Base. The 342d NVA Division attacked to the south at the same time, blocked Highway 1, and cut Quang Tri City off from the Thua Thien Province. Communist artillery, armor, and infantry pushed the defenders back toward Highway 1 and south toward Quang Tri City. Giai had issued orders for a general withdrawal to positions near My Chanh on 29 April, but was overruled by Lam. This plan apparently formed the basis for most of his actions that followed.[18] The various accounts of events merge intent and action from this point, so that it is hard to recreate Giai and Lam's command dynamics. Vietnamese General Vien commented the Quang Tri debacle involved some intricacies "that only the principles could clarify."

Early Sunday morning, 30 April 1972, a regimental-sized enemy force supported by armor was assembled southwest of Ai Tu. Up to this point, Lieutenant Colonel Nguyen Nang Bao's Brigade 147 used artillery and tanks to stop North Vietnamese attacks, but now ammunition supply was critical and the supporting 20th Tank Battalion was parceled out below the Thach Han River to keep Highway 1 open to the south. Naval gunfire could not be used against the staging area as it was near maximum range. The Marines called in aircraft with sorties striking close to the front lines. Even heavy air attacks could not save the untenable salient north of the Thach Han River.[19] Seeing armor moving south, the remaining army infantry abandoned their positions, all types of vehicles ran out of fuel, and rumors were rampant. Colonel Metcalf recalled several thousand troops and hundreds of vehicles all gridlocked on Highway 1 "with no escape route except into the withering fire" and then panic.[20] At this stage, according to Colonel Metcalf, the higher headquarters — I Corps, Rangers, Marines — added to the confusion by passing contrary instructions, and Giai was unable to sort out the situation.[21]

At dawn on 30 April 1972, Colonel Pham Van Chung of Brigade 369, sent a battalion up Highway 1 to try to get through to Quang Tri City in accordance with orders from division and corps. It was hit by heavy automatic weapon and recoilless rifle fire, delayed for air strikes, and then reached a bottleneck between the O'Khe Bridge and Hai Lang, where the Communists had installed themselves alongside the highway. With the destruction of this enemy force, down the road "came an exodus of refugees fleeing south" and the battalion's prospects of linking up with units in Quang Tri City faded. It was over-extended, low on ammunition, and unable to move up the road into the flow of refugees. Colonel Chang ordered the battalion back to the O'Khe Bridge to hold it for units breaking out from the north.[22]

At noon, 30 April 1972, Giai withdrew the Marines from the Ai Tu Combat Base. General Giai felt the only chance of holding Quang Tri City would be with Brigade 147, the only tactical unit remaining in any condition to fight. Metcalf said it would be "our last ditch defense."[23] Remaining division units would form a defensive line south of the Thach Han and the armor would be committed to open the highway toward Hue.[24] General Lam was notified of this plan and accepted it, but "no specific approval" was provided and no orders were issued.[25]

Lieutenant Colonel Bao, with brigade advisor Major Jim R. Joy, had been briefed by the division staff and the plan began smoothly enough as the Marine brigade headquarters and artillery battalion departed Ai Tu.[26] Marine advisors effectively directed and controlled tactical air strikes, artillery, and naval gunfire missions, slowing enemy pursuit and permitting the brigade's orderly and covered withdrawal.[27]

This went well until the column approaching Quang Tri City discovered that division engineers had destroyed the bridges across the river. The Marines tried to tow their artillery across a ford, but the swift current and soft bottom frustrated their efforts, forcing them to destroy 18 howitzers and 22 vehicles. Marines swam and waded the river at the bridge site and moved directly into their positions. By dark, the brigade occupied its planned defenses in Quang Tri City. The 1st Armored Brigade fared worse, when its recently assigned commander destroyed 10 howitzers and 12 tanks because of lack of fuel and ammunition. Fortunately, 16 of the remaining M48 tanks of the 20th Tank Battalion forded the river a kilometer north of the brigades.[28]

On the morning of 1 May 1972, General Lam informed General Giai that all positions were to be held and no withdrawal of any kind was authorized. This directive was from Saigon with Lam receiving his orders from President Nguyen Van Thieu.[29] New intelligence reports indicated that the city would be hit by a heavy artillery attack that evening and Giai and Metcalf were in conflict, with Metcalf insisting that the Marines could hold the Citadel with American supporting arms "indefinitely." General Giai was now convinced that further defense of Quang Tri City would be fruitless and to protect the lives "of all of you," he let units fall back to My Chanh and at this point he could not stop them.

At 1215, the 3d Division's chief of staff walked into Team 155's bunker and, using American radio circuits, called all the subordinate commanders and their advisors and said "General Giai has released all commanders to fight their way to the My Chanh River!" Within 30 minutes, the I Corps commander, General Lam ordered "stand and die." General Giai's subordinates, all his brigade-level commanders according to General Kroesen, refused to obey and said Giai could withdraw with them or be left, "a threat they proceeded to carry out."[30] Other units did not acknowledge the change or openly refused to deviate from their original orders. Shortly afterwards, Colonel Metcalf radioed Brigade 147 and said "the ARVN are pulling out; advisors may stay with their units or join me" for evacuation. Major Joy responded that the Brigade 147 Marine advisors would stay with their units. Colonel Metcalf watched the division staff and found his counterparts packing their belongings or "totally unaware or concerned of the situation."[31]

Lieutenant Colonel Bao declined to defend what all others were leaving, recalling his brigade's previous abandonment at Mai Loc by the division. Certainly the sight of the 3d Division soldiers with their families did nothing to engender the attitude necessary for a last stand.[F] A little after 2:30, the brigade headquarters was southwest of the Citadel where it was expected to be joined by the division commander and staff and

---

(F) Most Marines had dependents in MR-III, unlike most ARVN units who fought and lived in the same areas. The presence and safety members were a constant drain on manpower and commanders' attention.

then push on to the south to link up with Brigade 369 at My Chanh.[32] In the confusion, Kroesen stated the brigade left the division commander, Colonel Metcalf, and the other advisors at the Citadel, and Bao was holding the bag for both.[33] Major Joy had talked with Colonel Metcalf earlier in the afternoon to coordinate this. After the division staff failed to join the brigade, Metcalf radioed Joy that the linkup could not be made and that the advisors with the brigade should resort to their own devices. In what had to be taken as a proforma, Metcalf reiterated that the Marine advisors could join him for the helicopter lift out and Major Joy again declined. The departing Team 155 senior advisor replied "Good Luck."

At 4:35, Brigade 147 moved east towards the coast and then turned south. After making several difficult stream crossings, the column arrived in the Hai Lang area, ten kilometers south of Quang Tri City. It was thought that at least a reinforced North Vietnamese regiment held Highway 1 at Hai Lang and had engaged the fleeing division forces, halting all movement south. One Communist soldier reported, "the people were moving on bicycles motorbikes, and buses.... No one was able to escape."[34] The interdiction of the road by the artillery and infantry weapons earned it the title of the "Highway of Horror" for the estimated 2,000 civilian and military dead left among this three-quarters of a mile stretch of road.[35] The intermingled civilian and military stragglers prevented maneuver on the highway; and the cross-country route used was extremely difficult for Brigade 147's attached M48 tanks and vehicles, most of which were lost trying to ford the Nhung River. Bao, after a long and heated discussion with his battalion commanders, established a tight perimeter for the night to resume the march the next day. In the course of this it was ascertained that all units in the brigade were still organized and combat effective. To the south, Brigade 369 had been unsuccessful in keeping the road open between Quang Tri and Hue, although it had inflicted heavy losses on the enemy and was not pinned down.[36] Brigade 369's efforts were directed at keeping the bridges over the O'Khe and My Chanh open to withdrawing troops and civilians. Major Robert F. Sheridan, Brigade 369's senior advisor, had followed Joy's radio traffic closely in the days preceding the mass exodus.

General Khang and the Marine Division headquarters were ordered by the Joint General Staff to assume command of all Marines and to defend at My Chanh. Two brigades, 147 and 369, were engaged with the enemy. Brigade 258 was in reserve, and the situation was "very confused as to who and what, if any" were left.[37] Khang, his staff, and advisors went into action to play the hand they had been dealt as the defense of Hue began.[38]

In light of this crisis, the Vietnamese National Security Council met with President Thieu on 2 May and took drastic action to restore order.[39] The next day, General Lam and his deputy were sacked and on 4 May, President Thieu went to Hue to place Lieutenant General Ngo Quang Troung in command of I Corps. General Khang moved to the Joint General Staff on 5 May as J3 Operations, after being offered II Corps. The Vietnamese Marine Division remained under his deputy, Brigadier General Bui The Lan, to defend the province, lost in part because of American and Vietnamese interservice rivalry.[40] By 6 May, the 3d Division could account for only 2,700 of its men and General Giai was under arrest, later tried for disobeying orders and abandoning a position in the face of the enemy.[F] His defense was that with food and ammunition gone, he saw "no further reason why we should stay in this ruined situation."[41]

Conclusion

The actions and motivation of the Vietnamese Marines were subjected to various interpretations: Metcalf stated the Marines lost Quang Tri City, Kroesen implied it, and General Abrams' ire was against both Marine and armored units — at least until he left in June 1972.[G] For claims that Brigade 147's withdrawal on 1 May precipitated the collapse, the fact it was the last to leave and stayed long enough to allow the division commander and his advisors to escape must be considered.[H] It maintained itself as an effective force by saving lives and equipment, the same logic given by Giai in his mitigation. The presence of the Marine Division staff and General Khang provided only a backdrop to these events and even the U.S. Army belatedly recognized the Marine's drive for division status "was correct and valuable."[42] Real questions should have been directed at the performance of the ARVN units, particularly the 2d and 57th Regiments, and General Lam's conduct. In an interesting final note, General Kroesen felt the Communists' inability to pursue and destroy routed South Vietnamese forces as evidence that Quang Tri City would not have fallen if defended. The enemy did not have the resources or organization to do "what the ARVN forces had done to themselves" with American counsel.[43] The North Vietnamese doggedly held Quang Tri City Citadel for five months after its capture.

(F) I personally recall the highly visible sandbags and posts for firing-squads set up by military police along QL-1 outside of Hue as a draconian reminder of duty for stragglers from Quang Tri City.

(G) Even General Westnoreland got into the act in his memoirs. An extreme example of this viewpoint was presented by Australian Army Brigadier General F. P. Serong, "The 1972 Easter Offensive," *Southeast Asian Perspectives*, Summer 74, pp. 32-34.

(H) The 28 April decision to pull Brigade 369 off of Fire Support Base Jane to reopen Highway 1 was probably more critical in that it exposed the division's southern flank.

APPENDIX N ENDNOTES

Author's Note

1 This information is based on records generated by the events and participants, but depends on American rather than South Vietnamese impressions. Unpublished material is from Washington, D.C., to include the Marine Corps Historical Center (MCHC), the U.S. Army Center for Military History (CMH); the National Archives and Records Administration (NARA); unless otherwise noted.

General references are Jeffrey J. Clarke, *Advice and Support: The Final Years, 1965–1973* (Washington, D.C.: U.S. Army Center for Military History, 1988); Editors' *Air Wars-Vietnam* (New York: Arno Press, 1978); Editors, *The Marines in Vietnam, 1954–1973* (Washington, D.C.: HQMC, 1985); LtGen Ngo Quang Truong, *The Easter Offensive of 1972* (Washington, D.C.: U.S. Army Center for Military History, 1979).

Background on the Marine Division is from: Senior Marine Advisor, "Vietnamese Marine Corps/Marine Advisory Unit Historical Summary 1954–1973," dtd 22Mar73 (MCHC), American Embassy, Saigon, "Command Histories and Historical Sketches of the RVNAF Divisions," dtd 6Feb73 (Author); Col Victor J. Croizat, "Vietnamese Naval Forces: Origin of the Species," *U.S. Naval Institute Proceedings*, Feb73, pp. 45-48.

Riverine Commandos to Marine Division

2 MajGen L. Nguyen Khang, "Republic of Vietnam Marine Corps," Marine Corps Gazette, Nov66, p. 68; LtGen Le Nguyen Khang intvw dtd 30Sep75 (MCHC); Clarke's *Advice and Support: The Final Years, 1965–1973* documents the politics of both the Vietnamese and MACV in the "complex network of political and professional, and familial relationships" that shifted, pp. 21ff.

3 Operations in Cambodia and Laos deserve a closer look than is possible in this paper. Problems arose between the VNMC brigade commanders and the acting brigade commander, Colonel Bui The Lan. Friction also occurred with the respective VNMC and the ARVN command structures. The Marines learned from combat with the North Vietnamese Army and adjusted their outlook accordingly, and even the ARVN noted that they retained unit integrity regardless of losses; MajGen Nguyen Duy Hinh, *Lam Son 719* (Washington, D.C.: U.S. Army Center for Military History, 1979), p. 154; Graham A. Cosmas and LtCol Terrence P. Murray, *U.S. Marines in Vietnam, Vietnamization and Redeployment* (Washington, D.C.: HQMC, 1986); Col John G. Miller, "Born in Battle," *The Marines* (Harrisburg: NHS Publications, 1989,) pp. 123-129.

4 Marine Advisory Unit File, Lam Son 719 Critique Folder; *Senior Marine Advisor*, "Combat Operation After Action Report Lam·Son 719," dtd 21Mar71, pp. 4,6 (MCHC); Col John G. Miller comments dtd 19May72 (Author)

5 Clarke, pp. 476, 508

6 MGen Frederick J. Kroesen, Jr. "1972 Vietnam Counteroffensive," USA Command and General Staff College, 1974, p. 7-4 (CMH)

7 MACV, "The Nguyen Hue Offensive," study dtd 7Jan72 (NARA). Information from the North Vietnamese has not fully been exploited, sources available include: PAVN Military Institute, Vietnam: The Anti-U.S. Resistance War, 1954-1975 (Hanoi: PAVN Publishing House, 1980); Nguyen Khac Vien, editor, Indochina: the 1972-1973 Turning Point (Hanoi, Xunhasaba, 1974); ColGen Van Tien Dung, "Some Problems Concerning the Art of Military Campaigns of the Vietnamese People's War," *Army Magazine*, Dec73, pp. 18-29; PAVN Senior Military Academy, "Quang Tri-Thua Thien Offensive Campaign," *Collection of Sketches and Battles* (Hanoi: Ministry of Defense, 1986), pp. 18-19.

8 FRAC Intelligence Summary 125-72 (MCHC)

9 Khang intvw; Senior Marine Advisor, Operations Summary Report VNMC, dtd 11Apr72-1May72, *Marine Corps Gazette*, Mar73, pp. 18-29 (probably the best summary of Marine Division operations by the G-3 advisor).

10 Col Donald J. Metcalf, "Why Did the Defense of Quang Tri Province, SVN, Collapse," U.S. Army War College, Oct72, p. 29 (CMH)

11 General Cao Van Vien, *Leadership* (Washington, D.C.: U.S. Army Center for Military History, 1981), p. 130; Kroesen, p 7-7

12 Col Gerald H. Turley, *The Easter Offensive* (Navato: Presidio Press, 1985), pp. 213 & 245.

13 *Leadership*, p. 132; LtCol Louis C. Wagner, 1st ARVN Armor Brigade After Action Report, May72, p. 16 (NARA).

14 Kroesen, p. 7-9.

15 Maj Jim R. Joy memorandum dtd 3May72, p. 16, Senior Marine Advisor Personal Evaluation of NVA Easter Offensive folder; Col Charles J. Goode and LtCol Marshall R. Wells intvw dtd 19Jan84 (MCHC).

16 Metcalf, pp. 18-20, Marine Advisory Unit, Command Chronology, May72 (MCHC).

17 *Leadership*, p. 132; Kroesen, pp. 7-8, 7-9

18 Wagner, encl. 4, 3dARVNDiv "special" msg dtd 212529Apr72.

19 Maj Glen Golden intvw dtd 3Jul75, Tape 6026 (MCHC).

20 Metcalf, p. 25.

21 Metcalf, p. 25-26.

22 Col Donald Price, comments on ms, dtd 10Oct90 (MCHC).

23 Col Donald J. Metcalf intvw by MACV dtd 15Sept72, p. 8 (NARA); *Leadership*, p. 133.

24 Kroesen comments; Kroesen, p. 17; Metcalf intvw; Maj David A. Brookbank, USAF, Special Report of Air Liaison Officer, dtd 31Jul72, p. 20 (MCHC).

25 Kroesen, p. 7-10.

26 Marine Advisory Unit, Command Chronology, May72 (MCHC).

27 LtGen D'Wayne Gray, comments on ms, dtd 9Dec89 (MCHC).

28 Joy, p. 14.

29 Gen Fredrick J. Kroesen, Jr., comments on ms, dtd 3Jan90 (MCHC); Vien, p. 133.

30 MajGen Kroesen msg to Gen Abrams dtd 2May72, Abram's Papers (CMH).

31 Metcalf, p. 27.

32 Joy, p. 11-12.

33 Metcalf intvw, p. 9; Kroesen. P.19; Joy, p. 17.

34 RVN Ministry of Foreign Affairs, The Communist Policy of Terror (Saigon, 1972), pp. 41-42; also RVN Ministry on Information La Route De L'Horreur (Saigon, 1972) (Edwin Beach).

35 Maj Anthony P. Shepard, comments on ms, dtd 11Jan90 (MCHC).

36 Maj William T. Sweeney memo dtd 8May72, Senior Marine Advisor Evaluation folder (MCHC).

37 Marine Advisory Unit File, Brig 258 Advisor's Log, 2May72 (MCHC).

38 LtCol Robert F. Sheridan, comments on ms, dtd 20Mar90; Senior Marine Advisor, Historical Summary 1972, p. 13 (MCHC); Price comments.

39 *Leadership*, p. 134.

40 Command General, First Regional Assistance Command, Senior Officer Debriefing Report, MajGen Howard H. Cooksey, dtd 25Jan73 (NARA); Officer in Charge, 1st Air and Naval Gunfire Company - Su1, Meritorious Unit Commendation, Recommendation for, dtd 12Nov72; Senior Marine Advisor, Senior Officer Debriefing Report, dtd 23Jan73; Senior Marine Advisor, Marine Advisory Unit Historical Summary, 1972, dtd 20Feb73 (MCHC); this is another area for more research.

41 Turley, p. 203.

42 BDM Corporation, *A Study of Strategic Lesson Learned in Vietnam, Volume VI - Conduct of the War, Book 1*, dtd 20Mar80.

43 Kroesen, p. 7-11.

INDEX

Hellgate Press

Hellgate Press is named after the historic and rugged Hellgate Canyon on southern Oregon's scenic Rogue River. The raging river that flows below the canyon's towering jagged cliffs has always attracted a special sort of individual — someone who seeks adventure. From the pioneers who bravely pursued the lush valleys beyond, to the anglers and rafters who take on its roaring challenges today — Hellgate Press publishes books that personify this adventurous spirit. Our books are about military history, adventure travel, and outdoor recreation. On the following pages, we would like to introduce you to some of our latest titles and encourage you to join in our celebration of this unique spirit.

Hellgate Press
P.O. Box 3727
Central Point, Oregon 97502-0032
(800) 228-2275

IN THE NAME OF ADVENTURE

NIGHT LANDING

A SHORT HISTORY OF WEST COAST SMUGGLING

David W. Heron

Night Landing reveals the true stories of smuggling off the shores of California from the early 1800s to the present. It is a provocative account of the many attempts to illegally trade items such as freon, drugs, AK-47s, sea otters, and diamonds. This unusual chronicle also profiles each of these ingenious, but over-optimistic criminals and their eventual apprehension.

Night Landing

Available from Hellgate Press
ISBN: 1-55571-449-8
$13.95, paperback
6 x 9", 200 pages

Army Museums:
West of the Mississippi

Available from Hellgate Press
ISBN: 1-55571-395-5
$17.95, paperback
8 ¼ x 11", 250 pages

ARMY MUSEUMS

WEST OF THE MISSISSIPPI

Fred L. Bell, SFC Retired

A guidebook for travelers to the army museums of the west as well as a source of information about the history of the sites where the museums are located. Contains detailed information about the contents of the museum and interesting information about famous soldiers stationed at the location or events associated with the facility. These 23 museums are in forts and military reservations represent our colorful heritage in the settling of the American West.

"Mr. Bell not only covers what exhibits and displays can be found in this collection of museums, but gives an informative and enlightening history lesson as well. This book is a must read for museum enthusiasts."

Wayne C. Heinold, Sr.
Command Sergeant Major
U.S. Army Criminal Investigation Command

From Hiroshima
With Love

Available from Hellgate Press
ISBN: 1-55571-404-8
$18.95, paperback
6 x 9", 318 pages

FROM HIROSHIMA WITH LOVE

Raymond A. Higgins

This remarkable story is written from actual detailed notes and diary entries kept by Lieutenant Commander Wallace Higgins. Because of his industrial experience back in the United States and with the reserve commission in the Navy, he was an excellent choice for military governor of Hiroshima. Higgins was responsible for helping rebuild a ravaged nation of war. He developed an unforeseen respect for the Japanese, their culture ... and one special woman. From his research prior to his arrival, he was able to better understand and treat the surrendering people of this devastated country with dignity, and the respect that they deserved. Firsthand accounts of Japan's astonishing defense system verify that had the United States chose invasion rather than the bomb, the results would have been drawn out and disastrous. These accounts also reveal a secret mission to secure hidden uranium for the making of Japan's own atomic bomb.

GULF WAR DEBRIEFING BOOK

AN AFTER ACTION REPORT

Andrew Leyden

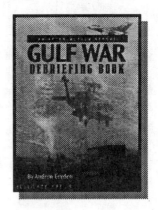

Now you have access to the complete story of what unfolded during the seven months of late 1990 and early 1991, with the *Gulf War Debriefing Book: An After Action Report*. Whereas most books on the Persian Gulf War tell an "inside story" based on someone else's opinion, this book lets you draw your own conclusions about the war by providing you with a meticulous review of events and documentation all at your fingertips! Includes lists of all military units deployed, a detailed account of the primary weapons used during the war, and a look at the people, places, and politics behind the military maneuvering. This resource also gives a day-by-day chronology of the events that took place during Operation Desert Shield/Storm and afterwards.

Gulf War
Debriefing Book:
An After Action Report

Available from Hellgate Press
ISBN: 1-55571-396-3
$18.95, paperback
7½ x 10", 320 pages

BYRON'S WAR

I NEVER WILL BE YOUNG AGAIN

Byron Lane

Based on letters that were mailed home and a personal journal written more than fifty years ago during World War II, *Byron's War* brings the war to life through the eyes of a very young air crew officer. It depicts how the life of this young American changed through cadet training, the experiences as a crew member flying across the North Atlantic under wartime hazards, the nostalgia and awesome responsibility assigned to a nineteen year old when leading hundreds of men and aircraft, bombing targets where success or failure could seriously impact the conduct of the war.

Byron's War:
I never will be young again

Available from Hellgate Press
ISBN: 1-55571-402-1
$21.95, paperback
5½ x 8¼", 300 pages

Order Directly From Hellgate Press

You can purchase any of these Hellgate Press titles
at most book sellers or directly through us with this order form.

TO ORDER CALL,
1-800-228-2275
FAX 1-541-476-1479

FOR   INQUIRIES
AND INTERNATIONAL ORDERS,
CALL   1-541-479-9464
EMAIL   info@psi-research.com

Hellgate Press

P.O. Box 3727
Central Point, OR
97502-0032

TITLE	PRICE	QUANTITY	COST
Night Landing	$13.95 — paperback		
Army Museums West of the Mississippi	$17.95 — paperback		
From Hiroshima With Love	$18.95 — paperback		
Gulf War Debriefing Book	$18.95 — paperback		
Byron's War	$21.95 — hardback		

IF YOUR PURCHASE IS:	SHIPPING IN THE USA:
$0 - $25	$5.00
$25.01 - $50	$6.00
$50.01 - $100	$7.00
$100.01 - $175	$9.00
$175.01 - $250	$13.00
over $250	please call

SUBTOTAL $
SHIPPING $
TOTAL ORDER $

Thank you for your order!

SHIPPING INFORMATION

Ordered by:
Name:

Street Address:

City/State/Zip:

Daytime Phone: Email:

Shipped to: *Fill this out only if the information is different than above*
Name:

Street Address:

City/State/Zip:

Daytime Phone: Email:

PAYMENT INFORMATION

Indicate your preferred payment method below. Rush service is available, call for details at **(800) 228-2275**. Overseas and Canadian orders: Please call for a quote on shipping.

☐ CHECK   ☐ AMERICAN EXPRESS   ☐ MASTERCARD   ☐ VISA

Card Number: Expiration Date:

Signature: Exact Name on Card:

For additional information, related web links, and news about
our latest releases be sure to visit the Hellgate Press Web site at
http://www.psi-research.com